# Teaching Kids with Learning Difficulties in Today's Classroom

**Revised & Updated Third Edition**

free spirit
PUBLISHING®

# Teaching Kids with Learning Difficulties in Today's Classroom

**Revised & Updated Third Edition**

## How Every Teacher Can Help Struggling Students Succeed

Susan Winebrenner, M.S.,
with contributing author Lisa M. Kiss, M.Ed.

free spirit
PUBLISHING®

**Library of Congress Cataloging-in-Publication Data**

Winebrenner, Susan, [date].

[Teaching kids with learning difficulties in the regular classroom]

Teaching kids with learning difficulties in today's classroom : how every teacher can help struggling students succeed / Susan Winebrenner, with contributing author Lisa Kiss. — Revised and updated third edition.

    pages cm

Includes bibliographical references and index.

ISBN 978-1-57542-480-4 — ISBN 1-57542-480-0  1. Learning disabled children—Education—United States. 2. Mainstreaming in education—United States.  I. Kiss, Lisa M. II. Title.

    LC4705.W56 2014

    371.9'0460973—dc23

                                       2014014100

ISBN: 978-1-57542-480-4

Edited by Pamela Espeland and Christine Zuchora-Walske
Cover and interior design by Tasha Kenyon

10 9 8 7 6 5 4 3
Printed in the United States of America

**Free Spirit Publishing Inc.**
6325 Sandburg Road, Suite 100
Minneapolis, MN 55427-3674
(612) 338-2068
help4kids@freespirit.com
www.freespirit.com

FSC
www.fsc.org
MIX
Paper from
responsible sources
FSC® C005010

**Free Spirit offers competitive pricing.**

Contact edsales@freespirit.com for pricing information on multiple quantity purchases.

This book is dedicated to all the teachers, parents, and grandparents who have struggled for many years, looking for ways to understand and help their children with learning difficulties experience success in their efforts to become educated.

# Acknowledgments

We are deeply grateful to the dedicated and creative educators who have so generously shared their teaching strategies in this book. In addition, thanks go to:

Free Spirit Publishing—for a constantly satisfying 22-year association.

Christine Zuchora-Walske and Marjorie Lisovskis—for your editing skills and support.

Judy Galbraith—publisher extraordinaire and encouraging friend and associate.

The entire staff at Free Spirit Publishing—for the magnificent ways you help your authors.

Karen Hess—for helping us understand and use your Cognitive Rigor Matrix.

Norman Webb—for your Depth of Knowledge (DOK) model and for participating in our telephone outreach.

Frank Lyman—for your models that teach kids and teachers how to learn and teach with rigor.

Charles Williams and the University of Oregon—for Dynamic Indicators of Basic Early Literacy Skills (DIBELS).

Chris Wigent—for your response to intervention (RTI) triangle and research.

Jeanette Van Houten—for your technology input and development of the ievaluate app rubric to assess apps for meeting student needs.

Sherry Milchick and the Pennsylvania Department of Education—for developing the functional behavior assessment (FBA) and giving us permission to use it.

Tulpehocken School District in Pennsylvania, including superintendent Edward Albert, the school board, and administrators—for encouraging Lisa to share her knowledge and experiences.

Dr. Marie Carbo—for helping struggling readers learn that they actually can read after all, and for your friendship and support of our work for this book.

Delta Kappa Gamma, especially Lisa's Nu Chapter sisters—for your encouragement while this book was being written.

Salman Khan—for founding the amazing Khan Academy to assist learners of all ages by allowing free online access to educational videos that help students better understand concepts in a wide array of subjects. Your work has had a positive impact on American education.

Personally, Susan thanks her husband, Joe Ceccarelli, whose seemingly limitless patience and ongoing support often made the difference for her between forging ahead and throwing in the towel. Susan also thanks Paul Ginsberg, her uncle, friend, and mentor, for his lifelong modeling of understanding and respecting all the people in our lives. Interacting with Paul and his wisdom over the years has created ongoing blessings.

Lisa thanks her husband, Doug, and her two children, Michelle and Brian, who showed how amazing they really are throughout this entire adventure by giving their complete support and unconditional love.

# Contents

# List of Reproducible Pages and Digital Content

You may download these forms at **freespirit.com/tkld-forms**. Use password **2succeed**.

## Digital Content

Additional Content Organization Charts

PDF Presentation for Professional Development

Reproducible Pages from the Book

# Foreword
## by Richard D. Lavoie

Parents and teachers need to come to the profound understanding that *kids go to school for a living.* It is their job. The classroom is their workplace. Their world. In fact, "school" is their entire identity.

Consider. When you bump into an 11-year-old from your community who you have not seen for a while, what is your greeting to him? *"Hi, Jason. How's school?"* His answer to that question determines his self-esteem, self-concept, and worldview.

Now imagine being a youngster who—through no fault or choice of his own—has marked difficulty learning at the same rate and in the same way that his classmates do. When you consider all this, it is small wonder that we find that kids with learning disorders are proportionally far more likely to abuse drugs, to have low self-esteem, participate in self-destructive behaviors, withdraw, act out . . . or drop out.

When I was trained in the early 1970s, these troubled and troubling kids were shunted off to special classes in isolated rooms in distant hallways. The inclusion initiatives of the 1980s changed all of that and now they "belong" to all of us. They are no longer the exclusive wards of special education; they now have a place in *every* classroom in *every* public school in America. And bravo for that!

But with the positive and humanistic goals of inclusion also come significant challenges for teachers. How do we deal effectively and fairly with these struggling students while—simultaneously—providing their classmates with the stimulating, fast-paced curriculum that they need and deserve?

This latest edition of *Teaching Kids with Learning Difficulties in Today's Classroom* by Susan Winebrenner and Lisa Kiss goes a long, long way toward answering that question. As I consumed this readable and user-friendly text, I was struck by one recurring theme: the antidote to misbehavior, frustration, anxiety, withdrawal, lack of motivation, and passivity for the "mainstreamed" student is SUCCESS. If you were to do a word cloud on the pages of this book to find the word that the authors used most frequently, I would bet that "success" would be in the top five.

Ensuring that a child is successful in a classroom does *not* mean that you provide the student with an easy curriculum, non-fail strategies, and unearned praise. Quite the contrary. As Susan and Lisa so brilliantly demonstrate, the key to the student's *true* success is careful balance of support and challenge.

*Support* and *challenge* are the two cornerstones of effective special education. The teacher's job is to continually *challenge* the child by providing a demanding curriculum and, simultaneously, the *support* the student needs to meet those demands.

Support without challenge is meaningless. Challenge without support is destructive.

This balance of support and challenge is the essence of special education. Success must be a fundamental ingredient in every lesson plan. We must replace the timeworn phrase "If he only tried harder he would do better" with the more effective phrase, "If he only *did* better he would try *harder.*"

This theme is embossed on every page of this extraordinary book. The authors cover all aspects of special needs, from testing to reading to behavior management to organizational skills to homework. Particularly outstanding is their innovative approach to learning styles that goes far beyond the traditional VAKT (visual, auditory, kinesthetic, tactile) approach that the reader may be familiar with.

So many curriculum guides begin with the premise that all the researchers, practitioners, and experts who preceded the author were wrong and the author has *the* solitary answer and solutions. Susan Winebrenner and Lisa Kiss take a far more enlightened view by building upon and expanding on some classic curricular approaches with a generous nod to the original authors. We all stand on the shoulders of giants.

This book will be an invaluable guide to the educator who is willing to commit the time and effort required to truly meet the unique needs of kids who struggle. This journey is not an easy one, but what important journey is?

With every good wish,

Richard D. Lavoie, M.A., M.Ed.
Author of *The Motivation Breakthrough* and *It's So Much Work to Be Your Friend*

# Introduction

Has there ever been a more challenging time to be a teacher? Teachers face constant pressure to be sure all students can demonstrate they are learning at expected levels and to embrace and master ever-changing teaching models in a short period of time. Add to that the challenges that come with having a widening range of student achievement levels in any class, and you can understand how absolutely amazing teachers are!

In order to be a successful teacher for students who are struggling to learn, you need to understand that these kids are not necessarily less intelligent or less capable than the successful students. Many are simply less *lucky*, because they have rarely experienced a match between the way their brains comfortably process information and the way they have been taught. (Chapter 3 will tell you more about this hypothesis.) Although many of these kids have been labeled "learning disabled," a more accurate description is that they are "learning *strategy* disabled." Many have never been taught strategies that are compatible with the way they think and learn. Once we teach them the appropriate techniques that help them compensate for their areas of weakness, their learning problems diminish significantly, and achievement success is in their grasp.

When the right methods are used, it is not necessary to water down content or repeat it endlessly. For example, for many years students who failed to learn to read with a phonics-oriented program were given remedial phonics. The assumption was that everyone had to understand phonics to be able to read. When we taught outlining, we assumed that all kids should learn it the *right* way, in a sequential process. Now that we understand more about how the human brain functions, we know that rather than remediate, we must work to make matches happen between the content to be learned and the learning styles (modalities) of our students. When the right matches are found, the message we send to struggling students is "You can be successful learners by using the learning strategies your brains find most comfortable and can more easily understand."

In addition to the obvious benefit of getting better achievement from students with learning difficulties, discovering how your students learn and teaching different kids in different ways provides other advantages. The consistent availability of differentiation opportunities shows your students that being different is just fine. It shows that you understand all kids don't learn the same way and that you happily accept all students exactly the way they are. Knowing that makes it less necessary for many students to mask their weaknesses with inappropriate behavior, so behavior may improve over time. Acts of bullying may also decrease, because it is harder to tease or ridicule people who are proud of their individuality.

> Although many of these kids have been labeled "learning disabled," a more accurate description is that they are "learning *strategy* disabled." Once we teach them the appropriate techniques that help them compensate for their areas of weakness, their learning problems diminish significantly, and achievement success is in their grasp.

Regardless of the curriculum you are teaching, the differentiation strategies described in this book will facilitate better learning success for students with learning difficulties. Meeting the Common Core State Standards (CCSS) should provide numerous opportunities for you to use many of your favorite teaching methods—with a new emphasis on providing rigorous learning experiences for all your students, not just those who are advanced. The standards include many opportunities for students to interact with activities that integrate content areas and stress higher-level thinking where appropriate. For example, math lessons might correlate to the study of a U.S. region or to the implications of worldwide population growth while the U.S. birthrate is declining. The possibilities are endless.

Never lose sight of the fact that a crucial 21st-century job survival skill is a positive attitude toward being retrained. Retraining is a lot like going back to school. All the students you teach will have to change careers numerous times before they retire. The people who will be successful at this are the ones who enjoy their formal schooling and therefore look forward to becoming students again. So our goal as teachers should be to instill in all our students a drive to be lifelong learners.

> Never lose sight of the fact that a crucial 21st-century job survival skill is a positive attitude toward being retrained.

## A Positive Learning Experience Leads to a Love of Learning

To put differentiation in a positive light, we have used the following differentiation rationale for students with learning difficulties, which you might choose to share with your colleagues. If they agree with most or all of the statements, they are demonstrating readiness to do their very best to guarantee a consistently positive learning experience for all their students, including those with learning difficulties.

1. All students should experience learning at their own personal challenge level every day.

2. High self-esteem, and therefore learning productivity, comes from being successful with tasks the students perceived would be difficult.*

3. When students feel they have some control over what happens in school, they are more likely to be productive. This feeling of control comes from opportunities to make choices. Teachers can make choices available by offering several options for the type of expected task or product.

4. When learning modalities are attended to and curriculum is challenging and meaningful, students are more likely to choose appropriate behaviors.

5. The first place an educator should look to explain inappropriate behavior is the curriculum. Is it appropriately challenging? Does it incorporate students' interests wherever possible? Does the student understand why it must be learned? Does it allow access through students' learning modality strengths?

6. All students must feel they are respected and accepted for who they are and what they need in order to be successful learners.

This book presents a wide variety of teaching methods, so you can find the right match for every student in your classroom. We have collected these practical, easy-to-use strategies, techniques, and activities from a variety of sources. Actually, that is what makes this book unique. You don't have to do your own research on what works for teaching kids how to read or how to remember their math facts. We've done the research for you. This book contains the most effective methods we have found for helping students with learning problems become much more successful learners. Simply diagnose the learning weakness a particular student exhibits, find the right chapter in this book, and match the strategies to the student. Using these strategies, you can help bring learners up to the level of the content rather than lowering expectations for some students.

All the strategies in this book have been proven effective when intervening with students whose academics or behavior do not reflect expectations. You will find these methods are effective with any curriculum type you may be using. They make curriculum differentiation much easier for you and more helpful for your students.

Throughout this book, we emphasize our belief that high self-esteem can be achieved only through hard work and genuine accomplishments. As author and educator Dr. Sylvia Rimm says, "The surest path to high self-esteem is to be successful at something one perceived would be difficult." Rimm goes on to say, "Each time we steal a student's struggle, we steal the opportunity for them to build self-confidence. They must learn to do difficult things to feel good about themselves."

When we combine Rimm's work with that of Dr. Carol Dweck, we fully understand the importance of training our students to welcome, rather than resist, hard work. Both experts agree that convincing students to welcome learning challenges is the key to their developing a lifelong appreciation for the link between serious effort and desired outcomes. When we praise young people for their effort and hard work, rather than their outcomes, such as grades or class rank, students are much more likely to develop the belief that hard work is more important for success in school and in life than innate ability.

Dweck's research is described in her book *Mindset*. She has found that learners who believe they have a fixed amount of ability have a *fixed mindset* and may conclude that they can never meet their desired goals because they lack the essential ability. Her work cautions us as adults to avoid using labels to describe young people. Adults can create fixed mindsets by calling attention to a person's innate advanced abilities or to a student's persistent trouble with creating successful learning outcomes.

---

*Rimm, 2008.

Labeling students sends the message that they have only a certain amount of intelligence and must be careful not to use it all up. However, students who attribute their success in school to their own hard work learn that they have more control over learning outcomes than they originally thought, and they exhibit a *growth mindset*. They notice the link between their willingness to work hard and the likelihood of getting the outcomes they desire. When we emphasize this link, students are more motivated to work hard to learn, and they are more likely to stay engaged in a learning experience, believing that hard work will lead to better outcomes. When you combine Rimm's and Dweck's research with the "Goal Setting" section in this book (page 61), you will see amazing improvement in student attitudes and learning outcomes.

Nothing is quite as powerful as our ability to communicate high expectations for success to our students. Over the years, many studies have shown that we get what we expect. For example, the Pygmalion study in the 1960s demonstrated that kids could improve dramatically if their teachers were told they would do extremely well in a given year.*

No one knows for certain how many students in our past have been labeled "slow" or "remedial" whose learning outcomes might have been improved by choosing a teaching strategy that was more brain-compatible. For example, some kids face remediation due to their lack of fluency with multiplication facts year after year. However, when they are taught finger multiplication (described on page 162), many can learn the facts in just a few days.

One of the most helpful features of this book is that the strategies may be used with *any* students who are frustrated in their attempts to learn *any* academic content. Keep trying strategies until you find the right match for that particular student. Really! The strategies are generic and are presented as a menu of options for you to use as you empower *all* kids to become successful in your classroom. They are just as effective with students in poverty and with English language learners (ELLs) as they are with kids who have been diagnosed with learning difficulties.

The Common Core State Standards bring many of the guidelines formerly associated with gifted education to regular classrooms, at various levels of complexity, thus setting higher expectations for all students. Of course, differentiation will still be necessary, but as the curriculum for all students increases in rigor, students and parents will no longer complain that only the kids at the top get to do the "good stuff." With Common Core, *all* students will be engaged in learning activities they feel are stimulating and respectful ways to spend their learning time.

You have nothing to lose and everything to gain by trying some of the methods described in this book. You know that your struggling students will continue to struggle if they don't get the help they need. When you find and use strategies that work, teaching and learning become mutually successful experiences.

We promise these methods will work for you and your students. They have been used by us and by many other classroom teachers with delightful success. After all, this is the third edition of this book. It has been in constant print and has been read widely since 1996. We have received feedback from many educators telling us that they have used multiple strategies from this book with great success with many types of students. Often, teachers have told us they wish they had known about some of these strategies throughout their entire teaching careers.

This book will help you become an even better teacher than you already are. All you have to remember is this: *If students are not learning the way you are teaching them, find and use a more appropriate method, so you can teach them the way they learn.*

# What's New in This Edition

If you are familiar with earlier editions of this book, you may have noticed that the title has changed slightly. The previous edition was titled *Teaching Kids with Learning Difficulties in the Regular Classroom*. The new title reflects this edition's emphasis on current teaching and learning philosophies and practice. *Teaching Kids with Learning Difficulties in Today's Classroom* is your guide to specific strategies you may use to be sure your teaching and learning practices are compatible with current thought and newly emerging curricula. Specifically, this book is updated in the following areas:

**1. Learning difficulties:** Learning difficulties are described as "disabilities" by the *Diagnostic and Statistical Manual of Mental Disorders, Fifth Edition (DSM-5)*. This manual is considered the universal authority for psychiatric diagnoses. *DSM-5* describes specific categories of mental health disorders and descriptions of each. It has long been used to help professionals in the fields of education and mental health recognize the many different categories of behaviors that identify persons who need specific interventions to put them on the road to emotional or academic recovery.

One of the most significant changes in *DSM-5* is that Asperger's syndrome no longer exists as a separate condition. It is included as part of the autism spectrum

---

*Rosenthal, Robert, and Lenore Jacobson. *Pygmalion in the Classroom: Teacher Expectation and Pupils' Intellectual Development*. Norwalk, CT: Crown House Publishing, 2003.

disorder (ASD) category. As you probably know, the number of kids who qualify in the category of ASD has exploded. In 2014, experts estimated that 1 child in 68 births would have ASD. To address the rapid growth in ASD diagnoses and the expectation of some parents for full inclusion in regular education programs, we have included sidebars throughout called "Unlocking Autism." They are devoted to students with ASD. They describe how teaching and learning strategies impact students who are on the autism spectrum, and some other students as well. Additional in-depth information about this disorder is in Chapter 2.

**2. Common Core:** At this book's writing, the Common Core State Standards (CCSS) are the emerging national initiative. They represent the first time in U.S. history that most of the states have agreed on the essential standards that students in preK through 12th grade must learn in order to be prepared for the workplace of today and the near future. These standards have moved away from the skill-based focus of No Child Left Behind (NCLB). Although NCLB's expectation that all students make "Adequate Yearly Progress" (AYP) produced measurable benefits, many in education were frustrated that NCLB left little room for higher-level thinking or problem-based learning experiences. In contrast, CCSS focuses on teaching skills through the study of much more rigorous content and more meaningful, exciting learning experiences. Our recommendations for ways to make that happen for your students with learning difficulties are found throughout this new edition, especially in Chapters 3 through 8.

Although the CCSS are being implemented in many states, some readers will not be experiencing them as soon as others. We want to reassure you that the strategies and information in this book are timeless and will be useful regardless of the content you are teaching. You will always need differentiation for some students for various reasons. This book provides dozens of user-friendly interventions you can use with little preparation. These interventions will be highly effective with any of your students who experience frustration in keeping up with the adopted curriculum.

**3. Response to intervention:** Response to intervention (RTI) is a program that was created to help educators achieve successful learning outcomes with all students. The goal of RTI is to increase rigor in both teaching and learning and to provide the structure through which differentiation can occur. Three tiers of instruction are geared to meet all levels of students' academic needs. Whether a student has learning difficulties or is proficient at grade level, high-achieving, or gifted, RTI helps you collaborate with your colleagues to be certain all students can eventually demonstrate mastery of any required curriculum. More RTI information may be found in Chapters 2 through 8.

**4. Professional learning communities (PLCs):** You may have heard the saying *There is nothing new under the sun.* Many years ago, Susan taught in a graduate program in Illinois that prepared candidates for their master's degrees in ways that were highly interactive and relied a great deal on candidates coaching each other throughout the process. Back then, the process was called action research. Susan watched it transform her graduate students into much more professional practitioners with their students. That experience caused Susan to always integrate a peer coaching component into all the professional development work she does.

> Although the CCSS are being implemented in many states, some readers will not be experiencing them as soon as others. We want to reassure you that the strategies and information in this book are timeless and will be useful regardless of the content you are teaching.

In PLCs, members use group meetings to discuss and refine their interventions with their students. That ongoing flow of ideas and suggestions between the PLCs and the classroom events greatly increases the sense of professionalism in the participants. This book is structured for ease of use in PLCs, and the digital content includes a PDF presentation to facilitate that process. In addition, we have written a PLC/Book Study Guide which can be downloaded at www.freespirit.com.

**5. Technology:** For years, most of students' interaction with computers took place outside the regular classroom, usually in a library media room or a computer lab. Current best practice requires students to use technology as an integral part of the learning process. So the Common Core has come at the exact right time, since its expectations are greatly enhanced by students' abilities to get right to the primary sources in their learning of all subjects and topics. Technology information is included in most chapters of this book, with a special in-depth section in Chapter 4. Sidebars titled "Tech Tips" appear throughout the book. These describe technologies that are very helpful for kids with learning difficulties.

**6. Behaviors of students with special needs:** In the years since the first two editions of this book were published, the emphasis on behavior has moved on to school-wide positive behavior management models. In this edition, we focus on behavior adjustment strategies linked to RTI in a model called Positive Behavioral Interventions and Supports (PBIS). According to the national PBIS website (www.pbis.org), PBIS is an implementation framework designed to enhance academic and social behavior outcomes for all students by emphasizing the use of data for informing decisions about the selection, implementation, and progress monitoring of evidence-based behavioral practices. Attention is focused on creating and sustaining positive behaviors school-wide in ways that are mutually rewarding for everyone in the school community, including on school buses and playgrounds and in halls and the classrooms themselves. All the information in Chapter 10 about behavior is compatible with the PBIS Guidelines and IEP Positive Behavior Support Plans.

Here's a glimpse of the valuable information you'll find in this book:

- **Chapter 1: Creating Active Learning for All Students** contains tips for helping all students feel welcome in your classroom, since kids who feel like outsiders are candidates for misbehavior and underachievement. It presents tried-and-true ways to get all students involved in all learning activities.

- **Chapter 2: Understanding Learning Difficulties and Intervening Effectively** describes various types of learning difficulties and offers suggestions for responding to students' special learning needs.

- **Chapter 3: Using Students' Learning Styles (Modalities) to Facilitate Learning Success** helps you enhance the learning success of your struggling students by matching your teaching to their learning modalities.

- **Chapter 4: Ensuring That All Students Make At Least One Year's Academic Growth During Each School Year** presents state-of-the-art ideas on how learning happens and how teachers can create learning success for all students.

- **Chapter 5: Teaching Integrated Language Arts, Including Literature, Sounds, and Writing** provides numerous concrete strategies to use with students whose reading fluency and comprehension need improvement in an integrated language arts approach.

- **Chapter 6: Reading and Learning with Informational Text** offers strategies for students who face many challenges in figuring out the important information and the meaning of content in informational texts such as in science, social studies, and so on.

- **Chapter 7: All Students Can Be Successful in Math** is full of easy-to-learn strategies for students who are working behind their grade-level peers in math.

- **Chapter 8: Using Assessments to Support Student Learning** contains strategies for both formative and summative assessments.

- **Chapter 9: Improving Students' Executive Functioning Skills** contains many practical strategies to help students become better organized and use effective study skills.

- **Chapter 10: Helping Students Choose Appropriate Behaviors** offers ideas for successful behavior management by involving students in monitoring their own behavior.

- **Chapter 11: Helping Parents Become Partners in Their Children's Learning** offers suggestions for involving parents as part of the learning team. It describes several ways to reach out to parents—including those who don't seem interested—and make them welcome at school.

Each chapter also includes a "Questions and Answers" section with responses to the questions we hear most often from educators. The book concludes with a "References and Resources" section that points you toward additional sources of information and materials. These are the best books, articles, videos, organizations, associations, programs, and resources we have found, and we encourage you to seek them out.

Finally, all the reproducible forms in the book are provided as digital content available to you online; you may customize many of the forms for your classroom and students. Also included in the digital file are additional content organization charts from our work in the field and a PDF presentation useful for introducing and exploring the book in study groups, PLCs, and other professional development settings. You may download the content and print the documents when you need them. See page xii for information on how to access the digital content.

# Teacher Effectiveness Leads to Student Success

Evidence shows that certain programs and practices have been successful in the last decade in significantly improving achievement scores for students who were previously unsuccessful in school. Dr. Martin Haberman, author of the book *Star Teachers of Children in Poverty*, has documented the importance of teachers having the ability to consistently use highly effective teaching methods. He believes that "for children in poverty, success in school is a matter of life and death, and they need teachers who are mature people who have a great deal of knowledge about their subject matter, but who can also relate to them as persons." Haberman also documents how essential it is for struggling students to have highly effective teachers. He is convinced that if struggling students have ineffective teachers two years in a row, the students can never recover from the deficits they have experienced.

Finally, research findings from the Tennessee Value-Added Assessment System (TVAAS) database demonstrate that the effectiveness of the teacher is the major determinant of student academic progress. In a 1996 study, William L. Sanders and June C. Rivers tracked thousands of elementary students' test scores year to year and used them to rate teachers as "effective" or "ineffective." They found a 50 percent difference over three years in the average test score changes of the two groups. The kids who had the effective teachers scored significantly better.*

The negative consequences of an ineffective teacher to a student's learning progress cannot be underestimated. The quality of classroom teachers is the most important factor that a school district can influence. It's more important than class size or school facilities.

What does this mean to you, the reader? Since you are reading this book, you are demonstrating that you are a person who always seeks to be as effective as possible. You understand that it is useless to continue to use strategies that are not working, and you are willing to try another strategy when you have reasonable hope for better learning outcomes. In our opinion, that is the definition of an effective teacher.

The strategies described in this book will help students with learning difficulties be more successful with the adopted curriculum of all states, whether or not your state is using CCSS content and suggested practices.

We believe this book can make teaching more pleasant and effective for you, and it can make learning more enjoyable and successful for your students with learning difficulties. We'd love to receive any feedback that you care to share with us. If you have feedback to offer or questions that are not addressed in this book, write to us c/o Free Spirit Publishing, 6325 Sandburg Road, Suite 100, Minneapolis, MN 55427-3674. Send us an email at help4kids@freespirit.com.

Let's get started.

Susan Winebrenner and Lisa Kiss

---

*Sanders, William L., and June C. Rivers. "Cumulative and Residual Effects of Teachers on Future Student Academic Achievement." TVAAS, November 1996.

# CHAPTER 1
# Creating Active Learning for All Students

Do you remember how you felt on the first day of a new school year when you were a student? Can you recall the questions that were spinning through your brain? "Will the teacher be nice to me? Will the other kids like me? Will anyone want to sit with me at lunch? What if the work is too hard?" If you can relate to those concerns, you can easily understand how most of your students feel as they enter your class.

Students with learning difficulties have the same worries, greatly magnified. Purposefully creating experiences that help students feel welcome and cared about in your classroom will go a long way toward providing a supportive learning environment for all kids.

## Welcoming Activities
### Say Hello to Someone Who . . .*

On the first day of class, students should participate in activities that help them learn about one another. "Say Hello to Someone Who . . . " is an enjoyable way to share and discover interesting information. Afterward, all students will know the names of several other students. Recognition in the halls, in other classes, in the cafeteria, and on the playground helps make each student feel like part of a group, which may prevent alienation.

Give each student a copy of the "Say Hello to Someone Who . . . " handout (page 19). Allow 15

*This activity and the handout on page 19 are adapted from *Patterns for Thinking, Patterns for Transfer* by Robin Fogarty and James Bellanca. © 1991 IRI Skylight Publishing, Inc., Palatine, IL. Used with permission.

minutes for students to circulate around the room and collect signatures from people who match descriptions on their handouts. (*Examples:* If Emilio stayed in town all summer, he's a match for the first box on the handout and signs his name in that box. If Sarah went on a trip, she signs her name in that box.) Explain that each student can sign another student's handout only once, and no students can sign their own handouts. All students should try to collect as many signatures as they can. After one student has signed another student's handout, both say, "Hello, [NAME], glad to meet you!"

### Getting to Know You

Whenever you ask students to work in groups, give them time to get to know one another. Here's one good way to do this.

Distribute stick-on nametags. Have students write their names in the center. Then have them write answers to the following questions in each of the four corners (or substitute your own questions):

- In the top left corner: "Where were you born?"

- In the top right corner: "What is your favorite food?"

- In the bottom left corner: "What is your favorite thing to do?"

- In the bottom right corner: "What is something you are very proud of?"

7

After students complete their nametags and put them on, have them pair up, interview their partners, then introduce their partners to four to six other students.

## The Name Game

Have students sit in a circle. Explain that one student will say his first name, then briefly describe one thing he enjoys doing. (*Example:* "Bobby. Shooting hoops.") Going around the circle, the next student will repeat what was just said, then add her first name and something she enjoys doing. (*Example:* "Bobby. Shooting hoops. Maria. Going for bike rides.") The third student will repeat what the first two students said, then add his own information, and so on around the circle.

Make sure the students understand that they must repeat everything that has been said before adding their information. **Tips:** If you know that some kids have memory problems, arrange for them to take their turn early in the game. If you think smaller circles are better, divide the group in two.

## Interest Survey

During the first week of school, send home copies of the "Interest Survey" handout (pages 20–21) as a homework assignment. Tell students they can ask family members for help in completing their surveys.

Read the returned surveys carefully and refer to them often throughout the year. You will find many ways you can use the information from the surveys. (*Examples:* Suggest school projects based on the surveys. For kids who seem *unmotivated* to learn, take a few seconds each day to speak to them about their interests outside of school. This shows that you like and respect them even when they are not being successful in their schoolwork.)

## Picture This: A Gallery of Ideas

If possible, obtain students' school pictures from last year and make photocopies to use with some of these suggested activities. Or take your own photos.

- Give all students space on a wall or bulletin board to display anything they want—photographs of themselves, their families, or their friends; work they feel proud of; or other categories. This eliminates the anguish struggling students experience when their work never makes it to the "Our Best Work" display.

- Have students make personalized bookmarks with their photos at the top, then decorate their bookmarks however they choose.

- With permission from the students' families, make copies of students' photos, add addresses and phone numbers, and create a classroom directory for kids to keep at home.

- Take and display photos of the class engaged in various activities. Make sure that all kids are included.

### Unlocking Autism 🔒

Autism spectrum disorder, or ASD, affects both verbal and nonverbal communication as well as social skills development. The most common communication and social problems include difficulty in making friends, verbal misunderstandings in conversation, difficulty in reading body language and understanding emotions, limited or repetitive speech, and unusual responses to the environment. Consult page 32 for details.

Throughout this book, you will see "Unlocking Autism" sidebars specifically devoted to strategies for students with autism. We've included this information to help our readers, who are dealing with the rapid growth of ASD diagnoses and some families' expectations for full inclusion in regular education programs.

## People Packages*

The "People Packages" activity has been used successfully in primary grades to help kids learn to respect and appreciate individual differences. Many adults may remember this activity as part of the Developing Understanding of Self and Others (DUSO) program they experienced in school as kids. Its goal is to help kids understand the crucial importance of teamwork by considering that all people on a team have important contributions to make to the team effort.

1. Collect a variety of nice items (*examples:* book, toy, costume jewelry, game) and ordinary objects (*examples:* spoon, paper napkin, sock). Wrap some of the ordinary objects in beautiful packages and the nice presents in plain brown paper or newspaper and string. The wrapped packages should be different sizes and shapes. Put them in a large carton and bring them to class.

---

*Marlene A. Cummings, Fitchburg, Wisconsin, author of *Individual Differences*, published by the Anti-Defamation League of B'nai B'rith, 1989. Used with permission. Demonstration by Doug Peterson available on YouTube.

2. Have the students sit in a circle. Spread out the packages in front of them. Ask, "Can you guess which packages have the nicest presents inside?" Most students will guess the beautifully wrapped packages.

3. Have students open the packages. Discuss with them how we can't tell what's inside a package by looking at the outside.

4. Call on several students, one at a time, to stand beside you while the other students describe them—in a nice way—as if they were packages. The other students should mention hair color, eyes, height, clothing, skin color, and so on. Then have the students standing beside you share with the class something interesting about themselves that doesn't show in their outer "packaging." These might be thoughts, feelings, experiences, pet peeves, personal likes or dislikes, hobbies, interests, or talents.

5. Draw this analogy for the students: "Just as we can't tell what's inside a wrapped package by looking at the outside, we can't tell what's inside a person, such as thoughts, feelings, or personality, from appearance alone."

Repeat the "People Packages" experience intermittently throughout the year, especially if students engage in name-calling.

## Ready, Set, Go

Sometime during the first week of school, take your students into the gym. Have them form a line facing a wall 20 or 30 feet away. They should all be the same distance from the wall. Tell them that when you say "go," they should all run as fast as they can to the wall. Say that as soon as someone reaches the wall, you'll blow a whistle as a signal for everyone to freeze where they are.

Give the "go" signal. As soon as the first person touches the wall, blow the whistle. Then say, "Now notice where you are standing and where you started. Walk until you get to the wall." When everyone is at the wall, say, "We all started in the same place, and we all ended up in the same place, but we got there at our own pace. We'll do the same with our schoolwork this year. So don't be concerned about anyone's pace but your own."

## Walk in Your Own Shoes*

Exchange shoes with one of the students. The more extreme the exchange, the better (*examples:* high heels for high-tops, large loafers for small sneakers). With the rest of the class as your audience, try to walk around the room in each other's shoes. Feel free to be silly. Discuss why people should wear their own shoes.

*Linda Reynolds, teacher; Elgin, Illinois.

Tell the students that their job is to make sure that the "shoes" they are asked to wear (the learning tasks you provide for them) "fit" them. Explain that your job as their teacher is to see that they are always wearing the correct shoes—that is, that students are doing learning tasks that provide the most comfort and that best enable them to move forward. Students should be concerned only about the shoes they themselves are wearing. They are not to worry about anybody else's shoes. If their shoes don't feel right for a particular learning activity, they should talk to you.

# More Ways to Create a Welcoming Environment

1. Every day, greet your students by name at the door to your classroom. For students who are very shy or who are not working up to grade-level standards, use information from the "Interest Survey" on pages 20–21 to speak to them about something in which they are personally interested. This communicates that you like and respect them even if they are not doing well academically.

2. Students of all ages love to put personal touches on their classroom to make it their home away from home. (*Example:* One teacher writes her room number in outlined block letters on a large sheet of tagboard, cuts out the numbers, then cuts each number into a jigsaw pattern. Each student gets one piece of the jigsaw puzzle. The students illustrate their pieces in ways that describe them. The teacher reassembles the pieces and displays them.)

3. Use your students' names in scenarios and examples you give to illustrate different subject areas.

4. Avoid using labels to describe your students, especially those with learning difficulties. (*Example:* Instead of saying, "Will the kids who need help with their reading come to this table?" simply say, "Harold, Jessie, and Sam, we need you to work with Miss Armstrong at this table for a while.")

5. Work with the school to make sure that the student handbook meets the needs of all students, including new students and those with physical or cognitive difficulties. (*Examples:* Include maps to the cafeteria, office, school counselor, library, and so on. Indicate elevators, ramps, and doors that are wheelchair accessible. If your school doesn't publish a student handbook, perhaps this could be a class project.)

6. Contact families early in the school year with good news—something positive you have noticed about their child. For students with low academic skills, you might

comment on personality traits or behaviors that have made a positive contribution to the class. It's much easier to get family assistance with school-related problems after they have heard something positive from you. All students will feel more welcome in your class when they realize you are looking hard to find their positive qualities.

**7.** Consistently model and teach respect for individual differences and needs. (*Example:* When you consistently offer differentiated learning tasks, you model respect for individual differences and demonstrate that you expect all students to follow your lead.)

**8.** Identify and honor individual learning modalities and personality strengths. (See Chapter 3 for specific strategies and suggestions.) Once you understand your students' learning modalities, and once you allow them to demonstrate what they are learning in a manner compatible with their strengths, it's easier to notice what they do well.

**9.** Avoid emphasizing competition and individual grades. Encourage students to help one another as they learn together on all phases except certain assessments.

**10.** Take every opportunity to show that mistakes are valuable for the learning opportunities they present. (*Example:* When you notice that someone seems confused, say, "You're confused? Good for you! How exciting. Since confusion comes before learning, we know that learning will happen soon."\*)

**11.** Help students maintain their dignity and sense of worth at all times. (*Example:* When you see someone doing something wrong, ask, "What are you getting ready to do?" instead of "What are you doing?" Most kids will stop their inappropriate behavior or switch to a more appropriate task, but the way you ask allows them to maintain their dignity.\*)

**12.** Avoid words or situations that could be interpreted as put-downs. Some of the things we say in jest are not funny to kids. (*Example:* Something as innocent as "Let's look around and see who we are waiting for now" sends a message that it's okay to tease a poky student. It's much better to say, "I'm happy to see so many of you ready to move on to the next subject," and hope that poky kids will get the message. It's also helpful to put your hand on a student's shoulder and say, "We're moving on to math now. Please get ready." Private verbal transactions are always better than public reminders.

**13.** At the end of the school year, have your students write letters to kids who will be coming into your classroom next year. Explain that the letters should help the new students understand you, the rules of your classroom, and the special things that make your classroom exciting and wonderful. Collect and read the letters. Note any ideas that you might want to incorporate into your teaching. Make plans to distribute them to your new students at the start of the next school year.

# Welcoming English Language Learners into the Classroom

English language learners or ELL students—also known as students with limited English proficiency (LEP), students learning English as a second language (ESL), and students in language minorities—are a rapidly growing population in many schools. Who would have imagined that one day we'd hear nearly 400 different languages in our classrooms, including Spanish, Hmong, Cantonese, Arabic, Tagalog, Farsi, Lakota, and Urdu? Here are several ways you can welcome ELL students into your classroom:

**1.** Pronounce the student's name; check pronunciation with the student or family.

**2.** Introduce the student to several classmates, one at a time. Seat the newcomer beside an introduced classmate. Seat the pair near your desk for a while. Make sure that the ELL student has company during recess and lunch.

**3.** Allow new students some time for silent observation of the class and its routines. Take time daily to talk to new students, even if you need to enlist language help from another person.

**4.** Within a week, expect new students to participate orally in class with the help of their partners, using the Name Card Method. (See "The Name Card Method," page 12.) It doesn't even matter if the partners actually understand each other. The new students will feel more like group members if you expect them to participate right away than if you wait until their language is more fluent.

**5.** Keep a routine to your instruction, and be consistent in how you give directions. Review routines often.

**6.** If two or more students who speak the same language work together on their learning tasks, they may feel more comfortable and be more productive.

**7.** Label everything in the classroom in English.

**8.** Use picture dictionaries.

---

\*Rita McNeeley, teacher, Port Huron, Michigan.

9. Present new ideas by starting with the concrete and moving to the abstract.

10. Use slower speech, occasional pauses, and controlled vocabulary, but do not talk louder or sound condescending. Avoid idioms and figures of speech. Allow extra time for students to process language.

11. Avoid yes-or-no questions. Always have students show you what they know or understand. Demonstrate a variety of methods students can use to show their understanding of a given topic.

12. Let students know when you do not understand them. Suggest that students draw pictures or symbols to communicate with you until they have better writing or speaking skills in English. When there is a communication issue, use printed letters rather than cursive to clarify. Use colors to draw attention to word or phrase features to which students should pay special attention.

13. Structure lessons so that students can demonstrate understanding using various language arts skills (reading, writing, speaking, and listening).

14. Give assignments one at a time, using short steps.

15. Reteach, repeat, and review frequently, making adjustments as needed. If a teaching strategy does not work for a specific student, always choose a different approach for reteaching.

16. Be aware of and modify approaches you use in assignment and test directions. ELL students often don't understand terms such as *match*, *identify*, *discuss*, and *compare* until the task is demonstrated.

17. Maintain high expectations. Expect students to do high-quality work and grade them on forward progress. Provide specific praise for things students do correctly, as well as for not giving up easily and for being willing to work hard.

18. Teach, model, and expect all students to accept their peers' mistakes without laughing or teasing. Karen Brown, a teacher from Phoenix, always tells her whole class, "It's not about the grades; it's about the learning." She has her students chant the second part of that phrase in unison. Students quickly understand this important message.

19. Provide adaptations for all assignments regarding the number of examples students must do, the amount of time they should work on a specific task, and the amount of help they can receive while working. ELL students often respond positively to the same strategies we use successfully with visual, tactile, or kinesthetic learners.

20. Whenever possible, use graphic organizers with consistent topics. See "The Content Organization Chart" (page 144).

21. Provide hands-on materials and manipulatives.

22. Structure activities so students can apply their newly acquired understanding.

23. Hold the same behavioral expectations for ELL students as you do for other class members.

24. Create opportunities for students to share their native languages and customs with the class.

25. Encourage families to speak or read in their native language at home. For school events you want families to attend, send notices home in the family's native language, and indicate whether translators or childcare will be available.

26. Provide different types of assessments at different levels of literacy development to measure growth in understanding.

27. Find and use any available technology that will speed up the student's English acquisition.

Many of these suggestions are also helpful for making new English-speaking students feel welcome in your classroom.

# Getting Everyone Involved in Learning

Because all students are capable learners, you as a teacher must demonstrate that all students are expected to fully participate in all activities. Sometimes you will want to offer options for students to choose from, but everyone should be involved in learning. Students who are allowed to disengage from active participation in your class are less likely to be successful than those who are highly engaged.

> Because all students are capable learners, you as a teacher must demonstrate that all students are expected to fully participate in all activities.

Some of our teaching behaviors actually encourage *dis*engagement. When certain students we call on don't respond and we move on to other students, those we leave may assume that we don't see them as capable. They may not realize that our reason for moving on is to save them from embarrassment. Our good intentions send the wrong message.

# The Name Card Method*

The Name Card Method communicates our expectation that *all* students will be active in class discussions. It gives kids a chance to develop friendships and fulfills the following expectations:

- No students will ever be able to hide from you again by being uninvolved.

- No students will ever be able to dominate class discussions.

- Blurting or calling out answers will dramatically decrease.

- Listening behaviors will dramatically improve.

- You will have nearly 100 percent participation in all discussions.

- You will not unconsciously engage in ethnic, cultural, or gender bias as you lead discussions.

- Students of all ages and abilities will find this method preferable to traditional hand raising and will even remind you to use the name cards if you forget. Most students recognize how fair this method is to all.

Well-meaning teachers often unintentionally communicate low expectations for some students by always asking them the easier questions or by letting them off the hook during class discussions. Unfortunately, the message students get when we do not hold them completely accountable is that we do not really believe they can handle the material. The Name Card Method makes certain that we communicate only the highest expectations—that all students will be able to participate successfully in discussions.

## Getting Ready

**1.** Tell your students that there will be no more hand raising during class discussions unless you specifically ask them to raise their hands.

**2.** Write each student's name on a three-by-five-inch card and gather the cards into a deck. **Tips:** Some teachers have kids make their own name cards and decorate them, but you may prefer to have some space on each card for jotting down information about the student. Some junior and senior high school teachers use color-coded cards with a specific color for each class period. Some special education teachers with very small groups

make double and triple decks, with each student's name appearing several times in the deck. And some primary teachers use craft sticks rather than cards. Please avoid using playing cards. It is uncomfortable for some students to spend a class period as the king of hearts or the two of spades. Using their actual names will also help you learn them.

**3.** Group students in pairs and seat them together. Tell your students that the pairs will change every few weeks so they will not have to work with the same partner indefinitely.

Allow *some* disparity in ability but not large gaps. Research on role modeling by educational psychologist Dale Schunk indicates that a great disparity between partners inhibits the struggling student and robs the gifted student of opportunities to experience new learning.** You might place your most capable students with each other; place high achievers with more average students; or place kids who love to help others with students who struggle the most. If you have some highly capable students who want to work with kids who have learning difficulties, allow them to do so on a limited basis.

If your students are in rows, seat the pairs across the aisle from each other. During discussions, they move their chairs together; at other times, they sit in their regular rows. If kids come to a rug or other gathering place for discussions, have them sit beside their partners. If your students are already in groups, designate pairs within the groups. Students whose partners are absent should join another pair until their partners return.

## Using the Name Card Method

Explain to your students why you are using the cards. Feel free to adapt and use one or more of the reasons listed previously or come up with your own. Students who are reluctant to use the cards will be more likely to cooperate when they know the reasons.

To get the best results with the Name Card Method, start with a discussion that uses open-ended questions, such as a discussion of a book students are reading, a current events discussion, or some challenging questions from any subject matter.

**1.** Tell the class that you are going to ask a series of questions. Explain that you will call on several students for the answer to each question, so no one should talk or blurt anything out of turn.

**2.** Ask a question. Give the students 10 to 15 seconds to THINK about their answers. Do not acknowledge any blurting. Remind students who start to talk prematurely that thinking time is not up yet.

*Adapted from "Think-Pair-Share, ThinkTrix, Thinklinks, and Weird Facts" by Frank T. Lyman Jr. in *Enhancing Thinking Through Cooperative Learning*, edited by Neil Davidson and Toni Worsham. NY: Teachers College Press, 1992. Used with permission.

**Schunk, Dale H. "Peer Models and Children's Behavioral Change." *Review of Educational Research* 52:2 (1987), pp. 149–174.

3. At your signal—such as saying "Pair up!"—have the students PAIR up with their designated partners to discuss possible answers to the question you have posed. The first time you do this, describe the signal you will use to call them back to your voice. You may have to practice this with the students until it becomes a habit for them. (*Examples:* You might say, "Time's up!" or clap your hands.) As soon as you give the signal, they should stop talking—even in the middle of a sentence or a word—and return their attention to you.

Have the pairs discuss possible answers to the question for 30 to 45 seconds. Tell them to use soft voices. If they want, they can write down their answers. Explain that these notes are for their own use and will not be collected.

While the students are talking, walk around to monitor that they are all on task. If some students get off task, consider the possibility that you've given them too much time. It's always better if they feel a little concern about needing to finish their discussion before you give the signal.

You might also use this time to coach reluctant students to prepare answers in case their cards are drawn (an event you already know will happen, but the students don't). When the time is up, use the signal you practiced to bring them back to attention.

4. It is now time to SHARE. Call on the student whose name is on the top card in the deck. Don't show the cards to the students, because sometimes (as in the scenario on page 14) you may want to manipulate the cards for a specific reason. **Tip:** Don't look at the cards before asking the question. In this way, you avoid the possibility of trying to match a question's difficulty with your perception of a student's intelligence. When we ask difficult questions of students we consider capable and easy questions of those we think are less capable, we communicate low expectations for struggling students. Struggling students can usually answer challenging questions after conferring with their discussion buddies during pair time.

5. Once you call on someone, follow these guidelines to show students they are capable of answering after adequate support has been provided. Avoid asking the student to call on others for help or asking the class to help the student, because these actions send a message that you have low expectations. Instead, if no response is forthcoming *within 10 seconds*, invite the student to confer again with his or her partner and say that you will return in a few moments for an answer. Meanwhile, hold the student's name card prominently, so it's obvious that you will remember to come back to the student. It's imperative that you *do* return within the next minute or so. This shows that you absolutely believe the student is capable of responding. If the student still cannot respond, you may offer a choice between two options or give a hint. (*Example:* "See if you can visualize how the main character solved the problem about the dog in the film we saw yesterday.")

6. You might also allow the student to say, "I need a little more time. Please come back to me." By using these strategies, other students do not have to wait too long for any student's response, and you can avoid any expression of annoyance toward the students who need this type of scaffolding. **Tip:** When you are in the habit of repeating students' answers aloud, kids soon discover that they don't have to listen very carefully.

7. Receive three or more unique responses to the same question without indicating whether the responses are correct. It doesn't matter whether a response is the speaker's or the partner's idea. What really matters is that all students are thinking about their answers to every question you ask.

After each response has been given, say, "thank you" or "okay" or "mm-hm," but give no judgments or praise of any kind, then call on another student with the same question. When students see that you will request multiple responses to the same question, they keep thinking about the question even after someone else has answered it. They know their name cards might be next, and they'll have to come up with reasonable responses as well.

Throughout the discussion, shuffle the name cards often. If students never know when their cards might come up, they'll pay more attention. If you place the used cards on the bottom of the deck (or the craft sticks into a different container from which they were pulled), kids will learn that they can mentally go to sleep when their turns end.

8. Before moving on to the next question, and for the benefit of students who enjoy sharing their deep wealth of knowledge, ask, "Does anyone have anything to add that has not already been said?" Students with something to add should raise their hands.

Explain that the ticket to being allowed to add to the discussion is to listen well to everyone else's contribution. If students repeat something said earlier, you will simply say, "That's already been said." You will not call on repeaters again during this discussion unless their cards come up. Tell the class that you don't need any help noting repeated information. In other words, you don't want to hear a loud chorus of "That's a repeat!" each time it happens.

9. Remember to use the Name Card Method when reviewing for assessments. You will be amazed at how much more students remember for those situations because they have been paying much closer attention to the lessons and discussions.

Only very rarely do teachers report that their students resist the Name Card Method. If that happens with your students, try these ideas:

- Be sure that you have taken the time to assign partners and to let the partners work together during discussions as we have described on page 12. If you use the method without the partners, students' anxiety levels rise dramatically. Not much clear thinking goes on when anxiety is high.

- Be sure to explain the reasons you're using the cards. When students understand your goals, they are more likely to comply. You can use the list of reasons on page 12.

- If all else fails, tell your students you are taking a graduate class and must do this for an assignment. Ask them to please try it out with you for two weeks so you can complete your assignment and get your grade. At the end of the two weeks, have a discussion with them about the reasons for use and their experience with the experiment. Most students, by virtue of their positive experience with the method, will agree that it's okay for you to keep using it.

## Variations on Think-Pair-Share

As you lead your students through the THINK and PAIR steps of the Name Card Method, you can also help them practice the following thinking categories of the ThinkTrix model developed by teacher educator Dr. Frank Lyman. Chapter 4 describes this model in more detail.*

- *Recall:* Students simply remember what they have learned.

- *Similarity:* Students find ways in which ideas, people, or events are similar.

- *Difference:* Students find ways in which ideas, people, or events are different.

- *Cause-effect:* Students demonstrate that they understand the relationships between causes and effects of events, behaviors, ideas, and so on.

- *Idea to example:* Students give specific examples of ideas being discussed.

- *Example to idea:* Students draw conclusions, make summaries, explore themes, explain rules, and so on to show that they get the big ideas.

---

*Adapted from "Think-Pair-Share, ThinkTrix, Thinklinks, and Weird Facts" by Frank T. Lyman Jr. in *Enhancing Thinking Through Cooperative Learning,* edited by Neil Davidson and Toni Worsham. NY: Teachers College Press, 1992. Used with permission of Frank T. Lyman Jr., teacher educator and originator of the Think, Pair, Share method as well as ThinkTrix, Principle-Based Coaching Wheels, and the Problem-Solving Flow Chart.

- *Evaluation:* Students give their opinions concerning the value of something: good or bad, right or wrong, significant or insignificant. This usually involves analyzing for cause and effect.

Students can vary the time that they spend as they PAIR by:

- taking turns teaching each other what the teacher has just taught

- explaining to their partners their own thinking about the concepts being learned

- identifying the type of thinking being called for by the questions

- writing about what they have learned as a pair

- reading aloud certain passages to each other to gather information or answer questions

- reviewing information for upcoming assessments

Finally, students can vary the ways in which they SHARE by:

- speaking

- reading

- acting out their ideas

- finding connections between old and new ideas

- indicating their judgments of material they are learning

## Scenario: Jamar

Jamar was a very pleasant young man but a reluctant learner. Whenever he was put on the spot, he blushed noticeably. He was extremely nervous the first time Susan used the Name Card Method to review the state capitals, which all fifth graders in the district were required to know. When Susan called his name, he just sat there silently, daring her to do something about it. She asked if she could speak to him after class.

"Jamar," she said, once everyone else had left the room, "I don't think you like this Name Card Method."

Jamar replied sarcastically, "What was your first clue?"

"Well," Susan said, "I can see that you're upset, and I want to reassure you that my goal in using the cards is not to make anyone uncomfortable. Perhaps you are worried about too many things, like when your card is coming up and what state I will ask you about."

"Yeah," he replied. "Isn't everybody worried about the same things?"

"Well," Susan said, "they may be worried, but it certainly isn't affecting them the way it's affecting you.

So let's try to make this less stressful for you. Tomorrow, when your card comes up, I'll ask you to name the capital of South Dakota."

Jamar paused for a few seconds, looked at Susan suspiciously, and asked, "How do you know you'll ask me that?"

"Trust me," she replied. "I just know. But there's one rule that goes with this arrangement. You can't tell anyone else at school about it."

"Why not?" he asked.

"Because this is a special arrangement between you and me, and no one else needs to know," Susan stated simply.

For nine consecutive days, on his way out to recess, Jamar made it his business to toss something into the trash can near Susan's desk. As he walked by, she softly said the name of his state for the following day. On the tenth day, he looked as if he was going to leave without getting the prompt.

"Jamar," Susan called from the desk, "didn't you forget something here?"

"Oh," he said, smiling sheepishly, "I don't need that anymore."

And he didn't!

Imagine the outcome if Susan had thought, "Oh, poor Jamar, he blushes and he's embarrassed, so I guess I'll leave him alone." Excusing him from participation would have indicated her agreement with him that he was unable to participate. Insisting on his participation, with the appropriate support system, sent him a clear message: "You *can* participate. You *will* participate. This is something you can do."

# Cooperative Learning/ Problem-Based Learning

The principles of cooperative learning can dramatically improve learning outcomes in group work for students who are struggling to learn. Students with learning difficulties do much better in classrooms where carefully defined group roles are used regularly, because it becomes acceptable for kids to help each other learn.

## How to Integrate Students with Learning Difficulties into Cooperative Learning and Problem-Solving Groups

In classrooms where competition is expected, there is little or no incentive for students to help struggling students learn. In classrooms where cooperative learning is valued, every student's chances for success are enhanced. But if other students perceive that struggling students will lower the outcomes for everyone, resistance and resentment are predictable. We must create conditions that prevent these problems. Following are suggestions for integrating students with learning difficulties into cooperative learning or problem-solving groups.

### Group Gifted Students Together

Group your three or four most capable students together and give them an extension of the regular grade-level task. When gifted students are in mixed-abilities cooperative learning groups with struggling students, the gifted kids tend to take over and get bossy. They fear that if they don't take charge, the group product or outcome will not meet their high standards. When gifted students are not in the mixed-ability groups, other kids have a chance to show off their talents.

### Avoid Group Grades

Instead of giving group grades, set up the assessment so that all students earn credit for their own contributions, as well as a bonus for the group product. When everyone in the group achieves a certain level of learning, everyone gets a bonus. (*Example:* Add up to five points to each person's individual score.)

It is perfectly acceptable to make special agreements with struggling students so their presence does not create a hardship for other students in their groups. At the beginning of a group learning project, ask those students to set their own goals regarding what they expect to achieve. If they reach their goals—even if they are less than what you expect from the rest of the group—they can still contribute to the group's bonus. (See the "Goal Setting" section on page 61.)

### Assign Group Roles

Give students with special learning needs jobs or roles that allow them to demonstrate their learning strengths. (*Example:* Some students may be highly creative or good at assembling things. Try putting them in the leadership role in a group activity that relies on spatial, visual, or mechanical thinking, such as working with tangram puzzles. Traditionally, linguistically gifted kids do poorly at tangram-type tasks, while students who may struggle with typical learning tasks are often highly skilled at tasks that require visual-spatial ability.)

### Create and Use Home Groups*

Home groups give all kids an anchor group to belong to. A home group is the group in which the student sits for a few minutes each day at the beginning of class. Students move from their home groups to their work

---

*Adapted from *Cooperation in the Classroom* (7th edition) by David Johnson, Roger Johnson, and Edythe Holubec. Edina, MN: Interaction Book Company, 1998. Used with permission. The eighth edition was published in 2008.

groups for cooperative learning activities and tasks or for more independent learning activities. They return to their home groups at the end of class to make sure that each group member understands the homework and remembers to take it home.

A home group might be made up of students who live in the same neighborhood, so group members can take homework to absent students. If attendance is a problem at your school, you might offer a group incentive, such as points toward a prize each day that all group members come to school. If group members have each other's telephone numbers (with permission from families), they might actually call one another and provide encouragement to come to school so the group can earn its points.

Other ways for home group members to support each other include:*

1. encouraging perfect attendance except when sick

2. helping all group members gather the school supplies needed for the day

3. coaching one another on basic information that must be learned (math facts, spelling, and so on)

4. preparing for an assessment

5. brainstorming and listing what is already known about a topic (See "KWPL" on page 101 for more information.)

6. brainstorming solutions to class problems in preparation for class meetings

7. doing show-and-tell in small groups rather than for the whole class

8. collecting homework for absent students and delivering it to them

9. checking homework together by comparing answers and reaching consensus, then making corrections in a different-colored pencil or pen

10. turning in completed homework (*Example:* Students receive their own grades plus bonus points if all group members turn in completed homework, and they earn more bonus points if all homework meets specific grade or rubric criteria.)

Note: Be sure to read the section in Chapter 11 on homework for more information about this important issue (see page 229).

## Use Pair Practice**

Use this technique when you are lecturing or teaching something to the whole class. It's especially effective when kids are working on projects for an integrated learning unit, and you want to find out how much they know about the entire topic, rather than just their small portion of it.

Designate the students in each pair as Partner A and Partner B. After you have taught a small portion of information, ask Partner A to reteach it to Partner B using any method that seems comfortable. Use the Name Card Method to check how many students understand the concept. If most students understand it, teach another small portion, then have Partner B reteach it to Partner A.

# More Ways to Get Everyone Involved in Learning

**1.** In one school, each student was required to set one academic goal and one social-behavioral goal at a time and focus on these goals until they were achieved. The school purchased a button-making machine and made "Yes I Can" buttons for everyone. Kids set goals, talked about their goals, and learned how to congratulate one another when goals were accomplished. The program was most successful when kids set short-term goals for each week or grading period. You might start a yearlong campaign to focus on students' growth through goal setting. As part of your campaign, emphasize positive self-talk. Whenever kids speak negatively about themselves by saying, "I can't do this," other kids (and the teacher) chant, "Yes you can!" Then the students answer, "Yes I can!" Talking about this with family members at conferences provides a positive note for every conference.

**2.** Teach your students that meaningful success comes from the ability to set and accomplish realistic short-term goals. Remember that kids who perceive themselves as incapable are unlikely to reach lofty goals of getting high grades unless they learn how to reach those goals in small, doable steps. See "Goal Setting" on page 61.

**3.** Create an atmosphere in which making mistakes is always expected, always encouraged as an opportunity for learning, and never the object of ridicule. Regularly tell your students that if work is always correct, no learning is happening. Share stories from your own

*Adapted from *Cooperation in the Classroom* (7th edition) by David Johnson, Roger Johnson, and Edythe Holubec. Edina, MN: Interaction Book Company, 1998. Used with permission. The eighth edition was published in 2008.

**Adapted from *Tape 9: Biology—Visual Learning Tools (High School)*. The Lesson Collection. Alexandria, VA: ASCD Video, 2000. Used with permission.

life—especially your childhood—that illustrate how you use mistakes as learning experiences.

4. Set up a volunteer peer tutoring location in the classroom, where struggling students can meet with students who can help. Never coerce any student into being a peer tutor; ask for volunteers only. Keep in mind that some kids are better tutors if they are still trying to master a concept than if they have already mastered it.

5. Model, teach, and reinforce the concept that in your classroom, the word *equal* does not mean "the same." Explain that all students have equal opportunities to learn and move ahead, but they won't always be doing the same activities. Emphasize that it is each student's job to learn and not to worry about how other students are learning. In this way, you avoid creating an environment in which students accuse you of being unfair when they see that all students aren't treated the same. Instead, you create an environment in which all individuals are greatly respected.

6. Involve the whole class to work as a team to fully integrate students with learning difficulties. Share as much information as you have about how and why learning difficulties manifest themselves, so facts will replace rumors and misinformation. Whenever possible, support all students' efforts to make this full integration happen over time.

### Unlocking Autism 🔒

The entire system of formal schooling exacerbates the social and learning challenges faced by students with ASD. Working partnerships among all the school people and family members who have contact with the student support successful socialization. Goals are much more likely to be reached, and even transferred to other situations, when these supports are present.

## Ticket Out the Door

1. A few minutes before the end of a lesson, ask students to take out a half sheet of paper. Tell them not to write their name on it, but to write "boy" or "girl" at the top and their class period. (This will help you discover any differences in the way both genders respond.) Ask them to write:

   - two things they understand well about today's lesson

   - one thing they don't completely understand about the lesson, or a question they would like to have answered

   Explain that spelling and mechanics aren't important. Tell them that this is their ticket out the door. They can't leave the classroom unless they give it to you on their way out.

2. Stand at the classroom door and collect the tickets as the students leave.

3. Use the information from the tickets to plan the next day's learning activities.

Involvement improves when students know they have to create a written record of what they have learned.

**Variation:** If students don't leave the room between lessons, you can call these notes "tickets to the next lesson" and have kids complete them before you go on to the next lesson.

# Questions and Answers

*"Won't some students, particularly those in the upper grades, think that the welcoming activities are silly or weird?"*

Students with learning difficulties often perceive school as impersonal and uncaring. Many students who drop out of school feel alienated from their peers. Welcoming activities, like "Say Hello to Someone Who . . ." (page 7), can give students a vital sense of belonging. To make this activity more relevant (and less silly) for adolescents, create your own handout with different information in the boxes. If you need more ideas for use with older kids, brainstorm possibilities with your colleagues.

*"What if a particular child's parents don't respond to my attempts to contact them? Some parents seem totally uninterested in their children's school experience, and I feel I may be wasting my time with those parents."*

Some parents do seem to resist the school's efforts to reach out to them. (Chapter 11 discusses this problem in more detail.) Keep in mind that for many parents of students with learning difficulties, most of their previous contact with the school may have been unpleasant. Once parents realize that you are trying to bring out the best in their child, their attitude may change. Be sure to call or email home weekly with good news about some success their child has experienced in school. The more good news they get, the more likely they are to visit the school when invited. Ask your public librarian or university library to help you find information about programs designed to increase parents' participation in their children's school experience.

***"What do I do if kids refuse to answer when their name comes up in the Name Card Method?"***

This may happen the first few times you try this strategy, as certain students who have convinced some of their teachers that they can't talk or participate try to get you to believe the same thing. Jamar's scenario (page 14) describes one way to deal with reluctant or openly resistant students. *Always* allow students to confer with partners before you call on them; this goes a long way toward reducing anxiety. Call on reluctant students early in the process, when they still have answers left on their written list. Give them particularly supportive partners. In most cases, students become less anxious about the Name Card Method as it becomes more familiar to them. In cases of serious emotional problems, consult with the school counselor, psychologist, or social worker for advice on how to ease students into the process.

***"I've had some students who simply won't talk to anyone in the classroom—not to me and not to other students. What can I do about this?"***

Over the years, some people have referred to this condition as "selective mutism," since some of these students talk comfortably in some settings while totally refusing to speak in others. Observe your nontalking students to see if they talk in other classes, on the playground, in the halls, or in the cafeteria. Use the Name Card Method to hold them accountable for responding to classroom questions. Call on them early in discussions, so they have responses to share after consulting with their partners as described in "The Name Card Method" on page 12.

The longer we allow students to avoid actively engaging in learning, the longer they will hide. Research on this condition documents that such students may be experiencing anxiety disorders, so consult with your counselors or social workers if your attempts don't lead to improvement or if they increase students' anxiety. If students have anxiety disorders, do not make a big deal about whether they talk in your class. Do not mention that you heard them speak to other students or in other environments. Do not pressure them into speaking through incentives or through repeated asking. Simply make it clear that they may participate in established practices for class participation.

A variety of rating scales exists to assess student anxiety. Consult your school psychologist for more information. You can use anxiety assessments to develop strategies targeting high-anxiety situations, which usually occur during larger group activities. These should be the last areas in which you expect participation. You might want to allow audio or video recordings for oral presentations. Finally, remember that if you share the questions with some students in a private manner before the discussion and give them a few moments to talk to their partners about the answers, this can significantly reduce their anxiety.

***"Won't gifted kids develop an overinflated opinion of themselves if they are always in their own cooperative learning group?"***

Gifted kids often become more humble when their task is appropriately challenging and they realize they can't complete it alone with ease. Furthermore, the makeup of a gifted cooperative learning group often changes with different subject areas. For example, the most gifted artists are not always the most capable readers, so they may also benefit from the strategies described in this book.

***"Won't other students resent special arrangements you make with struggling students to earn credit in the cooperative learning group?"***

Other students are more likely to resent arrangements in which some students' severe learning difficulties are a disadvantage for their group. If all mixed-abilities cooperative learning groups have at least one student who needs special arrangements, or if the student who has these special needs is rotated among several groups over time, there should be no resentment.

# Say Hello to Someone Who . . .

| Stayed in town all summer | Goes to ball games | Went on a trip |
|---|---|---|
| **Likes cheeseburgers** | **Has more than three brothers or sisters** | **Speaks more than one language** |
| **Has been to Disney World** | **Can kick or throw a ball really far** | **Is new to our school** |
| **Can play a musical instrument** | **Wears glasses or contact lenses** | **Likes to read** |

# Interest Survey

1. Do you speak any languages besides English at home? If you do, please tell which languages you can speak and understand.

   _____

   _____

2. What types of TV or web programs do you like to watch? Why?

   _____

   _____

   _____

   _____

3. Does your home have a computer or tablet you are allowed to use? How do you do use it? Do you use a smartphone to go online? Describe two of your favorite websites or apps.

   _____

   _____

   _____

   _____

   _____

   _____

   _____

4. Tell about your favorite games or hobbies.

   _____

   _____

   _____

   _____

   _____

5. What kinds of movies do you like to see? Why?

   _____

   _____

   _____

   _____

6. Tell about a vacation you would like to take.

   _____

   _____

   _____

   _____

7. What is your favorite activity or subject at school? Why?

   _____

   _____

   _____

   _____

8. What is your least favorite activity or subject at school? Why?

   _____

   _____

   _____

   _____

9. What kinds of things have you collected? What do you do with the things you collect?

   _____

   _____

   _____

   _____

continued →

10. What career(s) do you think might be right for you when you are an adult?

_____

_____

_____

_____

_____

11. What kinds of books or magazines do you like?

_____

_____

_____

_____

12. How do you learn about the news in your neighborhood, city, state or province, country, or the world? Ask older people to describe the changes they have seen in how the news is delivered to people.

_____

_____

_____

_____

_____

13. What is your first choice for what to do when you have free time at home?

_____

_____

_____

_____

_____

14. If you could talk to any person alive today, who would it be? Why? Think of three questions you would ask the person.

_____

_____

_____

_____

_____

_____

15. Imagine that you could invent something to make the world a better place. Describe your invention.

_____

_____

_____

_____

_____

_____

16. What is something you can do really well?

_____

_____

_____

_____

17. Tell me something else about yourself that you would like me to know.

_____

_____

_____

_____

# CHAPTER 2

# Understanding Learning Difficulties and Intervening Effectively

With so many types of learning difficulties, entire books have been devoted to each type. After careful research, we have concluded that it is not the classroom teacher's job to definitively identify the specific category into which a struggling student fits—because of the high amount of crossover among categories, even experts are not always sure of their diagnoses. Rather, the teacher's job is to gather and apply as many teaching strategies as possible, with the intent of matching those that work best to each student's needs. This book does the gathering. The application is up to you.

This chapter summarizes characteristics of students with significant learning problems and offers suggestions for intervening with some of those problems. The material can help you better understand and meet the needs of students in your classroom who are having significant trouble learning, including students in special education who spend part or all of each day in regular education classrooms and students who are not fluent in English. To obtain more detailed information about specific types of learning difficulties, see "References and Resources" at the end of this book.

As you work with your struggling students, regardless of their specific diagnoses, keep the following points in mind:

**1.** Huge numbers of children who appear to have learning difficulties are not really learning disabled—they are learning *strategy* disabled. Once they learn to use effective strategies, their disabilities fade away. This leaves us with a small number of students whose brains perceive different messages than their senses do.

**2.** Never forget the important fact that kids with learning difficulties really *cannot* learn in traditional ways. They are *not* choosing to fail. The strategies presented in this book have been proven to help struggling students become more successful learners. Don't worry about using the wrong strategy or technique with the wrong category of student. Don't worry about whether a student has been formally labeled "learning disabled" or "special education." Just use what works and congratulate yourself for trying.

**3.** Many kids who struggle to learn have average or even above-average intelligence. Their learning challenges are unrelated to intelligence. Frustration with learning significantly increases inappropriate behaviors and might make students appear less competent than they really are. Many behavior problems improve notably when students perceive themselves as being successful in school.

Attention deficit hyperactivity disorder (ADHD) is one of the disorders most frequently experienced by students in the special education community. The *DSM-5* describes ADHD as being either "with or without hyperactivity." See page 36 for additional information about ADHD and working with students who have the diagnosis.

**4.** Ritalin and similar drugs are intended to be used with kids whose neurological impairments include hyperactivity or attention disorders, so they can focus better on academic subjects and appropriate social behaviors. However, chemical intervention should occur only after several modifications in curriculum and behavior management have been tried. For some students, the modifications are enough. For those who need chemical intervention, the dosage may be adjusted once compensation behaviors have been learned and have become somewhat automatic.

**5.** Before you take a stand for or against chemical intervention, talk to adults who have ADHD. They are in the best position to describe their life with and without medication. Read *Faking It* by Christopher Lee and Rosemary Jackson, *Making the Words Stand Still* by Donald E. Lyman, and *Driven to Distraction* by Edward M. Hallowell and John J. Ratey for additional insights. Also view the film *How Difficult Can This Be?* by Richard Lavoie. (See "References and Resources.") These resources can increase your empathy for the small percentage of students who actually have some neurological perceptual impairment.

**6.** Be assertive in asking for assistance from the special education staff and administrators when you face challenges in teaching students with exceptional learning needs. These professionals should provide the support you need, so you don't have to significantly reduce the level of attention and services you give to your other students. In our opinion, it is not ethical for the practice of inclusion to totally sacrifice the needs of children in regular education to the needs of students in special education.

**7.** Many of the strategies that help struggling students become more successful are also helpful with other students, including those who are not fluent in English. All your students—and their parents as well—will appreciate your efforts to improve learning success for everyone.

# Learning Difficulties (LD)

In this book, the term *LD* refers to all students with learning difficulties. We would rather use a term that contains more hope than the term *learning disabilities*. Over the years, concern has developed about overidentification (labeling students who are not truly exceptional) in some geographic areas or with certain physicians. Rather than focus on specific categories of need, this book allows you to stock your backpack of teaching strategies with a wide variety of interventions,

which you should feel free to use with any student who demonstrates a need for them.

The following descriptions will help teachers and parents understand student diagnoses as described in the evaluation reports they receive from the psychologists who have done the special education testing. (Note to readers: to special education professionals, the word *aurally* means "how a student hears spoken language.")

**1. Processing deficits** are problems recognizing and interpreting information taken in through the senses. The two most common areas of processing difficulty associated with learning difficulties are visual and auditory perception.

**2. Auditory sequencing** is the ability to order information received aurally, such as directions, lists, events, or sounds. Most sequencing tasks involve memory.

---

The teacher's job is to gather and apply as many teaching strategies as possible, with the intent of matching those that work best to each student's needs.

---

**3. Auditory memory** is the ability to remember information received aurally, such as directions, events, or lists. Using modalities other than verbal makes the task easier to recall for students with auditory memory difficulties.

**4. Visual sequencing** refers to the ability to see objects, such as a series of events, the alphabet, or spelling of words, in a particular sequential order. Most sequencing tasks involve memory.

**5. Visual memory** is the ability to retain and recall previously seen materials, including stories, words, or a series of events, after the visual images are no longer available.

**6. Dysgraphia** is a learning difficulty that makes the act of writing difficult. It includes problems with spelling, handwriting, and putting thoughts on paper. When students say, "I can tell you about this, but I can't write it down," they are telling the truth, and we should not infer that they are too lazy to write. The best accommodation for dysgraphia is to have students respond orally. They should get appropriate credit for the subject area in which they have been assessed, but their writing counts only in assessments if the target assignment is writing. For more about writing, see page 118.

**7. Visual-motor integration (VMI)** is the ability to see something and match an appropriate movement to it. An example is reading a word on an interactive whiteboard and writing it on a piece of paper.

**8. Auditory figure ground** is the ability to distinguish directions and other needed information given orally in the classroom from background noise, such as the hum of lights, children talking, and outside noise.

**9. Visual figure ground** is the ability to see and isolate such things as a detail, picture, word, or number from background visuals when presented with a lot of visual information at one time.

**10. Visual discrimination** is the ability to look at items such as letters, words, or numbers and note similarities and differences in what you see.

**11. Spatial orientation** is the ability to interpret correctly how an individual's body is situated and should move in the environment around it. Examples of spatial orientation difficulties include not walking "correctly" in the hall or in a line; students' lack of awareness about how they present themselves, such as with posture, lack of modesty, or wearing things that are inappropriate to certain situations; and respecting others' personal space.

**12. Expressive language** is how we share our knowledge, feelings, and thoughts with others through speaking, writing, or body language. Students with expressive language difficulties may have problems with fluency in speaking and writing, because their brains have improperly stored information at some time in the past. They may rarely get through a sentence without many stops and starts.

**13. Receptive language** is the ability to understand and comprehend what is being said or read to you.

## How It Feels to Have LD

The best place we know for adults to get an easy-to-digest understanding of what it really means to have a significant learning difficulty is the work of educator Richard Lavoie. His landmark work is a video titled *How Difficult Can This Be? The F.A.T. City Workshop*. This unique program allows viewers to experience the same frustration, anxiety, and tension that children with learning difficulties face in their daily lives. In the video, teachers, social workers, psychologists, parents, and friends who have participated in Lavoie's workshop comment upon their experience and how it changed the ways in which they interact with children who have LD. Another excellent source of information about what it's like to have LD is Lavoie's video *Last One Picked . . . First One Picked On*. Both videos are memorable and moving. Either can help people without LD understand those with LD and be more supportive of individuals with any type of learning difficulty. See "References and Resources" for more information on these videos. You may also explore Lavoie's work at www.ricklavoie.com.

By definition, many students with LD have average to above-average intelligence, but they experience processing problems when their brains receive stimuli from their senses. A significant discrepancy exists between their ability as measured on individual intelligence quotient (IQ) tests and their school performance as evaluated by their teachers. The difficulty reflects the area of the brain where processing problems occur. For example, some students misperceive symbolic language but may be highly capable when dealing with concrete representations. Words and numbers do not make logical sense to them when found outside a meaningful, concrete context. They become very frustrated when the adults in their lives plead with them, "Just *try* a little harder! You need to put more effort into this if you want to be successful!"

People with LD usually have some learning problems throughout their lives. One does not outgrow LD; one develops coping strategies. For example, many students with LD have developed an "I don't care" attitude to divert attention from their inability to perform school tasks. These kids are often immature, since their LD may also have affected their growth in the areas of physical coordination and emotional development. They may be unable to detect the subtle cues that enable people to function capably and appropriately in social situations, and may therefore exhibit socially unacceptable behaviors. Some students experience constant stress and tension as a result of their LD, which may cause physical symptoms and further inhibit their capacity to learn.

A poignant description of what it's like to have severe LD is found in Lee and Jackson's book *Faking It*. Following is a summary of some observations Lee makes about his experiences.*

Christopher Lee was in the second grade before he realized that something was wrong with him. He was pulled out of public school and placed in a school for so-called "special" kids. It didn't take him long to realize that the word *special* did not mean "extraordinary" and, in fact, did not have a positive meaning at all. He soon concluded that *learning disabled* was a cover phrase for "slow and stupid."

He experienced teasing and cruel treatment from his peers and even from well-meaning teachers who constantly admonished him to try harder, revealing their inability to understand that his learning problems were too complex to

---

*Summarized from *Faking It: A Look into the Mind of a Creative Learner* by Christopher Lee and Rosemary F. Jackson, pp. 21, 25, 28–29. Portsmouth, NH: Heinemann, 1992. Used with permission.

be solved by more effort. His coping strategy was to hide his inabilities from his teacher, his parents, and his peers—to fake being normal.

Christopher's learning problems affected his ability to see and hear letters correctly and to express his thoughts orally and in writing. Spelling was particularly painful for him because "words never seemed to be spelled the way I heard them and words never looked the same twice." For many years, he assumed that writing and spelling were synonymous, and since he could not spell, he felt he could not write. It was only after encountering a computer with a spell-check program that he realized that writing was connected more to content than to mechanics. In his words: "Spending so much time on trying to teach someone with a learning disability to spell might be detrimental to that person's ability to ever learn to write."

The mechanics of writing were very difficult for him to master. "When I am writing, I see a continuous line. I don't see punctuation . . . and so I don't stop when I read. I don't see where sentences and paragraphs begin or end. I never see any structure when I read, and therefore I don't know how to use it when I am writing." His thoughts went faster than he could speak or write them, and he had to stop and start often when trying to express a complete thought. At the same time, he was sidetracked by trying to find out what different words and phrases meant, and he eventually forgot what he wanted to write.

His auditory deficits made it almost impossible for him to attach the correct sounds to the letters that represent them, so a phonics approach simply didn't work for him. When the same words were written with a capital letter or a lowercase letter at the beginning or appeared in different typefaces, he perceived them as different words. His deficits in understanding language made it impossible for him to understand much of what people were saying when they tried to explain things to him, including his own disabilities.

Christopher concluded that labels of deficiency create fewer learning opportunities for kids. In effect, they become known and referred to as their disability. For example, Christopher became the kid with multiple learning disabilities. It can be very demeaning and frustrating.

---

Christopher concluded that labels of deficiency create fewer learning opportunities for kids.

---

# Ways to Intervene with LD

"If students cannot learn the way we teach them, then we must teach them the way they learn." These words, from Dr. Kenneth Dunn, coauthor with Dr. Rita Dunn of several books on learning modalities, sum up the essence of our book. Whatever methods you are currently using that are not leading to success for certain students should be abandoned and replaced, for those students only, with methods more likely to lead to learning success. Students who are currently experiencing learning success should remain on their successful path.

The most helpful outcome from learning what we can about all types of learning difficulties is that it helps us stop focusing on blame and guilt and start focusing on successful learning results from using the most effective compensation strategies we can find. We are confident that the strategies in this book, combined with the "References and Resources," will create educational success for teachers and students alike.

## Create Learning Modality Compatible Conditions

1. Teach to students' learning modality strengths. Involve all parts of the brain in all activities; physical movement, visualization, music, rhythm, and emotion all help learning. Have kids act or dance out words and concepts. Whenever practical, turn off some or all lights and play soothing instrumental music in the background. Encourage students to make mental pictures of what they are learning and to study those pictures with their eyes closed. Have them visualize what the subject looks, sounds, and smells like. Repeating visualizations many times improves memory. Use these interventions as your first-choice teaching methods rather than as remediation techniques.

2. Keep visual and auditory distractions to a minimum. Since some kids with LD are distracted by their surroundings, it's probably better for them not to be seated beside colorful, stimulating displays. Permit students to work in study carrels or screened-off areas if these arrangements lead to more productivity.

3. Allow students to listen to soothing instrumental music on headphones while they work.

4. Record lectures, presentations, and text material on CDs or in MP3 format, or contact Learning Ally or Bookshare. Both organizations offer digital versions of most of the texts and literature used in our schools. See "References and Resources."

5. Give hyperactive kids frequent movement opportunities during planned breaks and permission to use items that help them focus during instruction (*examples:* wall push-ups, jumping jacks, play dough, running errands for you, fidget seats, large ball seats, handheld "fidget items," or other items found on the Internet).

6. Make learning concrete. Almost all students with LD do extremely well when a learning task is something they can actually get their hands on and when it is connected to something they are interested in or curious about.

7. Whenever possible, find alternatives to large-group work. Have students work alone, with partners, or in small groups with no more than four members.

8. Find and use available technology assistance. Don't wait until students can do something on their own before allowing them to use helpful technology. For more technology ideas, please see the assistive technology chart on pages 80–81.

9. Keep in mind that kids with LD work more enthusiastically on projects than on skill work. They learn better if immersed in one topic for several days, as opposed to moving from topic to topic each day. Use the "Log of Project Work" (page 90) to help them stay on track and provide helpful scaffolding during their project work. At the start of each work period, students enter the current date in the left column of the chart and briefly describe the task they plan to accomplish that day in the center column of the chart. Five minutes before project work ends, provide a prompt for students to record what they actually accomplished for that single work period in the right column of the chart. For parts or tasks that were left unfinished, students record reminders in the center column of the next horizontal line of the chart. As they accomplish each task, they plan and record a new task.

10. Allow struggling students to take classroom tests in untimed situations. Let them either read a test item aloud or have someone else read it to them; in many cases, this leads to improved test results.

11. Never assume that kids who struggle to learn could do better if they just tried harder.

12. Consult Chapters 3 and 4 for more strategies and suggestions.

## Use Praise Effectively

Many teachers think that praise of any type is helpful for improving student motivation and self-esteem. Yet there is ample proof that in order to be effective, praise must follow these guidelines:

- It must happen almost instantly after the praise-worthy event.

- Praise must be specific—it must describe the exact act or behavior you want to see more often. (*Example:* Instead of saying, "I'm so proud of you, Juan!" say, "You are becoming much more accurate on your timed number facts tests. Good work, Juan!")

- Praise must be sincere—you must mean it, and the student must believe it. You can tell how the act makes you or someone else feel. (*Example:* "When you were helpful to your friend, I noticed how happy he was.")

- Praise should never be accompanied by a negative statement. (*Example:* Avoid saying things like, "Your desk is very neat right now, but I wonder if you can keep it that way.")

**Tip:** Coach your students on how to praise themselves. Perhaps they could respond to a visual signal from you when you observe some praiseworthy behavior. Your signal could be their cue to engage in some self-praise.

## Improve Students' Attending Behaviors

1. Put a large, easy-to-read room and teacher identification sign on or beside your classroom door, so students with spatial orientation problems can find the room easily.

2. Write daily schedules where all can see them. Check things off as they are completed, so students have a sense of progress. Teach students to use daily assignment notebooks.

3. Have students set goals for how much of a task they predict they can do in an allotted time, instead of expecting them to work as long as it takes to complete the entire task. Use the "Goal Planning Chart" (page 86) and goal-setting strategies (pages 61–63) to help students do this.

4. Provide students with copies of the "Daily Task Checklist" (page 43) to keep at their desks. Give them some control over choosing from among several tasks and deciding how much of a task they can do in the allotted time. Whenever they complete an activity, have

them indicate their progress on the checklist so they can receive positive reinforcement immediately instead of waiting until the end of a class period or school day. If a student procrastinates consistently despite the checklist, set up a behavior-consequence situation. (*Example:* "Josie, if you complete the items on your checklist by the time we agreed upon, you can work on a choice activity for ten minutes. If you can't reach your goal, you won't have time for the choice activity.")

**5.** Talk slowly. Some kids with LD, and certainly English language learners, process speech in slow motion. Give them advance notice (a physical cue, a special word) that you will be asking them a question. Use words sparingly. Keep conversations brief.

**6.** Be succinct in giving directions, and always model what you want students to do by showing them concrete examples of what finished products should look like. Never give a string of directions all at once. Instead, give one direction at a time, demonstrate it, and show an example of what the product should look like. Have students repeat the directions before they begin their work. Give positive reinforcement as soon as they complete the first task.

**7.** Establish eye contact while speaking to students, but don't insist that they maintain it if it makes them uncomfortable.

**8.** For students who are confused by too much to look at on a page, provide windows cut out of paper or cardboard that expose only portions of the page at a time. Students can also use these windows as line or place markers.

**9.** Use neon-type highlighters to call students' attention to important sections of handouts. Avoid using red ink to mark errors. This only reinforces incorrect responses in students' minds.

**10.** Use humor frequently, but be very careful not to use sarcasm. (*Examples:* Include students' names in silly scenarios in the content areas. Have a recording of a laugh track handy to play when things get too serious. Have kids bring in cartoons they think are funny or create new captions for funny pictures. Develop a "Good Humor" bulletin board. Joke with the class on a regular basis and show appreciation for the funny things kids say. Pretend to throw smiles for younger kids to catch and put on their faces instead of frowns.

**11.** Use digital and other game formats often to teach content and skills. Most students can learn significantly more material in a game or quiz-show format than with traditional paper-and-pencil tasks. Create or purchase generic game boards that can be used with various card decks of skill work; students advance playing pieces on the board for each correct response they make. As an alternative to game boards, let students keep each card for which they give a correct response. The student with the most cards at the end of the game is the winner.

**12.** Expose all your students to high-quality curriculum and learning experiences. It's much easier to teach necessary skills when they are attached to content that is meaningful and interesting for the students.

**13.** Never do for your students what they can do for themselves.

**14.** Consult Chapters 3 and 4 for more strategies and suggestions.

## Improve Students' Social Skills to Minimize Behavior Problems

As if having trouble learning weren't enough, many struggling students find it very difficult to behave in socially appropriate ways. Because of their learning delays, they appear immature. Their social-interactive skills resemble those of much younger children, so they may seem silly or babyish to those around them. Since children tend to socially reject kids who are different for any reason, students with learning difficulties often find it hard to make and keep friends.

Their hyperactivity and disorganization often make them stand out and become the objects of negative attention. They just don't seem to "get it" in social situations, constantly missing subtle clues that other kids pick up easily. They may seem unaware of things they say and do that might lead to being shunned or disliked by other kids. If their hyperactivity is manifested in talking too much, they may be perceived as wanting to dominate conversations. In many groups, it becomes fashionable for these kids to become the targets of teasing and bullying. If your school does not currently have an effective anti-bullying program, consult some online resources or colleagues from other schools for recommendations. State-of-the-art programs borrow elements from the work of David Olweus, a Norwegian educator. If you are considering a program, suggest that your administrator talk to administrators at schools that use it to see how it really works when implemented.

As teachers, we play a crucial role in how kids are treated by their peers. When we become annoyed, impatient, or angry about a child's irritating behavior, our other students may pick up on our negative feelings and infer that we are giving them permission to denigrate kids who are so different from the norm. If this is the situation in your classroom, you might seek help from specialists who know the learning needs and challenges faced by students with learning difficulties. The goal in all classrooms is for all kids to be accepted as very sensitive people, even though they may at times exhibit some behavior that needs changing. We need to lead the way so all kids can be noticed and appreciated first for their strengths.

Teaching social skills is important for a number of reasons. Students need to learn how to develop positive social relationships, interact effectively with peers in the school setting so that all parties feel accepted, and learn to cope with uncomfortable situations that they encounter at school. Research shows that teaching social skills reduces school adjustment problems, grade retention, truancy, dropouts, and mental health problems.

1. Find and use programs that teach social-interactive skills, such as those by Arnold Goldstein and Dorothy Rich. (See "References and Resources.") Seek assistance from a school counselor, social worker, special education staff person, student teacher, or paraprofessional.

2. Choose a particular social skill that needs improvement and teach it to those students who could most benefit from learning it. See "Directly Teach Social Skills" on page 207.

3. Use a subtle signal that indicates to students when they are engaging in inappropriate social behaviors. The signal can also prompt students to recall and use a more appropriate skill that has been taught.

4. Teach students to keep track of their own progress. They might use the awareness tallies method described in Chapter 10 (page 206).

5. Make sure that all students understand the consequences of inappropriate behavior. Consequences should be applied in an objective fashion, without anger or excessive emotion.

6. Expect that anyone who behaves inappropriately will make amends by apologizing directly to the injured party, and that the injured party will accept the apology—unless the inappropriate behavior is repeated over time, in which case apologies are meaningless. Never excuse inappropriate behavior by thinking or saying that students' learning difficulties make it impossible for them to follow expected procedures. If the undesired behavior is indeed characteristic of the learning difficulty, such as tics for students with Tourette's syndrome, then the teacher will be addressing it through a positive behavior plan in the student's individualized education program (IEP), which includes replacement instruction, self-monitoring, and praise.

7. Teach your students to ignore inappropriate behavior unless someone's safety (physical or emotional) is in jeopardy. If safety is an issue, the preferred response is to state, "I don't like it when you do that. I want you to stop doing that right now." Make it very clear that retaliation is not allowed.

8. Consult Chapter 10 ("Helping Students Choose Appropriate Behaviors") for more ideas on how to help students with social problems.

9. Teach yourself and your students to recognize and immediately reinforce positive behaviors. Always try to *immediately* "catch them being good" and describe to them specifically the desirable behaviors you noticed. (*Example:* If you see Neil walking down his aisle without touching anyone's person or desk, excuse yourself from what you are doing, go up to him, place your hand on his shoulder, and say, "Neil, I noticed that you were able to walk down your aisle just now and keep your hands to yourself. Keep it up! Thank you.")

---

The goal in *all* classrooms is for *all* kids to be accepted as very sensitive people, even though they may at times exhibit some behavior that needs changing.

---

10. Demonstrate ways for class members to ignore inappropriate behaviors. Help students develop consistent nonreinforcing responses. (*Examples:* Show students how to move away from others who are bothering them, end eye contact, and refuse to respond to taunts or insults.)

11. Seat students whose behaviors are distracting behind the vision of other kids. Seat them in the last row or the back of the room. To the left and right of them, seat students who can model appropriate behavior.

12. Establish and use predictable routines in class activities and in transitions. Give notice if a routine will be changed or interrupted. Unpredictability throws many struggling students off-balance. (This may be one reason they misbehave when a substitute teaches for you.)

13. Another way to notice desirable behaviors is what Lisa's school calls "the pat-on-the-back program." As part of a school-wide positive behavior support (SWPBS) program (see page 214), every month a specific behavior takes the spotlight. The behavior might be helping others, using the words *please* and *thank you*, or waiting your turn. When peers or teachers observe a student doing the desired behavior of the month, they give that student a "pat on the back." This is a cutout paper hand that is taped on the back shoulder of the student. This program helps shape a positive culture within the school community.

## Unlocking Autism 🔒

Students who lack appropriate social skills may include kids with or without an autism diagnosis. Affected children appear unable to understand social cues, to respond to the environment, to control emotions enough to think about an appropriate response, or to realize that more practice with a desired skill could lead to them choosing it more automatically.

Poor social skills for students with autism spectrum disorders include the following behaviors:

- yelling or calling out
- aggression or destruction
- echolalia (automatic repetition of vocalizations made by a person)
- inappropriate touching of others or avoidance of people and events
- covering their ears
- crying frequently
- talking to themselves
- behaving impulsively
- asking incessant questions
- staring
- refusing to respond
- appearing fearful
- having difficulty transitioning

These behaviors may be allowed, as they represent students' efforts to let off some steam, but you also can offer the following interventions to help students participate in instruction without disruption:

- giving clear, concise directions without too much information
- using pictures with few spoken words
- repeated practice of desirable behaviors
- using a preferred activity for five minutes before and after a required task
- sharing social stories that describe appropriate responses to fictional characters

# Students Who Are Twice Exceptional (2e)

Some students are clearly gifted in some areas and clearly in need of learning assistance in other areas. The gifted education world has labeled these students twice exceptional (2e). Historically, schools have ignored the gifts and concentrated almost all the students' time in school on remediating the weaknesses. However, the fairest way to handle this situation is to treat these students as gifted in their areas of strength, and not take time away from those strength areas to make more time for working on their difficulties. When learning in their areas of difficulty, they should be taught the same compensation strategies as any other student who needs them.

The learning difficulty might be as simple as not being fluent in English. It is safe to assume that other cultures have the same percentage of gifted students as the United States does among its fluent English speakers. Notice and recognize signs of gifted abilities in students of all cultures, and don't wait until English fluency is attained to provide appropriate learning challenges for these kids. For specific strategies on how to nurture the giftedness in children from other cultures, consult *Reaching New Horizons* by Jaime A. Castellano and Eva Díaz.

Many gifted kids with LD are not diagnosed as either gifted *or* learning disabled. Their LD often brings their school performance down into the average range, and it is difficult for teachers to notice the gifted behaviors they may exhibit. The families of these students may be perceived by educators as dreamers who wish that their perfectly average children could be intellectually gifted. But families are in the unique position of seeing how precocious their children are at home, where they can express their exceptional learning abilities in ways that are naturally fluent for them.

What alarms many educators (and parents) is that many of the characteristics that describe gifted students are strikingly similar to the characteristics of students with ADHD. Gifted kids may be restless and physically active when the tasks they are asked to perform do not capture their interest. Their intensity often leads them into confrontations with authority, because they need a good reason to conform. Their daydreaming may actually be directed toward the mental contemplation of complex and creative scenarios. They may present different personas in different situations: naughty at school but pleasant at scout meetings, restless at their desks but totally immersed in a book they are reading for pleasure, socially inept with their classmates but charming when talking to adults. If these students are mistakenly identified as having LD or ADHD, the danger is that their giftedness will go unnoticed because the deficit label usually takes precedence over other learning exceptionalities.

Some gifted kids do have LD, but most do not. Rather than worrying about the distinction, we should do everything in our power to ensure that we offer *all* students with LD learning modality compatible tasks that emphasize hands-on learning. We should make every effort to identify our students' passionate interests and find ways for them to work on these interests during school time. Gifted behaviors will be observable as students take simple learning tasks and make them more abstract and complex.

Generally speaking, gifted kids who *do* have LD:

1. usually show noticeably discrepant scores between the verbal and nonverbal sections of ability tests

2. have extremely uneven academic skills that make them seem unmotivated to learn and cause them to avoid many school tasks, leading to incomplete assignments

3. have auditory or visual processing problems that cause them to respond, work, and appear to think very slowly (This leads to great difficulty in explaining or expressing their ideas and feelings; they may talk around a topic and appear unable to get to the point.)

4. have problems with motor skills as exhibited by clumsiness, poor handwriting, and difficulty completing paper-and-pencil tasks

5. may be able to tell lots about what they know but greatly resist writing anything on paper

6. have trouble with long- and short-term memory

7. lack organizational and study skills and appear messy and disorganized

8. exhibit low self-esteem through anger, put-downs, crying, disruptive behaviors, and apathy

9. are extremely frustrated with school

Yet many gifted kids with LD also:

1. have scored in the gifted range on ability, achievement, or creativity tests

2. have a wide range of knowledge about many topics and can express their knowledge verbally

3. have wild and crazy ideas

4. express humor in unusual and sometimes bizarre ways

5. have fertile imaginations

6. have penetrating insights, superior vocabularies, and sophisticated ideas and opinions

## Intervening with Gifted Students with or without LD

1. First, find out what your students *already* know and give them full credit for it before you teach a specific lesson.

2. Find out what they are passionately interested in outside of school and allow them to work on related projects in school. Many of the standards you are teaching this year could probably be learned in the context of many topics.

3. Allow students to express what they know in ways that are compatible with their learning modalities. Allow them to be gifted in their areas of strength while accommodating their LD in their areas of weakness.

4. Provide alternate learning experiences instead of the regular work, and behavior problems may disappear. You will then have the proof you need that the learning difficulties of these students were really a combination of boredom and frustration.

5. Consult Susan's book *Teaching Gifted Kids in Today's Classroom* for more strategies to keep gifted students highly motivated and productive in school. (See "References and Resources.")

## Scenario: Toni

Toni always had something in her hands: pencils, toys, even gum. Unfortunately, the gum often found its way into her hair, requiring her teachers to be creative in the gum removal department. Her LD resource teacher addressed that problem by giving Toni a round, polished stone to keep her hands occupied, and that helped some.

In third grade, Toni had difficulty getting her thoughts down on paper, and she worked slowly and laboriously on all her assignments. Her writing was small and cramped, and her sentence structure was weak and disorganized. But if you let her tell you a story she had in her mind, that was another matter. She was always coming up with highly creative (if totally impractical) ways to solve classroom problems for other kids. She loved dominating class discussions so much that it seemed her tongue was one of her most hyperactive body parts.

Toni read at a sixth-grade level, but all her other schoolwork was below third-grade level. Her teacher was very frustrated, because he thought that Toni's advanced reading ability was proof that she could do the other work if only she applied herself and tried a little harder. The teacher feared that Toni was manipulating him by pretending not to be able to do the third-grade work.

When Toni's LD was documented, her teacher and Susan created learning modality compatible ways for her to express what she was learning. Although her drawing skills leaned toward the blood-and-gore genre, she was able to use these skills in a detailed study of killer sharks. The LD resource teacher located a retired media specialist who became Toni's mentor and helped her create a narrated slide show.

Classroom accommodations included teaching Toni to use word processing and spell-check support in her written work, allowing her to record and illustrate her marvelous stories, teaching her research skills in conjunction with the work she was doing with her mentor, and eliminating time pressures for activities and tests. At the beginning of each work period, Toni set a goal for her projected productivity, using the "Daily Task Checklist" (page 43).

As Toni became more successful with some school tasks, her attitude and behavior clearly improved. As she realized that others appreciated her for her creative strengths, she became more comfortable accepting help in her areas of weakness.

# Conditions That Make Learning Difficult

The Individuals with Disabilities Education Act (IDEA) is a law originally enacted by Congress in 1975 to ensure that children with disabilities have the opportunity to receive a free appropriate public education, just like other children. Revised in 2004, IDEA governs how states and public agencies provide early intervention, special education, and related services to eligible children and teens. A child is eligible for services if, after being evaluated, he or she can be placed within one of the following disability categories: intellectual disability, hearing impairment (including deafness), speech or language impairment, visual impairment (including blindness), serious emotional disturbance, orthopedic impairment, autism, traumatic brain injury, other health impairment, specific learning disability, deaf-blindness, or multiple disabilities.

The following sections describe characteristics of students who fall within some of those categories and who have conditions that interfere with their ability to learn. Each list of characteristics is followed by intervention guidelines. Suggestions for intervening with behavior problems are found in Chapter 10, which is entirely devoted to behavior issues. Whenever possible, consult with the teachers who have previously taught these students. As you adapt your teaching for students with special learning needs, you will be seeking more information constantly. Some of the best sources are the national organizations that exist to deliver support services for people whose disabilities present special life challenges. See "References and Resources" for several suggestions.

## Behavior Disorders Including Emotional Disturbances (ED)

Students with ED exhibit some, many, or all of the following characteristics. Some children with these behaviors have been diagnosed with oppositional defiant disorder (ODD).

1. They have a history of outbursts of serious misbehavior, tantrums, and general discipline problems, which are evident in many children with ED before age three.

2. They are restless, anxious, or irritable much of the time.

3. They may spend much of their school time in the hall or in the office of some person responsible for discipline. They are often truant and may have a history of needing police intervention.

4. They have short fuses and may become extremely angry at the slightest frustration or provocation. They act impulsively and appear unable to consider their options before they act.

5. They constantly test the limits on everything, from class rules to bedtime.

6. They defy authority, saying things like "You can't tell me what to do when I'm not at school" or "You can't make me stop." They argue constantly.

7. They deliberately annoy people, including both adults and other kids.

8. They may be extremely physically aggressive, using force to get objects from others or to do something before it is their turn. They may strike or kick adults. Many of their behaviors are labeled as bullying.

9. They may steal or destroy property. Some abuse animals and other children. They may justify taking revenge on others because they believe that the system has abused them.

10. They may appear somewhat paranoid, believing that no one likes them or that others are laughing at them. They don't usually want to work in

groups, partly because they think the other kids don't want them around. (Unfortunately, these perceptions may be accurate.)

11. They may express an inappropriate emotion at the wrong time (*example:* laughing when someone is hurt).

12. They may use terms like *dummy* and *weirdo* to describe themselves. Because their behavior so often interferes with their learning, they do, in fact, develop academic deficiencies.

13. Some kids with ED are almost invisible. They try to blend into the background and not be noticed. These kids may appear terrified when asked to recite or participate in class.

14. Some are unusually sad or depressed. They may develop physical symptoms or irrational fears when in school, a condition sometimes referred to as "school phobia," which may eventually become a panic or anxiety disorder.

15. Some seem unable to learn, even though they have no diagnosed LD.

# Autism Spectrum Disorder (ASD)

Autism includes all the autism spectrum disorders (ASD), also known as pervasive developmental disorders (PDD). This disability usually appears by age three. It significantly impacts an individual's verbal and nonverbal communication and social interactions.

The symptoms occur in different degrees in different people. Some have no oral speech; others can talk fluently but exhibit other behaviors that indicate they are "on the spectrum." Some have difficulty expressing their needs and coping with change. Some students with ASD may show repetitive, nonfunctional behaviors, such as hand flapping or walking on tiptoes. Some of these behaviors can even be violent or self-harmful. Students may also show extreme resistance to change in daily routines or habits. Sometimes they may perseverate on one or two particular topics, such as weather

## Unlocking Autism 🔒

*DSM-5* excludes Asperger's syndrome as a discrete diagnosis. It is now embedded in the category on autism spectrum disorder, in the hopes that it will be more easily recognized and treated. Asperger's syndrome would still, however, be included as a special needs descriptor in a diagnosis of a student being twice exceptional.

or dinosaurs. Extreme sensitivity to sensory input from sights, sounds, touches, textures, tastes, and smells is also characteristic. On page 33, we describe a planned, supervised time-out situation or place where students can use things that hug their bodies tightly and comfort them, listen to soothing music, and so on.

Typical communication problems of children with ASD:

- **Social skills problems:** Students may have difficulty interacting with others, may prefer solitude and show no interest in making friends, or may want to make friends, but not know how to approach others or hold appropriate conversations.

- **Verbal and language challenges:** Students may display a poor response to verbal instruction or misunderstand others' speech.

- **Speech limitations:** Students' abilities to communicate using speech range from none to adequate.

- **Echolalia:** Students may exhibit patterns of repeating a word or phrase out of context numerous times.

- **Mind blindness:** Students may have problems understanding the emotions of others and may respond inappropriately, leading to misunderstandings in communication and social situations with peers in regular education.

- **Sensory issues:** Certain sounds, tastes, or sights may bother or provoke an unusual response in students with an autism condition.

Types of communication challenges vary greatly with age, degree of disability, and treatment history. A speech and language pathologist can help you determine the greatest communication needs and most effective strategies for your students with ASD. Both visual and verbal information should be presented simultaneously whenever possible. Interaction with nondisabled peers is also important, because these peers provide models of appropriate language, social, and behavior skills. Finally, to overcome frequent problems in generalizing skills learned at school, it is very helpful for an IEP team to develop programs with families, so that learning activities, experiences, and approaches can be carried over into the home and community. For more information, contact the Autism Society and see this chapter's "References and Resources" section on page 247.

The needs of students with autism and other learning difficulties are likely to change daily. The goal is for students to develop self-awareness. They can learn to

## Unlocking Autism 🔒

### Sensory Breaks

Students with autism need sensory breaks. These are times when students can manage sensory overload from their surroundings. The type of sensory break depends on the students' needs and strengths. A sensory break might include:

- spinning
- rocking
- doing push-ups against the wall
- rubbing something with texture
- wearing a weighted vest or blanket
- listening to music
- sucking through a straw
- chewing something crunchy
- taking an auditory break in a quiet environment
- using an assistive technology

recognize when they need to stabilize, self-regulate, and take a sensory break and when they are stable enough to return to class.

A sensory break area can be an established location within your room or another location in the school. Some schools have sensory rooms that contain items such as sand tables, play dough, building blocks, and scooters. Students can also listen to quiet music, go into a tent or tunnel of some kind, put on a sleep mask, and enjoy peace and quiet until they calm down. Rocking chairs are helpful to a student who needs that motion for calming.

A sensory room can be staffed by a parent volunteer, a retired teacher, or a paraprofessional, if one is available. Sometimes pairs of teachers agree to allow children from the other teacher's classroom to take sensory breaks in their room. As kids enter the room, they go directly to the designated area and do whatever they have been given permission to do. Frequently, the sensory break space is in a corner of a classroom taught by a specialist in LD, intellectual disability (ID), or emotional support (ES).

## Intellectual Disabilities (ID)

Children who have intellectual disabilities (formerly labeled "mentally retarded" or "educationally delayed") behave and learn at far less sophisticated levels than their age peers. Much of their behavior resembles that of very young children. Parents and other family members of persons with ID report some very positive behaviors in their kids, including sympathy, empathy, friendliness, a strong willingness to help in almost any way, and a great appreciation for the kindnesses of people in general. Although they represent a significant range of abilities and characteristics, their learning difficulties tend to fall into the following categories.

### Attention Deficits

Students have trouble paying attention to the task at hand or to the person describing the task. Their attention span may be very short, and their attention may be easily captured by extraneous sounds or movements. Students have difficulty remembering what they learn from one day to another. However, once a particular skill moves into long-term memory, students may be able to remember it quite well.

### Academic Deficits

Students learn and perform well below average in typical academic subjects at any age. Most never achieve fluency in abstract and conceptual thinking. They have great difficulty generalizing what they learn in one situation and applying it to another.

### Language Deficits

Students may not be able to understand clearly what they are told. They are unable to express their thoughts clearly. Their speech may sound labored, and their voice quality may be unusual.

### Motor Coordination Problems

Students' development of gross motor skills, like running, skipping, or hopping, is delayed. Development of fine motor skills needed for writing, cutting, and other school tasks is much less mature than for their age peers. Many students with ID have significant vision or hearing problems as well.

### Social Problems

In their efforts to get attention, students with ID often behave inappropriately—sometimes even aggressively. They may act silly; make funny noises; push, hit, or kick other kids for no apparent reason; and annoy others by excessive displays of affection, such as hugging and kissing. Their behavior is inconsistent, unpredictable, and immature, and since it appears babyish to their peers, these students may not be accepted into the group unless teachers coach them and their peers.

## Intervening with ID

1. Most kids with ID can be taught to greatly improve their social skills. For one approach, see "Directly Teach Social Skills" on page 207.

2. You and the other students may have to concentrate for some time on helping these kids develop appropriate social behaviors. Students with ID need to be told consistently when their behavior is inappropriate. Any student who is the target of unwanted behavior by another child should say directly to that child, "I don't like that. I don't like it when you do that. I want you to stop doing that right now."

3. Once these students' social behavior is in the acceptable range, you may pay more attention to their academic growth. It is never appropriate to hold back the class to wait for students with ID to catch up. Rather, adjust the amount of work you give them and the methods they may use to learn. Students with ID need to work on simplified versions of what the rest of the class is doing, and they need more time to complete their work. Break tasks into small steps and sequence the steps from simplest to most difficult. As with all struggling students, consistently use concrete examples and experiences to teach abstract concepts.

4. Students with ID also need to spend time on life skills such as listening, sitting still, following directions, getting in and out of their outer clothing, and so on. You may need to teach some of these basic skills explicitly.

5. Ask for student volunteers to serve as learning buddies for students with ID. Be sure to rotate the buddies so many kids share in the responsibility of helping one another learn.

6. Teach students with ID how to use the "Daily Task Checklist" (page 43). If they can't print, have them use stickers to illustrate specific tasks.

## Orthopedic Impairment

Students with orthopedic impairment include those who are in wheelchairs; those with cerebral palsy, muscular dystrophy, and spina bifida; those with epilepsy and other conditions that result in seizures; those with arthritis and congenital malformations; and students with any other conditions that affect their mobility.

Students with orthopedic impairment exhibit some, many, or all of the following characteristics:

- They may have normal to above-average intelligence.
- They may suffer multiple related afflictions, such as vision or speech disorders.

- They may have to miss school regularly for long-term hospital care. If hospital teachers are available, you may be asked to guide them by keeping them aware of what the students would have been learning in school. Ask to be kept informed of the students' medical status and any changes. Hospital stays may also be accompanied by traumatic events, so expect some setbacks when the children return to school.

## Intervening with Orthopedic Impairment

- Don't assume that these students have had the same background experiences as their classmates, since their physical limitations may have prevented them from participating in many activities other kids have shared.

- Seek training in specific interventions for physical problems such as seizures. Ask the special education staff in your district; perhaps they can offer the training or refer you to someone who can.

- Make students' learning experiences developmentally appropriate by assessing which skills they possess, then teaching them at levels that cause them to stretch and move ahead.

- Sometimes these kids have become overly dependent on assistance from others. Use goal-setting strategies (see pages 61–63) and behavior contracts (see pages 209–210) as needed.

## Hearing Impairment

Students who have been identified with any degree of hearing loss, from mild to profound, are said to be "hearing impaired." If there are kids in your class whose attention to task consistently wavers, you should carefully observe them for indicators that their hearing might be impaired. These indicators include:

- frequent ear and respiratory infections
- family history of hearing impairment
- leaning forward, cupping their hands behind their ears, or turning their heads to hear better
- asking others to repeat what's been said
- moving closer to the sound source
- the appearance of inattention
- frequent daydreaming
- speech, voice, and articulation problems
- a noticeable change in academic performance

## Intervening with Hearing Impairment

1. Face the class while teaching. Rather than turning away to write on the board, prepare visual aids in advance and display them as the lesson progresses.

2. Use lots of demonstrations, exhibits, and hands-on learning experiences.

3. Allow students to work away from background noise, since they may have difficulty separating speech from other sounds.

4. Permit students to move around the room as necessary to get closer to what they want and need to hear.

5. Have students work with volunteer buddies who can jot down important points made during class discussions.

6. Allow students to use scripts of soundtracks for videos, movies, CD-ROM programs, and so on. Scripts may be available from the production companies or television or cable networks on request.

7. During class discussions, have kids raise their hands after they are called on so students with hearing impairments can identify the speakers and watch them as they speak.

8. Consult an audiologist to learn about technologies that can enhance communication for students with hearing impairments.

9. If some kids know and use the manual (finger-spelling) alphabet, have them teach it to several other students so they can communicate with kids who are hearing impaired. If no one in your classroom knows the manual alphabet, someone in your school probably does. Or contact your district office and say that you would like someone to visit your class and teach the manual alphabet.

10. Introduce your class to American Sign Language (ASL). Since this is a complete language, not just an alphabet, you probably will want to invite someone who is fluent in ASL to demonstrate it for your class.

## Visual Impairment

Students who are visually impaired may rub their eyes a lot, close or cover one eye, hold books close to their eyes, squint or frown frequently, and have significant difficulty reading. Their eyes may itch or burn, they may complain that things are blurry, and they may have frequent headaches. If they have been legally blind from birth, they may lack understanding of abstract terms such as *color* and *sky*.

## Intervening with Visual Impairment

1. Always face students with visual impairment when you are speaking.

2. Repeat aloud anything you write on a visual aid.

3. Make sure that all handouts are clear and readable, with dark letters and numbers and adequate white space between words and lines. Use a photocopier to enlarge written material for students with impaired vision.

4. Record your lectures so students can listen to them again later.

5. Provide concrete, hands-on learning materials.

6. Find and provide recorded versions of teaching materials. Check with libraries and national organizations such as the American Foundation for the Blind. (See "References and Resources.")

7. Seat students with visual impairments next to volunteer buddies who can help them follow along. Rotate buddies at least once a month.

8. Contact an association of optometrists or ophthalmologists for advice on helping students with vision problems, as some doctors have developed very effective methods. (*Example:* The Irlen Institute has successfully used color therapy for a condition called *scotopic sensitivity,* which makes print appear as if it is moving around. For some kids, placing a colored transparency over text keeps the print from moving and makes it easier to read and understand. To contact the Irlen Institute, see "References and Resources.")

### Tech Tip 🖥

Try the AIM Explorer at aem.cast.org/navigating /aim-explorer.html. This is a free computer simulation that helps struggling readers decide which supports—such as magnification, custom text and background colors, text-to-speech, text highlighting, and layout options—might help them access and understand text. AIM Explorer is designed for readers with low vision, physical challenges, and learning and attention difficulties. It does not address Braille use, and it assumes that a sighted adult is working with the visually impaired student.

# Traumatic Brain Injury (TBI)

Traumatic brain injury is an acquired injury to the brain caused by external physical force, resulting in total or partial functional impairment that adversely affects a child's educational performance. Accidents, severe sports injuries, or child abuse can cause traumatic brain injuries. These injuries can lead to problems in memory, language, attention, reasoning, judgment, abstract thinking, problem solving, emotional regulation, and social interactions.

# Other Health Impairments (OHI)

The disability category of other health impairments includes a long list of medical problems that can interfere with daily functioning. Diabetes, cystic fibrosis, HIV and AIDS, asthma, and ADHD are just a few of the conditions in this category. (You may think that this broad category is a strange way to address ADHD, which is such a pervasive and troublesome condition in many of our students. We think so, too. See the following section for more information about ADHD.) Students with these conditions may have limited strength, vitality, or attentiveness and may require special healthcare or educational accommodations. Some children have several simultaneous diagnoses, and OHI is often added to the IEP as a catchall category when specialists realize there is more to a diagnosis than the labels describe.

## ADHD

The Centers for Disease Control and Prevention (CDC) says that diagnosing ADHD is not easy and there should always be a confirming diagnosis after a pediatrician, parent, or educator indicates suspicion of ADHD. Because there is no single test that can diagnose ADHD, the diagnosis should be made by a medical doctor or a specially trained healthcare provider. The *DSM-5* lists criteria that can be used for diagnosing ADHD. School psychologists can identify ADHD "for educational purposes only," meaning they can qualify students for services under the OHI disability category if a student presents characteristics of ADHD. Ideally, classroom observation and collection of data from teachers and relatives will contribute to the final diagnosis.

Descriptions of symptoms are widely available online and may change as brain research progresses. Two of the best sites for this information are the National Center for Learning Disabilities (www.ncld.org) and the National Institute of Mental Health (www.nimh .nih.gov). Since you can locate current information about diagnosis and effective interventions by simply searching online for the phrase *ADHD in children and adults*, we do not list this information here.

Very interesting research indicates that the brains of young people impacted by ADHD may be maturing up to three years slower than the brains of their age peers. Scientists have also found that when students have to work on tasks they consider uninteresting, their brains show a reduced number of dopamine receptors and transporters. This explains why students with ADHD can concentrate for long periods of time on tasks that fascinate them. Further, and most intriguing, is the prediction that a good percentage of these youngsters can actually get better over time as their brains catch up to age expectations.*

---

There should always be a confirming diagnosis after a pediatrician, parent, or educator indicates suspicion of ADHD.

---

# Substance Exposure (SE)

Although substance exposure isn't a specific category within IDEA, children who were exposed before birth to alcohol or other addictive drugs create significant challenges for classroom teachers. Many experts believe that crack-cocaine-affected children need a minimum of two years in a special class before they are introduced into a regular classroom. The rationale is that without intervention in a separate environment, their problems are likely to last throughout their school career.

Students with SE exhibit some, many, or all of the following characteristics:

1. They engage in behaviors that appear hyperactive. They are impulsive and distractible and often abandon tasks before completion. Many appear to be in a constant state of high stimulation.

2. Some have an unusual walking gait. Some present facial and head malformations, especially head circumference too small for the body.

3. They may resist the basic kinds of nurturing that caring adults wish to give, because their nervous systems are already so sensitive and overstimulated that any added stimulation is painful. They may cry a lot because of this.

4. Since they are so needy themselves, it may be difficult for them to notice or respond to the needs of others.

---

*Mahr, "ADHD Kids Can Get Better," *Time* Magazine, November 12, 2007.

5. They may experience sudden mood swings and have more intense and less predictable outbursts than kids with ED.

6. Many appear to have no sense of limits. Some may be violent and may attack others for no reason or with no provocation. They seem unable to learn from experience, and they repeat destructive acts without visible remorse. They appear not to understand or care about the consequences of their behaviors. Some are labeled "asocial," as they appear to actually enjoy their inappropriate behaviors.

7. They may possess normal or above-average intelligence despite their serious learning problems.

8. They are often unable to learn independently or by imitating the behavior of other kids. They need to be directly taught all academic and social skills.

## Intervening with SE

1. Most of what works with students with ADHD should also work with kids who are substance exposed. Keep trying strategies until you find something that is effective. (Look back at "Ways to Intervene with LD" on pages 25–28.)

2. Many of these children are supersensitive to stimuli. In teaching and interacting with them, use only one stimulus at a time. *Either* talk to them *or* touch them *or* look at them; don't combine stimuli. And keep in mind that many can't tolerate much touching.

3. Remove highly stimulating objects in the classroom from their line of vision.

4. Limit choices; kids with SE are easily confused and overstimulated by too many choices.

5. Allow adequate space between students with SE and other students. In general, leave enough room for arms and legs to swing without touching anyone else.

6. Be prepared to physically restrain students during outbursts. Get permission in advance from families and administrators. Remove items from the classroom that could be used to hurt others.

7. Model or demonstrate exactly what you want students to do in work, play, and showing emotion.

8. Teach very directly, one thing at a time, until some progress is made. Teach the way each child learns best and use the same methods consistently.

9. Establish and use routines without variation. Transitions from one activity to another must be specifically taught and experienced as having a beginning, a middle, and an end. Always give ample warning before transitions. (*Example:* "In one minute, we will put our books away and stand up for brief exercise.") Always use the same words for each transition, even if you have to read from a script.

10. Make a simple list of essential class rules and give copies to students to keep at their desks. If students must leave the room, they should bring along the list of rules.

11. Celebrate (in a low-key way) each milestone these students reach. Abandon grade-level expectations in favor of indications of individual progress.

12. There should always be more than one adult in your classroom, since these children need so much attention and support. A major goal is for the child to develop an attachment to an adult. For this to happen, the student-teacher ratio should be lower than in a typical class. Students with SE require a lot of one-on-one attention. If you don't have a full-time aide, work with the student's family to advocate for one through the special education department.

# Attribution Theory and Learned Helplessness

Once we understand the various learning difficulties and how to intervene, it's also important to know what we shouldn't do. Many teachers and parents worry about overhelping kids with learning difficulties. This is a legitimate concern. Above all, we want to make sure we do not create a condition in these kids called "learned helplessness." Students who have learned helplessness exhibit some or all of the following behaviors:

- They are slow to start their work and often don't complete it.
- They act out inappropriately to keep others from discovering that they are not competent.
- They give up at the first twinge of frustration.
- They use body language (slumping, frowning, sighing) to describe their helpless feelings; they appear tired and depressed.
- They turn in their work facedown at the last possible moment.

As teachers, we can empower all of our students to become more successful learners. One teaching technique uses the psychology of attribution theory to

| Debilitating Help That Enables into Helplessness | Positive Help That Facilitates Autonomous Behaviors |
|---|---|
| Protecting | Setting clear limits |
| Rescuing from expected outcomes | Imposing agreed-upon consequences |
| Overcontrolling | Letting students experience their own lives |
| Overlooking errors and other problems | Discussing issues and creating solutions |
| Frequently reminding | Giving clear directions; providing visual examples |
| Nagging | Letting students set their own short-term goals |
| Speaking for | Waiting for responses; suggesting two alternatives |
| Making work and assessments easy | Teaching at challenge levels through learning strengths |
| Giving inflated grades | Using rubrics honestly |
| Accepting excuses | Making expectations clear; coaching to goals |
| Inconsistency | Consistency with fairness |
| Allowing inattentiveness | Holding accountable for paying attention |
| Allowing inappropriate behaviors | Teaching self-monitoring |

counter learned helplessness. Attribution theory defines to whom or to what we attribute our success or failure. Successful learners attribute their success to having exerted enough effort to succeed, and they likely conclude that a lack of effort caused any failure. To fix the problem, they simply have to exert more effort. Unsuccessful students expect to fail, since they perceive they lack the ability to succeed. They don't see any connection between effort and results. They believe that some kids are born smarter than others and never realize that successful students identify and use specific strategies to improve their learning outcomes.

Students who believe they will succeed begin a learning task by thinking, "I can do this. If I work hard, I will be able to complete this task." Students who believe they will fail begin by thinking, "I can't do this by myself. I need help. If no one will help me, then it is not my fault that I can't learn this or get this done." They create a self-protecting set of explanations for whatever happens to them, all of which give the control to an external source. When they fail, they tell themselves, "I did a rotten job on that assignment because the teacher never helps me." And *even when they succeed,* they rationalize, "I got a good evaluation on my story because my teacher helped me. Without the teacher's help, I could not have done a good job."

When people get too much help over time, the message they receive is that they really need help. They come to believe they are not capable, because if they *were* capable, they wouldn't need all that help. So the irony is that overhelpers are contributing to students' incapacities rather than strengthening their abilities to learn. The more we help them, the more helpless they become.

The way we respond to frustrated students shapes how they handle frustration in the future. When kids become convinced that they can't do things without help, they begin to take pleasure in having things done for them. They may become quite assertive in demanding our help. We reinforce their learned helplessness by giving in, thus enabling the helplessness to continue. The relationship actively becomes a codependent one. They expect constant prompts from us, we oblige, and that only proves they can't succeed without us.

According to Dr. Steven Landfried, who has studied this issue for many years, adults overhelp children in many ways. Landfried defines educational enabling as:*

- doing things for students they can learn to do for themselves

---

*The definition of educational enabling and the Debilitating Help/Positive Help chart are used with permission of Steven E. Landfried, Caring Accountability Workshops, 21 Albion Street, Edgerton, WI 53534; (608) 531-1716.

- allowing students to choose behaviors that do not lead to productivity

- overprotecting, coddling, rescuing, bailing out, and other behaviors that teach youngsters they will not be held accountable for their choices and behaviors

- practices done in the spirit of helping that foster codependency and lower the learner's self-expectations, competencies, and self-esteem

He describes enabling behaviors and suggests other actions—*true* help—we could choose instead. Both kinds are described in the chart on page 38.

*Caution:* When dealing with students who have learned to be helpless, it's easy to blame them for their own failures. But until we have taught them the way they learn best, they have no control over whether they succeed or fail. We can avoid learned helplessness by using all the strategies we can find to teach to students' learning modality strengths, thus empowering students to be successful with grade-level standards. We need to give kids the right kind of help—the kind that says and demonstrates, "Of course you can do this! We just have to find the method that works best for you, and success will be within your grasp."

---

Successful learners attribute their success to having exerted enough effort to succeed, and they likely conclude that a lack of effort caused any failure. To fix the problem, they simply have to exert more effort. Unsuccessful students expect to fail, since they perceive they lack the ability to succeed. They don't see any connection between effort and results.

---

# Least Restrictive Environment (LRE)

IDEA requires states to provide a free appropriate public education (FAPE) in the least restrictive environment (LRE) to all students with disabilities. This law requires that children with disabilities be educated "to the maximum extent appropriate" in the "least restrictive environment." IDEA recognizes that, *to the extent possible,* children with disabilities are entitled to the same educational experiences as their nondisabled peers. A student's IEP may determine whether a regular classroom is the best learning environment. The LRE is not always the regular classroom.

Once a student's areas of need are established, teacher teams work to choose the least restrictive location(s) for the delivery of the necessary services. For some students with LD, the general education classroom *is* the least restrictive. Given the proper accommodations and modifications, this is the environment in which the child can benefit from and learn with the highest degree of mastery.

Some students may participate in the regular classroom as well as visit a resource room for additional support. Other students with more severe cognitive or behavioral challenges may require all their direct instruction in core subjects in an alternate classroom or setting as needed to accommodate their IEP. Sometimes, students with severe disabilities can function well socially with their peers, in which case participation in some elective or enrichment classes such as art, music, or a contemporary living class may be the least restrictive and may provide a reasonable pathway to their participation in more heterogeneous classes over time.

## Scenario: Rosalinda

Rosalinda was one of Lisa's special education students in an inclusive elementary school setting. She was nine years old and had been receiving special education services for two years. In the third grade, she spent most of her day in the general education classroom, where she received some support from various service providers. Rosalinda's general education teacher was excellent at differentiating instruction to suit students with special learning needs. When the members of Rosalinda's multidisciplinary team met for her annual IEP, all of them agreed that services were being successfully provided in the least restrictive environment (her regular classroom). The recommendation was to continue to educate her the same way in fourth grade.

However, in fourth grade, Lisa soon discovered that the general education placement seemed inappropriate because Rosalinda was no longer succeeding. She could not function successfully with the same type of limited support she received in the third grade. She now needed a more restrictive environment, including more hours in the resource room. By the end of the year, however, Rosalinda was able to move back into the general education classroom through the collaborative efforts of her multidisciplinary team. Once again, the general education classroom became the least restrictive environment.

What we learn from this scenario is that the least restrictive environment is the place where optimum learning occurs for a student.

# Working as a Team with Special Education Teachers

Bringing students with specific learning or functional differences into the regular classroom can work for many reasons. Regular classrooms provide students with higher expectations for doing age- and grade-appropriate work, as well as more positive role models for behavior and learning. We prepare the so-called normal kids to live and work beside students with LD and to perceive them in a positive light. Seeing the benefits of integrating functionally challenged people into regular classrooms, these future parents will be able to provide high expectations for their own children to actualize learning potential.

Regular education and special education teachers must work together to create environments that promote optimum learning conditions. The degree of cooperation may be the key to learning success for students with significant learning challenges. When special education programs changed so that most of a child's education would take place in the regular classroom, it was with the understanding that the special education staff would serve as active advisors to the regular classroom teachers. If you are a regular classroom teacher with special education students who interact regularly with and get support from special education teachers, the inclusion program is working the way it is supposed to work. If your support from the special education staff is minimal, you have the right to ask for and receive assistance regarding specific classroom interventions that might make a positive difference. So do not hesitate to ask and continue asking until you get the assistance you need.

In the best situation, the regular and special education teachers work as teammates through a method called coteaching. The special education teacher does not focus only on the students with disabilities; rather, both teachers collaborate to teach *all* students. This model increases the intensity and differentiation of academic instruction and also develops needed social skills that students with disabilities may not have. Teachers also benefit by learning from each other's expertise and expanding their repertoire of strategies.

Many schools have created teams of specialists to act as resources for regular classroom teachers. Originally formed to reduce the number of kids who were being referred for separate special education classes, these teams may also be used to prevent learning or behavior problems from becoming unmanageable in the regular classroom. Called teacher assistance teams (TAT) or learning resource teachers (LRT), they are on call for regular classroom teachers and administrators. They go into the classroom, observe those students with learning or behavior difficulties, and assist the teacher with specific intervention strategies. Team members continue to provide support until the target student and the regular classroom teacher are able to manage the time spent in the regular classroom independently. Many schools have also implemented response to intervention (RTI). RTI is a three-tiered intervention model that allows for early remediation of learning deficits. Progress is monitored frequently so that students who need more intensive instruction receive it, and students whose weaknesses are remediated can then be given more challenging levels of instruction.

Do not hesitate to ask and continue asking until you get the assistance you need.

In the past, educators identified students with learning difficulties based on the "discrepancy model." In this model, a student needed to show a significant difference between ability (IQ) and academic achievement. Using the RTI model, if students are on a tier three intervention for two 10-week periods and do not show enough growth to move to a higher tier, they are then referred for a special education evaluation. You can find more details about RTI in Chapter 4 on page 63.

Plan with special education teachers to locate and bring into your school staff development programs that enable teachers to appreciate diversity that goes beyond multiculturalism. If you bring guest speakers into your classroom throughout the year, make sure that some of them are people with learning difficulties and other disabilities who have succeeded in life.

## Guidelines for Teaching Students with Learning Difficulties*

### General Guidelines

- Students may be listening even if they aren't giving you any verbal or visual feedback.

- Not all students with learning difficulties have comprehension problems.

*Adapted from West Virginia University, used with permission, 2004. SCIDIS (Science Discovery) Learning.

- Your special education staff person should be included in your efforts to create the most successful intervention plan.

- All LD diagnoses should come from multiple assessment sources. Students who are twice exceptional may appear neither advanced nor needy until they receive further diagnostic assessments.

- Make available to the students biographies of famous people who overcame learning challenges themselves. Then discuss in detail how these individuals found success through a combination of hard work and asking for help when needed.

### Tech Tip 🖥

Technology can be used to remediate and reinforce basic skills, but it can also improve the areas of critical thinking and problem solving. Almost all students love using tablets or computers. Students can start by exploring a topic in which they are very interested. Help students locate a website about the topic that includes opportunities for more rigorous thinking experiences. For example, consult the website for *National Geographic Kids* (kids.nationalgeographic.com). Direct students to watch short videos and create questions they would like to answer. They can then move on to some online research from there. See the "Question Starters" reproducible on page 126 for ideas.

Consult with your school's or district's technology specialist for similar resources, or do your own Web search. Also visit Webquest .org. Webquest helps a student quickly locate information about a certain topic and then incorporates higher-level thinking skills such as analysis, synthesis, and evaluation into the learning activity.

### Teacher Presentation Tips

1. Always activate a student's prior knowledge about a topic using "KWPL" in this book (page 101) or a similar strategy. Give particular examples that use the students' own names to engage learning.

2. Always accurately identify a student's entry level into the upcoming content.

3. With students who have severe learning challenges and reading problems, contact sites such as www .learningally.org or www.bookshare.org, which provide special learning aids for students with reading challenges.

4. Provide students with study guides or cloze exercises that cue them to key points in their readings.

5. Use interactive whiteboard technology to adapt the text for students' particular reading challenges or to illustrate new concepts and summaries.

6. Give directions for assignments orally and in written form. Provide rubrics and examples of the task.

7. Pace instruction appropriately with frequent review or cloze activities to assure prior learning is established.

8. Use the vocabulary attribute charts on page 114 or similar tools to teach selected vocabulary for each story or unit.

9. Provide and teach mnemonic strategies.

10. Present directions in small segments and ask students to repeat them to their name card partners or to one another in a small group of children with similar challenges.

11. Provide written assignments in an uncluttered format.

12. The learning environment needs to be inviting, but not cluttered and overstimulating so that it distracts from learning.

13. Frequently use concrete examples to teach concepts, such as role playing, modeling, using props, or giving demonstrations.

14. Play appropriate background music, such as any compositions by George Frideric Handel, Johann Sebastian Bach, Wolfgang Amadeus Mozart, or other composers of baroque and classical music. Cheri Lucas has an online article and Chris Brewer has a book called *Soundtracks for Learning* (see "References and Resources"), which describe specific information on how to use music to enhance learning. Although scientists have debated this theory for years, we have both seen dramatic results when we have used music with our students who have learning difficulties of various types.

## Questions and Answers

*"How can I teach kids with such exceptional educational needs? I've never had any special education training."*

It may help you to know that many labeled special education students don't actually belong in the categories in which they have been placed. Some gifted kids have been misdiagnosed as delayed learners because they wouldn't do their work. The learning needs of many diagnosed students are closer to those of kids in regular education classrooms. Most kids with exceptional learning needs benefit from the chance to learn with students who have a wider range of abilities than those found in special education settings.

Programs in which students with special needs spend most of their time in regular classrooms were designed with the assumption that special education staff would work as partners with regular education teachers to provide appropriate assistance. If you're not receiving the help you need, ask for it—and keep asking until you get results.

Invite someone from the special education staff to observe the dynamics in your classroom vis-à-vis a particular student and make specific intervention suggestions. Also ask that person to help you monitor the success of those changes. If you need more help, invite the principal to come in and make the same kinds of observations. Ask the principal to locate additional services that might be available for you, perhaps from a county or state special education agency. Beyond that, ask the principal how a change can be made to the student's IEP to get help from a paraprofessional who would work with you in your classroom. Also ask for input on how to access other appropriate support services.

According to the IDEA, all children who are eligible for special education services have the right to a free, appropriate public education in the least restrictive educational environment. For some kids with profound exceptional learning needs, the least restrictive environment may not be in the regular classroom. If you use several of the strategies described in this book with a particular student and see no improvement, document your intervention attempts and ask the appropriate administrator for a reevaluation of that student's placement in your class.

*"Isn't it better for special education kids to spend most of their time in programs with teachers who have the right kind of training?"*

It's better for *some* students to spend most of their school time in special education classrooms . . . but those students are very few. Inclusion practices resulted in part from the *over*identification of students for special educational services. We need to be careful not to recommend a student for out-of-classroom placement until we have consistently used appropriate intervention strategies without success.

*"I'm confused. So many of these kids have opposite needs. How am I supposed to know the right thing to do on the spur of the moment?"*

Remember, it's not necessary for you to match the correct intervention to each individual student's needs. Refer to the general suggestions at the beginning of this chapter (pages 22–23) first; many of them are effective with students in several categories of learning needs. Use whatever works.

*"If we make all these accommodations for struggling students, won't it hurt them when they get into the real world? Isn't there a time when they should learn basic skills without the aid of technology or extra help? Where will they find adult environments in which such deference is paid to their special needs?"*

Many colleges have special programs for students with learning difficulties. Programs also exist to provide lifetime coaching for people who need a little extra support to get to work and complete the tasks there. As teachers, we need only be concerned that these students leave school feeling confident that they can learn and that they are worthwhile members of learning communities. When they feel that way, they are much more likely to make their way successfully in the real world.

# Daily Task Checklist

Name: _____

| Portion of task you plan do for this work period | Check here when portion is done | Check here if you did not complete the portion |
|---|---|---|
|  |  |  |
|  |  |  |
|  |  |  |
|  |  |  |
|  |  |  |
|  |  |  |
|  |  |  |
|  |  |  |
|  |  |  |
|  |  |  |
|  |  |  |
|  |  |  |

# CHAPTER 3

# Using Students' Learning Styles (Modalities) to Facilitate Learning Success

The term *learning modalities* refers to the way the brain perceives and processes what it needs to learn. The students we teach best are those whose learning modalities match the teaching style with which we are most comfortable. Sometimes we underestimate the learning capabilities of students who don't learn the "right" way. In fact, there is no right way. The only way for each student is the one that works.

In recent years, there has been some chatter in professional articles about whether the concept of learning modalities actually exists. Suffice it to say that we use the term only as a vehicle for communicating the strategies throughout this book that we know are highly effective for students with learning difficulties. We happily leave the esoteric debates to the researchers.

This chapter will help you understand and appreciate how you can enhance the learning success of your struggling students by matching your teaching to their learning modalities. You'll discover that many of the differences you have with your students are not personality conflicts but clashes between your preferred teaching style and their preferred learning modalities. You'll see how certain easy-to-make modifications in the learning environment and in the way you teach will allow students with learning difficulties to improve their learning productivity. Of course, as your students become more successful, your attitudes and satisfaction about your teaching effectiveness will improve as well.

## Scenario: Eric

Eric was a fourth grader for whom school had not been a pleasant experience. Since his reputation preceded him, teachers dreaded hearing that they were getting Eric for the upcoming school year.

Eric was constantly moving—touching other students or fidgeting with a toy or some other inappropriate object. He was never in his seat. He jumped up often to sharpen his pencil (although he never seemed to use it), and he made funny noises while he worked—somewhere between a squeak and a snort. He always had something in his mouth, usually gum or candy. If the teacher took that away from him, in went a pencil, sleeve, or shoestring.

Eric's cumulative records folder showed a pattern established early in kindergarten. Most of the parent-teacher conferences his parents attended were filled with teacher observations of Eric's inability to meet expected behavior and productivity guidelines. As each year progressed, teachers became less tolerant of Eric's behavior and more insistent that he be evaluated by a doctor and put on some kind of medication.

Eric's fourth-grade teacher attended one of Susan's workshops on learning modalities. Once there, the teacher was quickly able to identify that Eric was a tactile-kinesthetic learner. (Tactile-kinesthetic learners' learning is noticeably improved when they have numerous opportunities to learn by touching and handling hands-on materials and by enjoying numerous opportunities to move about during the learning phase of any lesson.) After hearing more about that particular learning modality, she returned to the classroom and provided the following interventions:

- She moved Eric's desk to a place where his movements would be least likely to attract the attention of the other students.

- She used masking tape to define a perimeter around Eric's desk measuring roughly a foot and a half in each direction. Then she told Eric that he could move as much as he wanted to, as long as he stayed within that space.

- She began allowing Eric to do his work in his favorite position—balancing on one knee on his chair and leaning over his desk—rather than requiring him to sit up straight.

- She gave Eric permission to chew gum in class, since chewing helped him work off excess energy. However, he couldn't leave the classroom with gum in his mouth. He was required to wrap it up and throw it away in a designated lined wastebasket.

- Since Eric needed to tap a pencil as another way to release excess energy, his teacher showed him the simple trick of tapping his pencil on his sleeve, arm, shirt, pant leg, or other soft surface instead of his desk or chair. Now Eric could tap without disturbing his classmates.

Eric's teacher adapted as many learning tasks as possible into a tactile-kinesthetic format. This enabled Eric to learn by touching and moving and to express what he learned with products that were easier for a tactile-kinesthetic learner to create. Examples included:

- having him record his work in chart form with pictures and drawings

- always letting him see the end of a task before starting to work

- teaching basic skills through jingles, chants, and movement

- letting him act out events in literature and other subjects

- teaching him how to purposefully relax before beginning school tasks

- letting him listen to soothing music through headphones as he worked

- giving him a soft ball to hold and squeeze

These accommodations drastically cut down on Eric's distracting behavior. Because his basic learning modality needs were being met, his mind was free to concentrate on learning. Eric understood that as long as he followed his teacher's guidelines for appropriate behavior during work times, the choice about whether to move, chew, or lean was his. When he didn't follow the guidelines, the choice was taken away from him for a day or two until he could make another plan to follow the guidelines.

## Medication for ADHD

Students with ADHD will often need a combination of medication and classroom interventions to achieve optimum results. The school should never recommend the medication, since this would require them to pay for it. However, if educators observe that the student appears overmedicated, with signs of fatigue or inability to participate alertly, that information should be shared with the family.

# Understanding Learning Modalities

The human brain is a complex and fascinating organ given little attention in education until the 1990s. It is composed of three main parts: the cerebrum, the cerebellum, and the brain stem. Only the cerebrum—the most recently evolved part—is capable of learning academic material. The next-oldest part of the brain, the cerebellum, is in charge of our emotions; the oldest known functioning part, the brain stem, is our survival center. When we experience stress, our brain stem takes over the other two parts of the brain and orders us to fight or flee. When students are asked to engage in learning tasks that conflict with the way they learn, they feel stressed. Their brain stems send the message, "Put up a fight or get out of here!"

Learning experiences must be brain-compatible, or they cannot be mastered effectively. Since different kids' brains function and learn differently, it stands to reason that we must teach them differently. To make new learning happen, we must connect it to a pattern the brain already knows and recognizes. When we do this, the brain perceives the new learning in a language it can easily understand. Equally importantly, the learning environment must be comfortable. When the body is in distress, the brain stem focuses on the discomfort and no learning takes place.

Drs. Marie Carbo, Rita Dunn, and Kenneth Dunn have described three styles of learning: *auditory, visual,* and *tactile-kinesthetic.* *

- Auditory people learn by listening.

- Visual people learn by seeing. They must get a picture in their brain in order to understand what they need to learn.

- Tactile-kinesthetic people learn by touching and moving.

Auditory learners are logical, analytical, sequential thinkers. They are comfortable with typical school tasks, including analyzing sounds and numbers, following directions in order, and doing exactly what the teacher has requested. Since their learning needs are usually met in the classroom, they are considered good students. Auditory learners are perfectly comfortable in rooms that are quiet, well-lit, and equipped with desks for each student. For these kids, typical classroom arrangements work very well and actually enhance their productivity.

Visual and tactile-kinesthetic learners are global thinkers. They are not comfortable with logical, analytical, sequential tasks until they can see the big picture. They can learn to think logically, analytically, and sequentially, but they must do it by working backward from the whole to the parts. They must learn new material in a meaningful context. Their thought patterns tend to be random (nonlinear, nonsequential); classroom discussions lead them onto divergent thinking pathways, and they make creative and unusual associations with the subject at hand. When we call on them, they may say something that seems totally irrelevant to the topic. However, if we stop and ask them to explain their statement, they can usually help us see how they made a particular connection.

Visual and tactile-kinesthetic learners are actually distracted by environments that are quiet, brightly lit, and equipped with standard furniture. In order for their brains to concentrate, they need an environment with low light, background sound, and comfy furniture or permission to work on the floor. So the very rules we usually apply to all children actually work against the productivity conditions that global learners need.

It will come as no surprise to anyone that visual learners have become the largest group in any heterogeneous classroom. Before the general use of computers and video games, this was probably not the case, but it is definitely an issue all teachers and families must deal with now. The kids we used to call the "good

kids" because they would actually listen to and follow our directions—the auditory learners—are becoming fewer and fewer. Of course, the good kids are still in our classes—they just aren't auditory learners anymore. They *are* strongly visual, and we must accommodate that preference in all our teaching.

One way to understand the significance of these learning modality differences is by considering the conflicts we have with the people in our lives. You can do this by taking the simple learning modalities inventory titled "Analytical or Global?" on page 54. Write your initials beside those characteristics that describe you, then write the initials of your significant other (SO) beside those characteristics that describe him or her. For purposes of this test, your SO might be your spouse or partner, another adult you know well and have occasional conflicts with, a child so different from you that you're sure the hospital switched infants on you, or a family member with whom you often clash.

As you review your responses, you'll probably notice many glaring differences between you and your SO. Especially in the case of a spouse or partner, we tend to seek out people whose abilities compensate for our weaknesses.

When two people notice in each other certain qualities they wish they had, an intense, irresistible attraction can develop. What's ironic is that once we commit to spending our lives together enjoying each other's strengths, those same qualities slowly but surely become irritating. Instead of appreciating the differences that initially drew us together, we expend enormous amounts of time, energy, and emotion trying to make the other person better (in other words, more like us).

As you can see from the inventory, our thinking and learning modalities predict certain preferences in our environmental conditions. These environmental preferences are so innate that we can exert very little conscious control over them. Many disagreements between SOs are caused by conflicts in environmental preferences.

It shouldn't surprise you to learn that you can minimize conflicts with your students by adjusting their learning environment. Once the environment is more compatible with your students' learning modalities, their ability to learn improves automatically and dramatically. Your ultimate goal is to provide a brain-compatible environment for *all* students.

## Learning Modalities and the Hierarchy of Needs

Another way to understand the importance of accommodating learning modalities is through psychologist

---

*Used with permission of Marie Carbo, executive director, National Reading Styles Institute (nrsi.com), Syosset, NY.

## Abraham Maslow's Hierarchy of Needs

**Self-Actualization Needs**
To develop our talents and be true to our goals; to realize our potential; to have peak experiences

**Self-Esteem and Competence Needs**
To achieve; to gain approval and recognition from others for our achievements; to be able to trust in our own abilities

**Belonging and Love Needs**
To love and be loved; to have relationships and be accepted; to know that we are a valued member of a group

**Safety Needs**
To feel safe, secure, and out of danger; to feel confident that we will not be harmed either physically or psychologically

**Physiological Needs**
To have the food, water, clothing, shelter, sleep, exercise, and comfort we need to survive

Abraham Maslow's famous hierarchy of needs.* Maslow taught that needs on the lower levels of the hierarchy must be met before needs on the higher levels can be addressed. In other words, when we overlook the physiological needs of students who are struggling to learn, we actually contribute to their learning problems.

We already know some of this intuitively. For example, we would never try to teach a new skill to an infant who is desperately hungry or overdue for a diaper change. Babies can learn only after their physiological needs are met.

Working up the pyramid, we find that other needs can be assigned to certain age groups. Kids in the elementary grades can learn when their physiological needs *and* safety needs are met. Adolescents can learn when their physiological, safety, *and* belonging needs are met. Adults can learn when their physiological, safety, belonging, *and* self-esteem needs are met. To read a book, take a workshop, enroll in a continuing education course, or pursue an advanced degree, one must be confident enough in one's own abilities and achievements to take risks. Self-actualization needs are met once all the needs below them in the pyramid have

been satisfied. Maslow taught that very few people ever reach this level.

He further taught that no matter what level we are currently functioning on, all our energy and attention will immediately be drawn to any lower level for which we perceive an unmet need. For example, suppose that you are engrossed in this book (self-esteem and competence level) when you suddenly smell smoke. You will drop the book and refocus your attention on the safety level until you discover the source of the smoke and do what you must to feel safe again.

With this in mind, consider the typical classroom. There are certainly some tactile-kinesthetic students in every room. If we insist that they sit still while we lecture and they do their tasks, sooner or later their physiological need to move will take precedence over any other need. The longer we ignore it, the more stress they will feel and the less they will learn. Many students we label "hyperactive" are tactile-kinesthetic learners whose hyperactive behaviors can be diminished if their learning tasks allow them to move while learning.**

# Learning Modalities and School Success

Note: If you are using a different learning modality model, such as multiple intelligences, you will find that this chapter still contains much useful information that can be helpful to you and your students.

All babies are born with their tactile-kinesthetic learning modality predominant. Parents naturally acknowledge the fact that babies learn by doing—by getting into everything, touching everything, pulling things apart, and knocking things down. Although we might prefer that children learn by letting us tell them things, we understand that a tidy house and a small child simply can't coexist.

Imagine how inappropriate it would be to sit a toddler in a high chair and say, "Today I am going to show you the kitchen. I want you to watch and listen as I describe it, but I don't want you to touch anything." If we restricted young children from touching, feeling, moving, dancing, and jumping, we know we would impair their ability to learn.

Success at most school tasks requires children to make the transition from tactile-kinesthetic to auditory-analytical. The brains of girls are ready to make that transition at about age six, while the brains of boys might not be ready for that transition until as late as eight or nine years old. Guess which gender significantly overpopulates special education and remedial reading programs? Boys.

---

*Hierarchy of Needs from *Motivation and Personality*, 3rd edition, by Abraham H. Maslow. New York: HarperCollins Publishers, 1987. Reprinted by permission of HarperCollins Publishers, Inc.

**Marie Carbo, Rita Dunn, and Kenneth Dunn.

Are boys really less capable than girls? Are visual-kinesthetic learners less intelligent than auditory learners? Or are many unsuccessful students simply being taught in a manner incompatible with their basic thinking and learning modality? By the time some boys are ready to succeed with typical school tasks, school has so badly damaged their self-esteem that they may be emotionally incapable of perceiving themselves as successful students—and they may never catch up.

Since most school tasks require listening, following step-by-step directions, or analyzing the sounds in words, auditory-analytical learners are far more likely to be successful than global (visual or tactile-kinesthetic) learners, unless teachers make appropriate modifications for the global kids. You can use the following lists of preferences to design successful learning activities for both kinds of global learners. The lists overlap because the preferences of visual learners and tactile-kinesthetic learners may be similar at times and different at other times.

Remember that global learners prefer a learning environment with some sound, low light, and opportunities for movement. They tend to study in a relaxed posture, they like to eat or chew when concentrating, and they usually must see or hear the whole before learning the parts.

Students who are generally successful with academic learning are probably auditory-analytical, or they possess a combination of modalities that allows them to learn just about anything with ease. Since this book is about helping students with learning difficulties, we will not spend time discussing the auditory-analytical group.

## What Visual Learners Prefer

When the first edition of this book was published in 1996, best estimates were that in a typical class, about 35 percent of learners were visual. In 2005, that figure jumped to 65 percent or more. Presently, the data (according to research by Dr. Marie Carbo) suggests that 40 to 50 percent learn visually, 50 to 60 percent of learners are tactile-kinesthetic, and 20 to 30 percent are auditory. (The percentages add up to more than 100 because some students learn in more than one way.)

You probably know the reason: television, video and computer games, smartphones and tablets, and learning software with lots of action. What are the chances these influences will go away anytime soon? You know the answer to that as well: none. Regardless of how well logical, analytical, and sequential tasks worked for earlier generations of students, the predominant learning modality now is visual, with a significant amount of kinesthetic. And that's just the way it is.

In general, visual learners prefer:

- pictures rather than words

- viewing rather than reading (videos, demonstrations, and examples work well)

- being shown an example of what the finished product should look like rather than hearing an explanation of the task

- reading the end of a book or story first to see if it's worth the effort to read the whole thing

- stories with excitement, humor, and adventure

- visualizing scenes, characters, and actions while reading about them

- learning phonics, skills, and vocabulary in context after hearing or reading the selection

- finding visual cues in texts (charts, graphs, photographs)

- graphic organizers (mapping, illustrating in chart form what they learn)

- writing down what they need to learn (but they may never need to look at their notes again)

- writing in many media (different colors and textures, shaving cream, finger paints, and so on)

- using artistic means to express what they learn

- drawing or doodling while listening

- opportunities to write out words during spelling bees and games

- being shown the correct version of what they have gotten wrong (never circle or highlight their errors, lest you reinforce incorrect information)

- visual order in their workplace (visual learners are often quite neat and well-organized; however, some can work in a mess and find things right where they left them)

## What Tactile-Kinesthetic Learners Prefer

Between 50 and 60 percent of the students in your class are probably tactile-kinesthetic learners. They prefer:

- receiving concrete examples at the beginning of a learning experience

- hands-on activities (*examples:* building the volcano or the simple electrical circuit instead of reading about it or watching a video or film)

- moving while learning; acting out words and phrases; touching everything within reach

- learning academic tasks after doing some physical activity (One teacher took her students for a run around the building each morning before beginning regular instruction, which dramatically improved their learning. For some tactile-kinesthetic learners, their reading fluency increases if they rotate their arm in a circular motion while reading.)

- stories with lots of action, adventure, and excitement

- reading the end of a book or story first to see if it's worth the effort to read the whole thing

- creative dramatics and readers' theater (see page 104); acting out stories and events

- learning by doing; trying out rather than learning about

- using manipulatives whenever possible

- fidgeting or chewing while thinking (**Tip:** to greatly reduce the amount of moving around, let them hold and squeeze a small rubber ball, such as a Koosh ball)

- writing in many media (sand, salt, shaving cream, or pudding; with their fingers on each other's backs; and so on)

- word processing instead of handwriting

- figuring out math problems with finger multiplication and finger math (see pages 160 and 162), number lines, and other number manipulation systems

- not having to listen to long lectures, lessons, or conversations

- learning the shapes of spelling words, not just the letters

- learning verbs over nouns

- displaying what they know in chart form with actual pictures or objects rather than telling about it

- learning and creating raps, rhythms, rhymes, and jingles

- speaking as little as possible; being terse and succinct

- expressing their feelings physically

- developing their own system of organization instead of using one designed for analytical thinkers

## The Essential Rules

The key to letting kids do whatever they need to better concentrate on their learning tasks is to offer *any* options to *all* students as long as they follow the Essential Rules. Explain to your students that anyone who chooses to do their work away from the direct instruction area—or anyone who chooses to chew, eat, tap, or move around—must follow these rules or might not be able to continue participating in the preferred options previously described.

1. Don't bother anyone else.

2. Don't call attention to yourself.

3. Work on your chosen learning tasks for the entire period.

4. Keep records of your own work as directed by your teachers.

Explain to your students that as long as they honor all four of these rules, they can make their own choices. If they fail to follow any of the rules, you will choose their task for that day. Students can try again on the next day to enjoy their choices by meeting the rules for acceptable behavior. **Tip:** For students with serious concentration problems, try focusing only on the first rule for a week or two. Then add the other rules one at a time, expecting the students to keep following the rules they have already learned.

Since these rules apply to everyone, they do not limit access to what your students would consider privileges. Therefore, students do not resent those who choose certain options. So you can let kids who need to listen to music use headphones, and let kids who need to sit on the floor do so as long as they stay visible, and let kids who need less light sit in a section of the room where the lights are turned off. Those who need to eat snacks before lunch because they consistently skip breakfast can do so, and kids who don't want to eat don't have to. You can send a message home to parents telling them which snacks are acceptable and which are not. **Tip:** It may be a good idea to explain to your principal why you are making these allowances before the principal finds out during a visit to your classroom.

*Caution:* When testing time comes, you should try to keep letting kids enjoy the same learning modality accommodations they have on nontesting days. If kids are allowed to work on the floor, they might take their test on the floor. If kids are allowed to listen to soothing music as they work, they should have the same option while they take tests. Without these accommodations, stress increases. Brains do not function at their best in high-stress situations.

# Teaching Students About Learning Modalities

Early repeated failure to learn can be devastating. Once students are convinced that they are incapable of learning, their expectations of failure often become a self-fulfilling prophecy. The most effective way to convince struggling students that they can learn is to show them by teaching to their learning modality strengths.

We also need to teach them *about* their own learning modalities. This empowers kids to act intelligently when learning seems difficult for them. When they realize that their inability to learn is not their fault, they no longer feel guilty and stupid. Instead, they stop and think, "The method I've been using to learn this is not working for me. I need to try another method that matches my learning modality strengths. When I find the right way to work on this problem, it will be a lot easier for me."

## Scenario: Mrs. Potter's Classroom*

Teacher Ann Potter uses a highly effective method to teach students about their own learning modalities. First, she introduces them to environmental preferences like those listed in "What Kind of Learner Are You?" and "What's Your Learning Modality?" on pages 55–56. She explains that different people have different preferences when it comes to their learning environment, and that they learn more effectively when conditions are right for them. Then she has them experiment with light levels, room temperature, body posture, and so on to determine which conditions best enable them to concentrate and get their work done.

For example, her students spend several days exploring various sound conditions. Specific areas in the classroom are set aside for silence, soft talking, and listening to recordings of soothing music or environmental sounds. At the end of the third class period on sound conditions, Mrs. Potter tapes several sheets of paper together to form a chart, draws a long line (continuum) from one end to the other, labels the left end "Total Silence" and the right end "Listening to Recordings," and posts it along a wall. She asks her students to line up in front of the continuum according to where they perceive they can best concentrate, and then she writes their names on the chart.

Something amazing happened one October to demonstrate that Mrs. Potter's students were understanding and appreciating differences in learning modality preferences. She had assigned a sustained silent reading period. One of her students, a boy named Jason, had trouble finding his book in his desk and was late getting to the rug. After looking for a place on the floor with a pillow on which to rest his head, he carefully settled in and opened his book. Slowly he became aware that someone nearby was mumbling. Jason was a student who preferred total silence while he worked. But instead of getting upset, he looked around to see who was mumbling. It was a girl named Linda. Jason glanced up at the continuum chart and located her name. Then he said to her, "Oh, Linda, I see that you are an auditory learner. You subvocalize when you read. I like to read in silence. But you were here first, so I guess I'll move." And he did.

# Teaching Your Students About Their Learning Modalities

Use "What Kind of Learner Are You?" and "What's Your Learning Modality?" (pages 55–56) to help your students learn about and understand their own learning modality strengths and weaknesses.** When students appreciate that differences between them are often explained by learning modality needs and differences, they become much more tolerant of each other. Once your students have developed the vocabulary and understanding of learning modalities, they will appreciate everything you do to accommodate those differences. And there will be significantly fewer behavior problems when students' learning modalities are accommodated.

Imagine walking over to the desk of a kinesthetic kid who constantly drums on the desktop with a pencil or fingers. If your student knows nothing about learning modalities, you might say something ineffective: "How many times have I told you to stop doing that?" Instead, because the student *does* know about learning modalities, you can say something highly effective: "When you make that noise on your desk, it really bothers the auditory learners in here, including me. So, if you want to continue your drumming, please tap on your arm or leg so you can enjoy the physical activity without infringing on the rights of other learners." No power struggle.

Gum chewing can be handled the same way. Gum chewing is rarely allowed in school because kids stash their used gum in yucky places, which they do because they don't want to get caught with the gum. But what if you allow gum chewing in your classroom for students

---

*Ann Potter, teacher, Elgin, Illinois.

**These pages can be copied as a two-sided handout. It will be easier for kids to manage, and you'll save paper as well. Use the Internet to find other learning modalities tests.

who follow certain rules? In Susan's class, kids could chew gum if and only if:

- the piece was no bigger than a stick of Dentyne

- they did not chew fruit-flavored gum (Susan hated the smell)

- they deposited used gum in only one wastebasket— a plastic-lined vessel beside Susan's desk

- they always left their gum in the wastebasket when leaving the room

Anyone who wanted to chew gum in Susan's classroom could. And you can probably guess what happened. During the first few days, everyone chewed gum. By the fourth day, the only kids chewing gum were those who needed it. And the ones who didn't need it had absolutely no problem with the fact that other kids were chewing it.

The learning styles methods in this book are completely complementary to other learning modality models, including multiple intelligences. The box below illustrates those connections.

# Matching Teaching to Students' Learning Modalities

- When you want to remember what's most important in helping global thinkers become successful learners, use the acronym WHOLISTIC: Whole to parts; Hands-on learning; Organize information visually; Learning modalities focus; Immerse the senses; Seek patterns and connections; Technology assistance; Integrate skills into context; Concrete to abstract. On page 57, you'll find a set of WHOLISTIC bookmarks. Make several copies, cut the bookmarks apart, laminate them, and use them. Place them in your manuals, notebooks, and other teaching materials. Use WHOLISTIC as a checklist to plan learning experiences, to identify what might be missing when global thinkers are struggling to learn, and to remind yourself of what to do differently when your students are not learning successfully.

- Never conduct an entire lesson in any one modality. If you spend most of the class time lecturing and explaining, this clearly favors students with auditory learning strengths. If the entire lesson is hands-on learning, auditory learners will be uncomfortable. However, it is not necessary to include all learning modalities in every lesson. Use a variety of approaches over several lessons, and focus on methods that global learners favor during reteaching times.

- Incorporate visuals into every lesson. For example, you might talk for 10 to 15 minutes, then show a film or video for another block of time. Showing parts of films or videos is fine if you don't want to use them in their entirety. Check to see what types of visual aids are available from publishers of textbooks and teaching support materials. Use charts and interactive whiteboard resources whenever you can.

- Play appropriate background music while kids are working. For many students, learning is enhanced when certain types of music play softly in the background. Particularly effective are Johann Pachelbel's Canon in D Major and the largo (slow) movements of concertos by George Handel, Johann Bach, Georg Philipp Telemann, and Arcangelo Corelli. Some researchers have observed that listening to Wolfgang Mozart appears to improve math competencies. If the music bothers the auditory learners in your classroom, give them a portable music player with headphones and let them listen to a recording of environmental sounds or white noise, which may help drown out the music and other distracting noises, such as talking.

| Learning Modalities | Multiple Intelligences | |
|---|---|---|
| **Auditory** | Linguistic | Intrapersonal |
| | Logical-mathematical | Naturalist |
| | Interpersonal | Existential, spiritual, moral |
| **Visual** | Visual-spatial | Intrapersonal |
| | Logical-mathematical | Naturalist |
| **Tactile-kinesthetic** | Bodily-kinesthetic | Naturalist |
| | Visual-spatial | Existential, spiritual, moral |
| | Musical-rhythmic | |

■ Provide hands-on experiences as often as possible. Students could build models of what they are studying, play a game that requires some movement, or act out a particular concept. Remember the old, reliable Chinese proverb: *I hear, and I forget; I see and hear, and I may remember; I do, and I understand.*

■ Offer a good balance between cooperative learning and independent work. Remember that if kids strongly resist cooperative learning but get their work done independently, there is no reason to force them into cooperative groups all the time. Expecting all students to choose to work on at least one cooperative learning task each week is more appropriate than requiring students who work best alone to cooperate to the point of learning modality discomfort. For more on cooperative learning, see page 15.

■ Regularly give students time to reflect on what has been taught and learned. Some students will choose to record their reflections in a journal, while others may prefer to create a sketch or model. Insisting that all kids write in journals many times each week favors auditory and visual learners but discriminates against tactile and kinesthetic students.

■ Encourage all students to talk about their learning modality strengths and about how understanding those strengths improves their success with school tasks.

■ Expect all students to set goals from one grading period to the next. Be sure the goals include the language of learning modalities. (*Example:* A student might choose a goal of "using graphic organizers to help remember content I should learn" or "using graphic organizers to take notes.") Be sure to take time to check students' goals with them at each marking period, and help them set realistic goals for the next checkpoint. For more information, see Chapter 9, especially pages 192–193.

■ Find and use software that motivates students to be successful learners, especially software that provides individualized guidance so students can move ahead on their own personally designed path of achievement. One example is *SuccessMaker.* (See "References and Resources.")

■ For students who often seem confused, teach exercises that are cross-lateral. Cross-lateral exercises stimulate both sides of the brain to communicate with each other and prevent one side from being too dominant, thus opening the learner to more successful intake of learning material. More information and teaching materials are available from Brain Gym International. (See "References and Resources.")

## Unlocking Autism 🔒

Due to communication weaknesses, students with autism are predominantly visual, tactile, or kinesthetic learners. Being actively engaged in learning greatly increases the likelihood that these students will retain new skills and concepts. When you give instructions verbally, you need to pair them with another learning modality that is a strength. Being aware of learning modalities will help increase learning competence and decrease social and behavior problems that can occur when students are very frustrated with the work they are expected to do.

Some researchers claim that the benefits of considering learning modalities while teaching has never been proven in research. Our experience indicates otherwise. So it is up to you to try a few of these strategies with your students and make your own decision based on your experiences.

# Questions and Answers

*"How can I possibly differentiate the required standards to meet all the varied learning needs of my students?"*

The only thing you really *must* do is to constantly ask yourself this question: "If this student is not learning the way I am teaching, what environmental or curricular modifications might enable more effective learning?" You are not expected to rearrange your entire classroom, nor is it necessary to diagnose and teach to each individual student's learning modality. However, awareness of learning modality implications for learning success will make you more aware of the need for certain modifications as specific students indicate that they are not learning successfully. As you offer these modifications, you will observe that other students' learning success is also being affected positively, and you can generalize the effects of the modifications. Some teachers who regularly use learning centers orient them around specific learning modality categories and let students find the tasks that allow them to demonstrate best what they are learning.

*"Isn't it a bad practice to always teach to students' learning modality strengths? Don't we all have to learn to blend and understand stimuli from many different styles? Won't kids be at a disadvantage in the real world if we only teach to their learning modality strengths?"*

No, not really. Many struggling students believe that they are incapable of success in school.

The most powerful evidence we can provide to convince them they *can learn* is success in tasks they formerly could not do. The LD students for whom you are using strategies from this book may have gone through several other school years with little or no accommodations for their learning modality strengths. If this year the opportunities you provide in their strongest learning modality leads them to better learning success, they will be at a much greater advantage in the real world than they would be if all their school years were filled only with failures. We believe there is no reason to arbitrarily expect them to spend precious learning time with tasks that frustrate them.

*"Our school has rules against chewing gum, eating food, or bringing portable music players to class. How can I make appropriate modifications to the learning environment while remaining within these rules?"*

We've never claimed to follow all the rules we were expected to obey as classroom teachers. (There . . . our secret is out!) Rules are often made in reaction to misconduct. Schools ban gum because of where kids tend to hide it; of course, there's no need to hide it if it's not against the rules to chew it. Food creates grazing grounds for critters; when kids bring nutritious snacks from home, they should be responsible for cleanup. If there's a chance that kids' portable music players might get taken by other students, perhaps you can keep them locked in your desk between uses. When we tell our students that they can chew gum only in our room and must dispose of it only in a certain wastebasket, kids who follow those rules are allowed to chew; kids who don't follow them lose their chewing privileges for a while. Chewing releases excess energy, especially for tactile-kinesthetic kids; if you simply can't allow it, try letting students tap on spots that create no noise (such as their arms or legs) or letting them swing their legs into a space through which other students are unlikely to pass. Remember that the reason for offering these options is to improve learning outcomes; if that doesn't happen, there's no need to provide the options any longer. When kids understand this, they usually react in positive ways.

*"I'm concerned about how my principal and other adults will react to some of the modifications I've made to accommodate various learning modality preferences."*

Don't wait for their reactions; be proactive. Explain your reasons for allowing certain liberties *before* you expect a classroom visit. Send newsletters home to families describing these changes in the context of other teaching decisions. Keep reminding people that your goal is to improve your students' learning, and you will continue to use only those methods that lead to positive outcomes.

*"How can I undo the damage I may have done to some kids in the past because I didn't know about learning modalities?"*

If you are taking the time to read this book, you can assume that you have a generous and friendly attitude toward students. Teachers are not in the practice of purposefully harming young people. We all make teaching decisions based on the information available to us at a given time. As you try some of these techniques with your own students, start passing information about them to some of your colleagues—particularly the teacher who is being driven to distraction by a student you had last year, for whom you now know what to do differently.

# Analytical or Global?

| When it comes to . . . | Analytical thinkers tend to prefer . . . | Global thinkers tend to prefer . . . |
|---|---|---|
| **1.** Sound | Silence for concentrating | Some sound for concentrating |
| **2.** Light | Bright light for reading or studying | Very low light for reading or studying |
| **3.** Room temperature | Turning thermostat warmer; wearing heavy clothing | Turning thermostat cooler; wearing lightweight clothing (even in winter) |
| **4.** Furniture | Studying at a desk and chair | Studying on a bed or floor |
| **5.** Mobility | Sitting still for long periods of time | Moving around constantly |
| **6.** Time of day | Learning in the morning; going to bed early | Learning later in the day; staying up late (a night owl) |
| **7.** Eating | Eating breakfast and regular meals | Skipping breakfast; snacking while learning |
| **8.** Learning | Working alone or under the direction of one other person; being self-directed, independent | Working in a group or peer learning; discovering answers rather than being told |
| **9.** Tasks | Working on one job at a time until done; being somewhat compulsive | Starting more jobs than they complete; procrastinating |
| **10.** Planning | Making lists for everything; planning far ahead; putting tasks on a calendar; avoiding risk taking | Doing things when they feel like it; not planning ahead, but going with the flow; experimenting; trying things out |
| **11.** Deciding | Taking a long time to make decisions; second-guessing decisions | Being spontaneous in making decisions; doing what feels right |
| **12.** Time | Punctuality; wearing watches with large numbers | Running late; wearing fashion watches with few or no numbers, but they match one's outfit |
| **13.** Neatness | Neat, well-organized appearance; outfits that go together | Disorganized appearance; clothes may not match or may be very colorful |
| **14.** Perceiving | Seeing things as they are at the moment; noticing details | Seeing things as they might be; perceiving the whole; ignoring details |
| **15.** Assembling | Following directions step-by-step; starting over if they get stuck | Studying a picture of how something will look when complete, then assembling it their way |
| **16.** Thinking | Logically, analytically, sequentially; seeing cause and effect; perceiving differences; figuring out things step-by-step; understanding symbolic codes | Intuitively and nonlinearly; seeing similarities and connections; working backward from whole to parts, from concrete to symbolic |
| **17.** Learning | Sequential tasks and concrete, logical steps | Learning through open-ended tasks; creating new ideas; learning through simile and metaphor |
| **18.** Remembering | Remembering what has been spoken | Remembering images of what has been seen and experienced |
| **19.** Taking tests | Predictable test formats (multiple-choice, true-false, essay) | Opportunities to express themselves in ways other than writing |

# What Kind of Learner Are You?

## Did You Know?

When you have trouble learning, that doesn't mean you're not smart. It means that you haven't been using your strongest learning modality—the learning way that's best for your brain.

There are two main types of learning modalities: **analytical** and **global**.

**Analytical learners learn by listening.** They learn best when teachers tell them what they need to learn. If you are an analytical learner, you are usually comfortable with tasks that ask you to figure things out, that require logical thinking, or that are presented in order from easier to harder.

**Global learners learn by seeing or doing.** They learn best when information is presented with pictures, diagrams, videos, and other visuals. Some global learners enjoy learning actively instead of writing down what they learn. They like to see the whole unit or chapter before learning the parts.

Both types of learners are smart. Neither is smarter or better than the other. Both can have learning problems when they try to learn something new in a way that isn't comfortable for their brain.

The other side of this handout is a chart that describes things that analytical and global learners tend to prefer (like best). When you read the chart, which things sound more like you? Do you think you're an analytical learner or a global learner? Can you find statements that describe you in both columns? Draw a circle around the statements that best describe the way you are most of the time. Then come back to this page and read the next section.

## What Does It Mean?

If you're an analytical learner, you are probably successful in school. Not because you're smarter than other kids, but because most school tasks are comfortable for your learning modality.

If you're a global learner (either visual or tactile-kinesthetic), you may have trouble with some school subjects. Not because you're less smart than other kids, but because most school tasks are not as comfortable for your learning modality. **Tip:** You can ask your teachers to help you learn by giving you visual aids or graphic organizers, which will make it much easier for you to remember what you are supposed to know. You can also ask to learn things using music or rhythm. For example, maybe you can sing rhymes or jump rope while memorizing math facts.

If your modality is described almost equally in both columns, it means that you can learn in many different ways. That's a good thing. It makes learning easier for you, no matter what modality your teachers choose to use.

# What's Your Learning Modality?

| When it comes to . . . | Analytical learners tend to prefer . . . | Global learners tend to prefer . . . |
|---|---|---|
| **1.** Sound | Quiet in order to concentrate | Music or other sounds in the background |
| **2.** Light | Bright light; no shadows | Low light |
| **3.** Room temperature | Warmer | Cooler |
| **4.** Study space | Desk and chair | Cushions or floor |
| **5.** Movement | Sitting still for long time periods | Lots of movement; rarely sit down completely |
| **6.** Alert time of day | Going to bed early and getting up early | Staying up late (night owl); have trouble getting up in the morning |
| **7.** Eating | Three meals a day— want breakfast | Skipping breakfast; eating late at night; chewing on things |
| **8.** Time | Wearing a watch; are always on time | Not wearing a watch; are rarely on time |
| **9.** Neatness | Being neat and well-organized | Being messy; have trouble finding things |
| **10.** Planning | Making and following lists | No lists; just doing what feels right |
| **11.** Learning | Finishing one task at a time | Jumping around from task to task |
| **12.** Group work | Working and learning on their own | Working with others |
| **13.** Processing information | Sequential information, in logical steps | Focusing on the whole rather than details |
| **14.** Rules and directions | Complete teacher explanations | Clear examples to understand teacher's expectations |
| **15.** Studying | Remembering facts | Meaningful contexts |
| **16.** Phonics | Sounding out words | Learning whole words rather than words in syllables |
| **17.** Reading | Lots of reading | High-interest reading: mystery, adventure, fantasy, and humor |
| **18.** Sequence | Arranging ideas in his or her head | Manipulating ideas and information hands-on |
| **19.** Skill work | Figuring things out independently | Getting help while learning |
| **20.** Recall | Many facts and figures | High-interest words or phrases |

| Whole to parts | Whole to parts | Whole to parts | Whole to parts | Whole to parts | Whole to parts |
|---|---|---|---|---|---|
| Hands-on learning | Hands-on learning | Hands-on learning | Hands-on learning | Hands-on learning | Hands-on learning |
| Organize information visually | Organize information visually | Organize information visually | Organize information visually | Organize information visually | Organize information visually |
| Learning modalities focus | Learning modalities focus | Learning modalities focus | Learning modalities focus | Learning modalities focus | Learning modalities focus |
| Immerse the senses | Immerse the senses | Immerse the senses | Immerse the senses | Immerse the senses | Immerse the senses |
| Seek patterns and connections | Seek patterns and connections | Seek patterns and connections | Seek patterns and connections | Seek patterns and connections | Seek patterns and connections |
| Technology assistance | Technology assistance | Technology assistance | Technology assistance | Technology assistance | Technology assistance |
| Integrate skills into context | Integrate skills into context | Integrate skills into context | Integrate skills into context | Integrate skills into context | Integrate skills into context |
| Concrete to abstract | Concrete to abstract | Concrete to abstract | Concrete to abstract | Concrete to abstract | Concrete to abstract |

# CHAPTER 4

# Ensuring That All Students Make At Least One Year's Academic Growth During Each School Year

Each day, children come to school hoping to experience successful learning. Learning happens when the brain acquires a program—a fixed sequence of steps that is useful to the learner. For this to occur, the brain must be able to connect new learning to some pattern it already knows. Kids learn best when they perceive that certain skills or information will help them better understand something they know or are eager to know more about.

Children are naturally creative thinkers who construct fascinating theories to explain the world around them. While visiting Disney World in Orlando, Susan watched divers feed the sea life in a huge aquarium. A three-year-old nearby observed, "Look—there's a fireman feeding the fish!" Clearly, the child was trying to understand what she was seeing; she knew that firefighters sometimes wear masks and black suits, and she was applying what was true in one context to another. Her wise dad, instead of correcting her, asked her to explain why she thought the man was a firefighter. The father validated his daughter's thinking ability; she in turn wanted to know more. The stage was set for learning.

We thwart children's capacity to learn when we treat them as passive vessels waiting to be filled with knowledge. We invite low performance when we communicate low expectations for what they can achieve. One reason why kids in remedial education so rarely outgrow their need for remediation is because the curriculum is too easy. Remember the words of Kenneth Dunn: "If students cannot learn the way we teach them, then we must teach them the way they learn."

> If students cannot learn the way we teach them, then we must teach them the way they learn.

The way to help struggling learners meet required standards is to teach that content in the students' preferred learning modalities. When we allow struggling students to work on tasks they think are easy or babyish, we communicate our belief that they simply can't do the regular work. This confirms their worst fears—that they were born stupid and that even their teachers think they are incapable of learning. The longer they have to wait for successful learning to happen, the deeper and more destructive their fears become.

This chapter describes a variety of teaching strategies and techniques for you to try. All have been proven effective in real classrooms, where they have helped struggling students overcome their fears and free themselves to learn. When we demonstrate that a simple change of method can lead to learning success, students begin to regain the confidence lost over several years of failure.

# The Impact of Poverty on Learning*

Huge numbers of children who live in poverty have severe achievement deficiencies. As we mentioned in this book's introduction, several researchers have documented the hazards of struggling students having ineffective teachers. The hopeful note in this research is the fact that having high-quality teachers throughout elementary school can substantially offset or even eliminate the anticipated achievement disadvantages for children from low socioeconomic backgrounds. The strategies described in this book will be extremely helpful to you as you work to be as effective as possible.

Martin Haberman has done an intensive study of this situation and has reported on it in his book *Star Teachers of Children in Poverty.* He claims that for children in poverty, having "star" teachers, defined as outstanding educators in all of the ways valued by parents, students, and school personnel, is a matter of life or death.

Several recent studies have documented the positive effect that really good teachers have on students. What is even more surprising is evidence that if a child has an ineffective teacher for one year, it will take the child two years to catch up. If the child has an ineffective teacher for two consecutive years, the child might never catch up.**

The reason it is important to know this is that many schools have assigned the most difficult students to the newest and most inexperienced teachers. Of course, many new teachers are highly effective, and some veteran teachers are less effective. But schools must make an effort to match severely underachieving students with the most effective teachers. Ongoing evidence on the effectiveness of this practice is extremely positive.

Further, Haberman estimates that 3,000 students in poverty drop out of high school every day in this country. Just do the math, and you can imagine what a devastating effect this has on our society and economy. The dropout syndrome begins in elementary school. Students who are not fluent readers by the end of third grade are at great risk of not completing high school. Share this information with your principal, to help her or him make the most effective teacher-student assignments possible.

So what is it that makes a teacher effective, especially with children who live with many disadvantages? Haberman observes that star teachers truly feel that school success for *every* child is enormously important. They expect that their students will have issues, and they approach those situations proactively. They don't base their ideas of success on whether a student can work in a dysfunctional system. They simply take the responsibility to guarantee learning success for all their students.

## What Star Teachers Do***

1. They make school a positive place and make learning as enjoyable and successful as possible.

2. They do whatever is possible in school, regardless of the realities of students' homes, families, and neighborhoods. They never blame the victim.

3. They connect learning to students' interests and relevant issues.

4. They model and teach appreciation of learning for its own sake.

5. They convince students that the students are welcome in the school and in the classroom.

6. They speak daily of things in the real world that would interest the students.

7. They remain gentle while consistently firm; they manage well with much flexibility.

8. They seek to understand without judging.

9. They own up to their mistakes and try to fix them.

10. They carefully choose homework and assign it sparingly by elapsed time instead of amount of work. For more information about homework, see Chapter 8.

11. They base student evaluation at least partly on student effort and progress.

12. They acknowledge their students' interest in a problem-solving, real-life application approach to learning the curriculum; they use whatever methods are effective in building learning success.

13. They maintain positive ongoing contact with all parents and caregivers.

14. They use behavior management techniques that teach children to take responsibility for their own behavior; they avoid arbitrary discipline or punishment measures.

---

*Information in this and the following section is adapted from Martin Haberman, *Star Teachers of Children in Poverty.* Indianapolis, IN: Kappa Delta Pi, 1995. Used with permission of the Haberman Educational Foundation (www.habermanfoundation.org).

**Sanders, William L., and June C. Rivers. "Cumulative and Residual Effects of Teachers on Future Student Academic Achievement." Knoxville, TN: University of Tennessee Value-Added Research and Assessment Center, November 1996. Revisited online in 2002. This is a landmark study.

***Susan has summarized this list from her own reading of Haberman's book *Star Teachers of Children in Poverty,* which contains information on this topic in much more detail.

## Successful Schools

In 2004, the Prichard Committee for Academic Excellence in Kentucky released a study of that state's top-scoring elementary schools whose students included large numbers of children in poverty. These successful schools reported fewer than 15 points difference in achievement levels between majority and minority populations and between low-income and middle-income students. The schools shared the following characteristics:

- The faculty does not make an issue of students who live in poverty. Disadvantaged and advantaged students are treated in fundamentally similar ways.

- The relationships among adults in the school are caring and respectful. Decisions are collaborative.

- All staff work hard to meet their students' needs in nutrition, transportation, and other areas with enthusiasm and without complaint.

- Administrators carefully recruit, hire, and place teachers and staff. Staff assignments are based solely on students' needs.

- Staff show evidence of personal willingness to work with and believe in all students.

Haberman's work, the Prichard study, and other research prove that a school program can make a positive difference in achievement, even in the presence of other factors that might work against the attainment of proficiency for some students. Combining high expectations for all students with appropriate intervention strategies for students who need them can dramatically affect students' perception of their own learning abilities and can positively impact their achievement.

## The Revised IDEA

The IDEA (Individuals with Disabilities Education Act), revised in 2004, contains specific language for ensuring that students with learning difficulties get the help they need to succeed in school. A student with a specific learning difficulty has a disorder in one or more of the basic psychological processes involved in understanding or in using spoken or written language. The disorder may manifest itself in the student being unable to successfully listen, think, speak, read, write, spell, or do mathematical calculations. The legislation expects that there will be an ongoing relationship between the regular classroom teacher and the special education personnel. For the most recent policy expectations for your state, please refer to idea.ed.gov.

We believe that regular education teachers can actually *prevent* certain students from needing to be referred for special education testing if the teachers know how to provide helpful in-class interventions such as those described in this book. For students with IEPs, these strategies can be used in both the special education *and* regular education classrooms.

## Before Referring a Student for Special Education Testing

The regular classroom teacher might find that some referrals are unnecessary once appropriate curricular and behavioral interventions have been successfully applied in the classroom. For example, highly kinesthetic students who have a lot of trouble sitting still and are up and moving much of the day might respond favorably to being allowed to move back and forth between two designated desks in the classroom, so movement is part of their routine. They might calm down and be able to stay on task longer while chewing gum, squeezing a Koosh ball, or listening to soothing music. They might be more successful at showing what they know through active learning options, rather than always having to write their thoughts. Students could use any available digital devices for this purpose as well.

Students who are reading significantly below grade level might respond positively to Power Reading Online (see pages 98–99) or the language experience method (see pages 95–97). Students with spelling or vocabulary problems may greatly improve their work in these areas by using the Learning Words by Style method (see page 116).

When classroom teachers find and use methods that improve students' academic success in the regular classroom, the need for referral for special education testing can be significantly reduced. In fact, many school districts provide teacher assistance teams to work with classroom teachers to try many strategies before resorting to formal referrals.

## After Referring a Student for Special Education Testing

Once a student has been referred and evaluated and has received an IEP, the classroom teacher's ongoing efforts should be not only to follow the recommendations in the IEP but also to continue trying other strategies that may lead to better learning success. This can make the IEP implementation more effective. Of course, any strategies used successfully in the classroom with students who have IEPs should be brought to the attention of the special education teacher and made part of the IEP written plan when it is revised. These strategies may also be made available to other students for whom they would increase successful learning outcomes.

# Creating a Mindset for Success in Learning and in Life

Carol Dweck's research (see pages 2–3) has demonstrated that all learners have one of two mindsets. She found that learners who believe that their capacity for learning is preset before they are born have a *fixed mindset.* Therefore, they reason, there is no sense in trying harder. If, however, learners believe that their effort and attitudes *do* play a significant part in their learning success, then they have a *growth mindset.* These kids are much more willing to work hard to complete more challenging learning tasks, because they are convinced that effort does make a difference.

The most effective way for adults to help students develop a growth mindset is by monitoring how we praise or make other comments to children. For instance, saying "You are really smart" or "You really have a lot of trouble learning" supports students' beliefs that their effort cannot make much of a difference. By contrast, when we say "I'm very impressed with how hard you are working on this" or "Describe to me how your effort positively affected your learning outcomes," we help our kids develop and maintain a growth mindset, which they are highly likely to carry into all types of future learning situations. In classrooms where students know their teachers truly believe all students can learn successfully, students are more likely to be successful.

# Goal Setting

The most significant difference between students who are successful in school and those who are not is the ability to set and accomplish realistic short-term goals. Students who are unsuccessful either don't set goals or they aim for lofty goals that are beyond their reach. It's extremely important to teach *all* students that success is not measured by grades or by semester or school-year outcomes. Rather, success hinges on setting and reaching realistic short-term learning goals. When that happens regularly, success comes naturally.

**1.** Give each struggling student a copy of the "Goal Planning Chart" handout (page 86) with the "Subject Area/Task" column filled in.

**2.** Gather a group of students who share the challenge of rarely finishing their work. At the beginning of each work period, ask the students to set a personal goal for how much work they expect to accomplish within the allotted time. (Limit their time period to five minutes less than what the rest of the class will have, since you will need to talk to these kids before the other students require your attention.)

**3.** *For this method to work, students must set their own goals.* Have the students write their goals as ratios—predicted work to amount of time—on their charts. (*Example:* 3 sentences in 10 minutes = 3/10)

**4.** At the end of the designated time period, return to the group, and without commenting on the quality of the work, ask each student the following questions, while the other students are paying attention to each brief conversation.

If the student's goal *has* been met, ask the following questions:

- "What was your goal?"
- "Did you accomplish your goal?"
- "Who is responsible for your success in accomplishing your goal?" It may take patience and prodding, but the student must respond, "I am responsible for my success in accomplishing my goal."
- "How does it feel to be successful?" Again, you may have to prompt the student to say, "It feels good to be successful."
- "How can you congratulate yourself or give yourself some recognition for a job well done?" Offer suggestions if necessary. Remember that students who are accustomed to low achievement tend to credit their success to luck or to the people who helped them.

If the goal has *not been met*, ask the following questions:

- "What was your goal?"
- "Did you accomplish your goal?"
- "Who is responsible for the fact that you did not reach your goal?" The student will probably blame some external source, such as another talking student, or the fact that the teacher was unavailable for help. Don't ask how it feels not to accomplish the goal. Instead, prompt until the student can say, "I am responsible for not reaching my goal."
- "What plan can you make for tomorrow to prevent the same problem from happening again?" Have the student write this plan on the "Goal Planning Chart."

**Tips:** Never punish students who don't reach their goals. The best way to get kids on track is to help them learn to set realistic goals and feel satisfaction from reaching them. The inability to earn positive feedback (from themselves and from you) is all the "punishment" they need.

If you must grade students' work under this arrangement, we recommend the following:

- a C for reaching a goal that is well below the work you expect from the rest of the class

- a B for when the goal gets into the grade-level range

- an A only for exceptional work (When we give students high grades for work they know is below expected outcomes for their age peers, they conclude that we think they are not capable of improving.)

Finally, have students work on *one* area or subject at a time until progress is apparent and success feels comfortable to them. If you add other areas or subjects too quickly, students may develop a fear of success. ("Adults always expect more of you if you show them what you can do. I guess I should stop working so hard.")

## Scenario: Kirsten

Kirsten was a sweet eight-year-old who was prone to crying huge tears only seconds after a task was assigned. Looking up at her teacher, she would moan softly, "I don't know what to do. I didn't hear the directions. Where should I start? Help me!" She easily became discouraged and overwhelmed.

Her teacher, Mr. Vanya, began sitting with her for a minute at the beginning of each task, planning her goal in terms of how much she could complete in the allotted time period. Once, when the task was to write a short descriptive paragraph, Kirsten seemed paralyzed and unable to begin.

"We are going to work on this for 20 minutes today," Mr. Vanya said. "I'd like you to tell me how many good sentences you think you can write in 15 minutes."

She looked at him with soulful eyes and ventured, "Two?"

"So you predict you will be able to write two good sentences in the next 15 minutes?"

"I think so."

He showed her how to write her goal as a ratio at the top of her paper, with the completed work prediction as the top number and the amount of time as the bottom number—in this case, 2/15. Then he told her, "You may begin now, and I'll be back in 15 minutes to see how you're doing. Remember, Kirsten, that you will be successful if you can accomplish your goal for this time period."

At the end of 15 minutes, he returned to her and said, "Okay, time's up. Let's take a look at the progress you've made in accomplishing your goal. What was your goal?"

She looked at the ratio she had written at the top of her paper and replied, "Two sentences in 15 minutes."

"Did you complete your goal?"

She looked at what she had done and said, "Yes, I wrote two sentences."

Mr. Vanya's third question was, "Well, now, who is responsible for your success?" She looked at him quizzically, since this definition of success—the ability to set and accomplish realistic goals—was a new concept for her.

Finally, she said, "I think you are responsible."

"Why do you think that?"

"Because you let me choose a smaller number of sentences."

"That's true . . . but who actually completed the goal?"

"I guess I did."

"I agree! Now I'd like you to say that to me in a complete sentence. Tell me—who is responsible for your success in reaching the goal you set?"

And after much encouragement, Kirsten was able to say, "I am responsible for my success because I reached the goal I set."

Then he asked her, "How does it feel to be successful?" (The purpose of this question is to help students who are caught in a failure cycle to realize that success

| Goal Planning Chart | | | | | |
|---|---|---|---|---|---|
| Subject Area/ Task | Monday | Tuesday | Wednesday | Thursday | Friday |
| Journal writing | 3/10 | 3/10 | 3/10 | 4/10 | 4/10 |
| Math | 2/15 | 2/15 | 3/15 | 3/15 | 4/15 |
| Science | 1/10 | 1/10 | 2/10 | 2/10 | 2/10 |

can feel good. This may seem strange to people who are success-oriented, but we have to understand that kids who perceive themselves as failures actually come to *prefer* failure because it is comfortable and predictable. Success represents change, and we all know how scary change can be.) Mr. Vanya talked with Kirsten about how reaching a goal is worth celebrating, and he explained that there were several ways she might congratulate herself for achieving success—like getting a big handshake, patting herself on the back, or giving herself a thumbs-up. By the end of the discussion, Kirsten was smiling.

Each day for several weeks, Kirsten and Mr. Vanya repeated this procedure in all subjects. Kirsten's goals remained quite small for several class periods until she began to feel more confident, at which point she set her goals slightly higher. Within two months, her goals in most subject areas were near grade-level expectations.

# Common Core as It Impacts Students with Learning Difficulties

In 2010, the National Governors Association and the Council of Chief State School Officers released a set of Common Core State Standards (CCSS) that provide consistent expectations for all students in reading, language arts, and math at all grade levels. This means that all students, including students with special needs, will be held to mastery of these standards.

Many states have adopted CCSS, and some have not. The CCSS expect that even students with learning difficulties will be expected to make adequate progress working through grade-level standards and that students with disabilities eligible under IDEA must be challenged to excel within the general curriculum. However, the strategies in this book will be helpful for all students with learning difficulties, regardless of the exact curriculum you are using, by providing specific adaptations, accommodations, and assistive technology to help your students with special needs achieve the expected levels of mastery.

Your immediate concern might be: "How are we supposed to make more rigorous standards accessible to students who have usually worked significantly below grade-level curriculum?" One of the most effective strategies is to use scaffolding.

Scaffolding is a process by which teachers can determine students' entry level into more challenging new learning content and then move students forward in a way that always stretches their minds, while they know that help is available when needed. The teacher provides just enough support (scaffolding) to give students courage to take learning risks, but not so much support that students don't use their own abilities. When students are able to take more consistent responsibility for mastering a designated task, you may begin the process of fading, or gradually removing the support, which ultimately allows students to work independently.

The CCSS for reading, writing, speaking, listening, and language are expected to be woven into the standards in other subject areas, including history, science, technology, health, and mathematics. The CCSS for math focuses on problem solving, reasoning, and modeling of higher-level math concepts. We all need to understand how to prepare all students for the new test format that will document students' mastery of CCSS.

## Zone of Proximal Development (ZPD)

Inherent in scaffolded instruction is Lev Vygotsky's concept of the zone of proximal development (ZPD). Vygotsky believed that "good learning" is most likely to occur within a student's ZPD. ZPD is a name for the gap between what a student already knows or can do and what the student wants or needs to know or do. The student can attain the latter only with the help of a more knowledgeable person, who serves as the scaffolding in the learning process. A student's ZPD is always changing as the student gains knowledge, so scaffolded instruction must constantly be individualized to address that issue.

Paying attention to each student's ZPD is a natural part of the differentiation process. Each time you identify a student's entry level into newer learning, you are paying attention to the student's ZPD.

## Response to Intervention (RTI)

A complementary education model called response to intervention (RTI or RtI) helps create successful CCSS assessment results. The RTI process sometimes combines both academic and behavior programs, including Title I and special education programs, LEP, ELL, and gifted programs, to create a common goal of increasing rigor for all students. RTI's plan is to accomplish this through differentiation of instruction using three tiers of instruction. The model is illustrated on page 64.

- **Tier I** provides a research-based (core) curriculum with short-term differentiation that has the highest probability of success with most students (80 percent).

- **Tier II** provides targeted skill-based intervention in addition to Tier I, for students who do not respond to quality initial instruction.

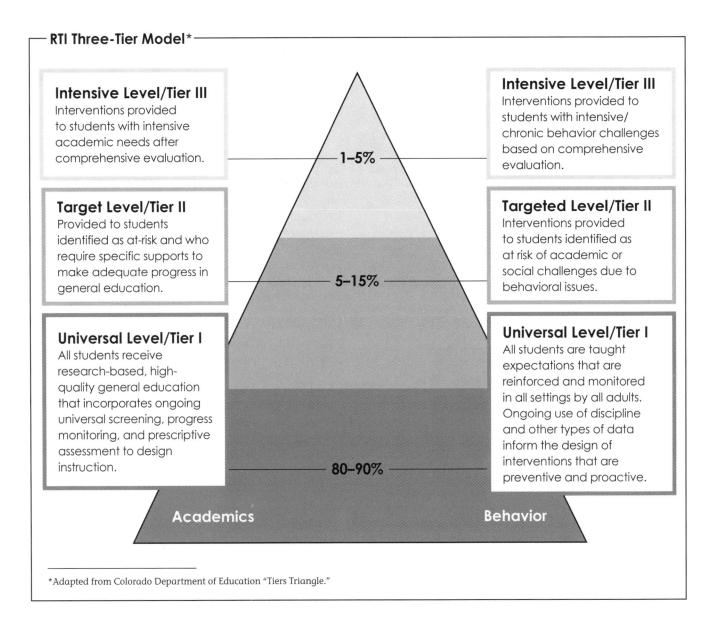

┌─ **RTI Three-Tier Model*** ──────────────────────────────────

**Intensive Level/Tier III**
Interventions provided
to students with intensive
academic needs after
comprehensive evaluation.

**Target Level/Tier II**
Provided to students
identified as at-risk and who
require specific supports to
make adequate progress in
general education.

**Universal Level/Tier I**
All students receive
research-based, high-
quality general education
that incorporates ongoing
universal screening, progress
monitoring, and prescriptive
assessment to design
instruction.

1–5%

5–15%

80–90%

**Intensive Level/Tier III**
Interventions provided to
students with intensive/
chronic behavior challenges
based on comprehensive
evaluation.

**Targeted Level/Tier II**
Interventions provided
to students identified as
at risk of academic or
social challenges due to
behavioral issues.

**Universal Level/Tier I**
All students are taught
expectations that are
reinforced and monitored
in all settings by all adults.
Ongoing use of discipline
and other types of data
inform the design of
interventions that are
preventive and proactive.

**Academics**                          **Behavior**

*Adapted from Colorado Department of Education "Tiers Triangle."

- **Tier III** provides intensive comprehensive intervention administered for a longer time period for students who do not respond to Tier II intervention.

Note: For students who can demonstrate mastery without as much teacher-directed instruction, Tier III time may also be used to flexibly regroup these advanced learners and allow them to work on learning experiences that are likely to challenge them more than remaining at the grade-level guidelines.

## Example of How to Use RTI

In Lisa's district, students receive 60 minutes of whole-group instruction on reading standards and 60 minutes of whole-group instruction on math standards. Following these whole-group times, students receive 30 minutes of small-group intervention time in each subject as well. If students are showing proficiency or are advanced with the standard, they are placed in a Tier I or enrichment group. If students are showing that they need additional practice or reteaching on the standard, they participate in a Tier II group during these 30-minute blocks. If the data collected by staff do not show that Tier II is providing the progress required, then students are moved to Tier III during these intervention blocks and receive instruction in the needed skills in an alternate approach not tried to date. As students make academic gains, they move from Tier III to Tier II and finally back to Tier I. Whether students are on Tier I, Tier II, or Tier III, all staff differentiate instruction and address the same standard for all students, at different levels of difficulty, during the 30-minute intervention time blocks.

Progress is evaluated frequently to determine if students are making adequate progress. If students are not showing growth on Tier II, they will need to move to Tier III interventions. This is the highest level of support, which may include significant amounts of time in intensive instruction in their areas of need. As students show success in learning, they may move through the tiers until no interventions are needed. If a student does not show growth on Tier III, a referral for a special education evaluation should occur.

In addition to classroom teachers, a variety of specialists, such as a reading specialist, math coach, or enrichment coach, become involved in teaching students. This requires more extensive documentation and more frequent formative and summative assessments.

## Scenario: What Size Are Your Shoes?

You may be wondering how students with LD will feel as they observe other kids doing work that is different from theirs. We knew one teacher who did a demonstration in front of the whole class in which she had the following dialogue with a student named Ivan, who had asked, "Why are some kids getting to do different work with words, but I am not getting to do what they are doing?" The teacher replied, "By the end of the demonstration, everyone will understand the answer to Ivan's question."

The teacher told the class that Ivan wanted to know why all kids in the class were not doing the same thing at the same time. She had luckily worn shoes with higher heels for the demonstration, even though it was unexpected. Ivan complied with her request to take off his shoes. She took off hers, too. She asked him to put on her shoes and take a few steps in them. He tried, but of course couldn't walk more than a step or two. "I can't walk in your shoes," he declared. The teacher said, "No worries—but now I'm going to walk a few steps in your shoes."

Ivan protested immediately. "There's no way that's going to work!"

"Why not?" the teacher asked.

"Because they are way too small for you and won't fit!"

The teacher thanked Ivan and then turned to the class and said, "Ivan and I have just demonstrated why you don't all do the same work at the same time. Because you are all quite different from each other in things like hair color, need for glasses, and favorite activities, I have to be sure I give each of you the exact work you need to move forward in your learning every day. If the reading shoes I give you are not the right size, that forward progress may not happen. If the work is too easy or too difficult, you should tell me that in private, and I will adjust your work to try a different level of difficulty. However, you may have nothing to say about the work—or the 'shoes'—I give to other kids. The correct fit of their learning shoes is a private matter between them and me."

After a brief discussion, the demonstration ended. A few weeks later, the teacher observed two students working beside each other at a table. Jordan looked at Emily's work, and then his own, and then said, "I just noticed that your work is different from mine. Why aren't we doing the same work?"

Emily looked at Jordan's paper and then her own and said, "Oh, this paper I am working on is not your size!"

"Oh yeah," Jordan murmured, and went back to work on his own task. We are betting that your own students will also like this explanation of why kids are not doing the same work at the same time.

Caveat: We should always be sure that all students are having equal opportunities for highly interesting learning tasks. When all students are actively engaged in work that is meaningful and interesting, there will be less envy or discomfort about one's level of work.

# Metacognition: Becoming Aware of One's Own Thinking*

Metacognition is paying attention to what you are thinking. This awareness enables you to monitor and analyze your thinking so you can increase your understanding of what you are trying to learn. Learners who can transfer their learning from one context to another are also applying metacognition.

The successful use of learning strategies is linked to motivation. When students fail, they tend to assign the cause to their own low innate ability—rather than to something they have the ability to change through effort and the application of specific learning strategies.** When they think out loud (use metacognition) as they work, they can feel they are doing something specific to help themselves use more effective learning strategies.

Use the "Thinking About What I Do" handout on page 87 to make metacognition more accessible to students. Students should use this handout every 15 minutes or so during a specific activity to help them monitor their thinking.

---

*"Metacognition: Study Strategies, Monitoring, and Motivation" by William Peirce © 2003.
**Dweck, 2006.

Long-term memory of learned material is enhanced by the brain's ability to seek and notice patterns, change from unsuccessful to more successful strategies, and realize that one is actually in control of one's own learning outcomes. The process of scaffolding helps us provide necessary supports to students from entry-level through challenging learning scenarios.

Teachers have to conduct an ongoing dialogue with students to determine what and how they are thinking, to clear up misconceptions, and to individualize instruction. An understanding of a student's prior knowledge and abilities helps the teacher connect the new knowledge to something the student already knows, which makes it much easier for the student to understand the content clearly and move forward with confidence.

# Providing a Meaningful and Challenging Curriculum

## Scenario: Brandon

When Brandon walked into Susan's fifth-grade class for the voluntary summer school program, he took a seat as far away from the front of the room as possible. He seemed quiet, shy, and reluctant to be there. Susan was teaching a specific approach to problem solving for gifted students, and she began the class with a series of brainstorming activities. Almost in spite of himself, Brandon became animated, and by the end of the half-day session he had contributed several unique and interesting ideas.

On the second day of class, he had a little smile on his face, and he chose a seat near where Susan had stood the day before to chart the brainstorming results. His sense of humor began to show itself, and he displayed a knack for piggybacking wild and crazy ideas onto some of his classmates' contributions. When the class broke into smaller groups, he volunteered to lead his group. His shyness had disappeared, and he was an eager and active participant in the day's activities.

On the morning of the third day, he walked into class with his mother beside him. His original shy demeanor had returned. "I had to bring Brandon to school today," his mother explained. "He skipped the first two days of the summer program."

"No, he didn't," Susan protested. "He was here both days and he has been doing great!"

"Well, now, I'm confused," she responded. "The remedial teacher called me yesterday to report that Brandon hadn't come to school."

After a brief investigation, the mystery was solved. The state was providing summer programs for two groups: gifted kids and those with remedial reading problems. Brandon had been signed up for the remedial class and had accidentally wandered into the class for gifted kids. Until Susan discovered he was remedial, he had behaved as though he was gifted and had fit right in with the other problem solvers.

We wish we could report that Brandon was allowed to stay with Susan's class, but at that time students could be either remedial or gifted—not both. Brandon's mom took him to the class where the state funding formula required him to stay. However, he usually stopped by for a visit on his way to or from class, and his remedial reading teacher was willing to try some of the techniques Susan was using with her students.

This experience has kept Susan humble ever since on the subject of appreciating each student's strengths even while addressing his or her learning weaknesses. It has also helped her respond to students when they complain something isn't "fair" in the teacher's practices. Rick Lavoie says it best: "Fair is not giving all students the same work to do. Fair is giving all students the work they actually need!"

---

"Fair is not giving all students the same work to do. Fair is giving all students the work they actually need!"

---

## Rigor

The CCSS expect students to move from the previous decade's emphasis on mastering specific skills to using those skills to develop deep conceptual understanding of essential content in both present and future situations. These expectations are to be held for all students. For students with learning difficulties, the challenge is to use specific strategies, such as those in this book, to access the more rigorous content they will experience. Rigor is the experience we have when we stretch our minds to understand ideas with which we are not immediately familiar or comfortable.

The Revised Bloom's Taxonomy (RBT) of thinking* is an update of the model educators have used forever to create challenging activities for all students. The chart below describes the definitions, activity design verbs, and possible products for all levels.

RBT uses verbs to describe what the learner *can do* and defines six levels of thinking. These levels include

---

*Anderson, L.W. (ed.), Krathwohl, D.R. (ed.), et al (2001), *A Taxonomy for Learning, Teaching, and Assessing: A Revision of Bloom's Taxonomy of Educational Objectives.* New York: Longman.

*recall, understand, apply, analyze, evaluate,* and *create.* Leaders in the field of developing rigorous curricula that complement the CCSS for all students have taken Bloom's work one step further to make certain that all students are always working at their challenge levels in all their schoolwork. The chart on page 68 summarizes the levels of the RBT that are then used in conjunction with Webb's Depth of Knowledge (DOK) work, and the two models are combined for your use in this chapter, using the work of Karin Hess and her Cognitive Rigor Matrix. Hess, a generous expert from the National Center for the Improvement of Educational Assessment (NCIEA) worked with us to develop the "Little Red Riding Hood DOK/Bloom Matrix" (page 68) that we recommend you use in your curriculum differentiation work. You should consider visiting www.nciea.org if you want guidance in making sure your curriculum is always providing rigorous learning experiences for all students. You can also access some helpful videos made by Karin Hess and her colleagues on YouTube.

The Common Core State Standards' suggested way to differentiate curricula for various students is to combine Webb's Depth of Knowledge (DOK) with the Revised Bloom's Taxonomy. The combination allows teachers to construct methods through which students can interact with any content at levels that provide more rigor than simply relying on the use of designated verbs. For example, at Bloom's "recall" level, the task is to simply recall information. However, at the DOK level 1, learners demonstrate that they can recall or restate information of expanded levels of difficulty, including recalling a fact, term, principle, or concept or performing a routine procedure. At level 2, learners are expected to explain why or how something actually works. Level 3 expects learners to demonstrate that they understand how to apply what they are learning to real-life situations. Finally, level 4 expects learners to integrate various types of information from multiple sources and disciplines to form new ideas or unique solutions to problems.

## Revised Bloom's Taxonomy

| Category | Definition | Activity Verbs | Product Possibilities |
|---|---|---|---|
| Recall | Remember something previously learned. | Tell, recite, list, memorize, remember, define, locate | Quiz or test, skill work, vocabulary, isolated facts |
| Understand | Demonstrate basic understanding of concepts and curriculum. Translate into other words. | Restate in own words, give examples, summarize, translate, show, edit | Drawing, diagram, graphic organizer, response to question, revision, translation |
| Apply | Transfer knowledge learned in one situation to another. | Demonstrate; use guides, maps, charts; build; cook | Recipe, model, demonstration, artwork, craft, playing a game by the rules |
| Analyze | Understand how parts relate to a whole. Understand structure and motive. Note fallacies. | Investigate, classify, categorize, compare, contrast, solve | Survey, questionnaire, prospectus, plan, solution to a problem, report, cyberhunt, webquest |
| Evaluate | Judge value of something against criteria. Support judgment. | Judge, evaluate, give opinion, give viewpoint, prioritize, recommend, critique | Decision, editorial, debate, critique, defense, verdict, judgment, roll-the-die, rubric |
| Create | Reform individual parts to make a new whole. | Compose, design, invent, create, hypothesize, construct, forecast, rearrange parts, imagine | Song, poem, story, advertisement, invention, movie, webquest, cyberhunt, other creative products |

## Little Red Riding Hood DOK/Bloom Matrix*

| DOK Level | Bloom Verbs | Lesson Objective | Questions for Students | CCSS Standard(s) | Assessment Purpose and Type |
|---|---|---|---|---|---|
| 1. Recalling and summarizing information and procedures | Tell, recite, list, remember, define, locate, translate, recognize, and use symbols. | Describe and locate literary elements in given text. | Describe the main characters, setting, and other story elements. | RI-1: Locate key details in text. | Formative: Check for understanding in class discussions. See formative assessments in this book on page 173. |
| 2. Basic skills and concepts and showing relationships (lower levels of depth) | Restate in own words, give examples, summarize, show, demonstrate the meaning of symbols, edit, demonstrate, classify, categorize, compare, contrast, hypothesize, forecast. | Explain how the literary elements in the story interact. | Summarize the story in the correct sequence. | R-2: Write summary. | Formative: Make a timeline of key events. Summative: Write text messages between Red and her mother explaining the wolf incident. |
| 3. Strategic thinking and reasoning | Conduct investigation and use data, solve, judge, evaluate, prioritize, recommend with justification, critique, compose an essay, design or understand patterns. | Analyze the character traits and explain how the author uses the characters' actions to reveal traits about each of them. | Justify your opinion about the degree of cleverness of the wolf. | RL-3: Describe characters in-depth. W-1: Opinion writing. W-8: Take notes, organize ideas. | Formative: Use the TBEAR graphic organizer to plan your writing with a peer. Summative: Write an essay. |
| 4. Extended thinking | Initiate or compose a research project or object of art, design a model, invent to solve a problem, imagine, create, synthesize. | Compare information across texts. Explore how authors might use source material to develop a text (example: using characteristics of a real wolf to develop a wolf character). | Support your viewpoint as to whether all wolves in literature are like the wolf portrayed in this story and support your response with evidence from this and other texts. | RL-6: Compare points of view. W-2: Explanatory writing. W-1: Opinion/literary critique. W-9: Draw evidence from texts. | Summative: Small groups prepare and deliver presentations to the class. |

* Used with permission of Karin Hess.

## Providing Meaningful Choices

The most potent motivator in any classroom is consistently giving students meaningful choices. Although educators have long included choice in programs for the gifted, we have overlooked the power choice has for all kids.

The easiest choices to give are those that relate to:

- what students will learn (*example: "You can learn about our moon or the moons that belong to other planets."*)

- how they will learn (*example: "You can read about your topic or watch a DVD about it."*)

- how they will express what they have learned (*example: "You can either write a paragraph or draw a picture and add a caption."*)

When kids make choices that reflect their learning modality strengths, and when teachers accept products other than written papers, we can almost always expect positive results. Most students will do whatever is necessary to learn something they really want to know.

The Common Core State Standards expect all students to be engaged in rigorous learning activities. The DOK model, previously explained, is one model that helps you ensure all students are experiencing rigor in their learning. Frank Lyman's ThinkTrix model, explained next, is another.

## ThinkTrix: A Critical Thinking Model*

ThinkTrix is an icon-driven model for helping students access rigor through specific critical thinking icons. It helps students who prefer to learn visually gain access to higher-level thinking activities. Each category of thinking has its own icon, so students can eventually use the visuals as a shortcut to the various categories of thinking. You can create questions that challenge students' thinking and use the model to demonstrate to your students the differences between various types of thinking and learning experiences. A sample ThinkTrix activity is on page 70, and a blank reproducible form is on page 88.

When you use ThinkTrix with the Name Card Method described on pages 12–14, you communicate your high expectations to all your students and give them easy access to more complex ways of thinking and learning. We see the model as a path to help struggling

students become more comfortable with higher-level thinking experiences, rather than spending most of their school time with simpler recall and comprehension experiences.

 **Recall.** Students simply remember what they have learned and talk about it. *Example:* "Tell the sequence of events in this story."

 **Similarity.** Students compare objects or phenomena to see what attributes they have in common. *Example:* "How are the causes of colds and the flu similar?"

 **Difference.** Students compare things to notice how they are different. *Example:* "How is a triangle different from a parallelogram?"

 **Cause-Effect.** Students look at how one action leads to or comes from another. *Examples:* "What causes a rainbow to be formed?" "What effects do rainbow sightings have on people?"

 **Idea to Example.** Students try to find facts, events, or objects to prove that an idea they have is supportable by evidence, or to deepen a concept. *Example:* "What are some examples of bravery in the stories in this unit?"

 **Example to Idea.** Students find patterns shared by events, sets of facts, or objects. *Example:* "What conclusions can be drawn from the evidence at the crime scene?"

 **Evaluation.** Students decide whether events, situations, facts, etc. are right or wrong, truthful or not, significant or not. *Example:* "Study recent Supreme Court decisions and give reasons why you agree or disagree with them."

## Presenting Exciting and Relevant Content

When students are presented with exciting and relevant content, much of their resistance to learning disappears. If you can answer "yes" to all or most of the following questions about your teaching, then you can probably assume that your students are motivated to learn:

- Am I able to modify the academic program without compromising appropriately high expectations? Am I teaching challenging content through my students' learning modality strengths?

- Is the content likely to intrigue my students? Is it about issues that really matter to them? Have I

*Adapted from "Think-Pair-Share, ThinkTrix, Thinklinks, and Weird Facts" by Frank T. Lyman Jr., in *Enhancing Thinking Through Cooperative Learning*, edited by Neil Davidson and Toni Worsham. NY: Teachers College Press, 1992. Used with permission of Frank T. Lyman Jr. A four-page laminated brochure on ThinkTrix may be found at www.kaganonline.com, including up-to-date commentaries and reviews.

## ThinkTrix on Global Warming

Objective: Help students understand global warming and its effects on human beings.

Required Standards:

a. Climate patterns are changing in our area and around the world.

b. Some scientists think a greenhouse effect is responsible for the changes.

c. Other scientists think the changes are simply a repeat of previous global patterns.

d. Some Internet sites can be helpful and reliable sources of information.

| Cause and Effect | | What are some conditions that are suspected to cause global warming? What would be the effect, in your life-time, of global warming on the environment, on growing things, on animals, and on humans? |
|---|---|---|
| Recall | **R** | What do you remember about global warming from our class discussion yesterday? |
| Similarity | | In what similar ways do all power sources impact the earth? |
| Difference | | How are the effects on the earth of coal and nuclear power different from each other? |
| Idea to Example | →EX | Give several examples of how you and your family would be impacted by global warming. |
| Example to Idea | EX→ | Given those examples, what is your hypothesis about people's responsibility to seriously address the issue now? |
| Evaluation | | In what ways might it be dangerous to continue the debate without carrying out effective interventions? |

considered their interests? (See "Interest Survey" on pages 20–21.)

- Is the emphasis on interpretive thinking and in-depth knowledge—on learning fewer things well?

- Am I presenting how-to-learn strategies within the context of meaningful content?

- Can my students see how to apply what they learn to other settings?

## Using Project-Based Learning

Many teachers are engaging students in learning the curriculum within the context of what has sometimes been called "problem-based learning." Essentially, a project where a problem is identified is assigned, and students work to solve it at the same time as they are learning skills and competencies. Here are a few examples:

**1.** Eighth graders worked to decide whether their town's main shopping area, which had been closed to vehicular traffic for many years, should be reopened to automobiles, since sales in the stores had been lagging. Students created a survey instrument, worked in teams to interview town residents, explored what other towns with similar problems had done, created a recommendation for the town council to consider, and presented it to the council at a regular meeting.

**2.** Fifth graders spent three consecutive days at an outdoor education program in a natural setting. They observed plants and animals in nature, discussed how pollution affects the natural environment, and learned how to survive in the forest.

**3.** High school students adopted a section of a local highway. They researched the costs of cleaning up litter from roads, developed an ad campaign for broadcast on local cable TV, and conducted a monthly cleanup mission on their stretch of road.

**4.** Third graders adopted grandparents from a local senior citizens' facility where people had been complaining of loneliness. They interviewed their grandparents and developed a historical narrative of life in their community over several generations. Then they developed biographies their grandparents helped them prepare and rehearse for presentation to a combined meeting of their class and the senior citizens.

**5.** Seventh graders took rubbing impressions from a local cemetery with graves dating back to the 1600s. They constructed a group story about life in those times, including information about diseases that affected people in the past but are no longer a threat today. Then they acted out their story in a presentation at the local historical society. They also made plans to help preserve the cemetery.

Project-based learning is returning to educational pedagogy, especially in the Common Core curriculum. It has the potential to turn on turned-off students. Teachers have discovered that they can teach the same objectives or outcomes to kids who are working on projects that they would have taught through the regular curriculum practices. For more on project-based learning, see Chapter 6 (page 142).

Some teachers worry that struggling students need *more* teacher control, not less. In fact, the best control comes from letting students immerse themselves in what they are learning. Many behavior problems decrease or disappear when students are deeply engaged.

For one week each month in an inner-city school in Pittsburgh, teachers set aside their normal routines and lead groups of students in projects that allow them an in-depth look at a topic of their choice. All projects are designed to teach kids the same skills they would get from the regular curriculum. The students work for an entire week without interruption; they don't even change classes. Classroom work is enhanced by library visits and field trips. The resulting projects demonstrate these truths:

- All students are capable of higher-level learning with in-depth study of a topic.

- Basic skills can be taught within the context of meaningful learning and critical thinking activities.

- Most students learn best in a community of learners. They also learn how to help each other learn.

Project-based learning is mutually satisfying to all the participants. This interdisciplinary approach connects learning standards from language arts, mathematics, geography, history, science, and social studies and gives students a relevant learning experience that encourages application to real-life situations. Technology is used as a motivating tool to collaborate with peers, acquire information, share resources, and be creative in a final product. Students' social skills, participation, and responsibility to a team are also fostered. Whether your students are recording results from a survey and graphing the data or creating a pamphlet for a sandwich sale, technology can be the vehicle to take this learning to a more realistic level. Technology also motivates students to become self-directed learners who plan, organize, and complete assignments with the teacher as facilitator. Technology as an integral part of project-based learning motivates students, because they have a choice in the product and are highly engaged. The final benefit to integrating project-based learning with technology is that it helps teachers design learning experiences that target students' learning modality strengths and improve student mastery.

Because project-based learning gives all students a high-quality educational experience, many students who formerly had negative attitudes about school decide that this type of learning is cool. In addition, they begin supporting one another as learners instead of disparaging the efforts of those who want to succeed in school.

**1.** Give each student a copy of the "Project Planner" handout (page 89).

**2.** Have students identify a topic they might like to explore. **Tip:** If they have trouble coming up with a topic, have them stroll through the stacks of a nearby library and peruse the school library shelves until a topic captures their interest.

**3.** Explain that a subtopic is a smaller piece of a larger topic. Give examples. Have students list at least four possible subtopics connected to their topic of study. Once students have listed their subtopics, have them choose one to focus on. Emphasize that this should be something they really want to learn more about.

**4.** Help students locate and collect sources of information about their subtopics. Ask the librarians at your local public library for assistance. They can gather resources across a wide range of reading abilities and lend them to you for an extended period of time. Consider inviting families to help kids search for information.

**5.** Provide a place for students to store the information they collect (*examples:* space on a bookshelf, a storage container, or a flash drive). Teach students to look through one source at a time and record important facts, phrases, and sentences on paper or notecards. Insist that they *not* look through several sources simultaneously. Explain that the goal of research is to learn new things about a certain topics and organize an appropriate amount of data one collects in a way that allows for easier sharing of the information with classmates. Model the use of metacognition (see page 65) to translate paragraphs and long sentences into short phrases. Encourage visual learners to use diagrams, maps, and other visual formats to record information. Investigate websites that offer coaching and support for notecard use, such as www.noodletools.com (for students of all ages).

**6.** Help students prepare a backward timeline to help them meet the expectations of the various parts of their project, including the due date. (See the example for science projects on pages 190–191.)

**7.** Have students select a method of sharing what they have learned. See page 73 for lists of products compatible with learning modality strengths. Don't expect formal written reports, since most struggling students have negative feelings about writing due, in part, to struggles they have experienced over their years in school. If some students want to prepare written reports, let them use a computer. Investigate programs like HyperStudio that allow kids to create polished-looking products. (See "References and Resources.")

**8.** Have students make their presentations. For projects that take a long time to complete, students can give brief progress reports every two to three weeks about what they have learned in that interval. **Tips:** Set a time limit for presentations so they don't run on forever. If some students need to share more information than the class needs to know, suggest that they meet with you privately or in a group to share other ideas they learned from working on their project.

To help kids stay on track during project work, have them keep a daily "Log of Project Work" (page 90). At the beginning of each work period, they enter the date and the task they plan to accomplish that day. Five minutes before project work ends, they record what they actually accomplished. Spillover work is written on the next line as their plan for the next day. As they accomplish each task, a new task is planned and recorded.

## Products Compatible with Learning Modality Strengths

Whenever students work on projects or other extended learning tasks, have them demonstrate what they learn in brain-compatible ways. See the following chart for possible products students can create. Also check with your technology specialist to see what software programs are available for students to use to create more sophisticated products. Ask about HyperStudio. (See "References and Resources.")

### Tech Tip 🖵

Younger students can use software called Kidspiration to collect and organize their research data. Students in grades five and up can use the grown-up version of this software called Inspiration. For information on both, visit www.inspiration.com.

| Products for Auditory Learners | Products for Visual Learners | Products for Tactile-Kinesthetic Learners |
|---|---|---|
| Give a speech or a talk. | Give a whiteboard presentation. | Create a diorama or a mobile. |
| Write a song, rap, poem, story, advertisement, or jingle | Illustrate songs, raps, or poems. | Create and produce a skit or play. Perform it for a class. |
| Hold a panel discussion, round-robin discussion, or debate. | Create a HyperStudio product. See "References and Resources." | Give a demonstration of something you enjoy doing. |
| Conduct an interview. | Create a video production. | Perform an experiment. |
| Present a "you are there" simulated interview or description. | Write, illustrate, and design a travel brochure. | Create a game for others to play to learn the required information. |
| Write an article or editorial for a newspaper. | Make a chart or poster or Web-based visual representing a synthesis of information. | Make a three-dimensional map. |
| Create a newspaper. | Create a diorama or a mobile. | Make and demonstrate a model. |

# Seal the Deal: More Strategies to Make This Chapter Title Become a Reality

## Group Response Methods

When we ask a question and get a response from one student, all this proves is that one student knows the answer. Think back to the last time you led a review for an upcoming test. If you discussed all the test questions, you probably felt confident that everyone would pass the test—but the distribution of grades didn't change much from the previous test, and there were still some failing grades. Why? Because there was only one person who actually responded to all the review questions: you.

When you ask "Any questions?" and no one raises a hand, this doesn't mean that everyone understands what you have just taught. Group response methods are a much more reliable way of determining how many students really get what you are teaching.

- Use the Name Card Method (see pages 12–14) to dramatically increase student participation, responsibility, and understanding.

- Teach nonverbal ways of responding to questions (*examples:* hand signals such as thumbs-up for "agree," thumbs-down for "disagree," thumbs sideways for "not sure"; holding up a certain number of fingers to indicate a choice between several alternatives). Instruct students to withhold their responses until you give a "show me" signal (*examples:* raising your right hand, snapping your fingers, clapping your hands). At your signal, all students respond simultaneously.

- Have students write their responses on handheld slates and raise them simultaneously when you give the signal. You can purchase small slates and chalk from school supply companies. Or make your own slates from shiny plastic-coated squares or similar material (available from building supply companies) and provide students with erasable markers.

- Give each student two three-by-five-inch cards— one green, one red. Holding up the green card means "I agree" or "true"; holding up the red card means "I disagree" or "false."

More strategies like this are described in Chapter 8.

## Peer Teaching

Peer teaching opportunities, whether formal or informal, allow students who already understand something to explain it to kids who haven't yet grasped it. Pair practice is an easy-to-implement peer teaching technique; see "Pair Practice," page 16. Of course, peer teaching should be limited to volunteers. Highly capable students should not feel obliged to tutor other students.

Some schools have peer assistance programs in which students help others with learning difficulties. Assistants are trained in peer tutoring techniques, and both tutors and those being tutored benefit from the experience.

## Flip Your Classroom

The 21st century has the potential to change teaching and learning strategies in ways we cannot yet imagine. One such strategy, the flipped classroom, turns typical teaching and learning practices upside down. It was created in response to the reality that instruction and learning often break down when the students can neither do their homework at home nor produce it in class when required to do so. Also problematic is the absence of homework help in some homes, which instantly puts those children at a learning disadvantage in classrooms where teachers rely on traditional homework products. The flipped classroom method is often the perfect solution to what many teachers erroneously describe as a serious lack of motivation on the part of some students. Our firm belief is that if the goal of our instruction is to avoid spending students' time in activities that are frustrating and nonproductive for them, we must seriously investigate emerging pedagogies to help bring about more positive learning outcomes.

A word about motivation is in order here. We don't believe that any students who don't do their work are unmotivated. On the contrary, they are *highly motivated* to *not do* what you are asking them to do. Many students' apparent lack of motivation is often frustration in disguise. We feel that each day struggling students show up at school is another day they're hoping they will finally experience successful learning. Our highest priority with these students should be to do whatever is necessary for them to become successful learners. (See the homework section in Chapter 11 for more information on this issue.)

In flipped classrooms, the content to be learned is delivered as videos to watch at home, and the "homework" is done at school, with the teacher as facilitator. Videos come from many sources, including online content centers, such as Khan Academy (www.khanacademy.org), some publishers, and the teachers themselves. Therefore, the *practice* to truly understand the lessons *happens at school,* where support and guidance are available. Student-teacher interaction occurs at a much higher level of cognition, and the opportunities for critical thinking are greatly expanded.

Students are much less anxious when they no longer have to do their homework under their families' guidance, and the playing field becomes more level between students whose families possess helpful resources and those whose families do not. Valuable help is much more available to students as they interact with the content and peers in flexible groups. Your role changes from a lecturer (or "sage on the stage") to learning coach (or "guide on the side"). You walk the talk of facilitating daily authentic learning experiences under your direct supervision.

In this method, the parents only have to facilitate their student's watching of the designated lessons. Teacher-family conversations shift from classroom behavior concerns or pressure for families to become more involved in homework to facilitating optimum learning and achievement for the students.

---

Many students' apparent lack of motivation is often frustration in disguise.

---

In classrooms and schools where the flipped classroom method has been used, typical concerns focus on the limitations experienced by children from low-income families. Some homes have serious technology shortages, some homes lack adult supervision, and some struggling students still operate at a disadvantage when compared to their classmates. In addition, some teachers need a lengthy time period to make the transition to a flipped classroom. However, as schools become more "wired," the availability of school-owned digital devices for students to borrow expands.

# Using Technology as an Integral Component of Effective Teaching

Children who watch lots of television and play computer and video games all the time expect to be entertained while they learn. They prefer to learn by viewing; they want color, sound, and visual effects; they anticipate speedy solutions to complex problems, because most TV crises are resolved in less than an hour. We can either wait until students once again become interested in traditional ways of learning, or we can train them for a workplace that will expect them to be comfortable and capable with all kinds of technology.

The effective use of technology in the classroom narrows the gap between potential and performance, especially for students who struggle to learn. Some educators have resisted using technology in the classroom, fearing that students will become dependent on the learning aids and unable to learn independently. This attitude makes as much sense as requiring kids with vision problems to take off their glasses in school. Students with learning difficulties can't become more successful learners simply by trying harder. We should be thrilled that so much technology is available, and we should use whatever we can get our hands on.

## Tech Tip 🖳

Always check YouTube for helpful videos for you or your students to watch. You'll find everything from finger multiplication demonstrations to a visual for a topic of interest.

All students can enjoy benefits from using various forms of technology. But students with learning difficulties can benefit dramatically when optimum matches are made between their learning needs and the most effective technology. Assistive technology has been developed to enable educators to find the most effective programs available and use them with students who are struggling to learn. The term *assistive technology* includes any device or software that will assist a student in mastering the standards needed for success in school.

Using computers in schools only to support the acquisition of traditional skills is a waste of time and technology. The current practice is to make computers an integral part of the learning process, so students learn *from* them instead of *about* them. Some schools have eliminated computer literacy classes altogether in favor of letting kids use computers to create exciting learning products. Students are illustrating and animating documents, creating multimedia presentations with PowerPoint, becoming filmmakers, designing their own websites and programs, and even helping their teachers with hardware and software. Many teachers are delighted to observe former troublemakers and struggling students turning out products that rival those of students considered to have higher ability.

Your success in using technology with students who have learning difficulties depends on how well you can match their learning needs to the assistive technology that is available. Your technology expert in your school or district, your state support agency, the technology consultant at your state's department of education, or assistive technology websites may be valuable resources to help determine this.

## Benefits of Using Technology for Students with LD

1. Students' enthusiasm and motivation to learn increase dramatically when technology is used.

2. Student productivity increases in all subject areas, and basic competencies are mastered sooner, causing teachers to scramble for material to fill up the balance of the year.

3. More spontaneous peer and cooperative learning happens when students are working together on technology-assisted instruction.

4. Most struggling writers, even very young children, become more fluent on the keyboard.

5. Standardized test results for struggling students who use technology are superior to those of students in control groups who do not.

6. High school students who use technology routinely have a higher graduation rate and a higher college participation rate. They receive more honors than other students.

7. Remember that kids need to learn how to use technology in the same way they learn everything else: through direct teaching that includes teacher-directed "think-alouds" in which teachers model how to do the task and verbally share what they are thinking throughout the entire process. Just as with any new or challenging content, scaffolding must be provided all along the learning paths. In the early stages, it's important to provide appropriate coaching so students don't become as frustrated with technology as they have been with more traditional learning methods.

## Simple Technologies

Following are very basic descriptions of technologies currently available. Any attempt to make more specific or detailed recommendations would likely be out of date by the time the ink is dry on this book. Stay in touch with your school's or district's technology person so you always know the latest ways to enhance learning success for your students with learning difficulties. You can also visit the websites of organizations that specialize in educational technology. The International Society for Technology in Education's website (www.iste .org) is an excellent source of educator resources, advocacy information, and more. From there, you can access numerous other organizations and resources, including companies committed to technology in education. See "References and Resources."

### Simple Computer Skills

Teach keyboarding to all students who have trouble writing, especially those who work slowly and tediously. Find a word processing program appropriate for the age group you teach. There is absolutely no reason to deprive kids of computer fluency until their handwriting improves to legibility or fluency. Some teachers have found that writing assignments finished on computers are much better and more polished than anything those students could have produced with pencil and paper.

Many kids with negative attitudes toward writing approach the task enthusiastically when they are given access to computers; many say that this makes them feel like real writers. Since emerging curriculum such as CCSS requires writing in all subject areas, any technology that helps students access the required learning standards should be made available to students.

## Calculators

Calculators are to math what word processors are to language and writing. For students who are dramatically less fluent in computation skills than their age peers, calculators enable them to progress to more authentic (and interesting) math tasks.

Calculators allow students to solve problems at a much higher mathematical level. Students who struggle with fact fluency in addition, subtraction, multiplication, or division can access a more complex math curriculum with the assistance of a calculator to compensate for this learning difficulty.

An article in a Pearson newsletter from 2010 states: "Clearly, prior research indicates that calculator use may increase student scores on mathematics tests, particularly when the test contains a large proportion of computation items. In addition, calculator use may be more beneficial for economically or experientially disadvantaged students. However, it is also clear from the most recent studies that judicial use of the calculator, use of the right type of calculator, and integration of the calculator into mathematics *instruction* are keys to maximizing the positive impact of allowing students to use them on standardized tests."* Perhaps the most significant finding is that students who use calculators are more inclined to be able to do better work when the focus of the test is on problem solving rather than computation.

When we keep struggling students from real problem solving while we wait for them to catch up on their fluency in math facts, we help create an ever-widening gap between them and their grade-level curriculum.

Students with LD or hearing impairments should have calculators with tape or paper printouts, so when they get a wrong answer, they can go back and check their work. Students who are visually impaired need calculators with large keyboards and readouts.

## Handheld Digital Devices

Handheld digital devices include electronic pocket spell-checkers and dictionaries, many of which have a synthesized speech feature; students can key in unfamiliar words, hear them pronounced, and access their

definitions. Some apps enable phones and tablets to perform the same operations. Tablets and e-readers assist students in numerous ways. Students can access textbooks and literature on e-readers. National publishing companies make recently published hardbound texts available in electronic versions for all subject areas. The text-to-speech feature helps students who struggle with reading participate in higher-level academic classes with success. Students can also use tablets to access many apps, such as Mental Note, which is used to take notes, draw diagrams, and organize assignments. Other similar apps have a text-to-speech option built in to assist students with vision impairments, reading difficulties, or note-taking challenges. In addition, tablets and smartphones may be used to help students organize their chaotic lives. Franklin Electronic Publishers also offers a wide variety of electronic spell-checkers, dictionaries, and organizers.

- Although CD-ROMs and DVDs are on their way out of the technology marketplace, many of us will continue to use those we have. Many manufacturers who have previously included CDs in their books now deliver the former CD content directly from their websites to anyone's digital device.

- Digital voice recorders have replaced traditional cassette recorders. They can digitally record sound from any source. However, many other digital devices, including smartphones and tablets, include this feature in their hardware.

- To assist LD students with note taking, several helpful products are available, including electronic capturing bars with embedded audio and handwriting recognition software, Echo or Pulse smartpens (with or without the additional use of speech recognition software) and SoundNote for the iPad.

If you have the opportunity to suggest topics for in-service meetings, ask for training on how to use technology resources to help you ease into the classroom of the future. Also, see "References and Resources."

## Interactive Whiteboards for Students with Special Needs

Interactive whiteboards allow interaction in learning for all students and have special applications for students with learning difficulties. Features that allow students to move items and ideas around through touch, as well as pens that record what is written on the whiteboard, allow students with limited motor skills to participate in this technology. Enlarged print helps students with visual needs, and touch activation allows for signing when instructing children with hearing

---

*Wolfe, Edward W. "What Impact Does Calculator Use Have on Test Results?" *Pearson Test, Measurement & Research Services Bulletin* 14 (May 2010): 4.

impairments. Interactive whiteboards increase motivation and decrease behavior problems because students are more successful at reaching their learning goals in all academic areas. Interactive whiteboards allow students to use thousands of websites designed to enhance their learning, including Boardmaker Plus, IntelliKeys, PixWriter, and One Switch.

As valuable as the interactive whiteboard is in enhancing classroom instruction, it is equally useful in IEP meetings. It allows the IEP team to view a student's present education levels, goals, and specially designed instruction modifications and design appropriate ongoing interventions for the student.

## Tech Tip 🖥

Before introducing a new technology tool to students, make sure that you know how all the functions work, so you can predict where your students will need the most assistance. Don't try to teach too much at one time. For instance, the first time you use a tool or a website, choose one or two learning goals (such as logging in or uploading a photo). If you ensure mastery of the little things by every student before you move on, you and your students will be able to experience increasingly challenging learning activities.

## Assistive Technology

One of the most dramatic changes in education in the last 10 years is the availability of assistive technology to most school districts. Students with learning difficulties require varied levels of assistive technology. Any form of technology that improves learning success for students with learning difficulties or ESL students falls into this category. Three levels of technology interventions are available. These are described here and in the "Assistive Technology" chart on pages 80–81:

- **Low technology:** An electronic planner is one example of a low-technology assistive device. It can assist in everything from remembering appointments to sequencing activities. Photographs or symbols help a student with learning difficulties complete a task sequentially. Be sure to look for online resources—especially YouTube, which has an amazing collection of short videos of teachers demonstrating highly effective strategies directly to students on a wide variety of topics, such as finger multiplication.

- **Medium technology:** Voice output communication aids (VOCAs), which contain visual representation systems for spoken information, help students understand a definition or a sentence read aloud to them. DVD recordings of kids demonstrating appropriate behaviors can help your students become aware of inappropriate behaviors. Students with LD might then ask to be recorded when they think they are demonstrating appropriate behaviors. Other useful examples of medium-level assistive technology include iPad and iPod Touch.

In addition to watching videos, you can make videos to assist your students. These videos may show tasks such as setting the table, or they may increase vocabulary words by naming objects or actions. You can use videos of your students to help them see expected and unexpected behaviors. You can model best practices for social interactions, such as smiling or saying hello to classmates. Your students can observe and discuss tone of voice, body language, personal space, facial expressions, and vocal volume. Your students will benefit from and appreciate the predictable outcome, often watching the same video for many consecutive days.

- **High technology:** Examples of high technology include text-to-speech or text-to-braille programs, personal amplification systems to help students with hearing impairment, touch screen devices, and voice recognition that allows a computer to write what a student speaks. ZoomText type programs provide a very large font size on documents. Learning Ally and Bookshare offer digital versions of most texts and literature used at various grade levels.

## Tech Tip 🖥

Involve students in the selection of appropriate apps. Make sure technology really addresses students' needs and is easy to use. The chart on pages 80–81 looks in detail at the functions of specific applications and helps the teacher determine which is the best fit to meet the student's learning needs. Simply use the chart descriptors to evaluate a potential app for your students.

For help in teaching students who have learning difficulties, this chart was created and is used in Lisa's district to provide a starting point for assistive technology options.

## Evaluate App Rubric

**Goal:** (What goal from students' IEP/504 does this app need to support?)

| | | |
|---|---|---|
| Name of App: | | Developer: |
| Content/Topic: | | Developer Website: |
| Date Reviewed: | Version: | Last Update: |
| Review by: | | Date: | Cost: |

| Domain | 1<br>Weak Quality | 2<br>Fair Quality | 3<br>Good Quality | 4<br>High Quality |
|---|---|---|---|---|
| **Curriculum Connection** | Does not meet expectation. | Limited or narrow scope of the topic. Underdeveloped. | Skills or concepts are practiced and reinforced. Limited level of consideration. | Very strong connection to the skill or concept being practiced. Levels of consideration offered. |
| **Type of Skills Practiced** | No skill practice, only "flash card" drill. | Skills are practiced in gaming format. | Simulated learning environment (virtual tasks). Scaffolds activities (beginner to advanced). | Problem-based learning with simulated environment. Program monitors and advances difficulty. |
| **Age and Grade Level** | Level is not appropriate for audience. Not suitable for age or grade level. Directions are incomplete or inadequate. | Level is often too easy or difficult for target audience. Features unsuitable material. Directions are unclear. | Level is appropriate, but some portions may be too easy or difficult. Most directions are clear but some are confusing. | Level is appropriate for target audience (age and grade). Directions are clear and complete. |
| **Languages** | Only 1 language | 2–3 languages | 4–5 languages | 6 or more languages |
| **Adjustable Levels** | Only 1 level | 2–3 levels | 4–5 levels | 6 or more levels |
| **Prompts** | No feedback offered. Moves forward with correct or incorrect responses. | Prompt is limited to indicating wrong answer. Student needs to get it right to move forward. | Prompt is specific preset number of tries (can't edit) before student moves forward. | Prompt is specific. Can set number of tries. There is a tutorial to help student. |
| **Ease of Use** | Very difficult to use. Limited or no instructions. Student needs support on every use. | Student needs to be cued through the process. | Student needs support (model) from adult or peer. | Intuitive; student can figure out independently. |

| | | | | |
|---|---|---|---|---|
| **Engagement** | Does not meet expectation. | Held the individual's attention for more than 2–3 minutes. | Held the individual's attention for more than 5 minutes. | Held the individual's attention for more than 10 minutes. |
| **Customization** | None. | Can turn off prompts and music. | Can add your own items and prompts. | All features, including fonts, are customizable. |
| **Alternative Access** | Has no access to alternative sources. | Specific interface access and works consistently. | App works with at least 2 access tools and works consistently. | App works with 3 or more access tools. Is consistent. |
| **Data Collected** | No data offered. | Data is collected in percentage only. Data cannot be printed or stored. | Data is collected. Number correct against total attempts. Can be printed. | Data is collected. Number of correct and incorrect responses against total attempts. Can be stored and printed. |
| **National Curriculum** | No | | | Yes |
| **Gender-Neutral** | No | | | Yes |
| **When was the app updated?** | 1 year ago or more. | Within the last 9 months. | Within the last 6 months. | Within the last 3 months. |
| **Total Points:** | | | | |
| **Total Points Divided by 14:** | | | | |
| **Rating** | Suitable for specific use. | Satisfactory. | Highly recommended. | Exceeds expectations. |
| **Strength of the app:** | | | | |
| **Weakness of the app:** | | | | |
| **Skills individual needs to have or learn before use:** | | | | |
| **Alternative apps to consider:** | | | | |

## Assistive Technology

| Instructional or Access Area | Standard Tools | Accommodations of Task and Expectations | Assistive Technology Solutions |
|---|---|---|---|
| **Writing:**<br>• Copy letters, words, or numbers<br>• Complete written assignments or tests with single-word responses (fill-in-the-blank), phrase or sentence responses, multiple-choice responses (circle or mark answer), or essay response (multiparagraph) | • Letter strip<br>• Computer with word processing software, including grammar and spell-checker | • Increased time for completing assignments<br>• Decreased length of assignment or number of responses<br>• Dictate story to scribe<br>• Word banks, sentence starters, and cloze format writing activities for supports<br>• Accepting shortened responses | • Pencil grip or other adapted writing aids<br>• Alternate paper (bold line, raised line, different spacing, secured to desk, paper stabilizer)<br>• Slant board<br>• Computer with word processing software equipped with spell-checker and grammar checker (such as Microsoft Word) or outlining or webbing software (such as Inspiration, Kidspiration, or Draft:Builder)<br>• Computer with talking word processing software (such as IntelliTalk, Write:OutLoud), word prediction software (Co:Writer)<br>• Speaking spell-checker or dictionary as a word recognition aid |
| **Reading:**<br>• Read names, sight words, functional vocabulary (community, emergency, grocery, and so on), or selected words within a sentence<br>• Comprehend age- or grade-appropriate reading materials, textbooks, computers, or interactive whiteboards<br>• Answer comprehension questions about text | • Textbooks<br>• Printed information from various sources<br>• Printed test materials | • Peer or adult reading assistance<br>• High-interest, low-reading-level materials<br>• Simplify complexity of text<br>• Color coding to emphasize key points<br>• Provide questions before reading short sections of text<br>• Customized vocabulary list<br>• Increase print size of material | • Reading pen<br>• Audiobooks (such as those from Learning Ally)<br>• Electronic books (eBooks)<br>• Computer with text enlargement software (such as ZoomText)<br>• Computer with text reading software (ReadPlease, Talk to Me, JAWS, Kurzweil 1000)<br>• Computer-based advanced reading aids (Kurzweil 3000, WYNN)<br>• Color overlays<br>• Highlighting<br>• Tracking strategies<br>• Closed captioning on non-caption-ready instructional materials |
| **Math:**<br>• Identify numbers in isolation and sequence<br>• Tell time and calculate elapsed time<br>• Identify coins and bills, their values, prices, appropriate change, or balance a checkbook | • Manipulatives<br>• Abacus<br>• Number line | • Change format of assignment (for example, write answers only)<br>• Reduce number of problems | • Computer-based on-screen calculator<br>• Electronic math worksheet software with adaptive input and output as needed (MathPad, Access to Math, or StudyWorks)<br>• Adapted measuring devices (devices with speech output, large-print display, or tactile output) |

| Objective | | | |
|---|---|---|---|
| • Comprehend and apply basic math concepts, calculations (addition, subtraction, multiplication, and division), complex math calculations, or word problems | • Math fact sheet (such as multiplication facts)<br>• Calculator | • Provide additional spacing between problems<br>• Change complexity of material (for example, separate problems by operations required) | • Scanner and software to create electronic practice activities<br>• Standard, talking, large-display, embossed-output (Braille 'n Speak), or large-keypad calculator |
| **Study and Organizational Skills:**<br>• Record assignments into assignment notebook<br>• Complete assigned task<br>• Request teacher or peer assistance when needed<br>• Have appropriate materials or supplies for class activities | • Crayon<br>• Marker<br>• Pencil<br>• Pen<br>• Clipboards<br>• Colored folders | • Provide outline or copy of lecture notes to student prior to delivery for student to use to follow lecture<br>• Student highlights key points on printed copy of notes rather than copying or recording lecture notes<br>• Webbing-concept mapping strategy<br>• Peer note taker<br>• Assignment sheet provided by peer or adult<br>• Student schedule or checklist<br>• Student self-monitoring sheets | • Print or picture schedule<br>• Organizational aids (color coding, appointment book, and so on)<br>• Voice-to-text software or dictated responses and note taking<br>• Interactive whiteboard for transferring teacher-written notes to student computer for viewing and printing |
| **Listening:**<br>• Follow verbal directions<br>• Listen to stories, books, classroom discussions, or teacher lectures and apply information (answer questions, record notes, and retell with correct sequencing and facts)<br>• Respond to environmental stimuli appropriately (someone knocking on classroom door, bell ringing, fire alarm) | • Headphones for clarity of sound and blocking of extraneous noises<br>• Closed captioning access to caption-ready television and visual presentations | • Repetition of spoken answers<br>• Positioning student strategically within classroom environment<br>• Use teacher proximity<br>• Elimination of extraneous noise (such as air conditioner)<br>• Break directions into smaller steps<br>• Use verbal prompts<br>• Interpreter | • Speech enhancing devices (amplifiers, clarifiers)<br>• Personal amplification or classroom FM system |
| **All Instructional Areas:**<br>• Increase engagement and ability to participate to the maximum extent possible in the regular classroom<br>• Use students' learning modality strengths | • Instructional materials, including software, to remediate and enhance specific writing, math, basic reading, or comprehension skills<br>• Television<br>• Visual media player<br>• Interactive whiteboard technology | • Modeling appropriate skills<br>• Cooperative participation<br>• Game participation<br>• Format of assignment changed to meet need of student (multiple-choice, matching word banks, fill-in-the-blank, short answer)<br>• Timer<br>• Use gestures | • Solutions for converting text into alternative format (scanner with optical character recognition [OCR] software, braille translation software, and so on) |

**Tech Tip** 🖥

Review a student's IEP or 504 plan (for kids who have some behavioral or educational issues, but who are not eligible for an IEP) to see if it includes provisions for assistive technology (AT), which is mandated by a federal law. Many students with LD are under-referred for assistive technology supports.

# Summary of Teaching Strategies for Students with Learning Difficulties and Those Emerging into English Fluency

The remaining chapters in this book address specific content areas (reading, writing, math), assessment, behavior, and family involvement. Before we move on, it will be helpful to summarize the 10 key strategies to use when teaching struggling students, to achieve proficiency with required standards. Keep in mind that these strategies are just as effective with students in poverty and learners of the English language as they are with kids who have been diagnosed with learning difficulties. The strategies are:

1. Actively reduce anxiety levels through attention to learning modality strengths and goal-setting instruction.

2. Teach from the whole back to the parts.

3. Enter standards through students' personal interests and include creative thinking activities.

4. Let students listen to soothing music as they work.

5. Use visual strategies throughout the curriculum, including graphic organizers.

6. Use color cues everywhere, from all content areas to all organizational strategies.

7. Allow learning in pairs or groups; use games, games, and more games.

8. Teach new material in meaningful contexts.

9. Combine verbal instruction with visual and kinesthetic cues; always show students an example of the completed activity.

10. Remember that active involvement is preferable to paper-and-pencil activities.

The methods in this book can be used with any content. It may feel as though you don't have enough time to try new methods. But the truth is, you can't afford *not* to try them. One thing is certain: When you keep doing things the way you are currently doing them, you and your students will keep getting the same results. To change the results, you must change the methods. You needn't change them for the whole class, and not for your successful students—but for students who are far behind expected standards, you really have no other choice.

## How Teaching Behaviors Can Improve Achievement

1. Consistently communicate high expectations for students' learning success.

2. Spend time activating prior knowledge. Use scaffolding techniques to be certain students always see how what they are presently learning is connected to what they already know. Be sure students know, at the beginning of a learning session, the exact standards they will be expected to learn. At the lesson's end, reinforce this information and demonstrate how the new learning was connected to those standards. (See "KWPL" on page 101.)

3. Continually adjust your teaching based on the feedback you receive from your students. (See the "Name Card Method" on page 12.)

4. When using rubrics, check to be certain the language is easily understood by your students. Offer rubrics in stages instead of the whole document at one time. (See Chapter 8.)

5. Use available technology to assist students in their learning, knowing that their real-world jobs will utilize myriad forms of technology. Even if the assessments are not delivered via computer, students who have had a highly successful year in school will be more likely to score at higher levels on assessments just because of the self-confidence their technology-supported learning experiences have provided.

6. Note to administrators: Be sure to include the special education teachers in all aspects of curriculum planning, classroom placements, and budgeting issues regarding necessary assistive technology or equipment.

## Unlocking Autism 🔒

Effective teachers communicate often with families. They also use appropriate and helpful assistive technologies. Examples used by students with autism in varying ways include visual schedules, iPads with such apps as Proloquo2go, and more intensive communication devices such as IntelliKeys. More suggested products are described in the chart on pages 80–81.

# The School-Wide Cluster Grouping Model (SCGM)

The school-wide cluster grouping model (SCGM) is a method for grouping all students at a grade level for optimum learning and achievement outcomes. Originally designed for the benefit of advanced or gifted learners, the research shows clearly that SCGM ultimately leads to higher achievement scores for *all* students at the grade levels that use the grouping model, taking care to assign students to classrooms using the chart below.*

During the school years of 2010 to 2014, when the SCGM was first implemented in Lisa's district, gifted identification has increased across all subgroups of students, including children of poverty, children from minority groups, and children who are twice exceptional. Most importantly, achievement test scores have improved for all students, including those with IEPs, when compared to students from a similar district that does not use SCGM. Since Lisa is the director of special education for her district, she is very impressed that this SCGM program has had such a positive impact on achievement for her students in special education.

Lisa has also noticed that the benefits of SCGM extend beyond student achievement. The training received by teachers includes attention to flexible grouping, curriculum differentiation, and classroom management procedures, which allows all students at all achievement levels to be consistently challenged in their learning.

In this model, *all* students at a grade level are grouped according to the chart on this page. The chart demonstrates how students are placed in the model when it is used at a specified grade level. Variations needed by unusual numbers of students in various categories are easily accommodated and are described in an article by Brulles and Winebrenner listed in the "References and Resources."

SCGM can address the needs of gifted students without compromising attention to struggling students. The model facilitates these outcomes with no significant budget requirements. A growing collection of data supports these claims.

Grouping categories consist of:

- **Group 1 (Gifted):** All identified gifted students, including those who are not fluent in English, not productive in school, and twice exceptional gifted students.

- **Group 2 (High Average):** Highly competent and productive students who achieve well in school.

- **Group 3: (Average):** Students achieving in the average range of grade-level standards.

- **Group 4: (Low Average):** Students who may struggle slightly with math or reading.

- **Group 5: (Far Below Average):** Students who struggle in most subject areas and score significantly below proficiency levels on academic measures.**

## Recommended SCGM Classroom Composition for a Single Grade Level

| Classroom | Gifted | High Average | Average | Low Average | Far Below Average |
|-----------|--------|--------------|---------|-------------|-------------------|
| A | 6 | 0 | 12 | 12 | 0 |
| B | 0 | 6 | 12 | 6 | 6 |
| C | 0 | 6 | 12 | 6 | 6 |

*Winebrenner and Brulles, *The Cluster Grouping Handbook,* Minneapolis: Free Spirit Publishing, 2008.

**Winebrenner and Brulles, 2008.

## Grouping Students in the School-Wide Cluster Grouping Model

With the SCGM, *all* students are grouped into classrooms based on their abilities and potential. Gifted cluster groups consist of approximately four to nine gifted students. When there are 10 or more gifted students identified at a grade level, a second gifted cluster classroom may be formed.

Prior to placing students into classrooms, all students in the grade level are assigned to one of the five groups noted here. Assignments to the various groups are determined using formal and informal methods that combine standardized test data on ability and achievement with teacher observations and other anecdotal data. All gifted students are automatically placed in Group 1, whether or not they are currently working at advanced levels. All other students are assigned to groups using the achievement-based descriptors.

Placing students into classroom groups occurs with teachers from the sending and receiving grades with assistance from the principal and special education teachers as needed. One method for making placements incorporates the use of colored index cards. Using this method, each student group at all grade levels involved is represented by a designated color, as determined by the student's gifted identification or achievement level. Each classroom teacher assigns his or her current students to the appropriate card color. Colored cards in the grade level are then combined to create the class combination as illustrated in the chart on page 83.*

Placement steps:

1. Cluster all gifted identified students into designated gifted cluster classrooms.

2. Next, group high average students into classrooms that have not been assigned the gifted cluster.

3. Place average students evenly in all classrooms.

4. Place low average students in all classrooms.

5. Place far below average ability students in the classes that do not have the gifted cluster.

Classroom compositions are carefully structured with two main goals: to ensure a balance of abilities throughout the grade level and to reduce the learning range in every classroom. These careful grouping practices allow teachers to more readily respond to the needs of all their students, to challenge gifted students clustered together in mixed-ability classes, and to engage in practices that lead to increased academic achievement for all their students.

---

* Winebrenner and Brulles, 2008.

The advantages for students with learning difficulties being placed in classes according to the SCGM are:

**1.** The teacher who has a cluster group of gifted students does not have the kids who are most needy academically, so that teacher can continue to provide ongoing attention to the gifted students' exceptional educational needs and challenge their learning on a daily basis.

**2.** The teachers who do not have a cluster of gifted students *do* have a cluster of high-achieving students who can provide positive academic role modeling for their classmates.

**3.** Students with learning difficulties are not likely to be intimidated when noticing the advanced learning abilities of kids at the top of the class.

**4.** Students who have high ability, but are not gifted, tend to be more considerate when coaching or tutoring their classmates.

**5.** Although all teachers still have heterogeneous classes, the student achievement range in all classes is slightly narrowed, which directly facilitates effective teaching.

**6.** An improvement in the high-stakes testing results has been documented, and has been credited to be the result of the narrower range of abilities in each class, along with the benefits of receiving training in essential differentiation strategies.

**7.** Because the classes created by SCGM contain a smaller range of achievement levels, the teacher who has students with learning difficulties but not gifted students has more time to pay attention to the struggling students. All classes have a group of high-achieving students to serve as academic role models for their classmates. Students who are twice exceptional—who have high capabilities in one or more areas of learning but also exhibit significant struggle in other areas—should be placed with the gifted cluster so their strengths will more likely be noticed and served by a teacher who has training in gifted education.

**8.** When a group of students with learning difficulties is placed in a classroom with students of other achievement levels, and with a teacher who knows how best to facilitate their learning success, the curriculum is more likely to be differentiated, partly because that teacher also has a slightly narrower range of achievement levels in her class, and measurable academic achievement will occur for all students at the grade level being targeted or piloted.

Note: See the "References and Resources" for more information on the SCGM, especially for use with advanced learners.

# Questions and Answers

*"How can I find time each day to work one-on-one with struggling students on goal setting?"*

Always give those students five minutes less to work on a task than you give the others, so you have the last five minutes of the work period to debrief their results. In other words, if the rest of your class has 30 minutes to complete a task, your struggling students will have 25 minutes. Have them use this figure in the ratio on their "Goal Planning Chart" (see page 62).

*"What can I do if the curriculum assigned to me is not very interesting for my students?"*

Be creative. If your school is using CCSS, students with learning difficulties are finding themselves engaged in very interesting work that combines standards from several subject areas to make it easier for students to understand how all learning is interrelated. If that is not the case, identify the skills and competencies your students are expected to learn, then figure out how to teach those skills and competencies in ways that are exciting and meaningful for your students. (*Examples:* If students find geography boring, try teaching it through current events. Have students watch a daily news program; use daily newspapers and weekly news magazines as your texts and point out or have students discover how different sources report the same stories from slightly different perspectives. Consult teaching manuals and journals and other publications for ideas. Seek out and use available Internet resources. Bribe colleagues to eat lunch together in your room by bringing chocolates to the meeting, then brainstorm creative teaching ideas together.)

*"How do I know what is reasonable to expect from students on the autism spectrum?"*

Students with ASD can have a wide range of academic abilities, from advanced to very low. Speaking with your special education teacher will help you set reasonable learning expectations for this student. The special education teacher will be able to share IQ levels and past achievement data that will guide your instructional decisions. The special education teacher will also be able to help you choose the best accommodations for meeting the student's academic needs. Students with ASD often have social needs as well. Your special education teacher can share with you strategies, such as visual schedules and sensory breaks, that work best with the student.

*"Our district has very little technology available. How can I use technology to help my students learn?"*

Focus on simple technology such as calculators, spell-checkers, iPads, and so on. (See the "Assistive Technology" chart on pages 80–81.) Many free educational apps are available for teachers and parents to access for students. The Internet has opened the door to many free educational websites that allow teachers to reinforce skills and enhance their instruction to meet the Common Core State Standards. Just search the apps at iTunes, or search for free apps or materials in a certain area of learning.

Many grants are available to help teachers increase their students' access to technology within their classrooms. Often local businesses will support efforts that promote technology use in the classroom. Parent-teacher organizations are also an excellent resource for providing funding for technology resources. Talk to your media specialist, public librarian, and the technology director at your state office of education to learn about grant opportunities as well.

# Goal Planning Chart

NAME: _____

Each day, predict how much you can do in the time you have. Use your goal information to discover how much progress you are actually making.

| Subject Area/Task | Monday | Tuesday | Wednesday | Thursday | Friday |
|---|---|---|---|---|---|
| | | | | | |
| | | | | | |
| | | | | | |
| | | | | | |
| | | | | | |
| | | | | | |
| | | | | | |
| | | | | | |
| | | | | | |
| | | | | | |
| | | | | | |

# Thinking About What I Do

Name: _____

Date: _____

**Directions: Answer each question by checking yes or no.**

| Questions to ask myself before I start: | Yes | No |
|---|---|---|
| Do I know what I am expected to do? | | |
| Do I have a plan for completing what I am expected to do? | | |
| Have I closed my eyes to visualize what I am supposed to do? | | |
| Have I visualized myself completing the task successfully? | | |
| If I accomplish this task, do I know what my reward is? | | |
| If I do not accomplish this task, do I have a plan for my next try? | | |
| **Questions to ask myself often while I am working:** | **Yes** | **No** |
| Am I following my plan? | | |
| Am I drifting off and losing my attention? | | |
| Am I focusing on the important content? | | |
| Am I working according to the goals I have set for myself? | | |
| Do I need a short break? | | |

# ThinkTrix

Objective: _____

Required Standards: _____

_____

_____

_____

| | | |
|---|---|---|
| **Cause and Effect** | ⟳ | |
| **Recall** | R | |
| **Similarity** | ◑ | |
| **Difference** | ◐ | |
| **Idea to Example** | 💡→EX | |
| **Example to Idea** | EX→💡 | |
| **Evaluation** | ⚖ | |

# Project Planner

**Name:** _____

**Date:** _____

**A Topic I Want to Learn About:**

Subtopics (list at least four, then circle the number of the one you choose):

1. _____    6. _____

2. _____    7. _____

3. _____    8. _____

4. _____    9. _____

5. _____    10. _____

Sources of information (list at least five, and use no more than one encyclopedia):

1. _____    6. _____

2. _____    7. _____

3. _____    8. _____

4. _____    9. _____

5. _____    10. _____

How I will use my learning modality strength to learn the material:

_____

_____

_____

How I will share what I've learned with the class in ways
that are learning modality friendly:

_____

_____

_____

# Log of Project Work

Name: _____

Project Topic: _____

| Date | Planned Work | Work Actually Completed Today |
|------|--------------|-------------------------------|
|      |              |                               |
|      |              |                               |
|      |              |                               |
|      |              |                               |
|      |              |                               |
|      |              |                               |
|      |              |                               |
|      |              |                               |
|      |              |                               |
|      |              |                               |

# CHAPTER 5

# Teaching Integrated Language Arts, Including Literature, Sounds, and Writing

Presently, the trend in language arts instruction is integration of literacy skills with one another and with other subject areas. What we formerly taught, sometimes with little or no integration, included reading stories and informational content, decoding sounds, and writing in various formats. With the present emphasis on training our students to be competent adults in their real-world jobs, we think integration of curriculum is very sensible.

## Reading

Reading is the ability to make meaning from printed words. How does meaning happen? The ability to derive meaning from text is related to whether the reader can activate prior knowledge about the topic. If we give kids a nonsense passage they can easily decode, no meaning is present. If we give them a passage and they understand the words but nothing about the topic, their reading is not meaningful. When kids can read the words but don't comprehend the meaning, they become frustrated and often conclude they are not good readers—and never will be.

Good readers automatically use strategies to adjust their reading rate to the material and check to see if what they are reading makes sense. Poor readers don't even know that such strategies exist. They think that good readers were born that way. This situation creates a barrier to school success, which depends on competence in reading. Reading stories, informational text,

math word problems, or explanations of math concepts all demand reading fluency with accurate comprehension. Fluent reading in the elementary grades is vital to a positive self-concept and feelings of self-efficacy in reading. Any student who is not a fluent reader by third grade is at risk of dropping out of school before high school graduation. Dropping out often leads to lifelong frustration in finding a satisfying career and earning a good income.

> Good readers automatically use strategies to adjust their reading rate to the material and check to see if what they are reading makes sense. Poor readers don't even know that such strategies exist.

All our efforts to improve student performance should begin with improving reading ability. Children learn to read by reading. An effective reading program is one of literacy development that combines several reading methods. No *one* reading method works for *all* kids, primarily because of the different learning modalities represented in our classrooms. Some reading programs are very prescriptive and contain multiple layers of activities students are expected to do. The reading program you use currently may be exactly right for most of your students. However, you probably still have some kids who have not adequately improved their reading ability using this program. It's essential to find the right method to bring each of your below-level readers closer to independent fluency and comprehension. Since all students do not respond positively to any one strategy, you may need to try several. When students discover that their reading problems do not stem from lack of intelligence, but rather from not having found and used the right strategies for them, their self-esteem gets back on track, and school feels like a good place to be.

This section describes a variety of methods you can use to improve success in reading fluency and comprehension for students with reading difficulties such as dyslexia, a severe difficulty in recognizing and understanding written language. You may apply these methods to selections from texts, anthologies, or literature. Start by identifying the reading skills that you know some of your students have not mastered, and instruct them in the methods you feel are most effective in facilitating the students' learning modality strengths. Identify a method described in this chapter and use it for a few weeks. For example, if you are teaching vocabulary, try the "Vocabulary Attributes Chart" (see page 114). When you're ready, add other strategies and methods. Make sure that your students spend some time each day with literature, informational text, understanding letter-sound relationships they need more practice to master, and then writing on topics related to what they've read. A reading program that ignores any of these aspects is incomplete.

# Guidelines for Helping Students with Reading Difficulties Become Successful Readers

**1.** Good readers automatically use reading strategies as they read. They use background knowledge and the context of the content to make meaningful connections between current and past texts and topics, make and continuously check inferences and predictions, make decisions about the relative importance of various sections, create images in their mind as they read, and give themselves permission to skip over unfamiliar words or ideas and find their meaning later. They are always checking to make sure what they are reading makes sense. They know when to reread and make clarifications throughout the reading process. In other words, they constantly practice metacognition. (See page 65). In contrast, struggling readers think that excellent readers were just born that way. They have little to no awareness that good readers are actually using strategies as

they read. Once struggling readers understand this, you can encourage them to believe that they, too, can become better readers simply by learning to use the strategies you will be teaching them.

**2.** The most effective way to hold the attention of students with learning difficulties is choosing high-interest reading material. When a selected topic is abstract, always introduce it in a way that has real-world meaning and refer back to those connections throughout the selection.

**3.** For ELL students and students of any age who are just entering reading instruction, provide some experience with big (or predictable) books. Many publishers produce giant books that make it possible for students to see the text and illustrations clearly while you read the words aloud. After repeated readings, students can read along with you. Through the use of repeated sentence patterns and action, students gain valuable experience in predicting story events that they will use as they read later on their own.

**4.** Accurately placing all readers at their personal instructional levels is critically important. Dynamic Indicators of Basic Early Literacy Skills (DIBELS), found at dibels.org, is our first choice for this purpose. DIBELS assessments are designed to provide a link between assessment and instruction by identifying a student's need for support early in the assessment process, monitoring progress toward individual goals, and evaluating the effectiveness of the intervention provided. The passages students read aloud may be used for screening, progress monitoring, and assessment purposes at reading levels from kindergarten through sixth grade. They are standardized, efficient, and extensively researched to help you identify students who may need additional literacy instruction in order to become proficient readers.

**5.** Once a story or article is selected, the first step is to read it aloud to nonfluent readers so they can get the big picture. Be aware, however, that competent readers often will not want to read a story once they know how it ends. Those students could do a prediction activity with a partner during the read-aloud, or they could use headphones with quiet music playing, so they don't hear the read-aloud. Similarly, the read-aloud can be presented through headphones to the students who need to hear it.

**6.** When students are ready for leveled readers, provide recorded versions of the stories for them to listen to as they are learning to read more fluently. Sometimes the publisher of your adopted reading series provides recorded stories. Another choice is to explore the National Reading Styles Institute (www.nrsi.com), directed by Dr. Marie Carbo. This company makes available numerous recordings of stories that are similar to those in reading anthologies. Carbo's method, which Susan has found extremely effective for students who struggle with fluency and comprehension, is called Power Reading Online (PRO). For more on this method, see page 98 of this chapter.

**7.** Do not teach vocabulary before students read the selection, since global learners need meaningful contexts to remember isolated terms. Some schools actually expect their designated reading teachers to teach vocabulary in context in their classroom to prepare students with reading difficulties for an upcoming story that will subsequently be read in the regular classroom. By the time the regular class is ready to begin the story, the reading support students are ready to participate with confidence. For more information, see the vocabulary section on pages 113–115.

**8.** Be aware that comprehension is the most critically important outcome of reading. It is not possible to create comprehension unless the student has fluently read the text.

**9.** Oral reading alone should never be used to assess comprehension. Assess students' comprehension only through activities related to text they are reading, and see if some oral reading segments might be better understood if the student uses silent reading instead. Note: This is also true for advanced readers, who often stumble through an oral reading sample because their eyes and brains are so far ahead of their mouths. A capable reader whose only shortcoming is poor oral reading skills should never spend time remediating that skill. If readers comprehend what they read, that's all they need to be allowed to move on to other stories or self-selected readings.

**10.** Use visual organizers and digital teaching aids whenever possible for the benefit of global learners. These tools create pictures for students to help them understand the whole before they must comprehend the parts. Story maps and character maps help them get the big picture of the selection. Compare-and-contrast circles clarify similarities and differences within categories of information. (See pages 103–104.)

# Three Components of Effective Reading Instruction

Some teachers, especially content area specialists, may not think of themselves as reading teachers. However, in the Common Core approach to teaching, *all* teachers are teachers of reading. That's because comprehending informational text makes up a huge portion of meeting general reading standards. The following guidelines can help you understand and address all three steps to improving reading and comprehension for students with learning or reading difficulties.

## Before Reading

- Activate students' prior knowledge.

- Describe the purpose for reading a certain selection.

- Guide students through a survey of upcoming content, calling attention to salient features such as bold or italicized print, font size, visual aids such as charts and graphs, pictures, and questions written into the text. Student partners ask each other questions about each feature and predict what the answer will be when they are later reading the text to gain meaning. Students may simply state their answers; it is not necessary to record them. For students in the primary grades, read the entire story aloud to them before they begin their own attempts. For older students, share the plot and read aloud a few of the beginning pages. As the survey proceeds, encourage student partners to make predictions of what might happen in the story or article. This is done so they can become emotionally connected to the events in the story as they check the actual content against their earlier predictions.

- Pronounce new vocabulary words as they are encountered in the text, but do not include any written vocabulary work at this point. Students with learning difficulties find it very frustrating to learn things that are presented outside a meaningful context.

- Locate places on maps, globes, or other media.

- A video program may be presented at this point, since it gives visual learners a context to which they can refer when needed. As before, good readers won't want to see the visual version until after they have finished reading the selection.

## During Reading

- Provide class time to discuss meaning and interpretations with partners and to check the predictions made before reading.

- Use predictable graphic organizers to help develop comprehension competencies that can be applied to other literature and informational texts.

- Summarize often, preferably using the same predictable graphic organizer each time.

- Learn vocabulary words in their meaningful contexts, using visual aids such as the "Vocabulary Attributes Chart" on page 133.

- Teach skills in the context of the reading material.

## After Reading

- Confirm or refute original predictions.

- Refer to the information recorded on graphic organizers to speak fluently about the information.

- Discuss connections between various sections of text.

- Summarize three to five big ideas (the most important concepts in the text) and keep them visible where students can see them if they read other selections related to the particular theme or section of study.

### Unlocking Autism 🔒

Students with autism have an extremely hard time acquiring language skills. They struggle with comprehending oral or written communication, texts, and questions that are not literal. Their struggles include learning to read and understanding such concepts as figurative language, inferences, and cause and effect. These language skills must be taught explicitly and reviewed often to be mastered.

Note: The following sections describe methods of teaching reading skills that have been proven effective with struggling readers. Of course, you might also look for apps that demonstrate similar functions.

## Big Books

Many publishers produce giant versions of books for young readers. These big books make it possible for students to see the text and illustrations simultaneously as you read aloud. Later, kids can read aloud together. Emerging readers of all ages especially enjoy anticipating and predicting repeated words or phrases.

1. Before starting to read, show the cover of the book, read the title, and discuss the cover illustration.

2. Have students predict what might happen in the story, based on the cover illustration. Later, they can predict a story by looking at all the pictures before you (or they) read the text.

3. Read the entire story straight through, using a pointer to indicate each word as you read it. Read in phrases to enhance meaning. Be very enthusiastic in your reading and pointing.

4. Reread the story immediately, asking the students to join in whenever they can.

5. Repeat the story several more times over several days until most of the students are familiar enough with the text to read it on their own.

6. If you have the related small books (regular-size versions of the big book), have students read to each other in groups. Encourage them to check out copies to read to family members at home. Demonstrate how they should point to each word as they read it.

### Variations

- Promote understanding of letter-sound relationships by having students point to all the words on a page that begin with a particular letter.

- Have students make a chart version of the story and work in groups to illustrate the text—one page per group.

- Have students create personal versions of the story by drawing their own pictures for it.

- For the benefit of tactile-kinesthetic learners, incorporate drama into the reading experience. Make masks representing the key characters or name cards for student actors to wear around their necks. The actors perform while the other students read the story aloud.

## Predictable Books

Originally used only in preschools and kindergartens but now available for older students as well, predictable books teach readers how to construct meaning from the printed page. The stories contain patterns that help students learn how comprehension is easier when readers make continuous predictions. These stories build fluency, teach about rhyming and word families, and create reading enjoyment. Note: Most big books are also predictable books; however, not all predictable books are big books.

Find any story in which a particular word or phrase is repeated often. *The House That Jack Built, The Three Billy Goats Gruff,* and similar stories lend themselves beautifully to this method. (Ask a librarian or reading specialist to recommend other titles.) Read the story aloud with great expression; stop just before each occurrence of the predictable word or phrase and let the students chant it together. Later, students can learn to recognize the words that represent a repetitive phrase and point them out.

# The Language Experience Method*

## Scenario: Jonathan

Jonathan was a third grader who could barely read at pre-primer level. His teacher, Mrs. Taylor, was extremely frustrated because all her other students were reading at or above third-grade level. Each day, she had to prepare a separate lesson for Jonathan using first-grade materials.

Jonathan was almost 10. He had repeated kindergarten because his teachers thought that he was too immature for first grade; he had repeated first grade because it was obvious that he was not learning to read. Although he was still a nonreader in second grade, that teacher passed him on to Mrs. Taylor, who referred him for evaluation by the special education team.

The team leader advised Mrs. Taylor to abandon the adopted reading program and spend almost all of Jonathan's learning time shoring up his skills in phonics. Since Jonathan was a global learner, and success in phonics requires skill in analytic thinking, this strategy did not work. His attendance became sporadic, and he looked sad and disheveled much of the time.

Then Susan met with Mrs. Taylor. During their meeting, Susan taught Mrs. Taylor how to use the language experience method. Mrs. Taylor agreed to a two-week trial period during which she would replace all her current methods with stories that Jonathan would provide from his own life experiences.

When Susan returned to the school a few weeks later, she poked her head in the doorway of Mrs. Taylor's classroom. Signaling to get Mrs. Taylor's attention, Susan whispered, "How's it going?" In response, Mrs. Taylor yelled, *"Jonathan! She's here! Get the envelope!"*

Jonathan glanced up to recognize Susan, left his desk with a funny smirk on his face, went to a shelf, and took down a huge manila envelope. In the two weeks since his teacher had started using the language experience method, Jonathan had dictated and learned to read three full stories about the beloved animals in his menagerie at home. The manila envelope contained about 20 sentences from three stories, each sentence cut into word pieces fastened together with a paper clip.

Jonathan approached Susan with the envelope, now smiling broadly. Mrs. Taylor said, "Show Mrs. Winebrenner how you read. Just choose any sentence." Jonathan dug his arm up to the elbow into the envelope, came out with one sentence, and said proudly, "This one."

"Let's go over to the table, and you can read it to me there," Susan suggested. She took the sentence from him, removed the paper clip, and turned all of the word pieces upside down on the table.

After mixing them up in a grand gesture, Jonathan chose one word, looked at it, and correctly read, "Was."

"Very nice," Susan said. "Try another."

He chose another word and correctly read, "His."

More than a little intrigued, Susan said, "Keep on going until you can tell me what the sentence says." The third word was *birthday,* and Jonathan immediately recalled the entire sentence that described the birthday of his pet hamster. He then repeated this performance with several other sentences. It was clear that Jonathan was not just saying words he had memorized, but was actually reading. By the time Susan and Jonathan were finished, he was grinning from ear to ear.

"What should we do next?" Mrs. Taylor asked.

"Why tamper with success? Just continue with what you've been doing, and I'll be back in a couple of weeks," said Susan.

During the next two weeks, eager third graders nearly drove Mrs. Taylor crazy volunteering to help Jonathan read his stories. By Susan's next visit, Mrs. Taylor had discovered that an upcoming story about dogs in the third-grade reader contained a lot of words that Jonathan had learned. "What would happen," she mused, "if we just brought him into the third-grade group to read this story?" She decided to give it a try.

Jonathan did quite well with the story and clearly enjoyed being able to work with the same material as his classmates. His self-esteem skyrocketed, since he had succeeded at something that was difficult for him. His physical appearance even improved.

One day, while Jonathan was reading one of his stories to Susan, he stopped suddenly in the middle of a sentence. An incredulous look came over his face and he softly said, "Oh! Now I see!"

"What do you see?" Susan prompted.

"You know all these words on all these papers in all these stories? They're just someone else's stories written down!" he exclaimed with awe.

Jonathan had unraveled the secret of reading. Until then, he had always thought that what his teachers called "reading" was completing workbook pages, preparing book reports, and answering teacher questions. Because he was able to read the stories he had written,

---

*Adapted from Russell G. Stauffer, *The Language Experience Approach to the Teaching of Reading.* New York: HarperCollins, 1980.

he finally understood the thinking-speaking-writing-reading connection that underlies successful reading experiences.

At about this time, the special education team finished its study of Jonathan and concluded that he had severe learning disabilities. The team suggested that he be moved to another class led by a teacher with special education training. Mrs. Taylor believed that this was not the correct placement for him. She met with his parents and explained how much progress Jonathan had been making in the regular classroom and how much his success meant to the rest of the class. She asked them to request a resource assistant to work with Jonathan in her classroom. They agreed, and Jonathan was able to spend most of his learning time with the class that had so lovingly nurtured him into becoming a successful reader.

Could Jonathan learn to read? Absolutely! His problem had resulted from the fact that the skill-based phonics methods that had been used with him in the first and second grades did not work with his global learning modality, which required more holistic methods. As soon as Susan and Mrs. Taylor provided a better match for his learning modality, he was able to become successful in reading—even though he had LD.

## The Language Experience Philosophy

This method has been known for decades. We believe it is effective not only with children who struggle with reading, but also with adults who are seeking literacy. The language experience method can be summed up with three simple affirmations:

- *If I can think about something, I can talk about it.*

- *If I can talk about something, I can write down my ideas.*

- *If I can write down my ideas, I can read what I have written.*

This method is especially useful for children who cannot read well, including those who don't speak English fluently. Obviously, their stories will lack proper syntax and grammar, but the point of this method is *not* to teach correct story construction. Rather, it is to help students understand how the elements that make up the act of reading relate to one another.

## Using the Language Experience Method with One or Two Students

Note for all versions of the language experience method: This activity should be done on paper, as the sentences must be cut apart and then each sentence cut into words. If you have only one or two struggling readers in your classroom, have each student create an individual story.

1. Ask each student to dictate four to six sentences about a subject from the student's personal life: siblings, pets, a favorite TV show, a proud moment, a memorable experience, and so on.

---

If I can think about something, I can talk about it. If I can talk about something, I can write down my ideas. If I can write down my ideas, I can read what I have written.

---

2. Print the sentences *exactly as they are dictated,* errors and all. The language experience method teaches students that reading is simply understanding thoughts that have been written down, and if you don't use students' exact thoughts, you can't lead them to that essential conclusion. Begin each sentence on a new line and space the lines and words generously, since both the sentences and the words will eventually be cut apart.

3. Have students read their sentences to you, pointing to the words and phrases while saying them aloud. If they get stuck on a word, tell them what it is. **Tip:** If students cannot remember what they wrote, use fewer sentences. When they can read the sentences in and out of order, perhaps even forward and backward, you will know that they are recognizing the words.

4. Cut the sentences apart. Spend several days having students read their sentences in and out of the correct order.

5. When students are able to read the sentences easily, cut them into word pieces. Paper-clip the words from each sentence together. Have students choose one sentence at a time. Place all the words for that sentence facedown. Turn over one word at a time for students to read aloud until they can infer the rest of the sentence. Then have them arrange the words in the correct order and read the sentence again. When all the sentences have been assembled, have the students read the entire story. **Tip:** If students turn over the words themselves, they will be more kinesthetically involved in the reading experience.

**6.** As students get to the point of easily recognizing the words out of context, have them create word files using notecards and recipe boxes. Throughout the learning process, they can continue to add words to their word files. You can use these words to teach letter-sound recognition, build vocabulary, teach meaning, and so on. Since these are the students' own words, they will enjoy learning more about them. Flash cards can be made with the word on one side of the card and the definition on the other. For visual learners, the definition can be a picture they have drawn.

*Variation:* Have students underline each word they read correctly when the story is intact. When a word has three lines drawn under it, students make a flash card for that word and add it to their growing recipe box collection.

**7.** When students become proficient with the language experience method, find real stories for them to learn to read. Choose stories that contain many of the words with which they are already familiar.

## Using the Language Experience Method with a Group

If a significant number of your students are reading below grade level, you can adapt the language experience method for group work.

**1.** Provide an in-school experience for the entire class (*examples:* taking a walk around the school grounds, viewing a film, selecting books at the library, or hearing a guest speaker). Giving the students a shared experience is an essential first step. We cannot assume that all children share similar experiences outside of school.

**2.** While the rest of the class is writing and drawing about the shared experience, call your students with reading problems together to create a group story about it. Have each student dictate at least one sentence for the story. Print the sentences *exactly as they are dictated.* Print the students' names at the ends of their sentences.

**3.** Continue by following steps 3 through 7 of "Using the Language Experience Method with One or Two Students," just described, adapting the steps as necessary for group work. Your goal is to have *all* the students in the group learn to read *all* the sentences in the story.

### Variation: Start with Art

Try this version of the language experience method with students who have trouble coming up with ideas for stories and with those who have had limited learning experiences outside of school. It's also a brain-compatible way for visual-global learners to create interesting stories.

**1.** Provide the class with a common experience.

**2.** Afterward, have students create drawings about the experience and arrange them in the proper sequence to make individual or group stories. All students will enjoy this experience, so you may wish to include everyone.

**3.** Once students have completed their drawing stories, have them dictate one or two sentences for each drawing. To include more details in the writing, suggest that students first add more details to their drawings. Better sentences come more easily from this process. Print the sentences *exactly as they are dictated.*

**4.** Continue by following steps 3 through 7 of "Using the Language Experience Method with One or Two Students," just described, adapting the steps as necessary.

# Fluency

Fluency is an essential competency for all readers. Fluent readers apply decoding skills automatically so they can concentrate on getting the meaning of what they are reading. They recognize many words by sight. They constantly make predictions about what's coming up, and they correct themselves if what they are reading is not making sense. They understand how to adjust their reading pace and strategies for different types of reading material.

Without fluency, comprehension is impaired. It is nearly impossible for nonfluent readers to remember the words and ideas they try to read. They are so concerned with pronouncing words correctly that they have little time to think about what the words mean. Furthermore, they are interrupted too often by teachers and peers who help them. Never help struggling readers unless they ask for it. Encourage them to use a trick most fluent adult readers apply automatically: they guess or skip unfamiliar words, coming back to these words later when the meaning of the entire sentence becomes more clear.

Silent fluency is much more important than oral fluency. If kids understand the meaning of what they read, but their reading *aloud* is flawed, do not remediate. The only valid test of reading ability is comprehension.

Believe it or not, some kids can read with increased fluency if they move one arm around in a big circle, ride a stationary bike, or pace while reading. This type of movement is called cross-lateral movement because it crosses the vertical center line of the body. According to research conducted by Jochen Donczik, exercises that cross the midline visually, auditorily, and physically improve reading rates and comprehension in children by activating or reestablishing communication between both sides of the brain. You can read more about this at www.braingym.org/studies.

Even more fascinating: students can often read words if they visualize the words in color, see them on colored paper, or read with the aid of a colored transparency sheet laid right over the words on the page. This phenomenon might be related to scotopic sensitivity. See page 35.

# Power Reading Online (PRO)*

Marie Carbo has adapted the learning modalities model created by Rita and Kenneth Dunn and applied it to reading. In recent years, Carbo has updated her methods in a body of work housed at the National Reading Styles Institute (www.nrsi.com). Her philosophy, however, remains the same as it has always been, since she has been able to document dramatic improvements for struggling readers who use her program. The program philosophy includes these principles:

- Speaking words in sentences with no comprehension is not a productive use of time.

- Comprehension is the key to understanding the written word.

- There is no comprehension without fluency.

These simple principles have allowed Carbo, her staff, and her supporters to create startling improvements in poor readers of all ages.

Formerly, Carbo's method asked teachers to make recordings of their own reading material. The updated method does that work for you and is available for your consideration at the website cited above as Power Reading Online (PRO). This program qualifies for federal funds under Titles I, II, III, V, and VI and is aligned with Common Core State Standards for kindergarten through twelfth grade.

Carbo has evidence of students making two to three years of growth in reading in nine months and will share that data with you when requested. Visit NRSI's website for all the specifics of the program and for access to the research.

Using PRO, students can listen to prerecorded stories at their instructional level. The recordings may be used in your classroom on a variety of digital devices. PRO asks students to first hear the entire story read aloud to them by the computer, then listen to a short segment of a professional recording done by the NRSI. Students listen to each segment two or three times while simultaneously reading the text and tracking the recorded phrases with two fingers of their dominant hand in "scoops" under each recorded phrase. This experience is designed so their exposure to the story

engages their auditory, visual, and tactile-kinesthetic senses simultaneously.

**Tip:** If the story is too long to be read aloud efficiently, have students use this method with only the first five to ten pages of the story. If using a novel, read the first one or two chapters aloud, summarize the rest, and use a story map (see page 103) to give students an idea of what to expect.

Using a laptop that contains a digital voice recorder, have students record themselves reading the beginning one or two paragraphs of the story. At the end of that segment, ask students to say, "This is how I sounded before I used PRO."

Have student then listen to the first recorded segment of the story, such as one provided by PRO staff at pro.nrsi.com. Student can listen to the first recorded segment of the story two or three times while reading along and making scooping motions on the page to correspond to the phrases as they are read on the recording. Then have the student make a second personal recording showing how the student sounds after listening to the taped segment.

Repeat the same process for personal recordings number three and four. After listening to all four personal recordings, including the first one made while reading the text cold, students will be able to hear how fluent they sound after listening to the professional recording one, two, and three times. Help students notice the improvements, if they are unable to do that themselves.

Based on the results, decide with the students how many repetitions they should listen to for the next section of text.

It isn't necessary to repeat this process with every student or every story. Once should be enough to motivate students to use PRO—including the repeated listenings—without much further prodding on your part.

## Learning Vocabulary with PRO

**1.** For low-interest selections, teach the vocabulary and skills in more interesting contexts. As long as vocabulary and skills are taken care of, it is not necessary for all students to actually read all selections in a unit.

**2.** Do not teach vocabulary words directly before students hear or read the story. Remember that global learners learn best in meaningful contexts. (See Chapter 3 for more information on this.) Being expected to learn the vocabulary outside the story context just doesn't work for this type of learner. As students read parts of the story, just supply the pronunciation and meaning of the words as they come up. After students have read a section fluently, have them learn the vocabulary from that section using the "Vocabulary Attributes Chart" from page 133 in this chapter.

---

*Adapted with permission from a personal interview with Dr. Marie Carbo, Chicago, IL 2013.

**3.** After covering points 1 and 2 with all the struggling readers, they are ready to discuss the story in a group, do the vocabulary work in a visual-kinesthetic method such as the Vocabulary Attributes Chart, and discuss the story elements using both lower- and higher-level thinking questions.

**4.** Repeat these steps until the entire story has been read and discussed.

## Essential Questions

Asking consistent and predictable questions about a story can strengthen the comprehension skills of your emerging readers. When you limit the number of questions you ask to those that are essential for understanding the material, students learn to prompt themselves with each new selection. These are the questions we suggest using with fictional text:

- *What was the basic problem that the character(s) had to solve?*

- *How did the character(s) solve that problem?*

- *How might you have solved the problem, if you had been in the same situation? Give details.*

You may use your own questions, but keep them brief and consistent. To make the information more accessible to visual learners, create a simplified version (with fewer shapes) of the story map on page 129.

**1.** For the first several stories, ask only the first question. *(What was the basic problem?)* Have reading buddies talk about the story until they can identify the basic problem. Call the class back together to discuss the problem. Use the Name Card Method (pages 12–14) to call on students for the discussion.

**2.** After students have mastered the identification and description of the basic problem, add the second question for subsequent stories. Have reading buddies address both questions. *(What was the problem? What was the solution?)* When the large group convenes, expect all students to have answers to both questions.

**3.** Once students are comfortable with the first two questions, add the third question. *(What would you have done to solve the problem?)*

In this way, students learn to approach each new story with the same questions. They automatically engage in comprehension activities while they are reading. Once students are adept at using the three essential questions, you can add other questions about the basic elements of fiction, such as setting, characters, plot, and action. Add them slowly, one at a time.

Try these essential questions for nonfiction:

- *What is the main topic of the selection?*

- *What major problem is being experienced by those involved?*

- *What causes of the problem are explained?*

- *What has been done already to solve the problem?*

- *What have been the effects of any action taken so far?*

- *What might you suggest as a more effective solution to the problem?*

- *What might be the author's purpose in writing the selection?*

## Scenario: Carlos

Carlos was a fifth grader with a negative attitude about reading—understandably, because his reading skills were very poor. It was painful to listen to him try to read aloud. He often hesitated, confused words, and started phrases and sentences over. His heavily furrowed brow indicated how hard he was working and how frustrated he felt.

Carlos was going to a special reading teacher every day. His teacher, Ms. Abbrogado, had learned about PRO and was using it with kids like Carlos to improve their fluency and comprehension. She had provided all the students with access to a digital recording device they could use to record how fluently they were reading before and after they listened to the PRO recording.

Shortly after Thanksgiving, Carlos told Mrs. Abbrogado he wanted to take home his personal recording.

"Why do you need this recording at home?"

"Because," Carlos replied with a little grin on his face, "I want to give it to my grandma for Christmas!"

Carlos had finally developed some self-respect regarding his reading ability. He was even ready to share his reading with his beloved grandma.

## Buddy Reading

Buddy reading, rehearsed reading, and choral reading are all highly effective techniques for teaching oral reading. Try any and all of them, or invent more of your own. Do whatever you can to communicate that reading aloud can be enjoyable for both the reader and the listener.

**1.** Give students an overview of the story or book they will be reading.

**2.** Read the entire story (or first chapter) aloud to the kids who need to hear it before reading it.

3. Before any discussion, questions, or vocabulary, pair struggling readers with more competent readers, but *never with the very best readers.* That type of pairing is not effective for either partner.

4. Assign each pair a small portion of the text to read aloud with their buddies. Guide them to divide the section fairly so each reads about an equal amount. Explain that when they are finished reading, they should talk to each other about what they think the main character's problem is. Or assign one or more of the other questions under "Essential Questions." (See page 99.)

5. Be sure to provide group discussion time frequently. If the whole class is reading the same story or novel, use the Name Card Method (pages 12–14) to ensure that all students are fully involved in the discussion.

6. Repeat steps 4 and 5 until the selection is completed. *Do not* ask struggling readers to read aloud to the entire class. This round-robin method is rarely effective and is often painful for both the exceptionally capable readers and those who find reading extremely difficult.

Buddy reading is also a helpful strategy for families to use when reading aloud at home, so offer to teach it to interested family members.

## Rehearsed Reading*

You can use this method to replace ineffective round-robin reading in both the literature and content areas.

1. Instead of calling on students at random to read aloud, assign each student a specific passage a day in advance.

2. Give students time to rehearse their passages, either alone or with a reading buddy. Be available to coach students in how to read with good volume and expression. Assign the practice experience as homework if someone at home is available to help.

3. When readers are ready, move them into higher thinking levels. Tell students they should also prepare one question to ask the class about their assigned section. Give each student a copy of the "Question Starters" handout (page 126), circling or underlining ahead of time the prompts you want them to use for a particular story.

**Tip:** For added interest, have students ask their questions before beginning their oral readings as well as at the end. Knowing what question they will eventually have to answer boosts the audience's interest and attention levels. A more alert audience makes the reader feel more valued and more intelligent.

4. On the following day, have students read their rehearsed passages aloud to the group, one at a time. While each student is reading, the others should have their books closed, using a finger or bookmark to hold their place. This allows the reader to make minor substitutions or changes without the whole group pouncing to point out errors.

**Tip:** Some highly visual learners won't be able to listen effectively without looking at the text. Allow those kids to keep their books open, but make them promise not to "help" the person who is doing the reading.

5. Allow time at the end of each reading for questions and responses.

## Choral Reading

Choral reading is an enjoyable way for students to improve fluency and learn to add expression to their oral reading. Certain texts include selections designed for choral reading; many readings in your regular curriculum may be adapted for this purpose. Type *choral reading* into an Internet search engine to find numerous selections.

1. Model reading an appropriate selection aloud with expression. Demonstrate proper phrasing, tempo, enunciation, rhythm, and volume.

2. Have students follow your example as you direct them. Point out any visual cues indicating how particular lines and words should be read. (*Examples:* Sections written in capital letters are usually read in unison, although the entire piece may be chanted that way. Larger or bold print means louder voices.)

3. As students become more capable choral readers, assign small parts to individual students, rows, boys, girls, and so on. It's also fun to add more voices with each line.

4. Add hand and body movements after the text is perfected.

5. Have students practice and polish a collection of readings and perform them for other classes or at times when families are visiting the class.

After kids have had some experience reading fun pieces, have them use choral reading for oral reading times. Teams can chorally read dialogue or take turns with paragraphs. Use your imagination—and use choral reading often.

Poetry lends itself well to choral reading. Try the following selection with your students and see how they like it.

---

*Vacca, Richard, and JoAnne Vacca. *Content Area Reading.* 10th edition. Glenview, IL: HarperCollins College Publishers, 2007. Used with permission of HarperCollins Publishers.

**The Kids at Our School***

We're the kids at *[insert school name]* School
We think we're great.
We think we're cool.
Our teacher's number one BIG RULE is:
"TRY AS HARD AS YOU CAN!"
We learn to follow our own school rules,
We read and write and calculate, too.
Our parents ask us each day, "Will you
TRY AS HARD AS YOU CAN?"
We try to please in every way,
To be real good at work and play!
'Cause we love to hear *[insert teacher's name]* say,
"THEY TRY AS HARD AS THEY CAN!"

---

### Tech Tip 🖥

Audio or digital books that read themselves aloud can be a huge help to students who struggle with a reading disability such as dyslexia. Excellent sources include www.nrsi.com, where all the information you seek about PRO may be found. Other sources for recorded books are www.learningally.org and www.bookshare.org.

---

# Improving Comprehension

Comprehension is the ability to understand what one reads. It can be aided by many techniques, some of which are described in this section.

Comprehension depends on the reader being able to connect what is read to prior knowledge and predict upcoming events. Prediction creates a purpose for reading, and students enjoy seeing how accurately they can foresee what will happen next in a story. Use story maps (see page 103) to help visual and tactile-kinesthetic learners see the big picture.

## Story Detectives

1. Make a copy of the "Predictions" handout (page 127) and use it to prepare a list of predictions for a story you plan to read. You will be asking students to respond to your predictions based on what they learn from the title, chapter titles, or pictures. Some of your predictions should be accurate, others highly improbable, and others somewhere in between.

2. Divide the class into small groups.

3. Have students read the title of the story and, based on the title, predict what events might occur. Or have the students browse through the story and make predictions based on the chapter titles or pictures.

4. Give each student or group a copy of the predictions you completed in step 1. Have the students respond to each prediction by checking "Yes" (they think the event will happen), "No" (they don't think it will happen), or "Maybe" (they think it might happen). Tell the students to be prepared to give reasons for their choices.

5. Get feedback from all groups and tally responses using a whiteboard or wall chart.

6. Keep the predictions on display as the story is read. Check regularly to see how accurate the predictions were.

## KWPL**

This method, originally labeled KWL by Donna Ogle, was expanded by Susan in the first edition of this book. The KWPL strategy is immensely successful in helping students with LD become actively engaged in all the steps of the three components of effective reading instruction described on pages 93–94 of this chapter.

The acronym KWPL stands for the following ideas:

- K: what we already **Know**
- W: what we **Want** to know
- P: what we **Predict** we will learn
- L: what we have **Learned**

Three of the four components—K, W, and P—are experienced before students actually read any text of a story or see any visual of a film or similar product. L is experienced after the information has been learned; it helps students summarize the big ideas from the lesson.

This easy-to-use method motivates students to read because it helps them understand the meaning of what they have read. It can be used for a reading selection—and also for any social studies, science, or thematic unit introduction—with a high degree of success. The Name Card Method (pages 12–14) is very effective when used with KWPL.

1. Draw four columns on the whiteboard or on a large piece of paper to use as the group chart. Give each column a heading, as shown on the "KWPL" handout (see page 128). Leave plenty of room for writing beneath

---

*Adapted from the work of Sue Rebholz, Shorewood, Wisconsin. Used with permission.

**Engaging in the Language Arts: Exploring the Power of Language* (2nd Edition) by Donna Ogle and James W. Beers, 2011. A valuable Web page is found at www.readingrockets.org. Type in *reciprocal teaching*; a video demonstration is also offered.

each heading. Be sure to emphasize the *K* in *Know*, the *W* in *Want*, the *P* in *Predict*, and the *L* in *Learned*, as shown. *Important:* Complete steps 2 through 4 *before* having students read the selection.

**2.** Give students their own desk copies of the "KWPL" handout. Have students work with partners to brainstorm all they KNOW about the designated topic. Use the Name Card Method to get responses to write in the "What We Already Know" column on the group chart.

**3.** Have students work with partners to decide what they WANT to know about the topic. Use the Name Card Method to list their questions in the "What We Want to Know" column on the group chart.

Include questions that may arise from disagreements about "What We Already Know." (*Example:* If the topic is alligators, one student might say, "An alligator has a very long snout," and another student might protest, "No, that's not an alligator, that's a crocodile." At this point, that topic becomes a question and moves into the "What We Want to Know" column, rewritten as a question: "Do alligators have long snouts?")

**4.** Have students use their own charts to PREDICT the answers to their "What We Want to Know" questions. It's okay if partners have different predictions. Use the Name Card Method to include their predictions in the "What We Predict We Will Learn" column on the group chart.

**5.** Have the students read the selection. During the reading, students check the accuracy of their individual predictions. They can use a plus sign (+) to indicate an accurate prediction and a minus sign (–) to indicate an inaccurate prediction. In this way, students become emotionally involved in what happens in the selection.

**6.** Discuss the reading. Then ask the student partners to write what they have LEARNED in the "What We Have Learned" column on their charts. Use the Name Card Method to complete that column on the group chart.

**7.** Discuss all four columns of the chart.

After students have experienced this process several times under your direction, they might enjoy working with partners on the same activity with a different selection, without using the group chart. Have more copies of the "KWPL" chart available.

## More Prediction Ideas to Try

**1.** If a story has pictures, have students page all the way through it, making predictions about the events, the main problem, the crisis, and the resolution. Several times during your reading of the story, stop, have the students close their books, and ask them to make predictions about what's going to happen next.

**2.** After students read a story (or you read it to them), have them close their books. Read the story again, leaving out words here and there. Have students predict and say the missing words. To turn this into a written exercise, copy a selection from the story, covering certain words. Write a list of possible word choices at the bottom of the page and have students fill in the blanks from the list of choices.

**3.** Some students enjoy writing their predictions and checking their accuracy as a story progresses. After students start reading a story, have them stop from time to time to predict the following:

- upcoming events
- the next word in a sentence
- a repeatable refrain (see "Predictable Books," page 94)
- how the story will end
- what might happen if a character chooses a different course of action

**4.** After completing a story, invite students to imagine:

- what happens after the story ends
- what would have happened if a character had chosen a different course of action
- how a character from this story might behave in a different story

**5.** Discuss how clues in a story lead to solutions and sometimes surprise endings. Have students reread a story a second time and locate those foreshadowing clues.

## Question-Answer-Response

The question-answer-response (QAR) strategy helps students understand how questions are raised in both fictional and informational texts. With this understanding, kids can better answer questions, learn to form their own questions, and practice metacognition to improve their reading comprehension.

This is accomplished through the following steps:

**1.** Students are taught that there are two categories of questions. "In-the-book" questions are text-explicit. "In-your-head" questions are text-implicit.

An in-the-book question is either a "right-there" question, with the answer found in one location, or a "search-and-find" question, with the information needed to form an answer found in multiple locations of the text. An in-your-head question is either an "author-and-you" question, which makes the reader predict or infer information about the characters or events, or an "on-my-own" question, which makes readers retrieve information from their background knowledge. Students who don't have these skills often find comprehension extremely difficult.

2. The teacher does a "think-aloud" with the class. The teacher models reading a selection and questions, and sorting the questions into their categories. As the questions are read, students and teacher work together to assign each question to its correct category. The teacher thinks out loud to help students understand the process. Questions are answered as they are discussed.

3. The teacher then gives pairs of students another short story to read with questions included. The pairs work together to assign the questions to the correct categories.

4. Pairs of students then repeat the process described in step 3.

5. When the teacher thinks the students are ready, they read a selection alone. They write their own questions in all four subcategories for their peers to answer.

# Visual Organizers

For global thinkers, visual organizers or graphic organizers are a brain-compatible way of improving integrated language arts skills. Story maps and character maps help them get the big picture of the selection. "Fishbone" diagrams organize details and events to help students write summaries, spider maps organize several main ideas and supporting details, and sequence charts put main events in order. Compare-and-contrast circles clarify similarities and differences within categories of information. Cause-and-effect diagrams clarify cause-and-effect thinking for students. This section describes many strategies regarding the use of visual organizers. There are many resources for finding and using these organizers, some of which are listed in the "Reference and Resources" on page 254.

## Story Maps and Character Maps

The more closely a story fits an expected, familiar structure, the easier it is for readers to grasp and remember the most important ideas. Before discussing the elements of a story, chart them on a story map; see the "Story Map" handout on page 129 for an example. Add spokes to the various shapes on the handout and use the Name Card Method (pages 12–14) to invite students to contribute details about each element.

Character maps are another way to visually organize important information about a story. Use a separate character map for each major character; see the "Character Map" handout on page 130 for an example. Add spokes and have students contribute the details

during a class discussion, again using the Name Card Method.

Once you have modeled the use of both handouts, students might enjoy working with partners to complete story maps and character maps for stories they read. Copy the handouts and distribute them to the students.

## The "Handy" Story Map*

This variation on the story map is perfect for younger kids. Give them blank sheets of paper and have them trace around one of their hands (fingers spread, palm down). Then have them fill in their "handy" maps with the following information about a story you have just read:

- thumb: story title
- index finger: setting
- middle finger: main character
- ring finger: main character's major problem
- pinkie: main character's major action to resolve the problem

## Compare-and-Contrast Circles

Two simple circles can be used to illustrate similarities and differences within categories of information.

1. Draw two large intersecting circles on the board and begin a class discussion, or have students draw their own circles and work independently.

2. List attributes of one element in the left section, attributes of another element in the right section, and attributes both elements share in the overlapping section (*examples:* characters in a story, characters' behaviors, events or experiences).

*Brenda Goffen, consultant in special education, Highland Park, Illinois.

**3.** To identify similarities, refer to the information in the overlapping section. To identify differences, refer to the information in the right and left sections.

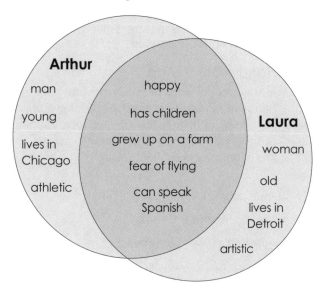

## Using a Story's Illustrations

Visual learners enjoy approaching a story's content by way of its illustrations. Try this strategy with your global thinkers and those who are artistically inclined. Have students:

1. Describe what they actually see in an illustration.

2. Predict what might happen next in the section, based on the illustration.

3. Find the similarities and differences among illustrations.

4. Study illustrations of the same story by different artists. Compare and contrast the different artists' illustrations.

5. Decide which illustration best captures the essential meaning of the selection.

6. Identify and explain any illustration that seems not to match the text it is supposed to illustrate.

7. Find other events that should have been illustrated, and create the illustrations.

8. Completely re-create all the story's illustrations in another style, or create illustrations for a story or document that currently has none.

## Creative Dramatics

An ideal comprehension tool for tactile-kinesthetic learners, creative dramatics is often overlooked because some teachers feel uncomfortable about using this technique. I encourage you to try a few of the following suggestions, just to see how they work with your students. You will probably find that the benefits outweigh your doubts or discomfort.

- Some kids have problems articulating their thoughts. An invitation to "show us what you are trying to say" may lead to a better description. Have students act out scenes from their lives that are related to the story characters' experiences. (*Example:* If the characters are dealing with an aging grandparent, students can act out short skits about their own problems with older relatives.) When students connect their reading with personal experiences, their reading becomes more meaningful and memorable.

- Have students dramatize story events; predict and act out upcoming events; act out vocabulary words; or portray specific characters. Older students can work in groups to demonstrate ways in which a character changes during a story.

- Have one student play the role of a major character in the story. The other students ask questions, and the character answers in the first person. It's easy to move students into interpretive levels of thinking when they start asking questions about how a character feels or demand that judgments be made.

Kids who become adept at dramatization can actually create plays from story material. They often enjoy video recording the results to show the folks at home or students in other classes.

### Variation: Readers' Theater

Some teachers find the readers' theater method more comfortable than creative dramatics. It's also very easy to implement.

Students read a story aloud as if it were a play. Each student takes a part; one part is always the narrator. Eliminate all the *he said*s and *she said*s. Students can use the rehearsed reading technique (page 100) to prepare their part before reading it to an audience. For more information about readers' theater, see "References and Resources."

## Summarizing

Use a fishbone graphic to teach summarizing skills. Write it on the board or create a simple handout. Students complete the fishbones by identifying the main topic of the selection and by finding and filling in answers to the categories *who, what, when, where, why,* and *how.* Afterward, students use that information to write a summary statement.

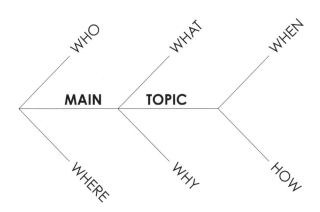

## Sequencing

Arranging story events in their proper order requires logical, analytical, and sequential thinking, which makes it a frustrating task for global thinkers. Begin teaching sequencing by having kids relate a series of action steps for some activity they know well (*examples:* getting dressed for school, tying their shoes, or making a peanut butter and jelly sandwich). Students can draw the events themselves or describe them as someone else writes them down, taking care to deliver them in the correct order. If the order is incorrect, have the students who drew or spoke the steps cut apart their pictures or sentences and rearrange them in proper order. Once students have learned the concept of sequencing from this activity, you can apply it to a story.

Following is a proven way to teach global thinkers how to sequence events in a story or those related to a historical era.

1. Have reading buddies list the events of a story on writing paper in no particular order. They should begin each event on a new line and leave spaces between. Model how to tell when a new event is being described by thinking out loud.

2. Have the students cut apart the event statements, then arrange them in their proper sequence by moving them around.

3. When the events are in their proper sequence, have the students number them and tape them to a larger sheet of paper, in order.

4. The students can now write the story or read it aloud in its proper sequence.

Note: Several websites can help kids with their drawing by providing samples kids can follow. Several apps do the same thing. Absolute Board and wSketch are helpful apps for learning basic drawing skills and are free for both Apple and Android operating systems.

## Variation: Comic Strips

1. Find a fairly long comic strip the student understands and enjoys (*examples:* a brief story from a comic book or a strip from the Sunday comics). Read it with the student.

2. Number each segment, then cut the segments apart and mix them together.

3. Have the student arrange the segments in the proper sequence by following the numbers. Mix and repeat several times.

4. When the student is capable of sequencing the segments independently, find a new strip, read it together, and cut it apart *without* first numbering the segments. Help the student reassemble the segments, then mix them together and have the student reassemble them without help. Repeat several times.

5. Practice with several more strips over time until the student understands this process and can complete it independently.

6. Demonstrate how students can do this with stories they read by drawing their own pictures and arranging them in their proper sequence.

Several comic strip websites are described in the "References and Resources" on pages 254–255. Some other helpful websites for working with comic strips are:

- www.makebeliefscomix.com
- www.readwritethink.org/files/resources /interactives/comic
- comicsintheclassroom.net

## Variation: Storyboards

Divide a large sheet of paper into several sections. Show students how to draw or write story events in each section in sequence. Let tactile-kinesthetic learners draw pictures on separate sheets of paper and physically rearrange them in the proper sequence. Storyboarding has gone digital. You can find several helpful websites if you search the term *storyboarding for kids*.

- www.storyboardthat.com
- kidsvid.4teachers.org

## Reciprocal Teaching*

Reciprocal teaching is an instructional procedure designed to enhance students' comprehension of text.

---

*The "Reciprocal Teaching" section is adapted from a manual regarding Reciprocal Teaching prepared by A. S. Palincsar, Y. David, and A. L. Brown. Used with permission of Annemarie Sullivan Palincsar.

The procedure is best characterized as a dialogue between teacher and students. The dialogue is built on four strategies: summarizing, question generating, clarifying, and predicting. The teacher and students take turns assuming the role of teacher in leading this dialogue. The term *reciprocal* describes the nature of the interactions, since one person acts in response to the other.

## Reciprocal Teaching Purpose and Components

The purpose of reciprocal teaching is to facilitate a group effort between teacher and students, as well as among students, in bringing meaning to the text. This method not only promotes comprehension, but also provides opportunities for students to monitor the effectiveness of their own thinking in getting the meaning of the text. As students become more skilled in these activities, they are experiencing metacognition (see page 65). Instruction that is conducted for the purpose of increasing students' awareness and regulation of their own activity is referred to as metacognitive instruction.

- **Summarizing** provides the opportunity to identify, paraphrase, and integrate important information in the text. Text can be summarized across sentences, across paragraphs, and across the passage as a whole. When the students first begin the reciprocal teaching procedure, their efforts are generally focused at the paragraph level. As they become more proficient, they are able to summarize larger portions of text. (Note: The fishbone diagram on page 105 can help with this component.)

- **Question generating** reinforces the summarizing strategy and carries the learner one step deeper into comprehension. When students generate questions, they first identify the kind of information that is significant enough that it could provide the substance for a question. Then they pose this information in a question form and self-test to ascertain that they can indeed answer their own question. Question generating is a flexible strategy, because students can be taught and encouraged to generate questions at many levels. For example, some school situations require students to master supporting detail information; others require students to infer from text or apply information from text to new problems or situations. (Note: The "Question Starters" handout on page 126 and the ThinkTrix critical thinking model on pages 69–71 can help with this component.)

- **Clarifying** is particularly important for students who may believe that the purpose of reading is saying the words correctly and who may not be

uncomfortable that the words are not making sense. When students learn to clarify, their attention is called to the many reasons why text can be difficult to understand, such as new vocabulary, unclear referent words, and unfamiliar or difficult concepts. They learn to be alert to the effects of such impediments to understanding and to take steps to restore meaning: reread, read ahead, and ask for help. (Note: The visual organizers on pages 103–105 of this chapter can help with clarifying.)

- **Predicting** requires students to hypothesize about what the author might discuss next in the text. In order to do this successfully, students must activate their relevant background knowledge on the topic. The students then have a purpose for reading: to confirm or disprove their hypotheses. Furthermore, students get the opportunity to link the new knowledge they will encounter in the text with the knowledge they already possess. The predicting strategy also facilitates use of text structure as students learn that headings, subheadings, and questions imbedded in the text are useful means of anticipating what might occur next. (Note: The "Predictions" handout on page 127 can help with this component.)

Each of these strategies is a means of helping students construct meaning from text and monitor their reading to ensure that they are, in fact, understanding what they read.

While the eventual goal is flexible use of the strategies, in reciprocal teaching they are typically used as follows: The discussion leader generates questions to which the group responds. Additional questions are raised by other members of the group. The leader then summarizes the text and asks others if they would like to elaborate upon or revise the summary. Any clarifications are discussed. Finally, in preparation for moving on to the next portion of text, the group generates predictions. Eventually, students rotate to other roles.

Reciprocal teaching was first developed by Annemarie Sullivan Palincsar and Anne L. Brown in 1987 as a strategy to help students bridge the gap between decoding and comprehension skills.* The target students are those who possess grade-level skills in letter-sound correspondence (sounding out words and chunking), but cannot construct meaning from the texts. Reciprocal teaching is an instructional activity in the form of a dialogue between teachers and students regarding segments of text. For that reason, it works

---

*(Palincsar, A. S., Brown, A. L. & Martin, S. (1987). Peer interaction in reading comprehension instruction. *Educational Psychologist, 22* (3 & 4), 231–253.

**Tech Tip** 🖥

The Reading Rockets website has a form called "Reciprocal Teaching Worksheet" you may wish to use to help students follow the assigned roles. Visit www.readingrockets.org.

best with small groups of students. This method has consistently received praise for its ability to improve students' comprehension of both fictional and informational texts.

Before you begin using reciprocal teaching in your classroom, you should introduce the four comprehension strategies—summarizing, question generating, clarifying, and predicting—individually to your students. You may use picture books or mentor texts, which are sample texts used to teach specific concepts, to introduce the parts of reciprocal teaching before using them in actual reading selections. After each of the strategies has been taught individually, you should start using all four together as quickly as possible. Too much precious learning time will be wasted if you attempt to teach each individual strategy to mastery before incorporating all of them through reciprocal teaching. Each strategy can be strengthened through mini-lessons as needed throughout the reciprocal teaching process.

Several Internet resources can help you practice this method with your students. Very helpful is one on reciprocal teaching at www.readingrockets.com. When you type in the term *reciprocal teaching*, a very clear summary of how to use the method is shown. There is also a link to a sample video lesson.

Many motivating ideas are available to support reciprocal teaching. For small groups of very young students, we recommend teaching students about the Fabulous Four characters Sammy Summarizer, Quincy Questioner, Clara Clarifier, and Paula Predictor suggested by Palincsar, David, and Brown. These comic book–type heroes show students how to defeat negative emotions they might feel by following the superheroes' examples. The website www.primaryconcepts.com (search for *comprehension puppets*) gives ideas for using puppets of the Fabulous Four. You can also find YouTube demonstrations of using this model—even some with kindergarten kids.

## Scenario: Mrs. Wu and Charlotte's Web

Mrs. Wu began the study of a novel by giving copies of E. B. White's *Charlotte's Web* to her students. She told them they would have 10 minutes to work with their reading partners to survey the entire book and write

down a few predictions, as time allowed. Next, she asked them to go back and survey only the first chapter. Their task was to write some predictions together about what might happen in this chapter. They were also to write a few guesses about the characters described in that chapter. She reassured them that no one else would see what they had written, so they shouldn't worry about the spelling. She also told them that she would use the Name Card Method to call on them to share what they had found. (See pages 12–14.)

Once Mrs. Wu received the students' predictions and recorded them so that they would be viewable throughout the chapter, she explained that they were going to use four strategies throughout their reading—summarizing, question generating, clarifying, and predicting—to understand the story. Mrs. Wu then asked, "How have we already used prediction today?" The students demonstrated that they understood it was on the prediction chart.

Mrs. Wu told the students, "As I read the first two pages aloud, please listen with your eyes closed and make a movie in your head that shows you what I am reading about. Please notice the images that come to your mind as I read this passage to you. As I read, please notice the answers to these questions, which we will discuss when I am done reading." She then announced the following questions: *What does the word* runt *mean?* (question generating, clarifying) and *Why did Fern's father have an ax?* (predicting, question generating). She posted the questions visually as she read them, and they remained visible as she was reading.

Mrs. Wu then prepared the students to listen to a second reading of the same text section. She said, "Please read along as I read aloud." She asked the class, "Which words or phrases helped you 'see' the passage?" Mrs. Wu continued, asking the following questions: *What is the story about?* (summarizing, question generating) *What do we know about Fern?* (summarizing, clarifying, predicting) *What are the clues that told us this?* (question generating, predicting) *What is the main idea of this section?* (summarizing, clarifying) *What do you think the next section will be about?* (predicting)

Mrs. Wu then read the next section of text aloud and asked more questions requiring students to summarize, question, clarify, and predict. After following this procedure for a few days, she chose five "teachers." She assigned one section to each "teacher" and told the teachers what days they would be teaching the class, so they could read and prepare questions for their sections in advance. The first teacher was Alma. Since Mrs. Wu had explicitly modeled reciprocal teaching repeated times, Alma knew exactly how to proceed. Students led the reciprocal teaching for the remainder of the text.

After reading the entire novel, the class took a reading comprehension assessment prepared by Mrs. Wu. Her students showed a high degree of mastery in summarizing, question generating, clarifying, and predicting and were better able to transfer the use of those behaviors to subsequent stories in literature.

# Literature-Based Reading

All the strategies described in this chapter work with real literature as well as with leveled reading materials. Some teachers use real literature for their entire reading program. Of course, if you do this, you will need to make absolutely certain that you include in your program all the assigned literacy standards for your grade level.

1. Whatever model or method you use, set aside at least 30 minutes per day for reading students' choice of literature or nonfiction texts. Don't call it "free reading" or "recreational reading." This implies that this reading time is not as valuable as time allotted for reading instruction. (Susan always used the term *reading choice time* with her students.) Always remember that the purpose of *all* reading instruction is to empower students to one day read anything they choose. In some classrooms, kids spend less than seven minutes during a typical reading period actually reading. How would you like it if someone nabbed your book, magazine, or newspaper after seven minutes and made you do skill work?

2. Help your students choose slightly challenging books by applying the three-finger rule. After they select a book they think they would like to read, they open it to a page somewhere in the middle—preferably one with few or no pictures. Then they read the page, holding up one finger each time they come to a word they can't read or understand. If by the end of the page they are holding up three (or more) fingers, the book is probably too difficult for independent reading, and they should make another selection. However, they may look at the book for other reasons.

3. Do away with any rule that forbids students to select books they have already read or books that are too easy for them. Adults frequently do both.

4. Before giving reluctant readers a story to read, tell them the story. This gives them a big picture to keep in mind as they read. Or read the story aloud until students know enough about it to pique their interest. Let them read independently from that point on.

5. Consider showing a video version of a story before and after your students read it. Later, have students compare and contrast the book and film. Allow analytic readers to choose not to see the film before they read the story themselves.

6. Avoid written book reports. Nothing is more likely to extinguish a growing flame of positive attitudes toward reading than a required written book report. All the language arts and writing objectives practiced in book reports can be experienced easily in other types of lessons.

7. Set aside a regular time for students to share books they are reading informally, even books they haven't finished. Don't adults do that all the time? Have you ever had a friend refuse to hear you talk about a book because you hadn't finished reading it yet?

8. One teacher begins each class session with an activity called "Let's Talk About Books." Students pair up to talk about the books they are reading or to read aloud a favorite passage. The teacher also works with a student partner, giving him or her some uninterrupted time together. All her students are more motivated to read.

9. Give each student a copy of the "Books I Want to Read" chart (page 131). Explain that the students should take out this chart whenever their peers share information about books they are reading. If students hear about books they might want to read, they list the books on their charts. When they visit the library, they carry their charts with them. Then they can select books independently without asking the question many librarians dread: *Do you have any good books?*

## How to Lead Group Discussions of Novels

Do whatever it takes to make class discussions about books challenging, engaging, intelligent, and meaningful. Teachers who have been trained in Socratic questioning, seminar leadership, or the Great Books program know how to pose challenging questions, probe for students' reasoning, direct students to find evidence for their opinions and conclusions, and keep discussions open by continuously asking questions rather than judging the rightness or wrongness of student responses. For another helpful model of higher-level thinking, see "ThinkTrix" (pages 69–71).

1. Start each discussion by having students summarize the novel so far and describe the part they have just finished reading.

2. Have them analyze and critique the characters' actions and decisions up to this point.

3. Have them predict events and actions that may happen in upcoming chapters. They should give reasons for their predictions.

4. Whenever possible, facilitate students' personal involvement in the novel. Structure debates where they take sides and argue a particular character's point of view. Then have them switch roles and take the opposite viewpoint. Or invite students to discuss the similarities and differences between their lives and the characters' lives. Call only on volunteers for this activity. Students should not have to share information about their private lives unless they choose to share it.

## Including Students with LD in Group Study of Novels or Literature Circles

In literature circles, small groups of students work together to understand and appreciate novels. Literature circles are an excellent way to meet the diverse needs of your students based on their ability levels and interests. Many Internet resources describe this method in detail, including:

- www.lauracandler.com
- www.proteacher.org

Because students with learning difficulties are usually thrilled to be fully engaged in reading full-length novels with a group, this is a highly motivating experience to include in their reading program.

Students' reading fluency, comprehension level, and interests can all be used to determine appropriate groupings for the students. First, use formative assessments to create groups based on academic levels. Then, divide students into subgroups according to results of interest inventories. Make accommodations to scaffold the students' areas of need so they can achieve success.

Students' learning in a literature circle is ongoing throughout the entire reading of the novel. Students must interact with the text and their peers throughout the book study to develop critical reading skills. Many rubrics are available in your district or online to help with this formative assessment throughout the entire process, such as:

- www.rcampus.com
- www.scholastic.com/teachers/lesson-plan/literature-circles-action

### Making Reading More Pleasant for Students with LD

You can differentiate the books that students read in their literature circles by using Developmental Reading Assessments (DRA). The DRA, published by Pearson, is a standardized reading test that determines a student's instructional level in reading. You or a reading specialist should administer the DRA individually to students. Students read designated sections aloud and then tell the examiner what they have read. Sections are available on many different levels of difficulty. Use DRA results, along with results from other appropriate assessments, to determine whether students are reading on, above, or below grade level.

By knowing student DRA levels, you can plan literature circles that include targeted interventions and support. Select materials to match students' instructional levels and provide appropriate instruction to challenge them. Ongoing teacher observations assure that the students comprehend what they are reading and are in the appropriate reading group.

### Helpful Accommodations for Students with Learning Difficulties

Some accommodations used for students with LD include:

- students who serve as writing scribes
- speech-to-text software such as Dragon NaturallySpeaking
- recorded books (www.nrsi.com)
- self-stick notes, highlighters, and bookmarks to draw students' attention to specific locations in the text
- story maps and other graphic organizers
- extended time to complete tasks in a supportive environment, such as intervention blocks in an RTI model

## Using a Reading Response Journal

Students who have a positive attitude about writing might enjoy keeping a journal about a book they are reading. A reading response journal is an excellent way to help students apply critical thinking to what they are reading. Students might write in their journals at the end of each reading session or during the reading process when their ideas are still fresh.

**Tips:** Don't require a written response every day. Even for students who like to write, this can quickly become an unpleasant chore. Remember that spelling accuracy and writing mechanics are not important in journal writing. Keep the focus on thoughtful reflection.

1. Give each student several copies of the "Reading Response Journal" handout (page 132). Explain that students may use several lines to respond to a particular event.

2. Some students appreciate topic suggestions, preferring those to the open-ended instruction *write about whatever you want*. You might design visual cues for specific types of responses.* Create handouts featuring each visual cue. Here are some examples:

- Write about what you see happening in the selection you will be reading today. When you finish reading, comment on the accuracy of your predictions.

- Write what you are thinking about the characters and events.

- Write about how what you are reading reminds you of your own experiences.

- Tell about something from a character's point of view.

- Write a letter to one of the characters. Tell what you like about the character, respond to something the character has done, and offer a suggestion about something the character might do differently.

- Write down your questions about things in the story you don't understand. Be prepared to ask these questions in class or discuss them with your teacher during conference.

- Make predictions about what you think will happen next in the story.

# Effective Guided and Independent Practice

Traditional use of consumables (workbooks and so on) is being discouraged in today's classrooms due to their high cost and concerns about their efficacy. The following suggestions will help you teach the skills of reading more effectively. **Tip:** Model any strategy by thinking out loud as you demonstrate it on an interactive whiteboard. Then your students can see that even the teacher uses strategies to be a good reader.

Guided practice gives you an opportunity to closely monitor students' practice of skills by assessing student progress, analyzing errors, and diagnosing next steps so students achieve continuous forward progress. Examples of guided practice activities include chorally reading a paragraph in a reading group, solving a few math problems together, or having a few students complete an exercise on the board while other students do the same exercise in their seats.

After students have developed at least 80 percent accuracy on the designated standards, they are ready to tackle independent work on these skills in the classroom, community, or home. The following strategies can help you monitor independent practice.

- **Praise, prompt, and leave**** is a strategy to help you structure your interaction with each student as you move around the classroom monitoring independent practice. The goal is to give clear, corrective feedback in the shortest amount of time possible.

  *Praise:* Tell students what they have done correctly. If work is incorrect, help students get back on the right track, and praise their effort in doing so.

  *Prompt:* Make sure students know how to move on to the next lesson segment.

  *Leave:* Leave students to work on the activity alone. Always return to check on student progress if corrections were needed. It takes much more time to reteach a skill because it has been practiced incorrectly than to learn it correctly before mistakes become deeply learned.

- **Drill and practice** is a strategy that facilitates mastery through repetitive practice. Activities need not be limited to paper-and-pencil tasks. Interactive whiteboard activities, computer software and websites, and visual-tactile-kinesthetic activities can also provide drill and practice. These formats especially benefit beginning learners and students with learning difficulties who need repeated exposure and additional time to acquire a new skill.

- **Real-life learning** is a strategy that promotes the transfer of skills. Practice must be varied and must progress at a student's own pace. Skills are presented in as many different contexts as possible, striving for higher levels of the Revised Bloom's Taxonomy (RBT). An example of this strategy would be teaching a student the skill of adding money and then making a shopping list and going to the store, clipping coupons and adding them together to determine the cost savings, or collecting money for a charitable organization and totaling the amount earned.

---

*Adapted from a method used by Linda Holt, teacher, Maui, Hawaii.

** (Fred Jones) Second Edition of *Tools for Teaching* – Latest Update: April 2, 2007

## Using Practice Activities More Effectively

Some teachers will continue to use consumables in various subject areas. Where possible, try to supplement that format with digital or Web-based activities. Students with LD have challenges in writing, and they will appreciate any variety you can provide.

Group your visual-tactile-kinesthetic learners in pairs for practice exercises. Assign tasks that convert easily to hands-on activities.

The following strategies might help increase students' interest in completing practice or workbook pages.

■ Any practice pages you use with your students should teach or reinforce skills that make sense within the context of what they are reading. Skip those pages for which you can't find a contextual connection, or rearrange the skills to teach them in meaningful contexts.

■ All practice pages must have clear directions. Read and discuss the directions with the students. Provide concrete visual examples of what the finished work should look like.

■ If some kids have difficulty understanding the directions for a practice page, offer them one at a time. Have students demonstrate their understanding of each direction before you add others.

■ Get students excited about practice pages by offering the five-in-a-row opportunity: Anyone who completes five consecutive questions or examples neatly, legibly, and correctly may stop practicing. This works best when students work independently rather than with partners.

## Teaching Reading: Sounds, Spelling, and Vocabulary

Most students can benefit from learning about letter-sound associations. Students with learning problems may have a great deal of trouble learning phonemic awareness and phonics because the sounds are often taught in isolation, and meaningful context is absent. Sometimes, these global learners are better off learning about phonics after they have learned to read by some other method, such as those described on pages 91–101. The thing to avoid is early failure in phonics, which leads students to conclude that they are not smart enough to learn to read.

## The Evolution of Phonics

Modern phonics methods include two parts: phonemic awareness and phonics. Phonemic awareness is the ability to recognize that a spoken word is made up of a sequence of individual sounds. Many reading specialists firmly believe that phonemic awareness is an essential skill for learning an alphabet-based language. They believe that even before children learn to read print, they need to develop an awareness of how the sounds in words work. Children must understand that words are made up of speech sounds, or phonemes. Phonemes are the smallest parts of sound in a spoken word that make a difference in a word's meaning. Whatever work with sounds that students can do with their eyes closed falls into the category of phonemic awareness. Phonemic awareness abilities include the understanding and application of these concepts:

■ Words are made up of individual sounds or blends of sounds.

■ Words can begin or end with the same sound.

■ Words can have the same sounds within them.

■ Words can rhyme.

■ Words have syllables.

■ Removing or substituting letters or sounds can create other words.

■ Some sounds are pronounced as blends.

■ Sentences are made up of groups of words.

Phonemic awareness can be developed through the following activities:

■ Identify and categorize sounds.

■ Blend sounds to form words.

■ Delete or add sounds to form new words.

■ Substitute sounds to make new words.

Phonemic awareness instruction is most effective when students are taught to manipulate phonemes by using alphabet letters. Phonemic awareness instruction should focus on only one or two types of phoneme manipulation rather than several. Phonemic instruction is usually done in kindergarten or first grade.

Children who cannot hear and work with the phonemes of spoken words will have a difficult time learning how to relate these phonemes to graphemes. A grapheme is a unit of a writing system—a letter of an alphabet or all the letters and letter combinations that represent a phoneme (*example: f, ph, and gh*). Early readers can show they have phonemic awareness in several ways:

- recognizing which words in a set of words start with the same sound

- isolating and saying the first or last sound in a word

- combining or blending the separate sounds in a word in order to say the word

- breaking up a word into its separate sounds

Most research in reading has shown that phonemic awareness is essential to learning to read. All reading instruction that occurs throughout elementary school is dependent on a strong foundation in phonemic awareness.

Various websites can provide concrete examples of activities that will give emerging readers practice in rhyming words, breaking words into syllables, phonemic segmentation, and other specific phonemic awareness skills. Here are a few good ones:

- www.starfall.com: activities and lessons for phonemic awareness

- www.rif.org (under "Kids" click on "Leading to Reading"): early literacy activities for babies and toddlers

- pbskids.org/island/activities: story and reading activities for preschoolers, including a reading activities calendar in English and Spanish

- www.sadlier.com/school/phonics: student early literacy to support phonemic awareness

- www.earobics.com (click on "Game Goo"): phonemic awareness activities

- www.familylearning.org.uk (click on "Phonics games"): links to a variety of preschool games to support phonemic awareness

- teacher.scholastic.com/clifford1/flash/phonics/index.htm: beginning letter sound activity

Phonemic awareness is different from phonics. Phonics is an instructional approach that teaches readers the relationship between letters and the sounds they make. Students are expected to make the connections between a letter and its sound.

If you compare this information with what you already know from Chapter 3 about the predominant learning styles of struggling readers—visual and kinesthetic rather than auditory—you may realize that for some students, other methods of learning to read may be more effective than phonics. Students who just can't discriminate all the subtle differences among sounds should never feel like failures in reading. Just because they can't easily master phonemic awareness or phonics doesn't mean they can't become fluent readers.

This chapter contains many methods that you can use to teach students to read. Your job is to connect each student with the strategy that will be most successful for that student. Remember that students who have not become effective readers by the end of third grade are at a significantly increased risk of not graduating from high school.

# Phonics Instruction

Phonics is a system of instruction in which readers learn the relationships between letters and their sounds in order to recognize and pronounce words, as well as to read and spell in isolation, in the context of words, and in sentences. Because poor word identification skills inhibit readers' ability to obtain meaning from text, phonics affects many areas of learning. For struggling learners, the essential issue is not *whether* they need phonics, but *when and how* phonics should be included in their reading program.

Students who appear totally confused and unable to learn sound-letter relationships in kindergarten through second grade should be taught to read by a more holistic method that will lead to successful outcomes. For these students, formal instruction in the rules of phonics should be postponed until they perceive themselves as successful readers. Somewhere during the second or third grade, you might offer to teach them some "magic tricks" that will enable them to pronounce unfamiliar words and improve their spelling ability. (Most seven- and eight-year-olds love tricks.) Students of all ages learn phonics much more easily when they are developmentally ready.

Global learners cannot learn sounds in isolation. It makes no sense to deprive them of meaningful reading experiences until they master the phonics component. Instead, we must teach all phonics-related skills in the context of meaningful words, phrases, and sentences. Whenever possible, use tactile-kinesthetic learning tasks that include a healthy dose of musical-rhythmic activities. And always remember how illogical and unreliable the English phonics system is. (*Example:* Why spell the word *fish* with the letters *f-i-s-h*? Why not spell it *g-h-o-t-i*? *Gh* as in *laugh* + *o* as in *women* + *ti* as in *nation* = *fish*.)

## Word Families*

- When students can say some letter sounds, move on to word families. (*Example:* If students can almost always recognize the short *a* in *pat*, say, "If you know *pat*, you know *hat* and *fat* and *rat* and *sat*.")

---

*Some ideas in this section are from Linda Holt, teacher, Maui, Hawaii. Used with permission.

- Teach families of words with similar sounds together. Print the target sounds in colored chalk, markers, or ink. Use one color for each word family.

- Collect word families on notecards in a word box. Highlight the target sound with a particular color to reinforce the visual image of the family pattern.

- Make learning about word families a tactile-kinesthetic experience. Use magnetic letters on a metal board and change the initial consonants. Have students write lists of the word families, perhaps using different colors for each family.

- Create a silly story filled with family words. (*Example:* "The purple turtle went to see the nurse because he got hurt going around the curve.") Have students add more words. Invite them to help you make up similar stories for other word families.

- Have students write stories using as many family words as possible. They can use highlighter pens to illustrate the repetitive pattern. Collect their stories in a book, make copies, and send them home for kids to read aloud.

- Once students understand simple word families (*example: cat, hat,* and *sat*), change the short vowel but keep the consonants the same. (*Example:* "If you know *cat,* you know *cot* and *cut.*") Next, work with blending sounds (*examples: flat, clap,* and *trap*).

- Reinforce the family words until students recognize the sounds and can speak them automatically.

- Design games and other enjoyable ways for students to practice their sound-letter skills. Most kids learn skills through games very quickly.

## Working with Words*

Give students a group of letters that make up a word they will learn in today's lesson. Have students arrange the letters to make several shorter words. Dictate the words you want them to make or provide a written list of the words. (*Example:* If the target word for the day is *weather,* give all students all seven letters. Don't tell them what the target word is. Say that the students are "word detectives," and their job is solving the mystery of how all these letters will fit together to make one word. Direct the students to use the letters to make *the, wet, hat, her, wreath, where,* and so on until someone figures out that all the letters together make *weather.*

**Variation:** Have students work in small groups to create as many words as possible from the letters in a five-minute period. One student acts as group recorder and writes down all the group's words. The team with the most words wins. Award bonus points for using all the letters in one word.

## The Word Wall*

A word wall is a large bulletin board or a designated spot on any type of large writing surface. Each week, you add to the wall five new words that students need for that week's reading and writing activities. Write the words on pieces of colored paper (or in colored markers or chalk) and arrange them alphabetically by the first letter only. Each day, select five words from the word wall for students to practice. Have them rhythmically chant and clap the letters in each word three times, then write the word and chant and clap again what they have written. For variety, use arm tap spelling (see page 117). Include any words from the previous "Working with Words" activity. Students might also practice words from the word wall using vocabulary flash cards (see page 114).

## Using Music, Rhythm, and Movement

- Raps and rhymes help kinesthetic students learn letter sounds more easily. Look for products that teach kids chants for phonics rules.

- Use rhythm cues to teach sounds and syllables. You might have students punch the air with their fists or clap each time they hear a syllable in a word. (*Example:* As you and the students say the word *pizza* together, fists go up on *piz* and *za.*)

- Have kids write words in the air using large hand and arm movements; using media such as shaving cream, finger paints, or salt; in different colors; or on one another's backs.

- Clapping the letters also helps kids remember correct spellings, as does hitting their arm for each syllable. Especially for global learners, rhythm clues are far more effective than the traditional syllable rules.

- It helps some students to act out a word while saying it repeatedly.

# Building Reading Vocabulary

If you went into your class tomorrow and gave a pop quiz on all the vocabulary words you have taught since the beginning of the year, what do you think the results would be? Generous estimates run as high as 50 percent, but most teachers predict somewhere between 20 and

---

*Adapted from Patricia Cunningham and Richard Allington, *Classrooms That Work: They Can All Read and Write.* New York: HarperCollins, 1994. Used with permission

35 percent. Since it's highly unlikely that our students will remember *all* the vocabulary words we teach them, and since they won't all remember the *same* 20 to 35 percent, it makes more sense to teach a smaller number of words so well that 100 percent of the students remember 100 percent of the same words. Be sure to search the Web for other vocabulary-building activities.

Traditional methods of studying vocabulary are largely ineffective for struggling students. As the mother of one second grader watched her daughter copy vocabulary words and their definitions from the glossary of a book, the mother asked, "What does that word mean? The one you just finished writing?" The child responded, "I don't know, Mommy. I don't have time to learn the words. I'm just supposed to copy them."

For all grade levels, the Common Core vocabulary standards are built on the three main principles of breadth, complexity, and depth of instruction. For students, especially students with learning difficulties, to master vocabulary as required in these standards, they need direct instruction and practice in a variety of contexts to transfer the words and their meanings to long-term memories. Students with LD need very explicit instruction with ample time to review. Coherent courses that integrate subjects and are coordinated across the curriculum provide the greatest increase in vocabulary knowledge.

Contrary to recent practices, global learners should *not* be taught the vocabulary from an upcoming reading selection *before* they read the text, since they find it very difficult to learn anything outside its meaningful context. Help students pronounce unusual names before reading, but don't teach vocabulary words until they appear in the context of a chapter. Above all, remember that global learners benefit most from visual teaching methods. Adding tactile-kinesthetic activities enhances the learning process even more.

Finally, please remember what we adults do when we come to an unfamiliar word in something we're reading: We spend a brief moment trying to infer the meaning from that context, and if that doesn't work, we skip it. We've always wondered why adults keep this secret from kids for so long. If we really want kids to be good readers, we have to give them lots of experience making educated guesses.

## Vocabulary Flash Cards

Make sure that students have seen and heard the vocabulary words in context *before* you have them work with flash cards.

- To create basic flash cards, have students write the vocabulary word on one side of the card and the meaning on the other. Some students might prefer to draw a picture of the meaning instead of writing it.

- To create more effective flash cards, have students write the word on the left side of the card and the meaning on the right, then cut the cards apart into jigsaw puzzle–like pieces. The mental image of the word will be reinforced by the shape of the puzzle piece. Matching words and meanings adds a tactile-kinesthetic component.*

- Have students group their vocabulary flash cards by categories or word families.

- Turn vocabulary mastery into a game. Students will need their own sets of basic flash cards (with their initials on each card). Group kids with similar words into pairs. To take a turn, a student reads a vocabulary word and tries to give the meaning. If the meaning is correct, the student receives the card. (Or have the students play the other way: first read the meaning, then give the word.) The person with the most cards at the end of the game wins. The initials make it easy to return the cards to the original owners when the game is over. Make this activity even more fun by giving each pair of students a game board, dice (or spinner), and playing pieces. When students read a vocabulary word and give the correct meaning, they spin the spinner or roll the dice and move on the game board.

## The Vocabulary Attributes Chart**

Vocabulary attributes charts can help students visualize and understand words and their meanings. Rather than teaching words as they appear in selections, you group words that share common attributes and teach them together. This method is effective with any subject area.

1. Make several copies of the "Vocabulary Attributes Chart" handout on page 133.

2. Decide on a category of words that share common attributes (*example:* nouns that describe things). Print a word that fits in that category in the center box of each chart, using red ink.

3. Create four subcategories of information that could describe attributes of all words in the category. (*Examples:* For nouns that describe things, subcategories might be *looks like*, *usual uses*, *unusual uses*, and *synonyms*.) Print these subcategories in the four boxes in the corners of the chart,

---

*Marie Carbo, Rita Dunn, and Kenneth Dunn. *Teaching Students to Read through Their Individual Learning Styles.* Englewood Cliffs, NJ: Allyn & Bacon, 1986.

**Several versions of vocabulary graphic organizers are free online at the West Virginia Department of Education website wvde.state.wv.us.

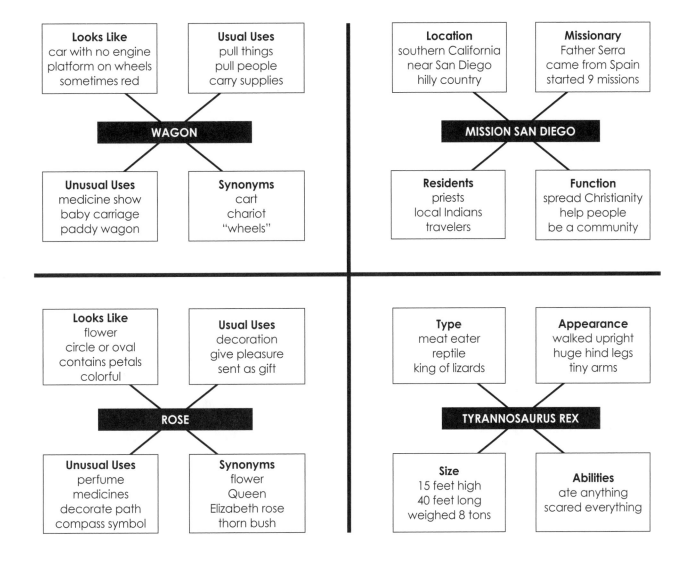

using red ink. These attribute boxes will stay the same for every word in the main category.

4. Have students brainstorm attributes for each category. Record them in blue ink on the lines.

5. When each chart is complete, hang it up where kids can see it. All the charts for a specific category should be displayed together.

See above for four examples of how this chart might look when completed. The "wagon" and "rose" examples show nouns and their attributes. The "Mission San Diego" example shows how this chart might be used for history. The "Tyrannosaurus Rex" example shows how it might be used for elementary science.

After students have experienced this process several times under your direction, they might enjoy working with partners on this activity.

# Spelling and Vocabulary Instruction

Students might ask, "Why do we have to learn to spell? We can use a computer with a spell-checker." The obvious answer is that knowing how to spell allows us to read and write with greater ease. Also, spell-checkers are often inaccurate, and there are many times when people have to complete an application or write a paragraph without the aid of technology. Poor spelling creates a poor first impression.

Spelling involves much more than memorization alone. Spelling is an integral part in achieving literacy. It should be taught in the context of reading and writing through an integrated language arts approach. Most students can become competent spellers if we teach them in ways that are compatible with their learning modalities.

## Learning Words with Your Best Style

Note: As we have mentioned earlier, the terms *style* and *modality* are interchangeable.

**1.** Choose four word lists that each contain 10 to 15 words that are reasonably similar in spelling or definition difficulty. Don't announce ahead of time which will be used.

**2.** Tell your students that you're going to take four weeks off from formal spelling instruction. During that time, you're going to teach the kids how to use their learning modalities to become better at spelling and vocabulary.

**3.** Give each student copies of the "Learning Words by Style" handout (page 134) and the "Learning Words by Style Record Sheet" handout* (page 135). Explain that for the next four weeks, they will use these charts to identify their preferred learning modalities in order to achieve the best possible spelling results. Reassure them that they will record their own scores privately and that none of the scores will count toward their recorded grades for word study.

**4.** Give the entire class a pretest of week one's words. Insist that everyone take the test and do the best they can, even though they haven't had a chance to study the words in advance. Again, reassure them that their scores will be private. Even you won't see them. Tell students that if they get just one wrong, they can pair up with another student with a similar score, select a list of challenging words to study, and learn the visual style on the "Learning Words by Style Record Sheet" along with the rest of the class.

**5.** Have students correct their own tests and record their scores in *blue* in the "V-Pre" (Visual Style, Pretest) column of the "Learning Words by Style Record Sheet" by coloring in the column up to and including the number they spelled correctly. Afterward, have them look at their "Learning Words by Styles Chart." Model the steps listed in the "Visual Style" box as you teach them. Explain that this is how visual learners study words.

**6.** Have students work in pairs to study the week one words the visual way. Monitor all pairs to make sure they are using the style correctly.

**7.** On Friday, give the week one test again. Have students correct their own tests and record their scores in *red* in the "V-Post" (Visual Style, Post-Test) column, as in step 5. This will show how well they can spell as a visual learner would.

**8.** Over the next three weeks, repeat steps 4 through 7 for the other three styles on the "Learning Words by Style Record Sheet," using the remaining word lists. Have students record their pretest and post-test scores on the record sheet. By the end of the fourth week, the colorful bar graph will show students the studying styles that give them the best results.

Challenge students to practice their preferred learning modality method in other areas (*examples:* learning state and world capitals, vocabulary words, number facts, and so on). Keep referring them back to the styles chart. When you return to the regular word program, encourage students to set and record their own goals for each week's word list.

## Scenario: Elaine

Eight-year-old Elaine had never gotten a score higher than 35 percent on any spelling test. Since most of her peers were already well set in their spelling patterns, and since their grades weren't changing much from week to week, Elaine's teacher, Mr. Pampas, announced that he would use the next four weeks of spelling time to teach the whole class about spelling styles.

He knew that Elaine studied her spelling words at home—her mother had confirmed that fact for him—but the results were invariably disappointing. During their four-week experiment, Elaine discovered that she was a visual-tactile-kinesthetic (multisensory) learner.

When the learning modality discovery activity ended, Mr. Pampas asked Elaine to set a goal each week for how many words she would learn to spell with 80 percent accuracy or higher by using her strongest learning style or modality. For the first week, she chose 10 words. Mr. Pampas choked back what he wanted to say: "Oh, no, that goal is too high! You would have to spell eight words correctly to get 80 percent, and the most you've ever gotten right on a formal spelling test is three." Instead, he helped her chart her goal. Then he coached her in using the multisensory style to study the words she selected from the spelling list. He affirmed her "yes I can" attitude—and watched in amazement as she got all 10 words correct on the test. She happily recorded her results, and he sent a note home to announce her victory.

Elaine gradually increased her goal until she was studying 15 words each week. She maintained good grades in spelling for the rest of the year.

*Caution:* The goal increase must be the student's idea, *not* the teacher's. Note to teachers: Vocabulary words can also be learned by using the "Vocabulary Attributes Chart" on page 133.

---

*Adapted from the work of Doris Brown, special education teacher, retired. Used with permission.

## More Techniques for Teaching Spelling and Learning Sounds

Most teachers never realize that they never really teach spelling and vocabulary, they just test for accuracy. Students have been led to believe that if they do all the test-related activities, they will somehow magically learn the words. And yet, teachers notice both the excellent and poor spelling and vocabulary students early in the year, and these students tend to stay in these categories for the rest of their time in the class. We must find ways to replace these ineffective methods with some that are varied by learning modality.

### Arm Tap Spelling

Have students spell words on their arm. They should extend the arm they don't write with and use the index and middle fingers of their writing hand to tap out each clustered sound, starting with the shoulder and moving toward the wrist with each sound, then slide out the whole word at the end. (*Example:* Model arm tap spelling with the word *arithmetic*. Tap *A* [pause] *R-I-T-H* [pause] *M-E* [pause] *T-I-C* [pause], then say the whole word as you slide your two fingers down your arm from shoulder to wrist.)

After much guided practice, students should be able to use this technique silently to figure out how many syllables are in a word and how it is spelled.

### The Fernauld Word-Tracing Method*

1. Ask students to identify a word they would like to spell accurately in their writing. (It's best to do this at a moment when a student needs a particular word—"Teacher, how do you spell _____?")

2. Using a soft, waxy instrument (like a thick crayon), print or write the word on a four-by-six-inch card. You should be able to feel the letters raised from the surface of the card.

3. Have students trace over the word with the index finger of their writing hand, saying the word aloud as they trace it. Pronounce multisyllabic words in syllables. After several practices, students should be able to turn the card over and write the word from memory.

### Functional Spelling

Struggling students are more motivated to learn something they consider meaningful and important. It makes sense to concentrate their spelling efforts on the words they need to function in their own writing.

1. Have students keep lists of their frequently misspelled words.

2. When they have collected five words, have them use the "Learning Words with Your Best Style" method (page 116) to study the words.

3. Have partners test each other. Words that are mastered are dropped from the list; new words are added until the list is five words long again.

Have students keep their word lists on a digital device or in a small spiral notebook. Once they accumulate 5 to 10 words on that list, they can study those words and then ask another student to test them at a time you suggest. Teach graphing skills for them to keep their own progress records.

### Spelling Baseball

Spelling baseball is a particular favorite of learners who need to move around. Students get to run the bases as they progress through the game.

1. Create two teams of students, with a range of spelling abilities on each team.

2. Draw a large diamond on the board at the front of the room to represent home plate. Designate the bases at labeled spots around the room, going counterclockwise as on a baseball field.

3. Have students go to bat and choose the level of difficulty of the word they will try to spell. A simple word is a single; a challenging word is a home run.

4. Each correct spelling is a base hit or home run. Each incorrect spelling is an out. Teams score a point each time one of their players comes home; after three outs, the other team is up to bat.

Of course, you can use this format to review any content, including or instead of spelling.

### Spelling Bees and Other Contests

It is imperative that students be allowed to use their preferred learning modality in spelling bees and other contests.

- If students are visual, allow them to write out the word rather than spell it aloud.

- If they are tactile-kinesthetic, let them write the word in sand or salt.

The only fair requirement is that *all* students be given the same amount of time to come up with the correct spelling. If these special allowances make your students ineligible for regional or national competitions, either conduct your own local spelling bee or have a

*Fernauld, Grace. *Remedial Techniques in Basic School Subjects: Methods for Teaching Dyslexics and Other Learning Disabled.* Austin, TX: PRO-ED, 1988. Used with permission. Currently reported by Susan Fondrk and Cheryl Frasca, Culver City, CA: Good Year Books, 2005.

separate competition for volunteers to qualify for those competitions.

### Studying Misspelled Words

Avoid circling spelling errors for visual learners, since that calls more attention to errors than to words spelled correctly. Instead, fold a piece of writing paper into three columns. Have students write their spelling words in the left column. On test day, have them fold that column over to the back and take the test in the middle column. Afterward, have them write in the right column the correct spellings of any words they got wrong in the middle column (on the same line as in the test column).

# Teaching Writing

Just as children learn to read by reading, they learn to write by writing. Almost all students can learn to write if we are flexible about the methods and the technology they can use. Remediation of handwriting or other writing skills beyond third grade without technology assistance is often a waste of everyone's time. Our goal should be to enable students to communicate in ways that are fluent and meaningful for them. When students perceive that writing lets them share exciting and important ideas, they may be more willing to do whatever it takes to learn how to write. This section describes many strategies and techniques that can turn your reluctant writers into willing and even eager writers.

Corbett Harrison, a writing teacher and online columnist on the subject of teaching writing, participated in the Northern Nevada Writing Project (NNWP). He claims that this program helped him know how to "really teach writing." It taught him the six traits of good writing: idea development, voice, sentence fluency, word choice, conventions, and organization. These same traits define effective writing in both typical writing lessons and those that are focused on informational text. Harrison favors using mentor texts to provide excellent examples of the six traits of good writing. Mentor texts are excellent examples of already published products. By focusing on one of the six traits for each mentor text, students gain the confidence necessary to improve their proficiency in writing over time.

NNWP is a program with counterparts in many other states. Check to see if your state has a writing project by searching online for *(your state's name) writing project*. To explore NNWP and a huge number of related writing lessons, visit writingfix.com. You can also visit Harrison's own website: corbettharrison.com. Here you'll find many articles he has written about writing, as well as references to his favorite motto: We write to prove we think!

Harrison realized that the way he had previously taught was totally ineffective in teaching students to write with enthusiasm and fidelity to the six traits of good writing. He became convinced that writing *cannot* be taught effectively using worksheets, through daily oral language drills, or with formulaic assignments that produce mostly voiceless writing from students.

# What to Do When Students Hate to Write

Frustrated students think they hate to write, but what they really hate is revising. When we give them more painless ways to complete their writing assignments, they develop more positive attitudes about writing.

From the first day children enter school, language experiences shape the way they perceive all communication skills. You might start by simply asking your students to write down a few ideas about something they did, saw, or heard. Obviously, students who aren't yet literate can't write real sentences. However, it's important for them to *think* they can so they begin to develop the critical understanding of the relationships among thinking, speaking, writing, and reading. As teachers, we must encourage them to write in any way they can. Some will just scribble; others will draw pictures; still others will write symbols that are incomprehensible to anyone but them. At this very early stage, the only criterion for acceptability should be whether students themselves can read what they have written.

Susan once worked with a group of three-year-olds who had just returned to preschool after a flood that had put most of their homes underwater. She asked the children to write about two things that had happened to them in the flood and to draw a picture about it. As they came up to read their stories, she modeled for them how a reader glances down at the text and looks up at the audience. By the time the third child came up, everyone was reading in this manner, even though most of their writing was illegible to others.

## Scenario: Walter

Walter was in a preschool class for four-year-olds who had been labeled "at risk." Each day, his teacher asked the class to write in their journals; at the end of the day, she translated their writing into acceptable English. When Susan suggested that she stop translating, the teacher expressed concern that her students wouldn't see good models of writing without her help. Susan explained that good models wouldn't be meaningful to the children until they themselves understood the thinking-speaking-writing-reading connection.

The teacher agreed to give it a try. The next day, she observed that Walter was spending an inordinate amount of time hunched over his journal. Curious about his entry, the teacher asked Walter to share what he had written with the class. Walter came up to stand beside the teacher. She looked over his shoulder and saw a series of chicken scratches that made absolutely no sense to her.

Walter started to read, "Last night before I went to bed —," then he suddenly stopped reading, giggled self-consciously, put his hand over his mouth, and said, "Oops, I made a mistake!" He turned his paper upside down (which for him was right side up) and continued reading his journal.

Emerging writers have a code that they understand perfectly well. When we interrupt their coding to show them the correct way to write, we may compromise their ability to achieve correctness at a developmentally appropriate time.

## Journal Writing

Journal writing is an important part of literacy development at any age. Most teachers allow students' journals to illustrate their writing progress over time. Although it's valuable to teach students the importance of keeping written records of their thoughts and experiences, the idea of having to write something every day can become very stressful for kids who find writing difficult in the first place. Here are a few suggestions for reducing that stress:

- Tell students to write a journal entry at least twice a week on whatever days they choose. This allows reluctant writers to skip some days when they just don't feel like writing.

- Many kids appreciate a suggestion from you about possible writing topics, but always allow students to choose their own topic if that is what they prefer.

- As you review student journals, respond in writing from time to time. This practice emphasizes the use of the written word as a communication device.

- If you want students to be candid in their journal entries, suggest a signal or symbol they can use to indicate when they don't want you to read a certain entry.

- Above all, avoid correcting what students write in their journals.

# What to Do When Students Don't Know What to Write About

How often have you heard someone say "the really good writers always write from personal experience"? Yet we teachers continue to compile lavish collections of story starters to aid creativity. This type of assignment is not authentic to struggling writers, who have yet to learn that writing is only part of the thinking-speaking-writing-reading connection.

In one class Susan worked with, she and the students spent two days compiling a list of possible writing topics. On the first day, they filled the entire chalkboard with ideas students brainstormed during a 20-minute period in response to the question "What can I write about?" On the second day, they took a six-foot piece of butcher paper and divided it into four sections titled "About Me," "About People I Know," "About People I Don't Know," and "Made-Up Stuff." Next, they put every item on the brainstormed list into one or more of these sections. Then they titled the chart "What I Can Write About" and taped it to a wall.

Students were encouraged to write their first story about a topic from the "About Me" category; subsequent stories could come from any other category. The chart stayed up all year. Whenever anyone said, "But I don't know what to write about!" Susan would simply point to the chart and say, "Check out our chart." The claims of not knowing what to write about ceased almost immediately.

| What I Can Write About | | | |
|---|---|---|---|
| About Me | About People I Know | About People I Don't Know | Made-Up Stuff |
| | | | |

## Improving Fluency by Just Writing

When students complain that they can't get started writing about a topic, suggest that they try the following:

1. Write your topic at the top of a sheet of paper.

2. Now just write for three to five minutes *without lifting your pencil from the paper.* You can write anything that comes to mind, even if it doesn't relate to your topic. If you really can't think of a single thing, write, "I can't think of anything to write." Keep looking back at your topic. Let your pencil do the work for you.

3. When the time is up, go over everything you have written. Underline any ideas that might be related to your topic.

4. Write the ideas you underlined on a clean sheet of paper. Skip several lines between each written idea. Work with a partner to brainstorm and list supporting ideas and details.

5. Use your ideas, supporting ideas, and details to write several sentences. Reorganize the sentences as needed into one or more paragraphs.

See "Making Writing Visual and Kinesthetic" (pages 122–124) for ways to help students organize sentences into paragraphs.

# Writing Programs

At the time of this book's publication, the methods to teach writing were undergoing a cosmic shift away from being a discrete subject area and toward the focus of preparing students for writing in their careers and other life paths. Many programs are in frequent use today, and some overlap. One of the most commonly used programs is the 6+1 Trait Writing Model. It is the current version of the six-trait rubric developed by the Northwest Regional Educational Laboratory in Portland, Oregon. It teaches what are now considered to be the seven most important traits of writing. They are:*

1. **Ideas and content:** This trait includes the main idea or theme, supporting details, clear purpose, and compelling information. Ideas must be of high quality.

2. **Organization:** This trait includes an engaging lead-in, logical order of ideas, smooth transitions, and a satisfying conclusion.

3. **Voice:** This trait includes the writer's personality, feelings, honesty, and sincerity. The reader or listener should believe what the writer is saying.

4. **Word choice:** This trait includes using memorable phrases, words that are appropriate for the intended audience, and specific parts of speech. Writing succinctly is the desired goal.

5. **Sentence fluency:** This trait includes rhythm and meter, variety in sentence length, rhyme, alliteration, and an easy flow of ideas through the entire piece.

6. **Conventions:** This trait includes appropriate grammar, correct spelling, meaningful punctuation, and effective paragraphs.

7. **Presentation:** This trait includes the form and layout of the text, and the ease of its readability.

For more information about the 6+1 Trait Writing Model, see "References and Resources" on page 253.

# The Writing Process**

The Writing Process is a method that helps students learn to write by emulating the methods used by professional writers. Just as in real-life writing, students are allowed to create many drafts without having to polish each one to the publication stage. Ultimately, they select a few to finalize for other eyes.

To use the Writing Process, give each student a copy of the "Steps to Good Writing" handout (page 136). Teach each step explicitly. Model any steps for which students need clarification. Be available to answer questions, teach skills, and provide encouragement.

*Caution:* It is imperative that students regularly select a piece of their writing to take all the way through the editing and publishing stages. This process may be useful in all types of writing, including those connected to CCSS. Whatever program, model, or method you use to teach writing, make certain that your students will be able to demonstrate mastery of the needed skills, perhaps through the use of rubrics that ideally will be used across all grade levels as students move through school and into their own adult pathways. Related information and resources may be found by searching the keywords *The Writing Process* online.

## Scenario: Damien

Damien was a fourth grader with diagnosed learning difficulties. When Susan met him, he was very fluent in expressing his ideas orally, but when it came to writing he dug in his heels and insisted, "I can't write! I hate writing!"

---

*6+1 Trait® Writing for the Common Core State Standards Institute

**Originated more than 40 years ago in San Francisco as the Bay Area Writing Project, the Writing Process has since been refined by many authors and teachers, including Nancy Atwell, Lucy McCormick Calkins, Donald H. Graves, and Donald M. Murray. See "References and Resources."

This situation with certain students—fluency in thinking and speaking combined with dramatic weakness in their ability to write down their thoughts—can often indicate that the students are twice exceptional: gifted in some areas of learning while experiencing learning difficulties in other areas. For more on this topic, see "Being Gifted and Simultaneously Having Learning Challenges" on page 29.

Like many kids with LD, Damien was a terrible speller, and his mental fluency was severely compromised by the halting manner in which he wrote. He would carefully consider each word, trying to determine whether he could come even remotely close to the correct spelling. He would lose track of his ideas in the middle of his sentences. He felt hopeless about his weaknesses and dreaded any writing assignment.

His teacher and Susan had decided to use the Writing Process with his class. They were curious about how that method would affect Damien.

First, Susan had to convince Damien that during the initial stages of the process, fluency was the only goal. Although he was skeptical, he soon figured out that she meant what she said, and he opened up on paper with such fervor that she faced a new challenge: how to stop him. He chose to write about his favorite activity—his family's annual summer camping trip to a remote site with lots of fishing. During their typical two-week outing, their routine was relatively constant from day to day. Damien wrote a bed-to-bed story for each day of their most recent vacation. He wrote furiously for the entire writing period every day for two weeks.

Finally, he agreed to choose one of his days to work through the other steps of the Writing Process. Susan assured him that he could finish the rest of the story some other time. Obviously, Damien was no longer resistant to writing. Like many other struggling writers, he had found success with the Writing Process.

# Penmanship and Handwriting

In a time when most people use keyboards or speech-to-writing programs to communicate, some educators believe that handwriting is no longer important to lifetime success. This country is undergoing a big transition in teaching kids how to create handwritten letters and words. As of this book's writing, many districts have abandoned teaching penmanship altogether. They reason that since kids rarely write by hand anymore, they have little or no need to learn how to form letters.

We believe that decision is very shortsighted. Gazing into our crystal ball, we can see a time in the future when the pendulum will begin swinging back toward the importance of writing by hand. People will recognize the loss to the histories of countries and families. They will realize how hard historians must work to find any personal records. They will notice the denigration of our once-lovely language, as it is reduced to abbreviations that texters favor but that have little meaning to other people.

Whether we call this skill "penmanship" or "handwriting," the ultimate goal of teaching it is enabling people to express themselves legibly using a specific writing instrument. So what can we do about the horrible handwriting of some of our struggling students? We can celebrate the fact that technologies are available to help them become legible writers. For kids whose learning difficulties make writing nearly impossible, ask your district's technology expert for assistance. See also the "References and Resources" on page 252.

In our opinion, Dr. Walter Barbe, a professor of language arts and an expert handwriting educator, has a very sensible philosophy about teaching handwriting. He thinks we should teach kids how to print in manuscript when their fine muscle coordination for writing is developed and teach cursive when kids are ready for that. He advises us to stop worrying about illegible writers and wasting their precious school time remediating their poor writing habits. Instead, he says, once both forms have been presented and briefly taught, we should allow each person to develop and use the method that is most fluent and legible for them. If that is using a keyboard, so be it. But at least we would have given those youngsters who want to use a more personal means of writing some simple instruction in how to do just that.

Just as in grammar, spelling, or mathematics, it is never okay to postpone children's interaction with meaningful writing while we wait for them to develop better handwriting skills. All students who have the necessary fine motor skills for writing should be taught printing. Children should learn to write when they are developmentally ready rather than at any specific age.

## Tips for Teaching Handwriting

Handwriting is more likely to improve with practice in actual writing than with handwriting exercises. However, if you are expected to teach handwriting as a separate subject, you should find the following tips helpful.

- Make sure that students' papers are properly positioned. Left-handed students should tilt their paper almost 15 degrees to the right so they can hold their pencils without hooking their hand to write straight.

- The Getty-Dubay Italic Handwriting Series has been successful for some students with handwriting difficulties. The letters have no loops and fewer flourishes, so the transition from manuscript to cursive is greatly simplified. Legibility and writing fluency are greatly improved. See "References and Resources."

- In his book *Making the Words Stand Still,* Donald Lyman includes a precise written alphabet. He suggests having students practice letters in the following families together: straight-line letters; straight and slanted letters; circle letters; circle-and-straight-line combinations; and circle-and-curve combinations. See "References and Resources."

- If spacing between words is a problem, have students place dice, other small objects, or one or two fingers between words to get an idea of the right amount of space to leave.

# Making Writing Visual and Kinesthetic

Although you can probably find many digital resources online to help kids with writing difficulties arrange the various parts of sentences to enhance meaning, we believe that the simple sentence construction chart below and paragraph centipede are effective for helping kids see and understand why various sentence parts are arranged as they are. These tools are helpful because the writers are involved with actual physical movement of sentences. Assigning specific colors to the various parts of a sentence allows students to actually move around until their bodies, holding their sentence parts, arrange themselves into an acceptable sentence.

## Use a Sentence Construction Chart

If students get stuck trying to write complete sentences, show them how to use a sentence construction chart. It's especially effective with visual learners. Of course, not every sentence will have all the elements on the chart. But all sentences should have at least a subject ("who or what") and a verb ("does or did").

| Which | Who or What | Does or Did | What or Whom | Where |
|-------|-------------|-------------|--------------|-------|
| my | dog | licked | the mail carrier | on the arm |

## The Paragraph Centipede*

Primary students enjoy this graphic approach to writing a cohesive paragraph—and with practice, their writing shows dramatic improvement. Have them work in groups on the paragraph centipede.

**1.** On a large sheet of blank paper, draw the body of a centipede. It should be large enough to allow for writing and also for several legs to be attached. On another sheet of paper, draw legs that are long enough and wide enough to fit a printed sentence. Make copies for each group of one body and several legs. **Tip:** Laminate the pictures so they can be reused.

**2.** Tell the students the main idea of the paragraph they are about to write. Have them write the idea on the centipede's body.

**3.** Have each group brainstorm as many details as they can to describe the main idea of the paragraph. Each student might suggest a detail and write it on a leg. If some students can't write, designate one student in each group to act as a recorder, putting each new detail on a separate leg. Explain that for now, fluency is the *only* goal. They shouldn't worry about correctness, spelling, mechanics, or the relevance or order of ideas.

**4.** After the groups have brainstormed several details, the selection process begins. Have students take turns reading the main idea (body) followed by their detail (leg). Students hold the leg up to the body while reading, and the group decides together whether a student's detail supports the main idea. Details that are meaningfully connected are put in one pile; details that aren't meaningfully connected are discarded.

**5.** When the groups have identified several details that fit, they decide on the sequence by ordering the legs from left to right. They keep rearranging the legs until everyone agrees on the sequence. At that point, they number the legs in order. Students take back their own legs and correct spelling, grammar, and punctuation, perhaps with the help of others in the group. (Have extra legs available for students who need them.)

---

*Adapted from James F. Baumann and Maribeth C. Schmitt, "Main idea-pede," in *The Reading Teacher,* March 1986, p. 64. Copyright by the International Reading Association. Used with permission.

**6.** The corrected legs are attached to the body in sequence, and everyone writes a complete paragraph and reads it aloud.

### Variation: The Paragraph Organizer

Try this approach with students in grades four through twelve. It's the same basic concept as the paragraph centipede, but it looks less childish. Have the students work in pairs or small groups.

**1.** Give each pair or group a copy of the "Paragraph Organizer" handout (page 137). Tell them to write the main idea in the space indicated. (Or you can write it in before you make the copies.)

**2.** Have students brainstorm supporting details, writing each detail on a new line in the "Sentence Suggestions" column of the chart. Make sure they understand that they are to put each idea on a new line (so they can easily cut apart the ideas in step 3). Explain that at this stage, fluency is the *only* goal. Tell them not to write anything yet in the "Sequence" column.

**3.** Tell students to cut the sentences apart, hold each sentence up to the main idea, and discard any that don't fit.

**4.** Have the students sequence the remaining details and number each one (under the "Sequence" heading). Teach them how to edit their sentences.

**5.** The final sentences are taped together in the correct sequence, and students write their paragraphs by copying the sequence on a clean sheet of paper.

## Story and Character Maps

The story and character maps on pages 129 and 130 may also be used to plan written descriptions of stories and characters. Students simply create sentences from each of the details charted on the map.

## Flip Books

To make sentence components for visual and kinesthetic learners easy to understand and change, try flip books. This method may be used to change any part or parts in the sentence. Flip books allow visual and kinesthetic learners a way of manipulating words to create various sentences. This method can start with the use of pictures and words and then fade to words only. Here are two websites that offer support in making flip books:

- suzyred.com/flip.html
- fabianacarters.blogspot.com/2012/09/sentence-flip-book.html

## "Hand In" a Perfect Sentence*

Students can do their own proofreading with this simple tool. Have them trace around one of their hands (fingers spread, palm down). Then have them write the following on the digits:

- thumb: *capitals*
- index finger: *punctuation*
- middle finger: *spelling*
- ring finger: *neatness*
- pinkie: *subject* (for staying on the subject)

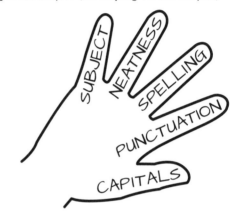

As students proofread a piece of their writing, they can use the hand prompts by touching each finger in turn and asking the following questions, one for each finger:

- thumb: "Does the sentence begin with a *capital* letter?"
- index finger: "Does it end with a *punctuation* mark—a period, question mark, or exclamation point?"
- middle finger: "Is the *spelling* correct?"
- ring finger: "Is the writing *neat* and readable?"
- pinkie: "Does it have something to do with the *subject* I am writing about?"

**Variations:** You can use the hand visual in countless ways in many different subject areas. Two variations for writing are:

- Each finger represents the components of a good narrative—"Who?" "What?" "When?" "Where?" "Why?"—and the palm represents "How?"
- To help students elaborate on character and scene descriptions, each digit is labeled with one of the senses—"What do we *see*?" "What do we *hear*?"

---

*Brenda Goffen, consultant in special education, Highland Park, Illinois.

"What do we *touch*?" "What do we *smell*?" "What do we *taste*?"—and the palm with "What do we *feel* (what emotion)?"

## Assistive Technology for Writing

Computer programs for writing help struggling writers develop and organize their ideas so their writing flows more fluently. Several kinds of programs are available. Some type the words as students speak them into a microphone. Some allow students to hear what they have typed. Spell-checking, word-prediction, and thesaurus programs also improve writing fluency. The more easliy that frustrated writers achieve fluency, the quicker their resistance to writing fades.

Some writing programs and applications use graphic organizers to build and strengthen writing skills, while others focus on writing conventions such as grammar. Many use time-saving devices such as predictive text. Please check out the "Assistive Technology" section and chart on pages 80–81 for more information about this topic.

# Assessing Students' Writing

As we all know, reading a piece of writing with excellent ideas, but mostly inaccurate use of conventions, is very frustrating for us and for students. Assigning a grade to such a piece is difficult. If you find that grading writing is difficult, you are not alone. Assessing writing is challenging for many teachers, especially when they are considering the work of students with LD.

Students with learning difficulties often think they hate writing. In our experience, what they really hate is revising.

Rubrics are a highly effective tool you can use to assess all types of writing. Rubrics help students become more competent by celebrating their strengths, such as being able to easily find evidence for their opinions and ideas in the text. Rubrics also help teachers and students target their needs for more instruction.

## Evaluating the Writing of Students with Learning Difficulties

Give each student a folder to be used exclusively for writing. Attach a "Writing Portfolio Record Sheet" (page 138) to the inside flap of the folder. Help each student select one writing skill in need of significant improvement. Explain that except for the target skill and previously mastered skills, you will not notice other types of errors. As the student shows significant improvement in the target skill, have a conference to decide what skill to

focus on next. Tell students that as they add new skills they are expected to maintain competence in the skills they have previously mastered.

Teaching struggling writers to use writing rubrics can be very effective in helping them internalize guidelines for good writing. Check to see what the publisher of your language arts or writing program offers. Find and use rubrics sanctioned by your district. Go online to find free rubrics. (See "References and Resources.") Be aware that complex rubrics can overwhelm emerging writers. The best approach is to use just one category at a time until some fluency is achieved. As other categories are added, students are expected to maintain the progress they have made in previous categories. For more information on assessment, see Chapter 8.

You can find many rubrics on the Internet to help you assess your students' competence in each of the 6+1 writing traits, or for any other program you are using. We recommend that you first consult your state's department of education website. Another excellent resource is the website for Education Northwest, as it gives samples at various grade levels. (Visit educationnorthwest.org /resource/464.)

# Questions and Answers

*"When can I start using these strategies, and how long should I use them?"*

All the strategies presented in this chapter can be used in conjunction with any reading or writing program you are currently using. In other words, you don't have to wait until they are approved or adopted by your school or district. You can start implementing them today with students who are not experiencing success with present methods. If other students also want to try these strategies occasionally, you can allow this, but your target students should use them consistently until they are ready to make a full-time transition to the adopted program. If they never become ready for that transition, remember that they were not doing well with the adopted program in the first place. These students are probably farther ahead because of your modifications than they would have been without them.

*"In what ways is the teaching of reading for students with LD changing when a district is using Common Core?"*

For students with learning difficulties to master the Common Core standards in language arts, you must provide targeted instruction that accommodates their exceptional learning needs. For example, students who struggle with comprehension must have direct instruction in how to interact with all the elements required for accurate comprehension to take place. For students to successfully participate in the regular education science and social studies classes, most publishing companies now have their textbooks available in online audio versions, along with high-interest texts with lower reading levels. Both these options should be supplemented with the same graphic organizers used by students who learn at or above grade level, so students with learning difficulties can still focus on the essential information. Formative assessment is critical in helping the students close the gap between their current level of learning and the grade-level standards they are expected to master during a given school year. IEPs should include annual goals aligned with grade-level academic standards.

Keep in mind that the teaching of reading is changing significantly for all students, not just those with learning difficulties. The CCSS bring a plethora of reading connections to informational text of all kinds, and you will have to continuously bring new teaching methods into your repertoire to create successful learning experiences for all learners.

### *"Won't some of these active learning strategies make my kids with high energy levels more uncontrollable?"*

Plan for students to work in 10- to 15-minute segments, with sensory breaks as described on page 33 between work sessions. If students need to calm down, have them listen to soothing music for a few minutes before returning to work. Keep classroom lights low as well. Make perks available for students who maintain on-task behavior.

### *"How can I use actual novels with students who read far below grade level?"*

All students enjoy stories they consider to be "good" and may even have better attitudes toward reading when they like the story content. All reading comprehension strategies described in this chapter may be applied to the study of high-quality literature, with or without literature circles. Check out the use of colored overlays or lenses for glasses described by the Irlen Institute at www.irlen.com.

### *"Shouldn't all students learn phonics in the primary grades?"*

Many adults learned to read by methods other than phonics and can read well. We should teach phonics when students are ready to learn phonics—usually when students are capable of discriminating between sounds. If a student's auditory memory function is impaired, or if some other form of LD makes it difficult or impossible for a student to understand and use phonics, use other methods described in this book to teach the skills needed for reading. Postpone teaching phonics until students perceive themselves as capable readers.

### *"What if some kids miss out on important vocabulary or skills because they aren't doing the same tasks as the other students?"*

Teach them the grade-level vocabulary in another format. (*Examples:* Incorporate the words into crossword puzzles or checkers games in which students are not allowed to move their checker until they say the meaning of the word on a particular square, which is approved by their opponent. Structure skill work to give the students practice in the skills that all the other students are working on, but in a more hands-on manner. Find and use apps that motivate them and hold their interest.

### *"Won't kids be unable to write in real-world situations if they always use the crutches described in this chapter?"*

Students who develop a positive attitude about their writing ability may eventually learn to write in more traditional ways. Those who never develop this attitude will always have problems with writing. Your goal should be to help your students perceive themselves as capable writers, using whatever methods are available to you.

We are aware of no standardized test on which students are not allowed to draw some type of graphic before they start writing. If visual learners need graphic assistance for their entire life, it's better for them to learn such crutches than to grow up believing there is only one correct way to write—a way they can't master.

Numerous colleges and universities provide assistance to students with learning difficulties. Our job is getting our students to want to continue their education. We should use any tool within our reach to make that happen.

### *"My students with LD resist journal writing. What can I do to help them?"*

Try using the goal-setting strategy described on pages 61–63 under "Goal Setting." This will give your students a sense of control over how much and what they write.

In our opinion, teachers often overdo journal writing. Some students are asked to journal for most or all of their subjects on a given day. We wonder how adults would feel if someone asked us to reflect in writing about every aspect of our daily lives. Give your students with learning difficulties choices about how often they will write in journals.

### *"How can I use technology to engage my students in writing?"*

Many websites offer free downloads that provide scaffolding assistance for students who struggle in writing. You can check out www.koyotesoft.com to get started.

# Question Starters

## Literal Thinking

"Demonstrate . . ." _____

"Explain in your own words . . ." _____

"Find . . ." _____

"Give a definition of . . ." _____

"Give an example of . . ." _____

"List . . ." _____

"See . . ." _____

"Summarize . . ." _____

## Interpretive/Creative Thinking

"Analyze . . ." _____

"Categorize . . ." _____

"Classify . . ." _____

"Compare . . ." _____

"Contrast . . ." _____

"Create . . ." _____

"Design . . ." _____

"Find similarities and differences . . ." _____

"Give the pros and cons of . . ." _____

"Imagine . . ." _____

"Judge . . ." _____

"Predict . . ." _____

"State and defend your opinion of . . ." _____

# Predictions

**Name:** _____

**For:** (story title) _____

| Prediction | Yes | No | Maybe |
|---|---|---|---|
| _____ | ☐ | ☐ | ☐ |
| _____ | ☐ | ☐ | ☐ |
| _____ | ☐ | ☐ | ☐ |
| _____ | ☐ | ☐ | ☐ |
| _____ | ☐ | ☐ | ☐ |
| _____ | ☐ | ☐ | ☐ |
| _____ | ☐ | ☐ | ☐ |
| _____ | ☐ | ☐ | ☐ |
| _____ | ☐ | ☐ | ☐ |
| _____ | ☐ | ☐ | ☐ |
| _____ | ☐ | ☐ | ☐ |
| _____ | ☐ | ☐ | ☐ |
| _____ | ☐ | ☐ | ☐ |
| _____ | ☐ | ☐ | ☐ |
| _____ | ☐ | ☐ | ☐ |
| _____ | ☐ | ☐ | ☐ |
| _____ | ☐ | ☐ | ☐ |
| _____ | ☐ | ☐ | ☐ |

# KWPL

**Name:** _____

**For:** (story title) _____

| What We Already **K**now | What We **W**ant to Know | What We **P**redict We Will Learn | What We Have **L**earned |
|---|---|---|---|
| | | | |

# Story Map

Setting

How You Would Have Solved This Problem

Major Character #1

How Problem Was Solved

Title

Major Character #2

Turning Point/Climax

Minor Characters and Roles

Biggest Problem Characters Must Solve

# Character Map

Physical Appearance

How You Would Have Solved Character's Problem

Positive Qualities

How Character Changed by End of Story

Name of Character

Negative Qualities

Barriers to Character's Plans or Wishes

Most Important Actions

Effect of Actions on Other Characters

# Books I Want to Read

**This list belongs to:** _____

| Author or Call Number | Title | Short Description |
|---|---|---|
| | | |
| | | |
| | | |
| | | |
| | | |
| | | |
| | | |
| | | |
| | | |

# Reading Response Journal

## A Record of My Thoughts

My name:_____

Title of the book I'm reading:_____

Author's name:_____

Date I started reading the book: _____

Date I finished reading the book: _____

| Event | My Reaction |
|---|---|
|  |  |
|  |  |
|  |  |
|  |  |
|  |  |
|  |  |
|  |  |
|  |  |

# Vocabulary Attributes Chart

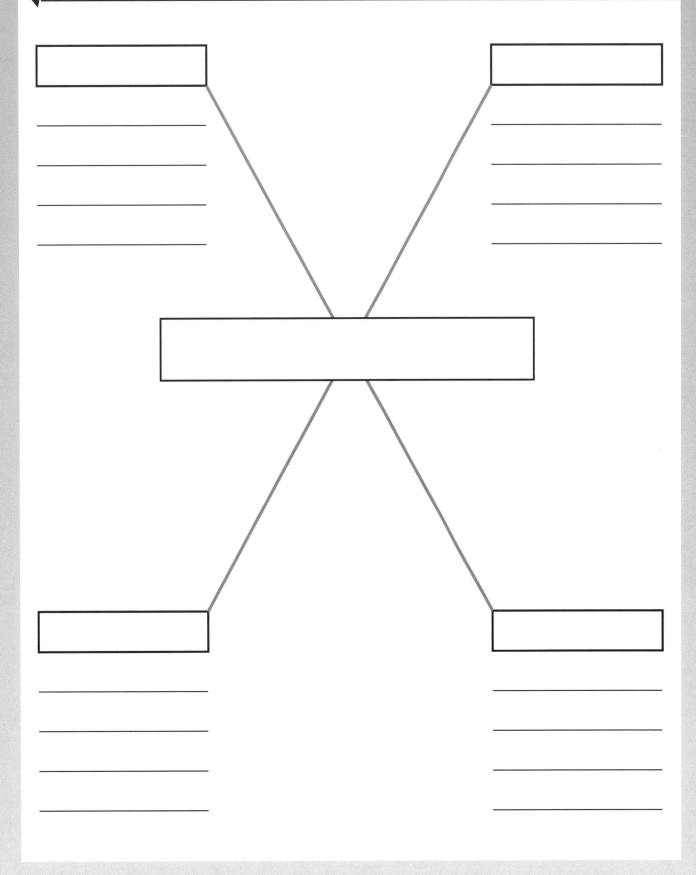

# Learning Words by Style

## Visual Style

- Look at the word and say it aloud, pronouncing every sound.
- Close your eyes and "see" the word.
- Open your eyes and write the word; check for accuracy.
- Write a definition in your own words.
- Look up to the left and "see" the word in a bright color; say the meaning aloud; write the word and check for accuracy.
- Repeat this process as often as it takes to remember the spelling.
- **Repeat these steps with all the words.**

## Tactile-Kinesthetic Style

- Trace the word with your index finger while saying the letters aloud.
- Draw a box around the word that follows the shapes of the letters; notice what the shape reminds you of.
- Sing, act, or dance the word (in your mind if you like).
- Use letters made from sandpaper; trace them as you say them; write the word; check for accuracy.
- Learn the meaning in your own words.
- Write the word in shaving cream, salt in a cafeteria tray, or other similar substance; each time the word is complete, say the meaning.
- **Repeat these steps with all the words.**

## Auditory Style

- Say the word aloud; notice each letter or blend, as well as any silent letters. Notice the syllables.
- Write the word as you are spelling it out loud.
- Write a meaning in your own words and read it aloud a few times.
- Sing the letters to any tune or song.
- Sing the meaning of the word.
- Write the word again, always checking for accuracy each time it is spelled out.
- **Repeat these steps with all the words.**

## Multisensory Style

(Multisensory style combines visual, tactile-kinesthetic, and auditory styles in any combination. One possible combination is described in this box. Teachers can create others.)

- Look at the word. Pronounce all sounds that should be spoken.
- Visualize the word in another color with your eyes closed.
- Trace the letters of the word in some other media or color or on a friend's back with your finger.
- Find the word's meaning and write it in your own words.
- Draw a box around the word and notice the shape the box makes.
- Close your eyes and visualize the word doing something that describes its meaning.
- Clap out the syllables of the word.
- Write the word several times; check for accuracy each time.
- **Repeat these steps with all the words.**

Name: _____

| Number of words | V-Pre | V-Post | T-K Pre | T-K Post | A-Pre | A-Post | M-Pre | M-Post |
|---|---|---|---|---|---|---|---|---|
| 15 | | | | | | | | |
| 14 | | | | | | | | |
| 13 | | | | | | | | |
| 12 | | | | | | | | |
| 11 | | | | | | | | |
| 10 | | | | | | | | |
| 9 | | | | | | | | |
| 8 | | | | | | | | |
| 7 | | | | | | | | |
| 6 | | | | | | | | |
| 5 | | | | | | | | |
| 4 | | | | | | | | |
| 3 | | | | | | | | |
| 2 | | | | | | | | |
| 1 | | | | | | | | |

## My strongest learning style is (check one):

☐ Visual   ☐ Tactile-Kinesthetic   ☐ Auditory   ☐ Multisensory

# Steps to Good Writing

## 1. Getting Ready: Prewriting

- Listen to soothing instrumental music in a slightly darkened room to let your ideas flow.

- Brainstorm your ideas about the suggested topic into a visual picture on paper. Do this in any way that feels comfortable. You might use a web or a mind map.

## 2. Writing

- Choose a subtopic from your picture, web, or mind map.

- Write your ideas in sentences as you think of them.

- At this stage, don't worry about putting your ideas in the correct order, using the correct spelling, or using the right punctuation, capitalization, or grammar. Just write!

- Continue this process until you are out of ideas.

## 3. Revising

- Read what you have written aloud to another student.

- Ask your listener to comment on **one** idea in your writing. Invite your listener to ask **one** question about something that is unclear.

- Have your listener make one suggestion about how to make your written piece better. You may accept or reject the suggestion.

- To make changes, try out different arrangements of the sentences and ideas. If you are working on paper, you can literally cut the sentences apart and tape them together in different orders. (Use removable tape.) If you are working on a computer, use a word processing program to move things around. You might save different versions of your piece and compare them.

## 4. Editing

- Work with a partner or the teacher to correct spelling, mechanics, and so on.

- If you feel that your writing needs a lot of help, focus on one skill at a time until you master it. Add other skills one at a time, knowing that all previously mastered skills should also be evident in your work.

## 5. Publishing

- For every three or four pieces you write, you must choose **one** to publish.

- Polish your chosen piece so other people can understand it.

- Write your final copy in pen (on a clean sheet of paper) or type it on a computer. If you use a computer, be sure to use any available programs to check your spelling and grammar.

- Arrange with the teacher to sit in the author's chair and share your work with the class.

**Repeat the writing and revising steps until YOU are satisfied with your writing.**

# Paragraph Organizer

**The main idea:** _____

_____

_____

| Sequence | Sentence Suggestions |
|----------|---------------------|
|          |                     |
|          |                     |
|          |                     |
|          |                     |
|          |                     |
|          |                     |
|          |                     |
|          |                     |
|          |                     |
|          |                     |
|          |                     |

# Writing Portfolio Record Sheet

**For:** _____

(student's name)

| Target Skill | Date Begun | Date Mastered | Comments |
|---|---|---|---|
|  |  |  |  |
|  |  |  |  |
|  |  |  |  |
|  |  |  |  |
|  |  |  |  |
|  |  |  |  |
|  |  |  |  |
|  |  |  |  |
|  |  |  |  |
|  |  |  |  |
|  |  |  |  |

# CHAPTER 6

# Reading and Learning with Informational Text

The content areas that extend the curriculum beyond reading, writing, and math present special problems to struggling learners, who usually have a negative attitude about the difficult reading they encounter in subjects such as literature, science, health, and social studies. Some students actually have a physiological response to any phrase that includes the word *read*. Their stress level rises, and their defense mechanisms activate. We try to substitute synonyms for the dreaded word *read* whenever possible, such as *skim, scan, find,* and *locate*.

If you think you're not a reading teacher, think again! When a student has trouble with a particular subject, poor reading skills usually are part of the problem. We are all reading teachers, since we all need to know how to help kids read and understand specific content. Although technology allows students with learning difficulties to receive the information they need from various digital sources, reading is still critical. Almost all 21st-century careers require some ability in the areas of reading and writing. (Note: Refer often to the "Assistive Technology" chart on pages 80–81 for technologies that may help you and your students in a variety of subject areas.)

The Common Core State Standards and other types of comprehensive curricula emphasize using informational text to develop the literacy skills students need to learn about science, social studies, and technical subjects. Informational text is an excellent resource for developing language and vocabulary. This is especially important for students with learning difficulties who have limited background knowledge and experiences to support their reading comprehension. To help these students become more successful in the content areas, we can boost their enthusiasm by letting them choose topics that already interest them or seem likely to interest them. We can teach them to approach all content-area reading with the question *How can I transform these words into pictures so I can remember the information visually?* We can enable them to use their learning modality strengths as they obtain and share information. We can give them ways to gather, identify, and organize the *maximum* amount of information with the *minimum* amount of reading. (Remember, if they're not learning the way we teach them, let's teach them the way they learn.)

> We are *all* reading teachers, since we *all* need to know how to help kids read and understand specific content.

This chapter focuses on the explicit teaching of strategies for reading and studying in the content areas. As you try them with your students, keep in mind the acronym *WHOLISTIC* (see page 51) to be sure you are using as many strategies as possible that are comfortable for global learners. If these strategies seem like a lot of time-consuming work, please don't be discouraged. Once your students know how to learn, you'll save time later on. Use as much time as is necessary to help students learn these strategies so they can use them independently. Since you will be teaching the strategies in the context of the required standards, you will not actually lose any learning time.

### Unlocking Autism 🔒

Some students with ASD struggle to adjust to a full-time regular classroom setting but show a high interest in nonfiction text. With accommodations, almost all these students can meet their IEP goals and make progress toward mastering Common Core State Standards. Some students have IEP goals that direct them to gain social experiences with age peers in a regular classroom setting, which is commonly accomplished through participation in science and social studies classes. Intensive accommodations are sometimes needed when the student has little to no speech. Remember, visual, tactile, and kinesthetic approaches greatly improve learning outcomes for this population.

## Scenario: Elizabeth

By the time she reached tenth grade, Elizabeth had lost faith that she would ever succeed in school, and she was seriously considering dropping out. Her failure was not from lack of trying. She went to school nearly every day, carried an assignment notebook and dutifully filled it out before leaving each class, brought home books from every subject every night, and spent 30 minutes per class per night on homework. Neither she nor her frustrated parents could understand why she kept getting low grades.

Elizabeth's special education teacher worked to find the causes for this dilemma. He discovered that when Elizabeth was trying to take notes from any source, her notes were simply too lengthy to be helpful.

He suggested that she use graphic organizers to take notes. He coached her on how to use those forms most effectively. Elizabeth learned how to notice and separate the most important information from the less important information.

The day Elizabeth came home after her first successful quiz, she told her parents gleefully, "I now realize I'm a visual learner. When I take notes and study in the way that matches my learning modality, I can actually understand the material. For the first time in my life, I feel really prepared for a test." Then she added, "Maybe these methods will make me smarter in my other classes, too."

## Getting Ready to Learn

How many learning-how-to-learn strategies do your students know? On page 149 is a chart you can use to track their progress. Use the "Not Yet" column to identify strategies they need to learn, the "Learning Now" column to indicate strategies you're currently teaching, and the "Knows How" column for strategies they have mastered. Enter dates to mark their progress over time; update the charts as students acquire new strategies. Older students can keep their own records.

## The Magic of Using Graphic Organizers

Graphic or visual organizers are any learning tools that allow students to visualize information, rather than simply reading, hearing, or seeing it. Sometimes graphic organizers are called mind maps. Provide experiences for students to use various types of these tools with several types of information sources, including those with printed text and those with some type of pictures. Allow all students to use whatever methods lead to the best possible learning outcomes for them.

### Scenario

On a day when Susan was demonstrating model lessons in a middle school, she visited a class of 12 students whose learning disabilities were significant enough to warrant their placement in a self-contained special education class. Their frustrated teacher greeted Susan by saying, "I sure am glad to see you! We've been working on outlining for our last six meetings, and the kids still don't get it. How can you help?"

Susan had two immediate but unspoken reactions to this question. First, she knew that most of the students were probably global learners. Outlining is a practice only analytical thinkers are comfortable with. Second, Susan wondered why the teacher was wasting so much valuable teaching time on an obsolete skill. Outlining is not something most people need to do in their everyday lives; organizing information is.

It took only 15 minutes for those kids to learn how to organize information in a brain-compatible way. The students were using a written exercise in which three species of bats were described, each in its own paragraph. The job was to identify each species with a

Roman numeral, find three details about each species, and list the details as entries A, B, and C under each numeral.

Susan placed each student with a partner and asked the students to quickly skim (not read) the paragraphs to identify one species of bat. She called on one student at random. Predictably, the student identified the vampire bat.

From her desk, the teacher signaled Susan. "The vampire bat is the one described in the *second* paragraph," she whispered, "and I expect students to identify them in their proper order."

"Don't worry," Susan whispered back. "It will all work out in the end."

Using colored markers, Susan drew a red circle and wrote "vampire bat" in the center. Next, she asked the partners to *skim* the appropriate paragraph to find two to three details about vampire bats. She cautioned them to find at least that many, because she would call on them at random until several details were mentioned. She told them they would have 60 seconds, and that gave them a sense of urgency that kept them nicely on task the entire time. When the time was up, Susan called on several students at random and charted their responses as spokes on the red circle.

Susan and the students repeated this process for the other two bats, using a blue triangle for the fruit bat and a green square for the flying fox. (You've probably guessed that the reason for using different colors and shapes is so the information will make a lasting impression on the kids' brains.)

Next, Susan said, "Now, what your teacher wants you to do is organize this information the way the ancient Romans did. So look at the first paragraph and identify the bat. Since it's the fruit bat, we'll print a Roman numeral I in the blue triangle for the fruit bat. Next, let's identify the first fact and label it with a capital A. The second fact is B, and so on."

Susan and the students repeated the same steps until they had a picture of the details for all three bats. Finally, they transferred the information to the correct blank spaces in the outline form at the bottom of the worksheet, and the global learners were on their way to learning how to outline in a learning modality compatible manner—backward from the whole to the parts.

The kids caught on that outlining was easy if they were allowed to do it in a way that was comfortable for them—visually and holistically. Next, someone asked a shocking question: "Could we please do another one?" Their teacher, shaking her head in disbelief, quickly passed out another example. Working independently, it took most pairs only 12 minutes to complete the second outline in the same manner as the first.

## Using Simple Graphic Organizers

Graphic organizers include flowcharts, timelines, diagrams, cartoons, pictures, Venn diagrams, or any other tools that help students visualize information. Graphic organizers enable global learners to *skim* written text for indicators that important information is present, *skim* a particular section for the necessary information, and record that information in a visual way, creating a mental picture of what they need to learn. They can glean a lot of information with a minimal amount of actual reading, which they greatly appreciate. Recall that global learners must see the big picture before focusing on any of the parts. Show your students how to use simple graphic organizers:

- As you lecture or talk, draw what you are saying onto a simple picture format. Use as many shapes and colors as you can, and think out loud as you draw. (See "Metacognition: Becoming Aware of One's Own Thinking," page 65). In this way, students will be able to repeat the process you are modeling.

- Demonstrate how to summarize information into short phrases as spokes attached to a shape. Never write complete sentences, which may make students think it is okay to copy word-for-word what they read.

- Show students how to use graphic organizers not only to illustrate important information, but also as tools they can use to prepare for assessments so they can better remember what they have learned.

Even if some students are already using other note-taking methods successfully, encourage them to try this method once or twice. Give them the "Simple Organizer" handout on page 150. Explain that once they know how to do simple mapping, they will have this strategy in their learning toolbox if they ever need another way to learn especially difficult information. Let all students use whatever methods lead to the best possible learning outcomes.

## Vocabulary Mapping

The "Vocabulary Attributes Chart" (page 133) is a visual organizer for vocabulary. It's effective not only at building reading vocabulary, but also for teaching vocabulary in any of the content areas.

In one sixth-grade class, the teacher was trying to teach the vocabulary of ancient Rome. He was very frustrated because the kids could *write* the definitions but couldn't *remember* what the words meant. To solve this problem, we grouped the words into several categories (*example:* words describing jobs in the Roman culture).

Then we created a vocabulary attributes chart for each group. The chart for the job of senator looked like this:

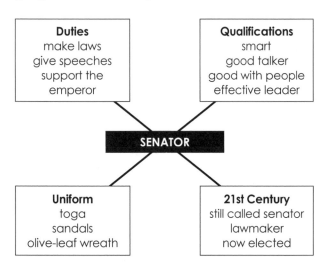

# Understanding Content from Written Sources and Lectures

Many content area teachers have never had any courses in how to teach reading. The KWPL method in Chapter 5 (page 128) is a good starting point. You can use this method not only to help students learn reading skills, but also to teach content area topics. The key is to complete the first three columns from left to right (KWP: what we already **K**now, what we **W**ant to know, and what we **P**redict we will learn) *before* students actually try to learn content from text or visual sources. These steps can take up most of a class period, so it is reasonable to assume that the actual reading of the content won't begin until the second day of the unit. Because students have had time to make connections to background information and to formulate questions, their brains will be much more likely to notice the important information when the reading begins.

## Projects and Reports, Including Project-Based Learning (PBL)

For various reasons, students with learning difficulties have often been denied opportunities for working on projects. Often teachers felt compelled to limit these students' work to mastering the basic skills required to perform well on assessments set up specifically to measure those skills. What teachers may not have realized is that projects actually motivate these students to learn, because students with learning difficulties find it much easier to concentrate on learning about topics they find interesting.

In contrast to traditional methods, project-based learning (PBL) creates a new relationship between learning and teaching. It requires you and your colleagues to work together to create and implement standards-based projects. Rather than you directing the instruction, your students guide their own learning through inquiry and exploration, following carefully explained instructions at several points throughout their project work. Your role in PBL is that of a learning coach. You are responsible for designing the guidelines for the project work and facilitating the students' ability to find the resources they need and to follow expected behaviors and procedures for the entire process.

Your students work to conduct their research, both answer and ask questions, collect and interpret data, develop and evaluate solutions to the designated problem, craft reasoned arguments, and present their findings to their classmates or another suitable audience. These steps are critical to meeting the rigor and perseverance required by the Common Core State Standards for informational text, as well as any curriculum that includes attention to rigor.

You can assess not only your students' final products, but also their performance throughout the entire problem-solving process. Students should have opportunities to assess their own critical thinking and problem-solving skills as well. Your structured feedback is critical to motivating and developing the perseverance your students need to meet the expected criteria for learning.

It is beyond the scope of this book to instruct you in all aspects of PBL, as many helpful resources designed for that purpose are available on the Internet. Our support for you and your students is focused on helping them be able to access and understand the information they seek. The "References and Resources" contain some specific sources that you may use to learn the steps and procedures associated with PBL. Arrange for your students to work with the media center or technology staff to locate and collect various sources of information about their subject. Public librarians and school media specialists are also happy to help with this process.

## Facilitating Students' Work When Using PBL

Students with learning difficulties can be very enthusiastic about doing projects or reports—until they realize a lot of reading is involved. The strategies in this section will help these students gather the information they need with a minimum of formal reading. You may notice that the following section is similar to one found in Chapter 5 on pages 93–94, but this one has been customized to help students reading informational text.

## Before Reading

Students must activate prior knowledge so they can make connections between what they already know and the new material they are about to learn. Have students:

1. Brainstorm what they already know about the topic. (See "KWPL" on pages 128.)

2. Describe and discuss the purpose for learning the material.

3. Survey the entire chapter, noticing important features such as pictures, maps, charts, diagrams, italics, and bold print. Make predictions along the way. (Use the "Predictions" handout on page 127.)

4. Read the questions at the end of each section before reading the section. This alerts the brain to what's important to notice while reading.

5. Read and pronounce the vocabulary words. Students should wait to learn or study words they don't know until they have read or heard the content. *Caution:* Writing dictionary definitions has been found to be completely ineffective in helping kids remember vocabulary words. It's much more effective to discuss the words in the context of the text and have kids write about the vocabulary in their own words. Graphic organizers such as the "Vocabulary Attributes Chart" on page 133 are a big help to visual learners.

6. Locate places and events on a map.

7. Watch a video, or other visual representation of the material about to be learned. This helps visual learners connect new information to the pictures now stored in their memory.

## During Reading

Students must make sure they understand what they are reading or hearing. Anything they don't understand must be clarified. Have students:

1. Notice headings and other features (pictures, maps, charts, diagrams, italics, bold print) that identify important information.

2. Get as much information as they can by skimming. (See "Skimming and Summarizing Written Material," next.)

3. Look away after a section is finished and say out loud, or write a summary of, what has been read or heard. (This may be done with a learning partner.)

4. Use graphic organizers such as the "Content Organization Chart" (pages 144 and 151) or the "Survey-Skim-Study-Question (3S+Q)" handout (page 152).

5. Learn to ask questions about the text. (See "Reciprocal Teaching" on pages 105–108 and the "Question Starters" handout on page 126.)

6. Check out earlier predictions. (Use the "Predictions" handout on page 127 or the P column in the "KWPL" handout on page 128.)

7. Summarize often what they are learning. (Use graphic organizers for this, such as the fishbone graphic on page 105.)

## After Reading

Students must be able to demonstrate their understanding of the text by answering the questions they surveyed before reading. They should also be able to connect information from several sections of text throughout the section or chapter. Have students:

1. Confirm or refute original predictions.

2. Summarize the major ideas in the whole piece by outlining, using a graphic organizer, or simply drawing what they want to remember.

3. Think about how this section is connected to what they have learned before.

4. Go back to their notes and combine the information there to describe five big ideas to remember from the entire section.

# Skimming and Summarizing Written Material

Have students:

1. Notice and read the heading for any new section.

2. Locate and read all questions that will have to be answered for that section.

3. Skim the first and last paragraphs of a section.

4. For other paragraphs in the section, read the first and last sentences and any key words that are italicized or highlighted in some way. Locate the information for the italicized terms. Illustrate one or two key points using a graphic organizer.

5. Write down the answer to a required question as soon as they recognize it.

6. To summarize a section, combine the key points from all paragraphs into one or two statements.

7. Write an introduction and conclusion for the summary.

Reciprocal teaching, explained in great detail on pages 105–108, is another strategy that can strengthen students' reading comprehension in the content areas.

Try it as a way to improve understanding of material from texts and lectures.

## The Content Organization Chart

Global students need a way to organize their thinking as they find and learn new content. For the brain to learn new information, it must first be able to connect what is new to what the brain already knows. Because the brain is a pattern-seeking device, we need to teach in visual patterns. Because the "Content Organization Chart" can help your students better understand any content they are learning, they will be more able to successfully participate in PBL.

The "Content Organization Chart" handout (page 151) is slightly different from simple graphic organizers because once the categories are in the visual forms, they remain the same for all other examples within that subject area. The following figure shows how you can use the "Content Organization Chart" to help your students follow along with the PBL steps you have chosen. A more in-depth description of the chart follows, starting in the next section on this page.

You're right—the "Content Organization Chart" looks exactly like the "Story Map" and "Character Map"

in Chapter 5. This basic format can be used for many different purposes. The chart lends itself to any subject area at any grade level, such as:

- the seasons
- the systems of the human body
- plants of a certain category
- the elements in a story or novel
- processes in mathematical equations
- the steps in a scientific experiment
- communities
- types of energy
- regions of the world
- types of government systems
- famous people from any category
- animals of a certain category
- artists of a certain style
- composers of a certain type of music
- the planets of the solar system
- the people of any country
- the states or provinces of any country

## Using the Content Organization Chart

The step-by-step description that follows illustrates how you might use the chart to teach students a unit on regions of their own country. The headings in the source material would be transferred to the geometric shapes on the chart. Once students complete a study of the region in which they live, they realize that the topics will stay consistent throughout their study of other regions.

First, demonstrate this method while all students are looking at the same source of information in writing. This method may be used to teach the structure of the text, which enables weak readers to get lots of information without having to read every single word. For example, when students realize all vocabulary words are italicized, or all section headings are always in bold blue print, they can let their eyes move more quickly than is possible when they think that all words and sections are equally important.

1. Prepare a large wall chart version of the "Content Organization Chart" handout on page 151, drawing each geometric shape in a different color. Of course, you can use other formats for the same purpose, such as an interactive whiteboard.

**Content Organization Chart for PBL**

- Setting the stage
- Become project designers
- Reflect on the PBL process and evaluate projects with rubric
- **Designated problem**
- Gather necessary background information
- Prepare and present the projects
- Students create their own projects
- Negotiate criteria for project evaluation
- Accumulate and store required materials

**2.** Group students in pairs. Give each student a personal copy of the "Content Organization Chart" handout. Explain that you will be using the wall chart to model what they should write on their handouts.

**3.** Tell students that they will be learning about their own region. (*Example:* If your school is in Wyoming, they will learn about the Great Plains.) Print the name in the center square of the wall chart. Students should write it on their charts, too.

**4.** Instruct students to look in the table or description of contents of their textbooks, eBooks, or online articles and locate the chapter or section on the selected region.

**5.** Have students survey the content by browsing through it, noticing how the text is organized, and asking each other questions about the pictures, charts, and other features. They don't have to answer the questions they ask. They should also read any questions that are listed in the chapter.

**6.** Working with partners, ask students to skim the content for about three minutes and notice the way(s) the text signals the presence of important categories of information. Print the name of the first category (*example:* "location") in the space at the top of the chart.

**7.** Direct students to skim the location section in the text and record three facts about that category on their charts or on the interactive whiteboard. They should record the facts on spokes attached to each figure on the chart.

**8.** Use the Name Card Method (pages 12–14) to call on students until you have four to six details about the region's location. Write them on the appropriate surface. Direct the students to add any details to their own charts that aren't already written there.

**9.** Call students' attention to the way the text signals the next category of information. Print the name of the category in the next shape on the wall chart or whiteboard, working clockwise; students also add it to their charts.

**10.** Repeat steps 7 and 8 for the new category. Proceed in the same way until all the categories have been charted. Call students' attention to the fact that they now have a completed chart they can use to prepare for any discussion or test on that particular region.

**11.** For the next region, hand out new copies of the "Content Organization Chart." You'll also need a fresh demonstration chart. Now choose a region of your country that is as different as possible. Print the name (*example:* "Pacific Northwest") in the center square of the chart. Call students' attention to the fact that informational texts often present content in very similar ways—from chapter to chapter and from subject to subject.

**12.** Using the Name Card Method, call on one student to *predict* a category of information that will be described for the new region. Write it on the demonstration chart—*in the same shape you used for that category on the first chart.*

**13.** If students are using textbooks, direct them to turn to the index, find the page that describes the predicted category, and chart the details for that category.

**14.** Repeat steps 8 through 10 for the new region.

By the third region, many of the discussion buddies will be ready to complete their own charts by using the textbook or other sources independently. Continue working with pairs that still need your assistance. Consistently point out that the same categories should always appear in the same places on the chart. (*Example:* If "location" was the top circle in the first chart, it should be the top circle in all charts.)

When you give an assessment, consider handing out blank copies of the chart and allowing students to fill them in with as many details as they can remember before starting the test. Since they will already have a visual image in their brain of a completed chart, they should be able to recall much more information about the topic than if they had used traditional note taking methods.

**Variation:** Older students might prefer using a chart without geometric shapes. At the top of page 146 is an example of a chart for studying the systems of the human body.

# Survey-Skim-Study-Question (3S+Q) Method

This method is very effective in its ability to help struggling readers choose the most important information from the text and record it in such a way that their note taking device becomes their study guide for assessments. When we tell students to study for an assessment, they will now know what to do.

In the acronym *3S+Q*, the three *S*'s stand for **Survey, Skim,** and **Study.** The *Q* stands for **Questioning.**

## 3S+Q Method for Note Taking

Here's how the 3S+Q method works for note taking:

**1.** Group students in pairs. Give each student a "Survey-Skim-Study-Question (3S+Q)" handout (page 152).

**2.** Demonstrate how to *survey* a section of text to notice all its features. These include but are not limited to italics, bold print, text size changes, use of color or symbols, maps, charts and all their captions, and so on. Each time one is noticed, pairs ask each other a question about the feature and the partner suggests an answer.

| Body System | Organs | Functions | Diseases | Caring For |
|---|---|---|---|---|
| Circulatory | Heart, arteries, veins | Pump blood to and from the heart | High blood pressure; blockages | Weight control; exercise; no smoking |
| Respiratory | Nose, lungs, bronchia, diaphragm | Deliver oxygen to blood; breathing | Cancer; chronic obstructive pulmonary disease (COPD) | Same as above |
| Digestive | Stomach, liver, gall bladder, intestines | Intake food; deliver nutrients to cells; eliminate waste | Ulcer; digestive disorders; Crohn's disease; cancer | Low-fat foods; low dairy; lots of water |
| Nervous | Brain, spinal column, nerves | Intellectual; controls other organs | Cancer; stroke, Alzheimer's disease | Avoid falls; engage in lifelong learning |

It does not matter if the answer is right or wrong. When the brain recognizes that feature later, the brain pays more attention to the feature.

3. Have pairs *skim* a section of text, record its general topic in the left column of their chart, then *question* each other about the meaning and write a brief summary of it in the right column using brief phrases—never complete sentences.

4. Continue in the same manner until you are done teaching about this topic.

5. Use the Name Card Method (pages 12–14) to call on kids for their topics and explanations. Invite several pairs to share. Assure the students that as long as they have the general gist of the idea, they don't need to use the exact words anyone else uses.

6. Continue in the same manner until students have taken a full page of notes.

### The Two-Column Strategy for Studying

To use the "Survey-Skim-Study-Question (3S+Q)" chart as a study guide, students should follow this procedure:

1. Cover each column with a sheet of paper.

2. Partner A uncovers the first topic and predicts the details that have been recorded about it.

3. Both partners check to see if the prediction is correct. If it is, they switch roles, and Partner B uncovers the second topic and predicts its details. If the prediction is incorrect, Partner A tries again.

4. When all the topics have been discussed, the partners repeat the process, this time uncovering the details first and predicting the topic.

In this way, students learn the information from both perspectives: topic and details.

Be prepared to model the 3S+Q method several times with students who have difficulty choosing the right topics and coming up with descriptions.

**Variation:** Create a new handout, labeling the left column "Question" and the right column "Explanation." Students take notes in the "Explanation" column for one segment of information at a time, then look back over their notes and create a question for each major point. They study those notes in the same way as described previously in steps 1 through 4.

Note: Students may use the same method to take notes from lectures or from a visual source. Before moving on to another topic, you might want to give student pairs a chance to compare their notes with other pairs, or you might want to use the Name Card Method to create a large version of the chart. This helps you ensure the accuracy of the student charts.

## Taking Notes for Projects and Reports

1. If there are hard copies of some resources, provide a space—perhaps on a bookshelf—for kids to store those materials.

2. Help students find a method of taking notes that will prevent them from being frustrated by trying to absorb too much information all at once. Create a content organization chart (see page 151), perhaps a digital version, so all students know exactly what subtopics they will be investigating. (Note: You may use fewer categories than shown in that chart. For example, in a study of the states, the categories might be topography, weather,

crops, industry, natural resources, recreation, regional cultural events, and famous sons or daughters.) Then the students will be ready to begin their note taking.

Some teachers use this method with an interactive whiteboard or other digital device. We recommend paper so you can display the completed forms in your classroom to show how all the categories of information remain consistent. This helps students develop the ability to predict important categories of information. Alternatively, if students record the information on their own digital devices, they will still be able to access it easily.

Some online resources exist, such as Evernote, UberNote, Google Docs, or our favorite, Ehow.com's subtopic for note cards. If that type of technology is not available for your classroom, teach students how to find important information in the sources they locate, and follow a chosen procedure for taking notes—in writing or digitally.

## Use Note Cards

Ask students to bring in four-by-six-inch note cards, highlighters, and colored paper in the same colors for each medium and in enough colors for the number of subtopics you have identified. Plan your teaching so you will have time for scaffolding, guiding, and encouraging your students throughout the process.

Teach students how to use note cards to take notes and organize information.

**1.** Give each student four to six note cards. Have them write a heading on each card. (*Example:* If students are studying the Spanish missions of California, they might choose four missions—perhaps San Luis Obispo, Santa Barbara, Santa Cruz, and San Juan Capistrano. Each location becomes a heading on a note card.)

**2.** Show students how to take notes in phrases or by paraphrasing what they read, hear, or observe. Insist that students not write complete sentences.

**3.** Have students take notes on the appropriate cards. (*Example:* As students learn information about San Luis Obispo, they locate the note card with that heading and record the information there. As they learn information about Santa Cruz, they record it on the note card with that heading.)

In this way, note taking becomes a kinesthetic experience. Kids with learning difficulties find this method much easier than writing everything on a piece of paper and reorganizing it later.

Students can also use note cards to prepare and study for tests. On one side, they write a question about a word or idea they need to know, using blue or black ink. On the other side, they write or draw the answer, using red ink. They can use the cards to review material on their own or with a partner. If they answer a question correctly, that card goes into a discard pile. If they answer incorrectly, it goes back into the main deck so it will come up again soon. The note cards should be shuffled each time they are used.

For middle school and high school students, please see "3S+Q Method for Note Taking" on page 145.

## Four-Step Research Method

Use this system for gathering and recording information on the selected topic:

**1.** Students select one topic and skim all their sources for information about that topic, highlighting relevant information in a designated color. For example, if the first topic is weather, students skim all their sources for weather information, highlight the information with yellow highlighter, and record the information in phrases on yellow note cards.

**2.** Students move on to another topic, using a different colored highlighter and note card. Note: If one of your goals for this activity is to give students practice in writing, you should use step 3. If that is not a goal, you may go directly to step 4.

**3.** To create a rough draft, students change the phrases into complete sentences and paragraphs on lined paper that is the same color as the highlighter and note cards. If you can purchase colored lined paper, do so. If not, reproduce lines on colored copy paper. Students use the sentences they have created in their final product.

**4.** Students turn the information from their note cards or rough drafts into a final product. The final product can be a presentation using software such as PowerPoint, a video, a poster report, a research paper, an essay, a three-dimensional display, or any of the other suggestions under "Products Compatible with Learning Modality Strengths" (see page 72). Consider your students' learning modalities and strengths when determining how the final product will be presented.

To help kids keep track of their progress on long-term projects, have them keep a daily "Log of Project Work" (page 90). At the beginning of each work period, they enter the date and the task they plan to accomplish that day in the middle column. Five minutes before project work ends, they record what they actually accomplished during that work period in the right column. Spillover work is written on the next middle line so they know where to start when they return to the project.

## Chunking a Science Fair Project

Lengthy assignments that require completing multiple items may overwhelm students with learning difficulties—especially students with poor executive functioning skills, which are defined and described in Chapter 9. A method called chunking divides an assignment into smaller tasks for a student to complete over an extended period of time. Dividing the work into manageable chunks helps the student complete the project successfully. The "Science Project Work Plan" handout (page 153) shows how you can chunk a science fair project for students who need it. The handout lists all the tasks required to complete the entire activity.

Note: You'll find a section explaining backward planning on page 190. This planning method will help students manage a long-term project, too.

Use one copy of the "Audience Rating Rubric" in Chapter 9 (page 197) for each person who is listening to the presentation. Send a copy of the rubric home for practicing the presentation with an adult.

# Questions and Answers

*"Won't all this drawing and mapping slow students down so much that they won't be able to complete their assignments?"*

Think of all the time kids waste when they don't know how to learn. It takes forever for them to find their books, paper, and pencils. Then they have to locate the right place to begin, after which they usually ask numerous questions of you and their classmates. As the use of graphic organizers becomes more automatic, your students may need less time to complete their learning tasks.

*"How is the 'Content Organization Chart' different from plain mapping or other graphic organizers?"*

Many graphic organizers or maps simply create a visual representation of printed text. The "Content Organization Chart" handout (page 151) is designed to illustrate the similarities among chapters or units. When students see and understand those similarities, they begin to anticipate them for upcoming content. Over time, they understand the importance of connecting new knowledge to what they learned in the past.

*"Shouldn't I teach vocabulary words in the same order as they appear in the written material?"*

You may teach them as they are introduced and used in the text, but keep in mind that students with learning difficulties cannot learn more than a few words at a time. That means you'll have to wait until later to teach some of the words. If you teach words by categories using the "Vocabulary Attributes Chart" (page 133), you'll be able to teach some words from the present context as well as other words with similar attributes from other contexts.

---

Dividing the work into manageable chunks helps the student complete the project successfully.

---

*"Won't there be some occasions when students will have to read an entire text rather than selectively skimming and mapping or charting?"*

If and when that time comes, students can still use visual or graphic organizers to make the text material easier to learn and understand. It's likely that students will eventually have many study methods at their disposal besides traditional reading and note taking. Always remember that students will succeed at real-world tasks only if they perceive themselves as capable learners. Use whatever means you can to develop positive self-perceptions, focusing on setting short-term goals (page 61) and on their ongoing effort as described in the section on Carol Dweck's work on page 2. The more successful students are with skimming methods, the more likely they will be to develop and maintain more positive attitudes about reading in general.

A high school English teacher in Midlothian, Illinois, devoted much time and effort during the school year teaching her students how to create visual mind maps of what they wanted to write before they actually started writing. She demonstrated how this strategy would enable them to be fluent in the idea-generation stage and more focused when they actually began to write. While supervising a written college entrance exam for some of her students, she was gratified to see that several of the kids were using the mapping strategy to plan the paragraph they had to write. The teacher knew then that she had taught them a skill they could use to survive in writing tasks even when she would not be there to coach them.

Any support techniques that your students with learning difficulties can learn from you will make them more confident adults and more capable students in post–high school learning situations.

*"What's the best technology available to help students with informational text?"*

Most publishers offer audio versions of current textbooks so that they are accessible to students with vision or decoding difficulties. Both Learning Ally (www.learning ally.org) and Bookshare (www.bookshare.org) provide audio versions of many texts used in schools.

# Learning How to Learn

**Student's Name:** _____

| Strategy | Not Yet | Learning Now | Knows How |
|---|---|---|---|
| Previewing content before reading or studying | | | |
| Using survey techniques such as noticing pictures, graphs, and italics | | | |
| Reading chapter questions before reading the text | | | |
| Predicting important information | | | |
| Taking notes in a manner compatible with learning modality | | | |
| Summarizing what was learned | | | |
| Understanding and remembering vocabulary | | | |
| Remembering what was learned | | | |
| Using various forms of reference materials | | | |
| Transferring learning to other situations | | | |
| Working and learning independently | | | |
| Asking for help when needed | | | |

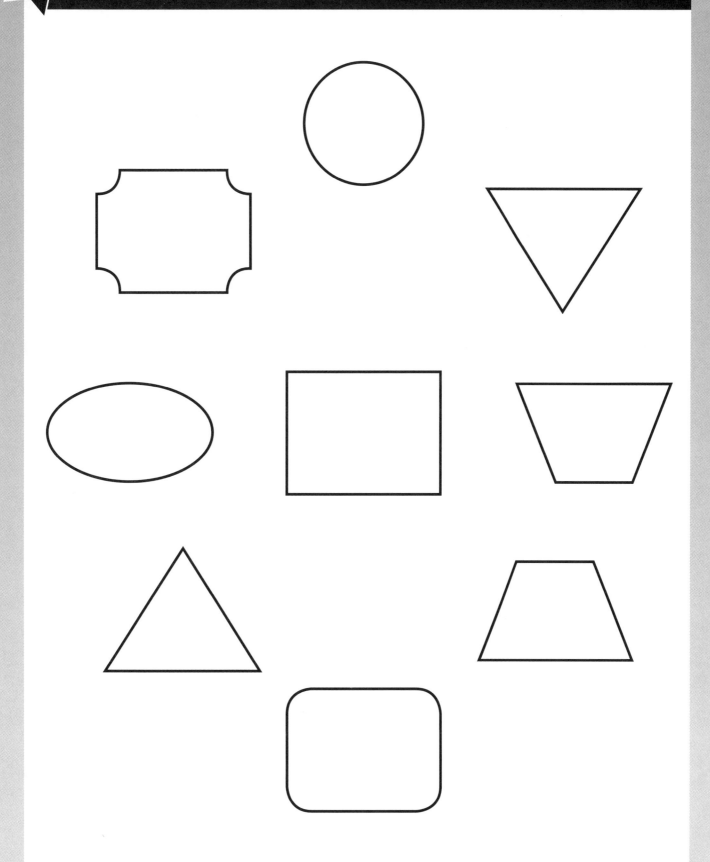

# Survey-Skim-Study-Question (3S+Q)

You can use this form to help you take notes and study the information for discussions and assessments.

- **S**urvey an entire selection to get the big picture. Ask **Q**uestions as you survey. You don't have to write the answers. Just think about them and tell them to your partner.

- **S**kim a small section of text at a time. Ask **Q**uestions as you skim to be sure you are noticing the most important information.

- When you find something you want to remember, take notes in phrases. Constantly ask yourself **Q**uestions to make sure the information is important.

- **S**tudy your notes using the two-column strategy. Ask **Q**uestions and answer them verbally.

| Topic | Details |
|-------|---------|
|       |         |
|       |         |
|       |         |
|       |         |
|       |         |
|       |         |
|       |         |
|       |         |
|       |         |
|       |         |

# Science Project Work Plan

| Tasks | Work Dates |
|---|---|
| **1. Select a topic.**<br>Choose a science project from sources approved by your teacher. Be aware that a science fair project is a method used to find an answer to a question, rather than to show what you know about a topic. Your teacher will help you in selecting your topic. | |
| **2. Gather background information.**<br>Gather information about your topic from books, magazines, the Internet, people, and companies. Use the note card method described by your teacher to record the important information and the sources. | |
| **3. Use the scientific method.**<br>Your teacher will provide a document that describes all the steps of the scientific method. Follow the steps in the order in which they are written. | |
| **4. Conduct a controlled experiment and record your data.**<br>Do your experiment according to the scientific method. Keep your notes in one place. Write down everything you think you might use later. | |
| **5. Make graphs and charts.**<br>Use graphs, charts, and other visuals to describe what happened in your experiment. | |
| **6. Construct an exhibit or display.**<br>Try to make your visual product fun to create and share, but be sure it also shows how you followed the scientific method. | |
| **7. Determine a presentation format:**<br>■ Tell the story of your project. Tell what you did and exactly how you did it.<br>■ Show where you gathered background information.<br>■ Using the rubric provided by your teacher, assess the quality of your work. | |
| **8. Practice your presentation.**<br>Practice with an adult to prepare for showing your project to judges. The more you practice, the more confident you will feel when presenting to the judges, who will be very interested in what you have learned and demonstrated. | |
| **9. Come to the fair and have fun!**<br>See you there! | |

# CHAPTER 7
# All Students Can Be Successful in Math

As you have probably noticed, the pendulum of emphasis in math curriculum and strategies swings back and forth between computation and problem solving, usually sacrificing much of one category for the benefit of the other. Of course, a well-rounded math program should contain a sensible amount of both. Above all, the required teaching strategies should allow all students to make at least one year's forward progress in math for each year they are in school.

The language of mathematics is just as symbolic as the language of reading, and we know that students with learning difficulties have a hard time with symbolic language. In general, struggling students exhibit some, many, or all of the following characteristics when it comes to math:

- They have difficulty seeing and hearing numbers correctly. Reversals and substitutions are common. For some kids, the numbers seem to move on the page.

- Students may be able to recite numbers fairly well, but they lack intuitive understanding about numbers and what they represent. They have very little number sense.

- Students fail to perceive patterns and relationships (*examples:* quantities represented by numerals, coin sizes and values, which signs represent which operations).

- Forming the numerals takes so much energy that students have none left for figuring out solutions. They misread and miswrite, have trouble counting, and can't stay within the lines. Motor problems make their papers sloppy and inaccurate. They mix up columns and digits. It's hard for them to keep their place on a page; this is made worse if work must be copied from the board. They lose manipulatives.

- Students have difficulty remembering number facts or vocabulary, problem-solving procedures, or previously learned material. Rapid-fire mental math is painful or impossible for them.

- Word problems are particularly daunting, since they include *three* layers of symbols: numbers, words, and operations. Students lose their train of thought in the problem-solving process.

- Students are confused by new math problems that include multiple concepts on each page of the textbook.

- Students do the same problem over and over or use only one problem-solving method repeatedly. (This is called *perseveration.*)

- Students can't ignore distractions like the sound coming from a group of students working with the teacher.

Many children develop an intuitive understanding of mathematical concepts during their preschool years. As they observe their world, they learn to understand numerals and the quantities they represent, how to divide things up fairly, and the appropriate clock times for going to bed, getting up, and eating meals. Since the brain seeks patterns, effective teaching in math focuses on demonstrating the presence of patterns and helping children connect new ideas to those they already understand. Since global learners must see the whole picture before understanding the parts, teaching them effectively requires moving from concrete, hands-on learning to the abstract applications of computation and other step-by-step procedures.

Students should not be required to learn basic math facts before engaging in problem solving. Just as kids learn to read by reading and to write by writing, they learn to do math by "mathing"—using mathematical concepts in scenarios based on real-life events. When teaching math to global learners, always begin with a concrete situation. (*Example:* "How many crackers should we take out of the box so all students can have one cracker?") When it is not possible to create an actual situation, use manipulatives to represent the problem. Ideally, you should move students with learning difficulties to the computation phase only after they understand the concepts involved. Some students respond well to memory tricks like "Does McDonald's Sell Cheeseburgers" on page 164, because these tricks make abstract concepts more concrete.

The National Council of Teachers of Mathematics (NCTM) calls attention to the rigorous levels of mathematical thinking and problem solving needed for college and career readiness. NCTM points out that those who understand and can do mathematics will have more and better opportunities than those who do not. The organization describes a suggested curriculum called *Principles and Standards for School Mathematics* (available at www.nctm.org/standards), which has been developed to meet current real-world math requirements. The first five standards present goals in the mathematical content areas of numbers and operations, algebra, geometry, measurement, and data analysis and probability. The second five describe goals for the processes of problem solving, reasoning and proof, connections, communication, and representation. The 10 standards are presented in great detail for students in preK to grade two, grades three to five, grades six to eight, and grades nine to twelve.

When you consider the NCTM standards plus the Common Core or your own state's standards, the prospect of bringing all students to proficiency may seem overwhelming. While successful students learn math concepts relatively quickly, and they easily see the connections among concepts, some students with learning difficulties take a long time to learn math, and they often fail to understand the connections among concepts, which makes retention elusive. Many math series complicate math instruction for struggling learners even further by presenting too many math concepts in one lesson or on one practice page. Very little time and only a page or two are devoted to explaining and developing new concepts. As a result, some students end up more confused than ever.

---

Just as kids learn to read by reading and to write by writing, they learn to do math by "mathing"—using mathematical concepts in scenarios based on real-life events.

---

It's essential to give students who are emerging into an understanding of mathematical concepts as much time as they need to learn how to manipulate objects so they can solve problems that have meaning in their daily lives (*examples:* dividing up treats for a class party, using money to buy real objects in a classroom store, physically manipulating shapes to see their relationships). Real-life scenarios must precede the shift to using abstract numerals. We must also remember to focus on what kids are doing well, not on their frustrations. Be patient. All good things take time, and for struggling students, a little more time may be just what they need.

This chapter presents strategies and techniques that facilitate math learning for students who find math difficult. Try several with your students, until you find one or two that make a noticeable difference in their success with math. Once again, remember Kenneth Dunn's advice: "If students cannot learn the way we teach them, then we must teach them the way they learn." Related self-talk that should be ever-present in students' minds is, "If this method is not making sense to me, I'll ask the teacher to help me try other methods until we find the one that works for me." Use the acronym *WHOLISTIC* (see page 51) as a reminder of how to promote learning success for struggling students in any subject area.

# Ways to Get Struggling Students Hooked on Math

- In our opinion, if a student has not mastered basic math operations and math facts with whole numbers by the end of third grade, accommodations need to be used so that all students can be engaged with higher-level problem-solving skills and experiences described by the standards, and not be held back by the lack of fact proficiency. When Susan was teaching upper elementary, every year she started the math text for struggling students at the chapter on adding decimals—then moved on to subtracting decimals, and so on. This enabled her students to skip the earlier chapters on adding, subtracting, multiplying, and dividing whole numbers. Same operations, same processes, but the kids felt very capable because they were allowed to skip some chapters and were starting the year with a topic few had ever been exposed to before: grown-up decimals!

■ Stay with hands-on learning until kids achieve understanding, then help them discover the skills they need to solve the same problem symbolically. In other words, they should see and manipulate the problem first with concrete objects, in real-world situations in the classroom, then translate the information into the symbolic language of numbers. Whenever possible, let students work together as they learn.

■ Remember that math happens all day long, not just during math class. Take every opportunity to show how math is present in *all* subjects (*examples:* the cost of fighting a battle, the number of calories people consume in a day, how sound is measured in music). Connect math at school to students' lives at home. (*Examples:* Have students observe and graph the TV-watching habits of family members; have students draw their bedroom or living room on graph paper, make furniture cutouts, and rearrange them to learn about scale.)

■ Call attention to how math is used in literature. Use math scenarios from stories you read aloud; fairy tales, folk tales, and children's books abound with potential scenarios. Ask a librarian for suggestions. (*Example:* How about the math in *Alice's Adventures in Wonderland?*) Have students create word problems from the books they are reading or from favorite classics. Find songs, poems, and jingles that incorporate repetitious math patterns; use novels and stories as math-related discussion-starters. (*Example:* A story about a runaway teenager can lead to an authentic exploration of how much it costs to live on one's own resources.)

■ Use the students' own names and actual life events in their math problems.

■ Since global learners need to see the big picture before learning the parts, always show them how a completed problem or task will look. (*Example:* When you want students to fill in a grid of number facts, show global learners the completed grid and have them work backward to understand the relationships and patterns.)

■ Use music, rhymes, raps, or jingles to help kids learn number facts in a way that is both fun and effective. "Schoolhouse Rock" has always been helpful for this.

■ Have students set their own goals for what part of a math task they will attempt or how many problems they will solve within a given time period. (See "Goal Setting" on pages 61–63.) If this doesn't motivate them to work on math, you might try allowing them to accumulate points they can trade in for incentives. If they meet their goal, they get all the possible points. If they achieve 70 percent or more of their goal, they get 70 percent of the possible points. If they beat their own goal, they get bonus points.

■ Consistently emphasize and model that asking questions and making mistakes is the only way to learn.

■ Teach estimation and expect students to use it in the math they do.

■ Use the Problem Solver materials at www .mheonline.com. The teacher materials are available at many grade levels and provide practice in applying the 10 most often used problem-solving strategies. Students can solve several problems using only one strategy, or they can solve one problem using several strategies. Teachers can use one problem-solving approach, such as Guess and Check, at several different grade levels simultaneously for students at various instructional levels in the class, making this resource a fabulous tool for differentiation.

■ Revisit ideas often after they have been learned. Each math period should include a review of one concept students already know.

■ Find and use any helpful technology that is approved by your district without being prohibitively expensive. Ask your technology support person for assistance. When teaching math to students with or without learning difficulties, the use of technology can be the key to motivation and mastery of the required standards. Interventions needn't be elaborate or high-tech. Basic math skills can be taught with the use of calculators, computer games, tablets, apps, and online resources such as Khan Academy. See the "Assistive Technology" chart on pages 80–81 and the following section for more ideas.

## More about Khan Academy

Lisa's district has found Khan Academy (www
.khanacademy.org) to be a wonderful free website for
all learners, including adults. Khan Academy provides
simple, 10-minute video tutorials on a multitude of
topics in math, science, and other subject areas. In the
math demos, each math problem is randomly gener-
ated, so students never run out of practice material.
If students need a hint, every problem can be broken
down step-by-step with one click. If students need more
help, they can always watch a related video or view the
same video as often as needed. Another exciting feature
is that gifted students can use the lessons to move into
more advanced lessons on a many topics.

Adults can get password-protected access to the lessons their students have been visiting. Adults with the
correct password can see detailed information about
students' learning activities, can access class reports for
all students using the site, and can gather precise data
for creating helpful classroom interventions. Several
large corporations have been working with Salman
Khan and his staff to improve learning literacy for their
employees and community members.

## Teaching Techniques to Try

**1.** Always take the time to show students how the skills
they are learning are used in real life, both in current
daily life and in future occupations and responsibilities.

**2.** Show an example of the problem as it looks when
completed. Often, global learners can understand better when they see the end first.

**3.** Choose and use consistent color cues for algorithms.
(*Example:* In fractions, if the numerator is always green
and the denominator is always red, the colors can help
students remember and use the language of mathematics, which can be very confusing.)

**4.** When doing project-based learning (page 142),
notice and discuss the mathematical applications in all
aspects of the work.

**5.** Model how to do a problem as you think out loud
the steps you are going through. Repeat this process
several times and always follow the same steps in the
same order.

**6.** One teaching method that is often successful with
struggling students is the concrete-representational-
abstract sequence of instruction (CRA). The idea is that
when this particular sequence is followed faithfully, better learning outcomes in math and reasoning occur. The
concrete stage uses manipulatives. The representational
stage uses pictures and other visual aids that relate
directly to what was done with the manipulatives. The
symbolic stage demonstrates how the concrete and representational stages appear numerically. The abstract
stage follows naturally as the students first engage in
guided practice and eventually practice independently
what they have learned. All stages should include thinking out loud, so students are aware of what they are
learning. (For more on metacognition, see page 65).

**7.** Another teaching method that has found favor among
teachers and students is cognitively guided instruction
(CGI). Teachers use Socratic questioning to lead students
to describe their thinking about how they solved a problem. Students learn that there are many ways to solve
problems, to value risk taking in their thinking, and to
honor the thinking of their classmates. CGI is based on
the belief that children's knowledge is central to instructional decision making. The teacher is the guide on the
side rather than the sage on the stage. Students who are
taught using CGI appear to have a deeper understanding of the way math works than do kids who spend most
of their time with computation. Training in how to use
CGI is available from the National Center for Improving Student Learning and Achievement in Mathematics
and Science (NCISLA). See "References and Resources."
Note: The Socratic method is equally useful in other subjects, including literature, social studies, and science.

**8.** Use the Name Card Method (pages 12–14) to check
homework and to check for understanding as you teach.
Use the cards to send kids to the board to demonstrate
math examples. Now and then, allow students to go
to the board with their math discussion buddies. After
writing the problem on the board, the students explain
how they got their answers. Then the whole class votes to
show whether they agree with their particular answers.
One secondary geometry teacher told his students that
when they put work on the board, they could choose
do it correctly or incorrectly. That way, if the class disagreed with an answer, the students could explain that
they knew it was wrong but were just trying to fool their
classmates. This gave kids a way to save face if they put
the wrong answer on the board.

**9.** As often as you possibly can, have students describe in
writing what they are thinking as they solve their problems. This practice is extremely useful in demonstrating
that there are many ways to solve a given problem, and
that every child's thinking deserves to be heard and
processed. Take class time to discuss these descriptions
and have kids appreciate and enjoy each other's mathematical thinking.

10. Teach in small chunks so kids get lots of practice with only one step at a time. Don't expect struggling students to do concept development and computation simultaneously. Supply a learning aid, such as a number facts grid, or a formula model, until kids have grasped the meaning of a new concept. Make sure they understand the words you are using to describe the concepts. (*Example:* When teaching the concept of perimeter, make sure students understand what the word *perimeter* means before asking them to compute actual perimeters.)

11. Be sure to teach and assess often in the same format that will be used on any important assessment activities in which students will be expected to engage. Students must be familiar with the format so they are not distracted by it. (*Example:* Since students will have to use computer-based assessments, provide experience with this type of assessment in their regular math class.)

12. Assign number values to letters of the alphabet. Have students compute the "cost" of different words and sentences.

13. Bring mail-order catalogs to class. Give each student a mystery amount of money to spend on purchases from a catalog. Instruct them to include tax and shipping when deciding what to buy.

14. Bring restaurant menus to class or have students access them online. Have students practice ordering, computing the bill (including tax and tip), and averaging the cost of each person's meal.

15. Dissect a daily newspaper or magazine—hard copy or digital—for math applications. One day's paper could keep your class busy for a week. If you don't know how to create lessons from the newspaper or a magazine, contact the publication's education editor and ask for assistance. Choose only activities that relate to your required standards.

16. Have students figure out time changes throughout the world, including the loss or gain of an entire day when one crosses the international date line.

17. Involve students in the study of economics. The Council for Economic Education is eager to share free materials for use with students in primary grades through high school. (See "References and Resources.") You might even go into business. Math comes alive when the entire class gets involved in manufacturing, selling, and earning a profit. Contact professionals in your community in banking, investments, engineering, manufacturing, retail, and other fields. Invite them to your class to show students how math is used in their daily work.

18. Whenever feasible, let students choose a smaller number of problems to do within an assigned time period. It's better to assign problems by the available time than to assign the same number of problems to all students. Encourage students to use the "Goal Planning Chart" (page 86) to set and reach goals.

19. Use math games whenever possible to bring some excitement to math. In deference to your kinesthetic learners, choose games where kids move around. Too many paper-and-pencil activities are frustrating for struggling students.

20. Use whatever tricks are available to you. See "Finger Multiplication" (page 162) and "Finger Math" (page 160). Both are fabulous aids that students can take into any testing situation with them, since the only tools they need are their own fingers.

For more information, check your teacher's manual or your publisher's website, or ask for assistance from your math support staff.

# Teaching Computation and Operations

## Computation

- Always show the solution first, so students can see the whole pattern at once. After the pattern has been shown several times, begin asking students to compute the solution independently.

- Never ask struggling students to copy work from the board or textbook. Math is about number relationships, not about accurate copying.

- Use number lines when kids begin to work with numbers, as well as when you're introducing new concepts. Commercially produced number lines are available in almost every educational catalog of teaching tools. Or use a large clock face with hour and minute markings as a number line; some kids find it easier to count back and forth on a clock face. Use colored markers for the 5-minute chunks and different-colored markers for the 15-minute chunks.

- *Always* expect kids to estimate a reasonable solution before they do any computation.

- For practice problems, less is more. Never assign more than six to ten practice problems. Motivate students by offering this option: they may stop practicing as soon as they complete five consecutive problems correctly.

- Allow students to use graph paper for computation problems to keep columns straight. Prepare sturdy templates for students to use while working problems. Templates can expose one problem at a time or one column in computation. Draw circles in colored ink around the problems' numbers, so kids don't think those digits are part of the problem.

■ Find and use any technology that makes math facts mastery happen faster for some students.

## Teaching the Facts

Follow this sequence to teach addition and subtraction facts. **Tip:** Always start with concrete objects before moving to numerals.

1. Teach the doubles, such as 11 + 11.

   ■ Have students make equations for the doubles' facts.

   ■ Have students make word problems using everyday situations.

   ■ Have students share their word problems. Encourage them to explain their thinking processes out loud. Try having them act out the problems to enhance their understanding.

   ■ Have students journal about the process and then discuss their thinking about it.

   ■ Send home some work that repeats the same process, with a letter to parents explaining it. Invite feedback from parents.

2. Repeat this process for the doubles plus 1. (*Example:* "If 5 + 5 = 10, then 5 + 6 = one more than 10, or 11. Likewise, if 5 – 5 = 0, then 6 – 5 = one more than 0, or 1.")

3. Repeat this process for the doubles plus 2, the doubles plus 3, and so on.

4. Repeat this process for the doubles minus 1, the doubles minus 2, the doubles minus 3, and so on.

## Expanded Notation

Use expanded notation to make sure kids understand the numbers they are using in their math problems. (*Example:* 36 + 42 would be rewritten as 30 + 6 and 40 + 2. Add either the 1s or the 10s first: 30 + 40 = 70; 6 + 2 = 8. The answer is 78.

If regrouping is necessary, as in 39 + 25, follow the same process: 30 + 9 and 20 + 5. 9 + 5 = 14; 30 + 20 = 50; 50 + 14 = 64.

Once kids understand the expanded notation method, it is much easier for them to grasp the related algorithm.

## Partial Sums

Another quick way to solve an addition problem is by doing partial sums. (*Example:* For 49 + 57: Add the 1s first: 9 + 7 = 16. Add the 10s next: 40 + 50 = 90. Add both sums: 16 + 90 = 106.)

## Math Facts

■ Teach the facts in families (*examples:* all the combinations that add up to 10, such as 2 + 8, 8 + 2, 3 + 7, 7 + 3, and so on; all the facts that are associated with one another, such as 6 + 4 = 10, 10 – 6 = 4, 10 – 4 = 6, and so on).

■ Teach addition and multiplication together, since they are two aspects of the same concept. Teach subtraction and division together for the same reason.

■ Demonstrate everything with manipulatives. Think out loud and have students do the same.

■ Call students' attention to the ways in which math facts are used in their real lives.

■ Make math facts a game during every math period. Fold pieces of paper into a certain number of sections, then challenge students to write one complete math fact family in each section. Have kids set their own goals for how many sections of paper they can complete.*

■ Enlist parent helpers to prepare math facts flash cards. An entire fact is written on the front of a five-by-seven-inch card and cut in two in a unique jigsaw pattern, with the problem on one part and the solution on the other. This is especially helpful for visual learners, who can link the facts to the patterns.

■ Give each student personal laminated copies of math facts grids. Indicate notable patterns (odd numbers, even numbers) with different colors. Have students use the grids to estimate the reciprocal processes (subtraction for addition, division for multiplication). (*Example:* "Divide 14 by 3. Is 14 a number in the 3 line? No? Then what is the closest number?")

■ Make or buy digital recordings of math facts, one series at a time. Say the facts in order, pausing briefly after each one. Example: "6 . . . 12 . . . 18 . . . 24 . . . 30 . . . 36 . . . 42 . . . 48 . . . 54 . . . 60." Another inexpensive source is Mondo Math from Learning Quest, available at mondomath.com. You may download Mondo Math onto your MP3 player or purchase CDs.

---

*Susan Flynn, teacher, Christiansburg, Virginia.

## Finger Math

In our workshops about teaching kids with learning difficulties, participants are always amazed by the finger multiplication strategy (see page 162). Many have asked for similar strategies for other math operations. One highly effective method we recommend comes from *The Complete Book of Fingermath* by Edwin M. Lieberthal. Although the book is out of print, it is available used on Amazon. Even easier to access are several YouTube demonstrations. Simply search YouTube for the keywords *finger math, finger math addition,* and *finger math subtraction,* to name just a few. These demonstrations make basic math operations accessible to all students.

Finger math is related to the workings of an abacus, which in turn are related to the workings of the fingers of both hands. I would use it with students who have not become fluent with memorized math facts despite months of practice. Finger math allows students to use all 10 fingers to add, subtract, multiply, and divide numerals up to at least 100. Once fluency is reached (after lots of practice), students have a method they can use in both testing and real-life situations to perform basic number operations quickly and accurately. (One fan calls it "a calculator you can sneak into the SAT.")

## TouchMath*

TouchMath is a program that has helped many tactile-kinesthetic learners understand basic math operations. It provides hands-on learning without actual manipulatives.

Each digit from 1 through 9 is drawn with the same number of dots (touchpoints) as the number it represents. The numbers 6 through 9 are drawn with circled dots, each representing two dots.

1. The 1 is touched at the top while counting, "One."

2. The 2 is touched at the beginning and end while counting, "One, two."

3. The 3 is touched at the beginning, middle, and end while counting, "One, two, three."

*TouchMath, 4th edition. Innovative Learning Concepts, Inc. Used with permission.

4. The 4 is touched and counted from top to bottom on the down strokes while counting, "One, two, three, four."

5. The 5 is touched and counted in the order shown: "One, two, three, four, five." You might call "four" the "belly button" to help students remember it.

6. The 6 begins the use of dots with circles. The circled dots are touched and counted twice. So the 6 is touched and counted from top to bottom: "One-two, three-four, five-six."

7. The 7 is touched and counted from top to bottom: "One-two, three-four, "five-six," followed by the single dot at the top left, "seven." You might call "seven" the "nose" to help students remember it.

8. The 8 is touched and counted from left to right, counting the "head" first and the "body" second: "One-two, three-four, five-six, seven-eight."

9. The 9 is touched and counted from top to bottom: "One-two, three-four, five-six, seven-eight," followed by the single dot at the left (the "nose"), "nine."

Students learn addition and subtraction by touching the numbers to reinforce the concept of how many. To add numbers, count all of the dots and circled dots.

Several YouTube segments demonstrate this method. YouTube also has video demonstrations of touch addition, subtraction, multiplication, and division as well as touch-math money. Search for those topics to learn all the tricks described in this chapter—and probably many more.

## TouchMath Money

Just as in TouchMath, TouchMath Money provides the hands-on learning that many tactile-kinesthetic learners need to understand how to count and work with money.

The dots on the coins are counted by fives, and the line under the penny equals one. As long as students have learned to count by fives, they can use this method to count amounts of money easily. For example, the group of coins below would be counted 5, 10, 15, 20, 25, 30, 35, 36 to equal 36 cents.

| 5 | 10 | 15, 20, 25, 30, 35 | 36 |

## Timed Tests

Timed tests on math facts have been a common practice for decades in the United States. However, for students with learning difficulties, the method has not always led to the desired result of instant fluency. These students will get better results if we add rhyme, rhythm, or movement to the learning process.

The Timed Test Arcade is an online math facts fluency game available at www.hoodamath.com /mobile/games/mathtimedtests.html. It offers students

in grades kindergarten through five an alternative method to achieving math fact fluency.

1. It assesses the student's initial speed.

2. It keeps a record of student achievements, providing immediate, color-coded feedback to students to help them identify and be more accurate with facts that are usually troublesome for them.

3. The instant results provide immediate feedback, which is satisfying for the student.

4. Illegible writing is no longer an issue, as the answers are typed in.

5. Most importantly, the Timed Test Arcade app is fun. It rewards students with digital arcade game tokens for each timed test taken. It motivates the student to continue working on math facts fluency at home or even in the car.

Another helpful learning aid is "Schoolhouse Rock." These songs and videos have been helpful to students with LD for decades and are still available.

Instead of having all students try to complete an arbitrary number of problems in a certain amount of time, give your struggling students control over their own progress. The chart below gives students chances to demonstrate they can learn to set realistic short-term goals and take satisfaction and pride when those goals are reached. For more on this topic, see the "Goal Setting" section on pages 61–63.

Some teachers allow students to take both timed and untimed tests and use the untimed results for assessing classroom competency. You may provide incentives for students who make steady progress with their personal best scores. You can also give the tests two scores, one untimed and solely based on accuracy and the other score using the time to assess fluency as well.

| Date of Math Facts Fluency Test | Number Correct | Personal Goal: Predict Number Correct on Next Test | Is Goal Adjustment Necessary? |
|---|---|---|---|
|  |  |  |  |
|  |  |  |  |
|  |  |  |  |
|  |  |  |  |
|  |  |  |  |

# Multiplication and Division

### Number Arrays

The following array represents 3 groups of 4, or 3 times one group of 4, or 3 x 4. Once kids understand this, they learn the reciprocals: 4 x 3 = 12; 12 ÷ 3 = 4; 12 ÷ 4 = 3.

### Nines on My Fingers*

This method is for the 9s only and may not be necessary when using finger multiplication (next section), which includes the 9s. However, so many teachers and kids already know this trick that we include it briefly here.

Write the numbers from 1 through 10 on colored stickers or with erasable markers on kids' fingers. Rubber gloves can also work here; just write the finger's number on each glove finger. The left pinkie is 1, the left ring finger is 2, and so on, all the way to the right pinkie, which is 10.

To compute 9 x 4, the student holds up both hands, palms facing out.

1. Bend the left index finger (4). The fingers to the left of the bent finger represent the 10s. Three 10s = 30.

2. The six fingers to the right of the bent finger (including thumbs) represent the 1s. Six 1s = 6.

3. Add the 10s and 1s together. 30 + 6 = 36, so 9 x 4 = 36.

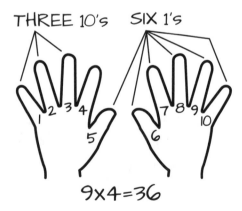

Try 9 x 7. Bend the right index finger (7). There are six 10s to the left of the bent finger and three 1s to the right of the bent finger, so 9 x 7 = 63.

---

*Adapted from Nancy S. Bley and Carol A. Thornton, *Teaching Mathematics to Students with Learning Disabilities.* Paperback edition, 2001. Austin, TX: PRO-ED. Used with permission.

### Finger Multiplication**

Use this method to help students learn the mutiplication facts from 6 through 10 with a method they can use forever, including in test taking situations.

We have found several websites and YouTube videos that demonstrate this method, which you may consult if your students need more visual and kinesthetic assistance. Search YouTube for "finger multiplication" or "Timothy Basaldua," who shows how to do the 4s with only one hand. You'll find a fantastic online article by Sidney Kolpas called "Let Your Fingers Do the Multiplying" at www.dccc.edu/sites/default/files/faculty/sid_kolpas/mathteacherfingers.pdf, which includes tricks up to the 15s.

Write the numbers from 6 through 10 on two sets of sticky colored dots (two 6s, two 7s, and so on). Have students stick the circles to their fingertips. The numbers may also be written on students' fingers with washable markers. The pinkies are 6s and should be the same color; the ring fingers are 7s and should be another color; the middle fingers are 8s (another color); the index fingers are 9s (another color); the thumbs are 10s (another color).

To compute 7 x 8, the student holds up both hands, palms facing the student, pinkies on the bottom.

1. Touch the 7 fingertip of either hand against the 8 fingertip of the other hand. The touching fingers, together with all the fingers below them on both hands, represent the 10s. Five 10s = 50.

2. Multiply the number of remaining fingers on one hand by the number of remaining fingers on the other hand to find the 1s. 3 x 2 = 6.

3. Add the 10s and 1s together. 50 + 6 = 56, so 7 x 8 = 56.

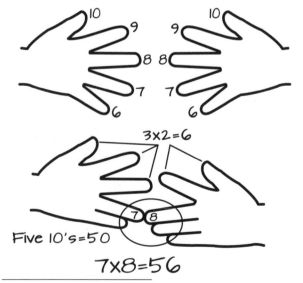

---

**Adapted from Martin Gardner, *Entertaining Science Experiments with Everyday Objects.* New York: Dover Publications, 1981. Used with permission of the author.

*Exceptions to teach last because these combinations take one extra step:*

- 6 x 6: Touching pinkies: Two 10's = 20. Multiplying free fingers: 4 x 4 = 16. 20 + 16 = 36, so 6 x 6 = 36.

- 6 x 7: Touching pinkie and ring finger: Three 10's = 30. Multiplying free fingers: 4 x 3 = 12. 30 + 12 = 42, so 6 x 7 = 42.

Most kids can do the multiplication facts for the 0s, 1s, 2s, and 5s easily. If some of your students need assistance for the 3s and 4s, try these tricks:

- **For the 3s, use the knuckle-knuckle-nail method:** To multiply 3 by any number up to 10, just hold up that number of fingers and count by ones on your knuckle, knuckle, and nail of each finger. (*Example:* For 3 x 6, hold up six fingers and count the two knuckles and nail of each finger. You will get 18.)

- **For the 4s, use the count-by-2s method:** To multiply 4 by any number up to 10, just hold up that number of fingers and count by 2s twice on each finger (*Example:* for 4 x 6, hold up six fingers and count by 2s twice on each finger to get 24 for your answer. So you would touch your right pinkie two times and count, "2, 4," touch your right ring finger twice and count, "6, 8," and so forth.

### Tech Tip 🖵

To teach the 11 times table and many other multiplication facts, visit the "Mr. R's Songs for Teaching" channel on YouTube at www.youtube.com/user/mathsongs1. If Mr. R's videos are not available, use your search engine to find other tricks for multiplying the 11s through the 20s. For more ideas, check out the "Reference and Resources" for this chapter on page 256.

### 19 Is as High as I Go*

With this method, students never have to add higher than 19.

Write out a problem of two-digit numbers to add. Whenever you get to 10, strike a slash through the number and write the leftover as a small digit. Here's an example:

1. Add the 1s column.

$$
\begin{array}{r}
78 \\
5\!\!\!/5\,^{3} \\
6\!\!\!/9\,^{2} \\
+\ 47 \\
\hline
9
\end{array}
$$

8 + 5 = 13; slash the 5 and write a tiny 3 beside it.

3 + 9 = 12; slash the 9 and write a tiny 2 beside it.

2 + 7 = 9; write the 9 in the 1s place of the sum.

2. Add the 10s column.

$$
\begin{array}{r}
^{2} \\
78 \\
^{4}5\!\!\!/5 \\
^{0}6\!\!\!/9 \\
+\ 47 \\
\hline
49
\end{array}
$$

Count the slashes in the 1s column: 2.
Write 2 above the 7 in the 10s column.

2 + 7 = 9; 9 + 5 = 14; slash the 5 and write a tiny 4 beside it.

4 + 6 = 10; slash the 6 and write a tiny 0 beside it.

0 + 4 = 4; write the 4 in the 10s place of the sum.

3. Add the 100s column.

$$
\begin{array}{r}
^{2}78 \\
55 \\
69 \\
+\ 47 \\
\hline
249
\end{array}
$$

Count the slashes in the 10s column: 2.

Write 2 in the 100s place of the sum.

### Partial Products

The partial products multiplication method is related to the expanded notation method for addition and subtraction (see page 159).

*Example:* 46 (40 + 6) x 23 (20 + 3).

$$
\begin{array}{r}
46 \\
\times\ 23
\end{array}
$$

1. Multiply the 1s: 3 x 6 = 18.

2. Multiply the lower of the 1s by the higher of the 10s: 3 x 40 = 120.

3. Multiply the lower of the 10s by the higher of the 1s: 20 x 6 = 120.

4. Multiply the 10s: 20 x 40 = 800.

5. Add 18 + 120 + 120 + 800 to get the answer: 1,058.

---

*Rita McNeeley, teacher, Port Huron, Michigan.

## Division Made Easy

With this method, students learn that division is progressive subtraction. They remember the steps by chanting a mnemonic device, *Does McDonald's Sell Cheeseburgers,*\* while adding tactile-kinesthetic support. Methods like these can make abstract algorithms easier to remember and use.

**1.** Students write the division problem, extending the division box by adding a vertical line at the right down the page.

$$25 \overline{)\ 2991\ }$$

**2.** Students chant "**D**oes" to remind themselves that the first step in the process is to **D**ivide. Simultaneously, they draw the division sign (÷) in the air. They estimate how many groups of 25 cheeseburgers can be made from a batch of 2991 cheeseburgers. Any estimate will do, as long as the total does not exceed the available supply. (*Example:* "I can divide 2991 into groups of 25 at least 100 times.")

**3.** Students chant "**M**cDonald's" to remind themselves that the next step in the process is to **M**ultiply. Simultaneously, they draw the multiplication sign (x) in the air. They multiply the estimate (100) by the number of cheeseburgers in each group (25), using up 2500 cheeseburgers.

$$25 \overline{)\ 2991\ } \quad 100$$
$$\phantom{25 )\ } 2500$$

**4.** Students chant "**S**ell" to remind themselves that the next step in the process is to **S**ubtract. Simultaneously, they draw the subtraction sign (–) in the air. They subtract the number of cheeseburgers they have grouped (2500) from the original available number of cheeseburgers (2991) to see how many cheeseburgers are left to be grouped. They discover that 491 are left.

$$25 \overline{)\ 2991\ } \quad 100$$
$$\phantom{25 )\ } \underline{2500}$$
$$\phantom{25 )\ } 491$$

**5.** Students chant "**C**heeseburgers" to remind themselves to **C**heck the remainder of cheeseburgers to be sure there are enough left to make more groups of 25. Simultaneously, they clap once loudly, signaling that the entire process is about to begin again.

**6.** Students repeat steps 2 through 5 until the remainder is so small that there are not enough cheeseburgers left to make any more groups of 25. Whatever is left is the remainder. The total number of groups is determined by the sum of all of the groups that have been made. Answer: 119 R 16.

$$25 \overline{)\ 2991\ }$$
$$\underline{2500} \quad 100$$
$$491$$
$$\underline{250} \quad 10$$
$$241$$
$$\underline{225} \quad 9$$
$$16 \quad \overline{\phantom{0}119}$$

\*Dave Wurst, teacher, Indian Prairie District, Illinois.

**7.** Use the same steps to illustrate that any number may be used to estimate, as long as there are enough items to form the required groupings.

$$25 \overline{)\ 2991\ }$$
$$\underline{250} \quad 10$$
$$2741$$
$$\underline{250} \quad 10$$
$$2491$$
$$\underline{1250} \quad 50$$
$$1241$$
$$\underline{250} \quad 10$$
$$991$$
$$\underline{250} \quad 10$$
$$741$$
$$\underline{500} \quad 20$$
$$241$$
$$\underline{225} \quad 9$$
$$16 \quad \overline{\phantom{0}119}$$

When kids are ready for the shorter regular method for long division, they can use the same prompts, with a slight variation (treat "cheeseburgers" as two words):

**D**oes = **D**ivide
Ask: "How many 25's in 2? 0. So how many 25's in 29? 1."

$$25 \overline{)\ 2991\ } \quad {}^{01}$$

**M**cDonald's = **M**ultiply
1 x 25 = 25

$$25 \overline{)\ 2991\ } \quad {}^{01}$$

**S**ell = **S**ubtract
29 – 25 = 4

$$25 \overline{)\ 2991\ } \quad {}^{01}$$
$$\underline{25}$$
$$4$$

**Chee**se = **C**heck to see that the remainder (4) is not larger than the divisor (25).

**Burgers** = **B**ring down next digit and **B**egin again.

$$25 \overline{)\ 2991\ } \quad {}^{01}$$
$$\underline{25}$$
$$49$$

Continue until the final remainder is smaller than the divisor and there are no digits left to bring down.

## Fractions

For some students, the study of fractions is extremely confusing, since the one-to-one correspondence they have come to depend on in whole-number computation is no longer present. The acronym *WHOLISTIC* (see page 51) can help you remember how to teach global learners virtually any content, including fractions.

- Have students find examples of fractions used in real life. Organize by categories on a chart.

- Create classroom situations in which kids need to use fractions (*examples:* dividing treats for a class party; dividing art materials for a project).

- Teach fractions first with concrete examples, such as filling a marked measuring cup with water, before moving on to visual aids that show equivalencies.

- Remember that hands-on activities and manipulatives always work best for teaching fractions to struggling students.

- Check out YouTube for demonstrations on fractions.

## Decimals

For many students with learning difficulties, decimals may be more confusing than fractions.

- Have students find examples of decimals used in real life. **Tip:** Have them look through the newspaper. Organize the examples by categories on a chart.

- Use different-colored blocks to show the equivalents.

- Give students practice using money—counting, buying things, making change, and so on. Use play money, including coins. Focus on the use of decimals by having students write money amounts accurately using a decimal point. This can be done using the interactive whiteboard, manipulatives, electronic tablets, touch screen computers, or with a pencil and notepad.

- Check out YouTube for demonstrations regarding computation with decimals.

## Liquid Measures*

The following visual helps students quickly understand liquid measures. It is easy to create. First, draw a giant black G. Then draw four red Qs inside the G. Then draw two green Ps inside each Q. Last, draw two black Cs inside each P. This drawing shows visual learners that there are four quarts in a gallon, two pints in a quart, two cups in a pint, four cups in a quart, sixteen cups in a gallon, eight pints in a gallon, and so on. This visual takes little time to prepare and is worth the effort.

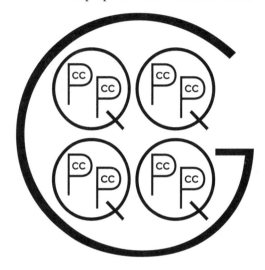

## Linear Measures

The following visual helps students quickly remember standard linear units of measure. One yard in front of a house has three feet. Each foot has twelve inchworms on it. Students can quickly convert between inches, feet, and yards using this visual.

---

\* Adapted from a strategy used by Melissa Matusevich, teacher, Montgomery County, Virginia.

# Word Problems

Create and display a permanent problem-solving strategies chart that lists the following suggestions:

- Make a model, diagram, drawing, table, or graph.

- Guess what the answer might be; compare your answer to your guess.

- Look for a pattern and use it.

- Work backward from the solution to the beginning of the problem.

- Make an organized list.

- Use simpler numbers.

- Write an equation.

- Act it out.

- Use a combination of strategies.

- Create your own strategy.

When teaching a word problem, start with a hook that ties the concepts in the problem to the students' personal lives. Use their real names in problem scenarios. Walk them through the following steps:

1. Read the problem aloud. Restate it in your own words.

2. Think about the problem. What do you know about it? What information does it give you? Take notes, draw pictures or diagrams, or use a graphic organizer to record your thoughts.

3. Circle the words that tell what the problem is asking you for.

4. Look at all the available information. Be sure that you understand all the words or symbols.

5. Cross out any unnecessary information.

6. Estimate the answer.

7. Choose a problem-solving strategy from the problem-solving strategies chart. Notice that the chart says you can also create your own strategy.

8. Solve the problem using the appropriate operation or operations—addition, subtraction, multiplication, or division.

9. Compare your solution to your estimate. Does the solution make sense? Is your computation accurate?

10. Try to get the same solution using another method.

Once students have chosen a problem-solving strategy, they may use the "Problem-Solving Box" handout on page 168.

## Using the Problem-Solving Box

Describe and demonstrate how this handout should be used. Students should write each step they use in the left column of the chart, then write a reason for that step in the right column.

Have students work in pairs to solve a problem and complete the handout, saying the steps and reasons out loud as they write them. Have them begin with simple problems they already know how to solve. Later, they can move on to more challenging problems. As always, pair struggling math students with helpful average students, not with the top math students. Ask the pairs to report to the class about the problem-solving methods they used.

---

When teaching a word problem, start with a hook that ties the concepts in the problem to the students' personal lives. Use their real names in problem scenarios.

---

You might find or create step-by-step processes for some or all of the problem-solving strategies listed previously under "Word Problems" (and on your classroom problem-solving strategies chart). Student pairs using the "Problem-Solving Box" handout could follow these processes or consult them when devising their own problem-solving strategies and steps.

# Questions and Answers

*"Math has never been my strongest teaching area. What can I do to strengthen my math teaching skills?"*

While researching the revised and updated edition of this book, we were amazed at how much help is available from software and the Internet for teachers who want to do a great job of teaching math. Check the "References and Resources" for this chapter. Take a class from someone who knows how to create excitement for math learning in kids. Study your teacher's guide for tips or call or email the publisher of the materials directly.

*"There is so much pressure to have students master all the assigned math standards that I can't find time to help the kids who are falling behind catch up. What can I do to make sure they don't get lost forever?"*

Remember the old Chinese proverb: *I hear and I forget; I see and I remember; I do and I understand!* We think the best thing to do is to teach today's new concept(s) to the entire class as a direct instruction lesson. Then, as stronger math students take the time to practice what has been taught, take a group of struggling math students aside and teach them, visually and kinesthetically, their number facts, all the basic operations, basic geometric shapes, and other essential concepts—and make it fun using the strategies in this chapter. Our belief is that kids who have had a positive experience in math this year are going to be more successful on the math portions of any test than students whose daily failures have convinced them that they can't ever understand math.

*"How will it look if these students have to use their fingers to help them compute when they are adults?"*

About as acceptable as it is for you to use the spell-check feature on your computer or the built-in calculator on your smartphone or other mobile device. Don't worry about how students will look years in the future. Let's focus on teaching our students to love math now!

*"Don't all students eventually have to commit the math facts to memory?"*

If there is no impairment of a student's memory processing, it's reasonable to expect the student to memorize the math facts. If a student's memory is impaired, this expectation may not be reasonable. Besides, many devices students already own include calculators, or small ones may be purchased for a very minimal cost. In either case, developing a genuine affection for math as a holistic learning experience is far more important than learning number facts.

# Problem-Solving Box

| Steps to Solve the Problem | Reasons for Each Step |
| --- | --- |
| | |

# CHAPTER 8

# Using Assessments to Support Student Learning

One of the greatest challenges today's educators face is how to assess the learning of students who begin a school year at an achievement level substantially below grade-level expectations. In the past, schools created and used assessment systems for students with special needs that were significantly different from the assessments applied to most other students. Students with LD were instructed and assessed in lower-level content and skills, often in an alternative setting. Instruction was often so far removed from the grade-level content expectations that assessments created were showing mastery of a different set of skills than those required by the general curriculum. Very little consideration was given to bringing their work up to grade-level standards, and very little attention was paid to using learning modalities in instruction and assessment procedures. Grading for special education students was often adjusted, with their effort taken into consideration as a way to give them higher grades for their work. The goal was to keep their self-esteem high in hopes that eventually that might lead to academic improvement. Many classroom teachers were uncomfortable with these practices, because students with LD were receiving special considerations that the teachers worried weren't fair to the other students.

Teachers, students, and parents are all profoundly affected by the importance of assessment data, both formative and summative. (For more information on both types of assessment, see pages 173–175.) Assessment data drives instruction by helping teachers decide what and how to teach, rather than simply following a set of curriculum topics in an inflexible order. For optimum assessment results, educators at all levels work hard to align what is taught with the expected standards, assess students often, and find ways to intervene as soon as achievement gaps are noted. Interventions are offered in several layers. Interventions are individualized according to the present needs of students.

This chapter describes ways in which teachers and students can work together to bring all students up to the required achievement level. These high expectations require all educators to examine, and perhaps change, their teaching, grading, and assessment practices.

## Effective Assessment Practices

Effective assessment practices include attention to the following principles.

### School Culture

1. Facilitate a school-wide focus on student achievement by precise alignment between required standards and the focus of instruction and assessment.

2. Actively involve students in communicating with their other teachers and their families about their achievement, focusing on improvements over time.

**3.** Consistently communicate high expectations for student work and behavior to demonstrate consistent forward progress rather than achieving high grades. Use the BUG Roll on page 183 to facilitate this outcome.

**4.** Remember that stimulating, meaningful curriculum motivates students to work hard; grading alone may not.

## Classroom Accommodations

**1.** Pay attention to students' strongest learning modalities and provide learning tasks to capitalize on those strengths.

**2.** For students with LD, provide more time for task completion and allow assistive technology access for students to use while they are learning.

**3.** Remember that methods that compare students to one another are not helpful, but those that compare student's performance to specific criteria, such as rubrics, are helpful and productive.

**4.** Provide scaffolding to help students continue to work on fewer tasks until they achieve higher levels of performance. This strategy is more effective than expecting students to work on too many tasks simultaneously.

**5.** Allow for testing accommodations and modifications, such as extended time, directions or test items read out loud, small group testing, frequent breaks, and even soothing background music played softly. (This allows easily distractible students to ignore other sounds or distractions.) Most importantly, any environmental accommodations, such as those described in Chapter 3, that are routinely allowed during regular learning times should also be available during formal testing. This can prevent additional stress students might experience if their normal accommodations are not available.

## Teaching Strategies

**1.** Show struggling students how to use goal setting so they can feel more in control of their learning and assessment outcomes. (See pages 61–63.) You might try what one school did: start a "Yes I Can" campaign. Have students make tags to wear that describe their specific goal(s) for the upcoming grading period. Display charts in the room that list students' goals, but not their progress. Students can keep their own private records of actual progress toward their goals. This allows students to recognize and reinforce one another's goal-related behaviors. When students work toward a goal, they declare, "Yes I can!" When students notice a classmate working toward a goal, they declare, "Yes you can!" If

your school has a button-making machine, you can also make "Yes I Can" buttons for your students to wear.

**2.** Before teaching content, always share with your students the exact standards to be learned. At the end of the lesson, come back to those standards to reinforce how the lesson related to them.

**3.** Always activate prior knowledge so students can understand how what they are about to learn is connected to what they already know and to real-life experiences.

## Homework

**1.** Never assign homework until students have had enough classroom instruction and practice so they know how to be successful with the homework.

**2.** Never grade homework, as it is a formative assessment process.

**3.** Give at least partial credit for returning any amount of homework to class. All students who bring something back to class from their homework time should get a reward, such as moving their game piece forward on a large version of a game board or recording a plus symbol (+) on a group homework return chart.

## Grading

**1.** Use grades as incentives, not punishments. Grades are somewhat effective as incentives but are almost never effective as punishment. (*Example:* A zero for late or incomplete work does not motivate students to work harder.)

> Grades are somewhat effective as incentives but are almost never effective as punishment.

**2.** Assess work or learning by specific criteria; this is more fair and effective.

**3.** Avoid grading curves. All students should be able to earn high grades and get the grades they have earned. When students perceive that only a few can get the highest grades, they may lose their motivation to strive for them.

**4.** Coach students on how to explain their grade reports to their families. In this way, families—and students themselves—have a much better understanding of what the reports really mean.

**5.** Make honors credit available to any student who shows capacity for learning at that level.

**6.** Do not offer extra credit. Extra credit is not useful for any student. The kids who really need it are those who have great trouble getting their regular credit. Students who have enough credit don't need anything extra.

**7.** Whenever possible, assess in the same format used on your state assessments. (*Examples:* If the state tests require students to fill in bubbles on answer sheets, use bubble answer sheets for your classroom assessments. If your state requires students to supply written responses for some test sections, be sure to give them practice in using that format as well.)

**8.** Assess often and adjust your instruction accordingly. Be sure your assessment procedures accurately reflect students' progress over time.

**9.** Report assessment data that are more descriptive than judgmental or punitive. (*Example:* Rather than just showing a grade that reflects the number of incorrect examples or problems, indicate the number of correct ones, and include comments that help students understand what they can do to improve their results next time on a similar task.)

**10.** When using rubrics, be sure your students understand the language. Offer rubrics in stages instead of all at once. (*Example:* If a writing rubric includes four categories—clarity, accuracy, idea development, and meaningful sequence—concentrate on idea development until students are scoring at average or higher levels. Then slowly add the other categories, one at a time.) As students become more comfortable with using rubrics independently, their assessment outcomes will improve.

**11.** Find (or create) and use student self-assessment tools that show progress over time.

**12.** Consider using the "Achievement Data Recording Chart" on page 182.

**13.** Observe your students systematically—daily if possible. This is a highly effective way of keeping accurate records to inform your instruction and coaching. Making notes subtly on a digital device will allow you to transfer that data to another record-keeping place at your convenience. This data is extremely useful when conferring with parents or support teachers. Constant record-keeping may seem awkward at first for you or your students, but after a while it becomes so automatic that you won't be able to observe anything significant without wanting to record it.

**14.** Do not give students grades for formative assessments, since these happen while students are at the beginning of the learning curve. To understand this, think about whether you would want to be graded by your supervisor during the first few weeks of trying to implement a new teaching skill.

**15.** Remember that low grades cause most students to withdraw from learning. Low grades entered in grade books should be changed to higher grades when students are able to show growth.

**16.** Make partial credit available whenever possible. (Even in some Olympic events, judges throw out the lowest score.)

**17.** Do not record a student's average grade. This practice is unfair. Recorded grades should always reflect student growth as well as the present level of achievement.

**18.** Do not grade effort. Only the student knows how much effort has been expended.

**19.** Use grading and assessment methods that enable students, families, and teachers to plan for improved outcomes on the next attempt.

# Technology

American education has finally moved away from using technology as a source of fun and games to understanding and applying its unique and powerful effects on the learning process. We should use everything we have that will move students forward. We should recognize that for students with learning difficulties, using technology as part of the learning process has the potential for dramatic gains in achievement.

As schools, and even towns, become "wired," making technology an integral part of the teaching and learning processes will help our students with LD become more successful in this century than they may have been when more traditional teaching methods were used. It will be interesting to watch this situation to see if it actually does create this advantage for visual and tactile-kinesthetic learners.

## Tech Tip 🖥

Assess students' progress as they learn how to use any new technology tool. Carry a student competency checklist on a clipboard, tablet, or other mobile device. As you stop by individual students, you might ask them to show you how to do one of the skills on the checklist. For example, when you're teaching students how to use presentation software such as PowerPoint, you might ask one student to show you how to create a new slide, another student how to insert a photo, and so on. This will help you intervene effectively before students become too frustrated to continue.

With education's focus on preparing students to be college- and career-ready, educators need to choose the best assistive technology that makes the standards accessible for students with learning difficulties. Refer to Chapter 4, pages 78–81, for two rubrics to help choose the most appropriate app for a student's need.

# Assessment and Grading

## Scenario: Noah

Noah was a seventh grader who had become increasingly negative about school in recent years. His mom sadly remembered how eager he had been to go to kindergarten. She also recalled how dismayed she had been to learn that his progress in school was seriously hampered by his inability to do simple things, such as understand letter-sound relationships or write his letters and numbers neatly.

---

When we *give* these students the highest possible grades, and they realize their grades are a gift from a teacher who has concluded that these students will never be able to reach exceptional levels of performance, they may give up.

---

Noah had always learned by listening to the conversations of older kids or adults, and he had been an avid fan of educational television. He loved surprising people with the information he knew just from watching those shows. Although he could tell great stories that demonstrated his creative imagination, he became sullen when he was expected to write down his thoughts neatly, legibly, and accurately.

His teachers in elementary school had offered him opportunities to work on shorter assignments or choose fewer spelling words. Although their gestures were sincere, Noah always rejected them because he worried that the other kids would find out about the special arrangements and tease him. His achievements were never good, but his fourth-grade teacher gave him all A's because he tried so hard. Since Noah knew his A's meant something different than they did for most other kids his age, he didn't take much pride in them.

When Noah reached middle school, he became a troublemaker. Perhaps the recognition he received for that role from his teachers and peers was safer than being recognized for his inadequacies with the regular seventh-grade work. He still watched shows on educational television, but he didn't talk about them anymore.

## Fair and Consistent Grading

"*I hate* doing report cards!" is a claim often made by frustrated teachers, who have long known that traditional grading methods leave much to be desired. Regardless of how well we keep records of student progress, the act of giving grades causes a lot of anxiety and worry. We wonder how adequate (and accurate) grades are and how effectively they communicate the actual progress our students are making. We realize that no matter how hard we try to be totally objective, we are often influenced by students' behaviors and attitudes.

Many parents hate report cards, too. Few families understand the often confusing and inconsistent information report cards bring. They know that some teachers give higher grades to kids who work really hard, while others conform consistently to the grading scale the school has adopted. Teachers' comments are often cryptic and full of incomprehensible jargon. Remarks like "Your son is not working up to potential," "Your daughter needs to use her time more wisely," and "Your child could do much better if she only applied herself" are so trite that their meaning has been lost. For grades to have true significance for families (and students), they must be interpreted the same way by everyone who sees them.

Most kids have no idea what grades actually mean or how much time their teachers spend trying to assign grades that are accurate and fair. Whenever Susan saw her students counting the total number of letter grades, check marks, or plusses and minuses, she wanted to scream, "No, that's not the way you're supposed to receive those grades!"

Struggling students hate report cards even more than teachers and families do. Once they realize that there won't be much good news for them to carry home at report card time, they develop a negative attitude about grades in general. Low grades usually don't motivate students to work harder and do better in the future.

Assessing and grading the work of students with LD has always been a complicated task. Some teachers feel that the highest grades should be reserved for students whose work either meets or exceeds grade-level expectations. Other teachers think that students with LD should be able to get the highest grades possible when evidence shows that they have given their best effort to the task. When we give these students the highest possible grades, and they realize their grades are a gift from a teacher who has concluded that these students will never be able to reach exceptional levels of performance, they may give up. They may infer that they have no hope of excelling according to grade-level standards.

We recommend that any student who is achieving competence with grade-level standards earn the equivalent of a B, since rubric descriptors at that level indicate the student is being successful understanding grade-level standards. A's should be reserved for work that demonstrates the highest levels described on grading rubrics. There is nothing wrong with getting a less-than-perfect grade. (Achievements below grade-level standards should, of course, earn the equivalent of grades below a B.)

### Tech Tip 🖥

A commercial program called Mastery Tracker is available at www.masteryconnect.com/learn-more/features.html. This program allows tracking of mastery of the Common Core State Standards.

Grading practices for schools using the Common Core State Standards are dramatically different from traditional grading practices. Students will be involved in ongoing self-assessments, sometimes doing them online, and will have access to the data that documents their learning progress. Teachers will use tools that allow students to *earn* their grades from rubrics, rather than being *given* a grade by a teacher. Grading practices in such a system are inherently more fair.

Our goal in grading should be to record successful outcomes that reflect actual learning, even for those who are accessing grade-level standards with lower-level materials. Grades that are expressed as a letter or percentage may not be the best way to document learning progress. Additional progress monitoring data is recorded on progress reports connected to IEP goals for students with LD. This provides a more detailed picture of the student's progress toward mastery of goals aligned to the standards. Alternate assessments are an encouraging and authentic way to measure and report students' academic growth.

# Types of Assessment Processes

Assessment practices are undergoing huge changes. We are learning how to make assessment practices work to improve student achievement, instead of just reporting it. In our opinion, this process is allowing us to do our jobs the same way other professionals, like doctors and accountants, do theirs. They do not treat all their clients the same. If they did, the clients would leave. Their process, for which they are well paid, is the following:

- They diagnose the client's present condition.

- They prescribe interventions that will move the client forward to health or solvency.

- After a time, they assess the process to see if it is working.

- If it is, they repeat the process.

- If it is not, they prescribe another method to move the client forward.

In this way, all clients get the personalized attention they need. We all know how impossible it seems to give that kind of attention to students in large classes. The following assessment practices provide ways to do what only *seems* impossible—to actually personalize assessment for each of our students. This section describes how formative and summative assessment practices help us work with our students to make certain they are all making measurable forward progress every day, week, month, and school year.

## Formative Assessment

Formative assessment is a collaborative process that allows teachers and students to check regularly on the degree to which students have mastered designated standards. Rather than giving grades, formative assessments should measure actual learning progress, which means moving forward with personally challenging work. The level of work, of course, will be different for students with LD than for students performing at or above grade level. During the formative assessment process, the absence of formal grading reduces stress for the learner and therefore increases the likelihood of success in the learning process.

Students with LD need more time and repetition to master new concepts and skills. The formative assessment process is very important for them, because it highlights what students must do in order to catch up to their grade-level peers. It shows students' individual areas of weakness, which teachers must target in their instruction, not wasting their learning time practicing content they have already mastered. In this way, teachers can eventually close the gap these students have traditionally experienced.

It's important to have evidence of student learning during class as well as through assignments and formal assessments. Several short activities that document student progress are described on page 174.

# Effective Formative Assessment Practices

## Activity 1: Brainstorming

1. Present an open-ended question for students to consider. Make sure students are seated beside their name card partners. (For more on the Name Card Method, see pages 12–14.)

2. Give all students 10 seconds to think of and briefly record their own ideas.

3. Have students brainstorm some ideas with their partner for 30 to 45 seconds. Use name cards to call on students, who are now much more likely to be able to make a contribution.

4. Record the ideas on a board. Use the information to form your ongoing lesson plans for the topic.

We have found that when students are allowed to simply call out their ideas while the teacher is recording them, the same students often monopolize the idea generation. When name cards are used instead, everyone's ideas can be considered.

## Activity 2: Concept Maps or Graphic Organizers

This activity promotes integration of ideas and provides immediate feedback about student understanding.

1. Provide students with a list of terms for the upcoming unit. Provide a blank concept map of your choice. Ask student partners to place the words appropriately into the concept map.

2. Provide time for several partner groups to share their concept maps with the whole class or with one or two other partner groups.

## Activity 3: Show Me

This strategy demonstrates a quick way to assess students' readiness to move on to more advanced content. It relies on group signaling method. As a quick assessment regarding content that has just been taught, use questions you have prepared in your lesson plans to determine how much has already been understood by which students. The students response should be simply yes or no, true or false, or a number from 1 to 10.

Model how students should use their hands to signal their responses. The most critical part of this method is to train students not to show their response until you give a verbal signal—often asking a question and then saying, "Show me." At that point, students use their fingers to show their answer. The real beauty of this is

that you don't have to even notice their signals. When students know that they must all signal at exactly the same time, you just have to pay close attention to which students' heads whip around at "show me," as they try to get help from their classmates. Be sure to use plenty of variety, including some signaling methods that allow students to stand up and even move around.

A variation of Show Me is called Give Me a Five. After finishing a lesson, ask your students, "Where are you with this material? Can you give me a one through five?" With a fist held in front of their chest, students show one through five fingers to indicate their level of comfort with the material. You can easily get visual information about how to group students for instruction at the time of the next lesson.

As you can see, this formative assessment method makes it very easy for you to look around at the students' responses and use them to form your flexible groups for the next day's lesson. You will easily know which students to group altogether for additional review and which for more direct instruction in a way that is suited to their learning needs.

Another variation of Show Me is a quick homework check. Designate five problems for the Show Me response, and give the correct answers to the students. At your signal, students hold up the number of fingers that describe how many problems they got correct. This provides an instant way for you to know who needs another direct instruction lesson and who is ready for extension work.

## Activity 4: Ticket Out the Door

This activity is extremely helpful for assessing the degree to which students have understood a class lesson. You can use that information to form flexible groups for the next day, some of which will be working on reinforcement and some on higher-level thinking activities.

1. Five minutes before the end of class, provide half-sheets of paper for students to write their tickets out the door.

2. Ask them to write:
   - their name (and class period for secondary students)
   - two things they fully understood about today's lesson
   - one question they need to have answered the next time this class meets

3. Use this data to plan the next differentiated learning experience for this class or subject area.

## Summative Assessment

Summative assessments are used for evaluation or grading after a particular section of content has been completed and formal assessment is needed. Summative grades should reflect student success with mastering the required standards, including those in the students' IEPs.

While formative assessments allow you to monitor progress and make appropriate interventions, summative assessments usually do not do so—unless the teacher has evidence at the end of a unit that reteaching is required. We generally receive the results of high-stakes summative assessments from testing agencies after the school year or term has ended. These assessments are mostly used to evaluate the effectiveness of curriculum and instruction for an entire class or grade level. They also evaluate the effectiveness of various school programs as they impact school improvement goals.

## Portfolios

Creating a portfolio is a systematic procedure that allows students to collect and display their work in a given subject area over time, much as an artist might. Portfolios emphasize students' strengths and illustrate how they learn rather than what they know. They allow attention to effort and progress, providing much more information about what students have achieved than grades and test scores alone do. Students (and their families) can more easily see how much progress they have made.

A portfolio might include a combination of regular work and work that represents any or all of the following:

- the same type of activity done at various intervals over time

- an unusual idea

- an in-depth understanding of a problem or idea

- a resourceful or clever use of materials

- evidence that a student has stayed with a topic for a long time and learned a lot about it

- products beyond paper-and-pencil tasks

Portfolio products can take virtually any form, from written papers and tests to drawings, photographs, audio recordings, videos or DVDs, electronic portfolios, certificates, reviews, CD-ROMs, and even three-dimensional objects. (*Example:* A math portfolio might include data about surveys students have conducted, observations about where and how math is used in everyday life, visual representations of something kids have designed that applies math functions, and descriptions of experiences with enrichment activities.) Each product should meet the following basic criteria:

- It should be selected by the student as an example of work the student is proud of or otherwise believes represents high-quality work.

- It should be edited and polished to preestablished levels of mastery, as described by rubrics that students refer to continuously as they work to achieve higher levels of performance. Unedited work can be sent home, but it should be stamped "not edited."

Once you have started using portfolios, set aside class time weekly for students to work on them. They should use that time to review the work they have done since the last selection time, choose something new that they feel should be included in their portfolio, and make any necessary changes or modifications that would enable a piece to stand as a representation of their best effort.

To keep parents up-to-date on how their children are doing in school, send them regular portfolio reports more often than report cards. Have children bring home their latest portfolio product to show their parents; be sure to coach students on how to describe their work to their parents. The "Portfolio Product Report" on page 181 is one example of a form you might use for families to complete and return to school. **Tips:** Introduce this form during a conference. Tell families that giving sincere verbal encouragement and celebrating small successes will motivate their children more than monetary or other tangible rewards. Discourage families from chastising their children or removing home privileges for unacceptable schoolwork.

## Performances, Exhibitions, or Demonstrations

In some schools, students are asked to perform what they have learned in virtual or real-life settings. Some educators believe that performance assessment is a more reliable indicator of student growth in learning than more objective tests. The problem is that performances are more difficult to create and evaluate than traditional assessments. The chart on page 176 illustrates typical assessment formats in both categories.

## Traditional Testing Compared to Performance Assessment

| Skill to Be Mastered | Traditional Testing | Performance Assessment |
|---|---|---|
| Math computation | Taking tests with paper and pencil. Solving word problems. | Using a catalog of merchandise, make a written plan to spend $1,200. Be sure to include tax and shipping costs. Do not exceed $1,200 and do not spend less than $1,175 total. |
| Biography | Read a biography of a famous person. Write answers on a biography report sheet. | With a partner, choose two biographies of people who lived during the same time period. Use an interview process to present what you learn. You play the role of one of the people, your partner plays the other, and you interview each other about events in your lives. For added interest, dress up as the people you are portraying. |
| Government | Complete a flowchart that shows how the balance of power works in U.S. government to prevent misuse and abuse of power. | Select a historic event in which persons in the United States tried to take more power than they were entitled to under the Constitution. Prepare a series of newspaper articles to illustrate how checks and balances stopped the potential abuse of power. |

### Unlocking Autism 🔒

For a student with autism, the IEP team will determine appropriate accommodations for assessing the degree to which students' goals have been mastered and for making sure the student is demonstrating continuous progress toward the IEP goals. Special education staff can clarify best practices for achieving these goals for students with autism.

## Rubrics for Determining Grades

Rubrics are useful for establishing a set of criteria by which to assess student work. Rubrics should be provided to students from the very beginning of their work on required tasks or products. This will help them always be thinking about their targeted category of achievement as they work. It will also help them understand the differences among the categories of achievement to decide if they want to raise their goals. Rubrics can also help teachers and peer partners be consistent in their evaluations. Finally, rubrics are helpful when giving students feedback on their assignments—especially if they are unhappy with their grades.

The publishers of your school's adopted materials may provide suggested rubrics. Other sources include:

- rubrics4teachers.com
- www.teachersfirst.com/lessons/rubrics/create-rubrics.cfm

## Ways to Make Assessment Less Stressful and More Accurate for All Students

1. Allow and encourage struggling students to use their strongest learning modality to demonstrate what they have learned.

2. Have an open invitation for students to earn credit for their work if they can show their thinking, even when their response is not what you expected.

3. When grading papers, mark correct responses instead of wrong responses. Write the score as a fraction, with the number correct over the total number of problems. (*Example:* A score of 6 correct out of 10 would be written as 6/10.)

4. When giving letter grades that relate to percentages, calculate the percent correct of the number of items completed rather than of the entire assignment.

5. Provide open-ended opportunities for kids to retake tests or redo assessments until they have achieved acceptable levels of performance. *Caution:* Be sure that this doesn't create lazy study habits in more capable students. Make attractive alternate activities available for those who reach acceptable levels of performance promptly.

6. Provide school-wide incentives for kids to bring up their grades. See "Use the BUG Roll" on page 183.

# Struggling Students and Standardized Tests

Standardized tests are especially challenging for students with learning difficulties, who are suddenly expected to do many things in a high-stakes situation that are difficult for them under the best of circumstances. They must read quickly, come up with answers, write, and solve several problems, all within a limited amount of time. Obviously these students need all the help we can offer.

- Give every student a copy of "How to Prepare for a Test: 10 Tried-and-True Tips" on page 198. (These tips can benefit all your students, not just struggling students.) Review and discuss each tip with the class. Explain that these strategies have worked for other students.

- Teach your students the STAR strategy for test success:*

  **S**urvey the test to get an idea of how much time you can spend on each question. Mark any questions you think you can answer quickly.

  **T**ake time to read the directions *carefully.*

  **A**nswer the questions. Start with an easy one to boost your confidence. Skip the ones you can't answer.

  **R**eread the questions and your answers. Make any needed changes. Return to any questions you've skipped and try again.

- Many students with learning difficulties do much better on standardized tests when they are allowed to take the tests in the same environments in which

they have been learning. If they usually work seated on the floor or while listening to music, they should be allowed to take tests under those conditions.

- Struggling students may also achieve better test results if they are permitted to read test questions aloud or have the questions read to them. You might arrange for those who want these considerations to take the test in another room, with an adult monitor present.

## Scenario: Seth

Seth, a second grader, always took a long time to work through any kind of test. He was so poky that he rarely completed even half of a timed test. Not surprisingly, the profile his teachers and parents got from his standardized test results was woefully inadequate and didn't come close to reflecting Seth's real abilities.

For example, on one standardized test, Seth considered the following question:

Which is harder?
    a) a feather
    b) a sidewalk
    c) a headboard
    d) all of them

Seth reasoned that a feather is hard to throw, a sidewalk is hard to walk on, and his headboard is hard when he hits his head on it, so he chose "d) all of them" as his answer. Naturally, he didn't get any credit for it.

When global thinkers take multiple-choice tests, they can invariably find reasons why *all* choices are correct. The suggestions on the following pages will allow you to learn much more about what your students know than standardized measures can tell you.

## Common Core Computer-Based Assessments

The following companies, Smarter Balanced Assessment Consortium (www.smarterbalance.org) and Partnership of Assessment for College and Careers (PARCC) (www.parcconline.org), are creating online assessments to assess student proficiency with the Common Core State Standards. States that are using CCSS must choose one or the other company to document their progress.

Both companies received federal funding to design assessments that are "performance-based" to fulfill Common Core's goal of college and career readiness. The tests will require students to demonstrate higher-order thinking through problem solving, essay writing, and research projects, as opposed to the multiple-choice, fill-in-the-blank tests of the past. PARCC has

---

*Adapted from *School Power: Study Skill Strategies for Succeeding in School,* by Jeanne Shay Schumm, Ph.D. Minneapolis: Free Spirit Publishing, 2001. Used with permission of the publisher.

developed diagnostic testing to be administered at the start of every school year. The results will provide teachers with baseline data to drive their instruction and student testing throughout the year. Smarter Balanced offers optional interim tests at the beginning and middle of the school year.

The key difference between the assessment companies' versions is that the Smarter Balanced model adjusts the line of questioning and difficulty in real time based on the responses of each individual student. In contrast, PARCC's tests adhere to a fixed format of questions for all students. In either case, the testing will be done during the same school year in which the students are assigned to their particular teacher. This ends the problem of teachers not being able to see their students' test outcomes until the beginning of the following school year, when it's too late to make adjustments in their teaching.

Students with learning difficulties may need some accommodations. Four types of accommodations are offered: presentation, timing and scheduling, response, and setting. Presentation accommodations include any change that needs to be made in the method or format of the test to help students access the questions more easily and accurately. For example, tools are available that can change the background and foreground colors of the screen, present the content using Braille, and translate the presentation of content into sign language or other languages for students with visual or hearing impairments or ELL students. Although there are no formal time limits to these online assessments, timing and scheduling accommodations allow for additional time, frequent breaks, or adjusting the time of day the test is given. This is helpful to students who have difficulty processing information, who have limited dexterity (which slows writing), who need assistive technology of any type, or who have difficulty maintaining focus. In the area of response, your students may provide their answers using assistive technology or a scribe. Students with physical, sensory, or learning difficulties may benefit from these accommodations. Accommodations allow students with LD to access the online tests in small groups at the same time their peers are experiencing them.

## Achievement Data Recording Chart

The "Achievement Data Recording Chart" handout on page 182 encourages students to take more control over their own assessment goals. It's best to begin using this chart at the start of the new school year, but you can also start using it at the end of the first or second report card periods.

Make a copy of the chart for each student. The language of the Common Core assessments might be different than it has been in the past, so take that into account. Fill in the student's scores (stanines or percentile ratings) from the end of last year. Explain and demonstrate how much progress is expected during a typical school year. (*Example:* If students scored in the 25th percentile in math computation at the end of last year, encourage them to set a goal of 50 percent or higher for this year to bring them into the proficiency range. The goal for the first report card might be 35 percent, the second 40 percent, and the third 50 percent or higher.)

Explain how students can set goals for their own achievement in each subject for your class. Then help students set specific goals for each report card. When the report card is issued, show students how to write their actual progress in a different color on their chart so they can see whether they reached their goals. Repeat this process between report cards until the end of the school year.

The "Achievement Data Recording Chart" handout helps students understand how one gets from one goal to another. Because the goals they set are their own, students are more motivated to move ahead than if they wait to see what the teacher gives them in each grading period. Of course, you can help your students with the process, but this method works best if the goals belong to them.

You might use the "Achievement Data Recording Chart" in conjunction with the "Goal Planning Chart" (page 86) and the "Yes I Can" strategy described on page 16.

## Use the BUG Roll*

Traditional grading systems are unfair in many ways. One of their most glaring weaknesses is that they do not always reward significant progress. Consider the typical classroom situation in which Student A moves from an average of 92 to 93 and gets recognized on the high honor roll for a net improvement of 1 percent. Meanwhile, Student B moves from an average of 42 to 68—a growth of 24 percentage points—and gets no recognition whatsoever.

The "BUG Roll"—the *BUG* stands for "Bringing Up Grades"—has motivated many struggling students to improve their grades. Although schools keep their top honor roll intact, a BUG Roll is added. To get on the BUG Roll, students must improve one letter grade in any subject area without going down to a lower grade than the one they earned in the previous marking period for any other subject. In an extreme scenario, a student who

---

*Felice Kaufmann. Talk given at the Illinois Gifted Education Conference, December 1987. Used with permission.

failed every subject in the first grading period would earn a position on the BUG Roll if she moved from an F to a D in science while still getting Fs in every other subject. Struggling students perceive that they have a good chance for positive recognition, while they would have no chance if they had to move from Fs to much higher grades to get on the regular honor roll. The parameters might require changes when using the Common Core language, but the idea should remain the same.

Students who make the BUG Roll realize some of the same perks that are given to regular honor roll students. Both groups enjoy seeing their names listed on an honor scroll that is placed where visitors can easily notice it. (The regular honor roll students are listed on one scroll, the BUG Roll students on another, but they are displayed side by side.) Both groups get tokens that entitle them to special privileges, such as days off from homework, purchases from the school store, or admission to special school functions. In some schools, special buttons are made and presented to kids as they become eligible for the BUG Roll. In one middle school, Susan heard students asking each other what subjects they were going to get bugged in.

If you would like to implement the BUG Roll in your classroom or school, you'll find a certificate you can use to honor your students on page 183. Be sure that regular honor roll students continue to be honored in special ways for their achievements as well.

# Interaction Between Assessments and the IEP

Assessment data from classroom work, both formative and summative, is an integral part of developing an IEP that is useful and effective. Baseline data is used at the beginning of the year to determine the appropriate level(s) for beginning instruction in the areas of need. Ongoing progress monitoring is carried out consistently and frequently to assure that the student is making measurable forward progress.

Summative assessments that illustrate the attainment of (adjusted) IEP goals also need to be recorded. These assessments and teacher observations are recorded in the "present education levels" section of the IEP. This record of progress is shared with parents through quarterly reports, conferences, and IEP team meetings. Good data collection makes student progress or needs for changes in programming clear for parents and teachers to understand.

# Assessment Checklist

Since this chapter contains so much information on assessments, we would like to offer the following summary, which you may use as a checklist whenever it's needed.

1. It is much easier to assess students' successful work. So always communicate high expectations of success for all students.

2. Students appreciate it when you highlight what they *are* learning, and *not* what they still need to learn.

3. Always spend time making sure students understand the connections between prior knowledge and new content to be learned.

4. Always share the precise learning objectives at the beginning of the lesson and before students engage in the learning experiences. Then, near the end of the lesson, take time to recap the connections between the required standards and the actual learning activities.

5. Use goal setting with students who struggle to learn and model your enthusiasm when there is evidence that even short-term goals have been reached.

6. Provide assessment opportunities in the same format that will be used in formal testing experiences.

7. Use formative assessments often as you teach, and continually adjust your instruction to accommodate weaknesses noticed during those assessments.

8. Be sure all students understand the language used in rubrics. Offer rubrics in cumulative stages rather than the entire rubric at once. Comfortable independent use of rubrics helps students assume more responsibility for their own learning mastery.

9. Actively involve students in communicating with their families and other teachers the evidence about their achievement, focusing on improvements over time.

10. Mastery that occurs from using technology is equal in value to mastery attained from non–technology-assisted learning.

## Unlocking Autism 🔒

Students with autism appreciate routines and predictable events. Providing simple tools such as rubrics to help them assess their own work is an effective way to involve them in the assessment process.

11. Assessment should be embedded in daily learning experiences through formative assessment strategies and should drive future instruction. Summative assessments are only the final step in the assessment process.

# Questions and Answers

*"Should students who work below grade level be able to earn top grades if there is evidence they are expending a lot of effort?"*

Review the discussion on this topic on pages 172–173. We believe that A's or other top grades should be reserved for student work that *exceeds* grade-level standards or that demonstrates ability to understand grade-level content from the perspective of higher-level thinking.

*"In post-secondary educational settings and the workplace, people are compared to each other constantly. When are these kids going to get practice experiencing comparisons if we personalize all the assessment techniques we use in the classroom?"*

Before students are ready to have their learning and productivity compared to that of others, they must have confidence in their ability to succeed. By personalizing assessment procedures, we are empowering more students to be successful—because they know what we expect before they start their work, and certainly before they hand it in. Today's workplaces combine collaboration and competition, and students should experience both. Balance is the key.

*"How can we expect parents to respond to assessment practices that bear little or no resemblance to what they are used to?"*

Parent reeducation is an important component of any educational change. Parents shouldn't have to interpret new assessment practices on their own. When we introduced cooperative learning and whole language, we probably shared our rationale and practices with parents. Send home ongoing bulletins or group emails to keep parents informed about grading and assessment procedures, and include this topic in conferences. You might also recommend websites that could help with this.

# Portfolio Product Report

**To be filled out by the student:**

Name: _____

Date: _____

Name/title of product: _____

Description of product: _____

_____

Why did you choose to include this product in your portfolio

_____

_____

_____

How does this product demonstrate that your schoolwork is improving?

_____

_____

_____

- - - - - - - - - - - - - - - - - - - - - - - - - - - - - - - - - - - - - - - -

**To be filled out by the parent/caregiver:**

How did your child share information about this product with you?

_____

_____

How did you acknowledge or celebrate your child's progress?

_____

_____

_____

Student's signature:

_____

Parent's or caregiver's signature:

_____

**Please give this form to your child to return to school. Thank you!**

# Achievement Data Recording Chart

Student's Name: _____

Current Grade in School: _____

| | Reading Skills | Reading Comprehension | Math Skills | Math Computation | Problem Solving | Writing | Other |
|---|---|---|---|---|---|---|---|
| **End of Last Year** | | | | | | | |
| **Start of School to First Report Card** | | | | | | | |
| **First to Second Report Cards** | | | | | | | |
| **Second to Final Report Cards** | | | | | | | |

# BUG Roll Certificate

Be it known that

_____

has earned the right to join the group of students who have been able to **Bring Up Grades** in the manner prescribed by our school.

## Congratulations!

# CHAPTER 9
# Improving Students' Executive Functioning Skills

As if students with learning difficulties don't face enough challenges, they are often profoundly disorganized and don't know how to study or see tasks through to completion. The competencies needed for self-control and self-regulation, as well as for getting through tasks with efficiency and effectiveness, are called executive functioning skills. The executive functions are processes for managing oneself and one's resources in order to achieve a goal. *Executive functioning* is an umbrella term for the neurologically based skills involving mental control and self-regulation.*

These skills are essential to success in school and in life. This chapter offers tips and strategies you can demonstrate and coach—concrete skills you can teach your struggling students and any others who could use some help in executive functioning. We could all benefit from methods that make our lives more efficient and rewarding.

## Bringing Order into the Disorganized Lives of Students with LD

*Teacher:* "Manuel, please number your paper from 1 to 10."

*Manuel:* "Do they have to be in order?"

---

*\*National Center for Learning Disabilities, "Executive Functioning Fact Sheet," 2005. www.ldonline.org/article/24880*

That really happened . . . don't you love it? Anecdotes like this illustrate what a big job it is to help struggling students get their learning act together. We ask them, "Did you do your homework? Did you remember to take home what you were supposed to study last night? Did you study for the test? Did you bring the materials you need today from home?" They answer, "No. I forgot. What test? What materials?" This causes great frustration for everyone involved.

Many students with learning difficulties are terribly disorganized. When we realize that students' organizational issues are connected in several ways to their learning modalities, we can appreciate the different ways in which they perceive and deal with organization issues. Since their brains are not based on sequential organization, typical advice on how to get and stay organized is often not effective for them. To help them in this area, we must teach organizational and time-management skills in the same explicit manner as any other skill. Begin with what will be expected at the end of a series of efforts, and work backward to help them learn the skills and tricks that will lead to a better-organized life for them. As always, start small and build slowly, one success at a time.

Above all, assume nothing. Never assume that these kids have executive functioning skills but choose not to use them. Never assume that anyone has taught them how to be organized and efficient. And even if students were taught these things, never assume they remember. Choose simple procedures; use them consistently; never give more than one or two directions at a time; offer sincere, specific praise when it is earned; and make sure written or visual versions of the directions are always available. With this type of assistance, visual learners can refer to customized directions to help them remember and actually do the tasks necessary to school success.

## Unlocking Autism 🔒

Students with autism need assistance to develop the executive functioning skills required for success in school and in transitioning to adult life. Visual schedules help with transitions throughout the school day. Graphic organizers help organize concepts by providing a visual representation for the student to use as a guide. Written instructions or modeling help students understand the steps in completing multistep tasks. This chapter describes many strategies that will assist students with learning difficulties in developing these skills.

## Use Routines

Create and follow routines for everything. Spend lots of time during the first two weeks of the school year reinforcing these routines so students follow them automatically without reminders from you. *Consistent* use of key words (*line up*) or signals (hand cupped behind your ear for "listen to me") should, in a short time, lead to students' habitual use of the expected routine. For students who don't respond well to verbal directions, provide visual checklists or picture directions for them to follow.

The more predictable and consistent your daily procedures are, the better struggling students will be able to cope with them. Start with simple routines that span a short period of time so students get frequent positive feedback. Begin with a one- or two-item routine; have students check off each item as it is completed. Add more items one at a time as students are ready for them. Add icons or pictures to each statement to make the message more visual. Some teachers even make the list as a timeline with pictures they find or create and use instead of words.

Here's an example: One of your students has great difficulty making transitions between tasks. Instead of keeping the entire class waiting, give that student a prearranged signal three to five minutes before the transition will take place. At your signal, the student stops what she or he is doing and consults a checklist that the two of you prepared together. The student goes through the procedures one by one:

1. Finish the word or exercise you are working on, but don't start any new part of your work.

2. Check to make sure that your name is in the upper-right corner of your paper.

3. Put your paper in the color-coded folder for that subject. Put it in the left pocket if the work is done, the right pocket if it isn't.

4. Put your pencil in the pencil slot at the top of your desk.

5. Put your books in your desk or container.

6. Watch and listen to the teacher for the signal telling what to do next.

At this point, the student should be ready to move on to the next activity with the rest of the class.

**Tip:** If your students use color-coded pocket folders for each subject, have them write "Completed Work" on the left pocket and "Work Being Done" on the right pocket.

## Promote the Checklist Habit

The simple act of creating and using checklists can bring order into many students' lives. See page 186 for examples. If kids need to bring certain things from home to school each day, a checklist attached to the door they use when leaving home can serve as a reminder. Icons or pictures can accompany the checklist. If a pencil hangs on a string nearby or is attached with Velcro, they don't have to waste time searching for a writing instrument. They can look quickly through their backpacks and check off each item as they notice it. (Several apps that serve this function are also available online.) The more wired your school becomes, the less students will be using materials they have to transport between home and school, and that will be wonderful for students with learning difficulties and the adults in their lives.

Checklists may be kept in a designated folder or may be taped to students' desks. If kids have lockers, prepare checklists to hang inside that remind students what they need to bring to each class. Students with learning difficulties should be allowed to visit their lockers before each class.

Give students "Daily Task Checklist" handouts (or apps) to use at their desks. (See page 43.) Physically checking off tasks as they're completed can be very satisfying. Award partial credit for partial success.

# More Ways to Get and Keep Students Organized

**1.** Use color everywhere you can to help kids with their organization: different-colored folders for each subject area, different-colored writing tools to indicate the type of correction that is needed, color categories on the "Content Organization Chart" (page 151), and so on.

**2.** If students in your school change classrooms for different subjects, you must develop a method to store their supplies in their homeroom that allows easy access for students throughout the day. You may use plastic containers stored on a shelf, in a cubby, or in a closet. Students may leave their supplies in this location and travel to other classes with only the supplies they need. With the increase in technology use, fewer supplies are required for students to store and manage. Many schools are moving to digital textbooks. Some schools are even issuing individual tablets, electronic notebooks, or laptops for all students.

**3.** Help students prioritize tasks by listing them in order of importance and working down the list. Students can feel good about accomplishing the most important tasks, even if they can't finish all the tasks.

**4.** Working at a desk may be overwhelming for kids with attention problems. Set them up at tables with study carrels. Students can work independently there and rejoin the class for discussions and group activities.

**5.** If at all possible, give students with LD a duplicate set of textbooks to keep at home, reducing the chance that they will lose their textbooks between home and school. Some teachers even provide their most hyperactive students with a second desk in the classroom, giving those kids another acceptable reason to move their bodies.

**6.** Attach often-misplaced or dropped items to students' desks with pieces of Velcro (*examples:* books, pencils, pens, erasers, or anything else that can be dropped).

**7.** Create a backward timeline for longer-term assignments. Coach parents to use this method at home as well. (*Examples:* If a story is due on Friday, show students how to plan the number of sentences they need to write on Thursday, Wednesday, Tuesday, and Monday, in that order. If a mobile display of the characters in a book is due in two weeks, work with the student to plan each day's activities, starting on the morning of the due date. Be sure to include those tasks on the student's daily task checklist; see page 43.)

## Things to Bring to School Each Day

| Item | Monday | Tuesday | Wednesday | Thursday | Friday |
|---|---|---|---|---|---|
| Books or materials I brought home | | | | | |
| Paper, pencils, pens, or digital device | | | | | |
| Homework | | | | | |
| Lunch or lunch money | | | | | |
| Permission slip | | | | | |
| Other_____ | | | | | |

## Things to Bring to Class Each Period

| Item | 1st | 2nd | 3rd | 4th | 5th | 6th | 7th | 8th |
|---|---|---|---|---|---|---|---|---|
| Book (or laptop or tablet) | | | | | | | | |
| Homework | | | | | | | | |
| Pencils, pens, paper | | | | | | | | |
| Other_____ | | | | | | | | |

**8.** Use assignment notebooks that are consistent from class to class. Parents and other caregivers should be told to expect that the notebook will come home every day, regardless of whether the student has homework. Then, part of the home routine should be to check the notebook with the student for homework assignments. If a backward timeline is in progress, that should go home, too, perhaps stapled to the assignment notebook so it returns to school the next day.

# Mnemonics

Mnemonics are strategies meant to help students remember related bits of information. For example, one of several mnemonics for remembering the notes on the lines of the treble staff in music (E, G, B, D, F) is *Every Good Boy Does Fine*. Many other mnemonics exist for teaching this same concept as well. Another common mnemonic for remembering the directions of north, south, east, and west on the compass rose is *Never Eat Shredded Wheat*.

## Acronyms

An acronym is a word or phrase made from the first letters of the words or phrases that students are trying to remember. For example, the acronym *HOMES* stands for the names of the Great Lakes: Huron, Ontario, Michigan, Erie, and Superior.

The think SMART acronym that follows is a mnemonic for remembering how to be prepared and how to select the most effective strategy for each lesson.

### Think SMART to Be Ready for Learning

S = **Smart** students use learning strategies.

M = **Materials** are ready (books, paper, folders, pencils, digital devices, and so on).

A = **Assignment** notebook or device is available.

R = **Remember** to ask questions when you don't understand.

T = **Think** positively. ("I can do it!")

Before beginning an activity, remind students to think SMART with a quick rhythmic chant. Slap each of your legs separately, then snap your fingers—first left, then right—while saying, "One, two, think SMART!" Students follow your model. Then review the letters of the acronym using the same four-beat pattern. For example, chant, "Smart students use strategies."

## Verbal Repetition

Just as in the old blab schools of the 1800s, students' memories are enhanced when the entire group chants together what they are trying to learn. Add rhymes or rhythms (beats), and the chances of remembering get even better.

## Chunking

Chunking reduces the strain on short-term memory. Instead of trying to learn and remember many individual things, one learns them in sets or groups. (*Example:* Have students learn the number facts in sets of three. To learn the 3s, students chant, "3, 6, 9; 3, 6, 9; 3, 6, 9," then "12, 15, 18; 12, 15, 18; 12, 15, 18," then "3, 6, 9, 12, 15, 18; 3, 6, 9, 12, 15, 18; 3, 6, 9, 12, 15, 18," and so on.)

It is also helpful for students to put up one finger to represent each math fact as they recite it. For the last example, the routine would be: Say "3" and hold up one thumb. Say "6" and add pointer finger; now two fingers are up. Say "9" and add middle finger; now three fingers are up. Keep adding one finger each time a new fact is called out.

## The Location Method

In this rather silly but effective method, students remember items on a list by imagining that each is located at a different place in a familiar room. (*Example:* To remember the names of three types of plant-eating dinosaurs, students might visualize themselves placing a stegosaur on the sofa, a hadrosaur in the hallway, and a sauropod in the sink. They would then visualize themselves retrieving the items in the same order.)

## Teaching Mnemonics

Teach any mnemonic metacognitively by thinking out loud and expecting students to do the same. For example, you might say, "I need a mnemonic for remembering the planets in the order of their distance from the sun. I'll start by making a vertical list of all the planets. Then I'll think of a word or phrase for each planet that starts with the same letter as the planet. My goal is to link the words into a sentence I can remember."

| **M**ercury | **M**y |
| **V**enus | **V**icious |
| **E**arth | **E**arthworm |
| **M**ars | **M**ight |
| **J**upiter | **J**ust |
| **S**aturn | **S**wallow |
| **U**ranus | **U**s |
| **N**eptune | **N**ow |

"Now, every time I want to remember the names of the planets in the correct order, I'll recall the sentence and remember that the first letter of every word or phrase is the same as the first letter of the planet's name." Challenge students to create their own memory sentences.

# Visual Learning Aids

Visual learning aids help students with receptive language difficulties function in their environment. The rapid comprehension required to process verbal information makes organizing steps in tasks difficult. Research shows that students are able to attend to visual information more successfully. The following are examples of visual aids for task completion, following directions, and a daily schedule.

## Task Card

This visual names the task, shows the materials needed to complete the task, and tells what needs to be done with the task when completed.

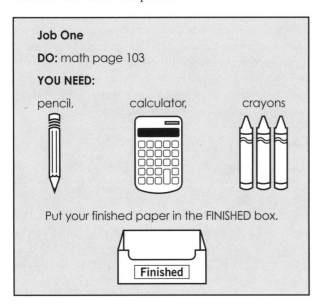

## First-Then Board

This visual (at the top of the next column) shows the student what the current task is and what comes next when that task is completed. The top-left picture says "first," and it points to the first kid in a line to illustrate what the word *first* means. From this picture, an arrow points to the top-right picture, which says "then" and shows a kid pointing to his personal choice board, from which he will choose the next task from limited choices. The bottom two pictures show two choices: messy play or outside play.

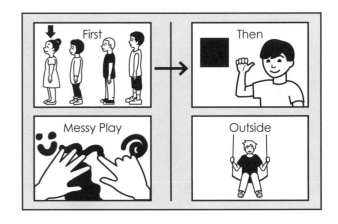

## Daily Schedule

This visual shows all transitions for the school day. As the day progresses, the completed tasks are removed from the Velcro schedule to help the student see the progression of the day.

# Teaching Students How to Study

Look back at "Getting Ready to Learn" on page 140. Do your students know these learning-how-to-learn strategies? Use the chart on page 149 to track their progress and determine which strategies you need to teach directly—or teach again. Use the "Not Yet" column to identify strategies they need to learn, the "Learning Now" column to indicate strategies you're currently teaching, and the "Knows How" column for strategies they have mastered. Enter dates to mark their progress over time; update the charts as students acquire new strategies. Older students can keep their own records.

## Material from Texts and Lectures

Teach students how to use these strategies and techniques metacognitively. (See page 65.) It's very helpful when students think out loud about the process they are using to learn.

### Skimming and Summarizing Written Material

1. Notice and read the heading of any new section.

2. Locate and read all questions that will have to be answered for that section.

3. Skim the first and last paragraphs of a section.

4. For other paragraphs in the section, read the first and last sentences and any key words that are italicized or highlighted in some way. Locate the

information for the italicized terms. Illustrate one or two key points using a graphic organizer.

5. As soon as you recognize the answer to a required question, write it down.

6. To summarize a section, combine the key points from all paragraphs into one or two statements.

7. Write an introduction and conclusion for the summary.

Note: Please see the "Survey-Skim-Study-Question (3S+Q)" handout on page 152 for an example of one type of application.

### Use Graphic Organizers

Use any graphic organizers with which your students are comfortable. Demonstrate how notes can be taken in short phrases and drawn rather than written out. Students who learn this method can often visualize the graphic organizer as they are taking an assessment, which helps them remember lots of information.

You may use the "Content Organization Chart" handout on page 151 as a graphic organizer for taking general notes on any topic. Simply retitle it the "Note-Taking Chart."

# Homework

A good homework guideline is that it should not exceed 10 minutes per grade level for all subjects combined. So first graders might have 10 minutes, fifth graders 50 minutes, and so on. This policy is supported by the National Education Association (NEA) as well as by many school districts. In all grades, teachers would have to work together to limit the total homework minutes per evening.

## Ways to Improve the Homework Situation for Struggling Students

1. Assign homework by elapsed time rather than as quantities of work to be done. In other words: instead of assigning numbers of pages to be read or problems to be solved or activities to be completed, tell students to spend 15 minutes reviewing math concepts or 20 minutes writing a story. Give them permission to stop working when that time has passed. Let parents and caregivers know of this homework policy and encourage them to assist their child *only* in writing down the beginning and ending times spent on homework each evening. The adults or an older sibling could also sign the paper at the end of the time, indicating they had monitored that the student paid attention to the time constraint.

**2.** Be sensitive with a particular student who has trouble remembering after school what has been taught during the day, or of conditions at home that deny support to kids working on their homework. Since homework is formative assessment, students should get some credit for having some portion of their homework done along with the recorded beginning and ending time of their homework attempts. Never punish a student for not finishing homework with recorded zeroes or any other method students would interpret as punitive.

**3.** Since homework should not be formally graded, students can earn a simple acknowledgment that they have done some work outside of class. You might record a plus (+) to indicate they returned something to the teacher or a minus (–) to show they did not. Some teachers give tokens for evidence that students worked for some time on their homework. Students may accumulate tokens and trade them for privileges, like taking the equipment out to recess or being the leader of a line.

**4.** To make the point that homework helps improve learning outcomes, some teachers give bonus points or extra credit for completed and returned homework, but never take away already-earned credit from students who do not return their homework. When you give partial credit for partial homework, students are more likely to complete at least some of their homework.

**5.** Talk to parents and caregivers to reassure them that it's not their job to be the teacher, and they should guard against overhelping their kids. Let them know how you want them to communicate with you if their child is having trouble understanding and doing the homework. (For more on this topic, see Chapter 11.)

**6.** The credit students earn in any particular subject should reflect their progress at school from one marking period to another. This is preferable to averaging grades over the span of a marking period. If you were being evaluated, you would want full credit for any improvement you have made from one observation to the next. You would not want the people evaluating you to average their observations over time.

**7.** For longer-term assignments and projects, help students create and use a Backward Calendar (page 196).

**8.** Using the flipped classroom model (page 74) can dramatically decrease homework challenges. The work students do at home is generally limited to watching an assigned and provided video lesson, which often is available on several types of digital devices. The work done in school facilitates students' understanding of what they have viewed at home the evening before. Practitioners of this model report that they perceive higher numbers of students who ultimately understand the required content than is the case when adults at home are responsible for the homework function. This method also creates learning situations that are less likely to discriminate against students from homes where homework support is absent.

## Use Assignment Notebooks

Provide and use electronic or paper assignment notebooks so all students are using the same format in each class for recording their assignments. All teachers who teach the same struggling student should use the same format for that student. On pages 194–195, you'll find a "Homework Assignments" handout that offers a suggested format. You may use or change this format as you see fit. In some schools, teachers provide homework information and help on their own Web pages.

Show students how to cross off completed assignments and star those that still need attention. Or students could use a color-coded system—blue or black for completed, red for incomplete. Teach parents or caregivers what their assignment notebook responsibilities are:

- Families should expect assignment notebooks to come home every night, regardless of whether students have homework.

- Families should ask to see the notebooks and have the students explain the assignments for that day.

- Families should consult the student's Backward Calendar to check the progress of any long-term assignments.

## Use a Calendar for Backward Planning

When you inform students that a science fair is being planned and all students must complete a project for it, many students with LD may feel anxious and resistant. They may think, "Oh no! How will I be able to complete an acceptable project by the day of the science fair? I don't even know where or how to begin."

A calendar is the best place to begin. Calendars for students with LD are most effective if students fill them in backward—from the final goal on the due date back through all the steps necessary to reach that goal. This method, called backward planning, will help your students plan out deadlines for all the tasks required to complete the entire project. This method takes a huge project and breaks it down into more manageable tasks. As each task is completed, students will likely discover they *can* accomplish large tasks using this method.

## Backward Calendar for a Science Fair Project

| | | | | | | |
|---|---|---|---|---|---|---|
| Sunday | Monday | Tuesday | Wednesday | Thursday | Friday | Saturday |
| | | | | 1 | 2 | 3 |
| 4 | 5 Select a science fair topic from the choices provided by your teacher. | 6 | 7 Gather background information on your topic using the note card method. | 8 | 9 Describe your topic using the scientific method vocabulary. | 10 |
| 11 | 12 Run controlled experiment and record data. | 13 | 14 | 15 | 16 | 17 |
| 18 | 19 | 20 | 21 Display your results in graphs and charts. | 22 | 23 Construct an exhibit or display. | 24 |
| 25 | 26 Choose a product to tell the story of your project, including your sources. | 27 | 28 Practice your presentation with an adult. | 29 | 30 | 31 Exhibit and present your project at the science fair. |

Above is a "Backward Calendar for a Science Fair Project." This method, also called chunking, can be adapted to any content area project that has multiple steps. See the "Science Project Work Plan" on page 153 for another example of how to help students manage a long-term project.

## Report or Project Presentation Aids

Note: We have found that when students report anything orally to an audience, the use of a listener's rubric helps them learn how to make the report much more interesting—both to the presenter and to the audience. The rubric provides items to which students can pay attention as they practice their presentation with various people. The rubric gives criteria for a listener to score a presenter's volume, expression, eye contact, clarity of content, focus to topic, and evidence of rehearsal.

During the formal report, audience members fill out the form. Additionally, presenters are expected to create an interesting question to write on a board before their presentation so listeners have a purpose for listening. You can coach your students on how to write higher-level thinking questions for this step using the ThinkTrix method on page 69. The presenter can use the name card method (page 12) to call on students to answer the question.

## Audience Rating Rubric

Give one copy of the "Audience Rating Rubric" handout on page 197 to each person who is listening to the report. Or designate six or so listeners who will fill out the rubric for each report or presentation. Send a copy home for practice with an adult.

# Ways to Improve Testing Outcomes for Students with LD

## Use Goal Setting

Just as students can use goal setting (see pages 61–63) to predict how much work they will do, they can use it to predict their performance on tests. Have students set a personal goal for each test: How many items do they think they can complete within the designated time? Have students write their goal as a ratio at the top of their test paper: predicted number of items to amount of time (*example:* 10 questions in 30 minutes = 10/30).

This ongoing exercise helps students see that they can actually influence their own outcomes by seriously setting and aiming to accomplish a short-term goal. The positive feelings gained from developing a habit of using this procedure are much more satisfying than grades could ever be. Students can graph their daily results in color, adding to the excitement.

## Address Test Anxiety

1. Talk about test anxiety with students who experience it. What is it? Where does it come from? What does it feel like? What are the symptoms?

2. Talk about the importance of getting enough sleep the night before a test and eating a healthful breakfast on the morning of a test.

3. Demonstrate deep breathing techniques and coach small groups of kids to use these techniques.

4. Demonstrate progressive relaxation—visualizing different parts of the body releasing stress.

5. Let students listen to soothing music through headphones during tests.

6. Teach positive affirmations students can repeat to themselves before and during tests.

7. Make sure every student has a copy of the "How to Prepare for a Test" handout (page 198).

## Teach Test-Taking Strategies and Tips

Teach and model the following test-taking strategies. They will help relieve test anxiety and provide the comfort of having a plan.

### For Any Test

- When you first get the test, take some time to look over all the items. Begin with sections that you think you will do well on, then go on to other sections as time permits.

- Read the directions carefully. If you don't understand the directions, ask the teacher.

- Ask the teacher if it's safe to guess on the type of test you are taking. (Sometimes it is, and sometimes it isn't.) If it is safe, then guess when you don't know the answer.

- Once you answer a question, don't change your answer later unless you are positive that your first answer is wrong.

- Never spend too much time on one problem. If you don't have a plan for solving the problem in mind within two minutes, move on to the next problem. Make a little mark next to any questions you skip so you can find them easily later.

### For True-or-False Items

- Statements with words like *always, never, completely, only,* and so on are almost always false.

- If any statement in a series of statements is false, the whole series is false.

- Guessing "true" is usually safer than guessing "false."

### For Multiple-Choice Items

- Answer the easiest questions first.

- Don't spend too much time on any one item.

- Cover the answers, read the question, and come up with your own answer, then compare it to the answers that are available.

- Read the beginning of the question separately with each of the choices, and think of them as true-or-false choices.

- Eliminate any choice you know to be incorrect.

- If two or more options seem true, and another option is "all of the above," choose "all of the above" as your answer.

- If any two options are the opposite of each other, choose one of them.

### For Short-Answer Items

- Look over all the questions first and jot down key words for everything you know.

- Come back and write sentences or complete phrases about the key words you wrote.

### For Essay Questions

- Take a few minutes to draw a graphic organizer and jot down your thoughts.

- Write a few sentences about each topic. Keep rereading the topic sentence to make sure the details you write are related to just that topic.

- It's better to have a few sentences for each of the required paragraphs than to spend all your time on just one paragraph. Leave open spaces between each paragraph as you are writing so you can fill in the space later with other sentences that fit.

## For Common Core Online Testing

- Students will need keyboarding skills to respond to test items. Special accommodations may be requested when they are documented in a student's IEP.

- The new formats should be examined and experienced by teachers and students well before students take the actual tests. School administrators will likely be involved in the process of switching teachers and students to updated assessment methods.

- Regular experience with critical thinking will be very helpful with CCSS testing formats.

- Students should have experience in being able to give reasons for their answers, as well as being able to explain why some answers are wrong.

# Questions and Answers

*"Where am I supposed to find time to help these kids with organizational tasks?"*

All students need to develop effective executive functioning skills for in-school and out-of-school situations. You can help students with LD become comfortable with these skills whenever more independent students are working alone or in small groups. Now and then, you may assign students to learning pairs with the intention of expecting the stronger student to help the weaker one, but that should be done only intermittently and with a variety of helpers over time. Please be aware that advanced learners are usually impatient in this type of situation, so it's best to avoid using them as the helpers on a regular basis.

*"What can I do when kids lose their forms and checklists?"*

Be proactive in planning for solutions to this very typical problem. Make duplicates so one copy can be kept at school while the other one goes home with the student. If families have access to email, set up a regular schedule for when they can expect to see emails from you. Many teachers maintain their own website, usually through the school hosting site, and can provide copies of forms there. Parents are invited to visit the site to find out the status of projects or other homework tasks without having to call the teacher.

If some of your students' parents appear unable to follow through with these parent access opportunities, find other ways to make the communications successful. Notes in backpacks, phone calls or home visits by appointment, and on-site homework assistance centers (provided by the school for after-school needs with homework or other issues) can all help you find solutions for unsatisfactory communication between home and school. Be certain your expectations are reasonable. If a student habitually leaves things at home, there may be a situation at home that is beyond the student's control to change. Be sensitive to such possibilities.

*"Isn't it possible that some kids are just lazy and could do much better if they only applied themselves to the learning jobs they have to do?"*

Think of something you tried a long time to learn, with little or no success. No matter how hard you tried, the task never seemed to get any easier. What happened over time to your motivation? Much of what looks like laziness is really hopelessness and frustration. When we keep sending the message to our students that we are confident they can learn, they may find the courage to try again. As soon as one strategy brings promising results, be sure to respond with specific and sincere praise. Use that success to encourage students to try a few more strategies. When we don't focus on matching the students to the most helpful strategies, the students have no alternative but to conclude they are simply not able to learn. We must prove that is not the case.

*"Many of my students get little or no help from parents. How can my students learn all they need to know without parental support?"*

The older we get, the more we understand how to differentiate between things we can and cannot change. The only way you *might* be able to change parents' behavior is to send home positive messages about their children. And even if you are never successful in improving your students' situation at home, you can keep demonstrating your firm belief that with the right match of strategies to their learning modalities, amazing progress can be made, with or without parental assistance.

# Homework Assignments

**Name:**_____ **Today's Date:**_____

| Subject | Assignment | Check if completed or explain why incomplete |
|---|---|---|
| Reading | | |
| English | | |
| Writing | | |
| Math | | |
| Social Studies | | |
| Science | | |
| Health | | |
| Foreign Language | | |
| Applied Arts | | |

continued →

| Circle what to take home | Circle what to bring back tomorrow |
|---|---|
| **Books:** | **Books:** |
| Math | Math |
| Reading | Reading |
| Social Studies | Social Studies |
| Science | Science |
| English | English |
| Foreign Language | Foreign Language |
| Other: _____ | Other: _____ |
| | |
| **Supplies:** | **Supplies:** |
| Pencils | Pencils |
| Colored pencils | Colored pencils |
| Markers | Markers |
| Pens | Pens |
| Paper | Paper |
| Ruler | Ruler |
| Assignment notebook | Assignment notebook |
| Other: _____ | Other: _____ |

Parent's/Caregiver's signature shows I spent _____ (time) working on all homework.

Parent's/Caregiver's Signature: _____

Comments from parent/caregiver:

_____

_____

_____

_____

_____

_____

# Backward Calendar

Month: _____

| Sunday | Monday | Tuesday | Wednesday | Thursday | Friday | Saturday |
|--------|--------|---------|-----------|----------|--------|----------|
|        |        |         |           |          |        |          |
|        |        |         |           |          |        |          |
|        |        |         |           |          |        |          |
|        |        |         |           |          |        |          |
|        |        |         |           |          |        |          |

# Audience Rating Rubric

| Report Elements | Yes | No |
|---|---|---|
| Presenter displayed an interesting question. | | |
| It was evident that the presenter had practiced. | | |
| The report had an attention-grabbing beginning. | | |
| The report was well organized. | | |
| Presenter explained well what he or she had learned. | | |
| Presenter spoke loudly and clearly with expression. | | |
| Presenter made frequent eye contact with listeners. | | |
| Presenter held the audience's attention. | | |
| Presenter answered questions clearly. | | |
| (Additional item) | | |
| (Additional item) | | |

# How to Prepare for a Test

## 10 Tried-and-True Tips

Hardly anyone likes tests, but everyone has to take them.
Here's how to make sure you're ready to do your best at test-taking time.

1. Before you leave the classroom, be sure you have asked questions about any words or ideas you don't completely understand.

2. Before you leave school, be sure you have all the materials you need to study for the test: your book, your notes, any extra material the teacher has given you, the homework hotline number or website address, and so on. (What else do you need?)

3. At home, find a quiet spot to do your studying. If it helps you concentrate, play soothing music at a very low volume while you study. Don't take phone calls, answer email, watch TV, play computer games, check social media, or text anyone. Just study.

4. Take time to review the content you have been learning, and use the typography of any text, such as headings, italics, bold print, or color, to help you notice important information. If you took notes, review those, too.

5. Take notes while you study. Use graphic organizers, different colors, mnemonics, or anything else that will help you remember the material.

6. Practice sample problems or exercises.

7. If you study with someone else, leave some time to review the material again by yourself.

8. Before you go to bed, put all the things you need to bring to school tomorrow in one place. (In your backpack? On the kitchen table? Next to the door?) Be sure that you have pencils or pens for the test. Is there anything else you will need? What about books? A calculator? A handheld device? What else? Have everything ready.

9. Go to sleep at a reasonable time.

10. Set your alarm so you wake up early enough to get ready without hurrying before you leave. If you don't usually eat breakfast, take a snack bar along with you unless the school provides snacks.

## Bonus: Quick Tips for Test Time

- When you get the test, take three deep breaths in through the nose and out through the mouth, which increases your blood oxygen level. Each time you exhale, think silently, "I'm ready for this test. I prepared for it, and I will do well."

- On the back of your paper (or on a piece of scratch paper), quickly write down anything you think you'll need for the test. Jot down key ideas, dates, vocabulary words, and names.

Sketch simple maps, vocabulary maps, or graphic organizers you have used for studying. Fill in a few details as you remember them.

- Skim the whole test. Then go back and complete the easier items first.

- As you work through the rest of the test, never spend more than two minutes on one item if it doesn't make sense to you or if it seems very hard. Make a mark in the margin so you can come back to that item if you have enough time.

# CHAPTER 10

# Helping Students Choose Appropriate Behaviors

## Scenario: Armen

Armen had been in the gifted program all through elementary school. His frustrated teachers recognized his exceptional intelligence despite his dismal record of class work completion, and most were happy to have him leave their rooms for a half-day each week for Challenge Class. They understood that one reason Armen resisted the work was because it wasn't *his* work; it was *their* work. Like other gifted kids, Armen would have been thrilled to do work that represented new learning for him. As his teachers moved him from the regular curriculum into projects connected to his passionate interests, he became more productive.

When Armen entered junior high school, the teachers there tended to perceive him as "lazy, stubborn, and someone who needs to be taught the lesson that in the real world, we don't always get to work on what we like!" Therefore, Armen spent most of his school time in an isolated cubby adjacent to the office, where he enjoyed entertaining teachers and other visitors. His teachers would not let him back into their classes until he promised to do his work. Some even asked him to write "I will not waste my time in school" hundreds of times—a significant waste of his time in school. The futility of their methods became apparent when, on March 30, Armen lost the privilege of attending the school picnic on May 31. Two months before school ended, the system had run out of ways to punish Armen. What would they do with him for the next two months?

## Looking Dumb or Being Bad: What Would Your Students Choose?

High on the list of things we are all concerned about is classroom discipline. When we are pushed to define the word *discipline,* it appears that what we worry about most is maintaining control. But discipline is not supposed to ensure mindless obedience. Rather, effective discipline should make good habits routine, so students can maintain proper behavior independently.

All behavior is a form of communication and is driven by a student's unmet academic, social, or emotional needs. When we say "behave yourself," we should be aware that students *are* demonstrating behaviors—just not the ones we would prefer they exhibit. We are actually asking that they change their behavior to conform to our specific expectations.

Why do some kids behave badly in school? One powerful reason is to avoid the embarrassment of being seen as stupid or incapable of learning. Every time we put kids in the position of fearing exposure for their learning inadequacies, we make them choose between looking dumb and being bad. The preferable choice is obvious; nobody wants to look dumb. Therefore, the simplest way to solve behavior problems is to help students become capable and successful learners.

Students who perceive over the years that they are almost always wrong in their efforts at their schoolwork may experience several attitudes from disappointment to hopelessness. So much of their poorly chosen behaviors are efforts to avoid the mental anguish that accompanies being asked to try harder on tasks that often make absolutely no sense to them. Procrastination becomes inevitable, and many distracting behaviors occur. Some kids hope that these behaviors will divert the attention of their teachers and classmates away from their inadequacies through laughter, and they may decide to become "clowns," because it feels much better when people laugh *with* you than *at* you. A predictable cycle results, which sometimes even helps the particular student feel better for a short period of time.

You probably know from personal experience how hard it is to make a change of any kind. Many adults remain in unhappy situations because they fear that a change will be even more miserable. If change is hard for us, imagine how tough it must be for kids. Once students are labeled "difficult," it may actually be more comfortable for them to stay that way than to change their behavior from bad to good. No wonder it sometimes appears that students are trying to sabotage their own lives and our sincere efforts to help them.

Anything you suggest to students must be perceived as safe enough to try. They must believe that they have some control over the outcomes of their behavior—even if that simply means they have learned to think more positive thoughts. Students need to know that the thoughts they allow into their heads control the behaviors they choose and the consequences of those behaviors. Rather than telling kids that they have chosen their negative consequences by their choice of behavior, help them understand that it is the thoughts they choose to focus on that have led to the consequence. This idea has been expressed for many years by Dr. William Glasser in

his work on reality therapy and by Dr. Albert Ellis in his work on rational emotive behavior therapy.

Sometimes students' misbehavior seems rooted in difficult home situations that we as teachers feel powerless to change. It's very frustrating when we don't get the cooperation or support from home that we know would make a big difference. Here's the bottom line: You have little or no control over what happens at home. What you *can* control is what happens to your students at school. We suspect that many parents who have never come to a parent-teacher conference have negative memories of their own school years. We believe that if we call those parents on a regular basis with good news about their children's achievement and behavior, school will seem like a friendlier place, and those parents might become more willing to get involved in their children's education. It's certainly worth a try.

# The Relentless Cycle of Threat

When we attempt to coerce children by scolding, threatening, revoking privileges, lowering grades, giving detentions, or calling their parents, we begin a vicious cycle of threat, and the only predictable outcome is revenge. Students may appear to comply for a short time, but their loss of dignity usually leads them to plan and carry out some way to get back at us. Often their retaliation is passive—forgetting things, appearing helpless, blaming others. Eventually their behavior forces us into another act of coercion, and the cycle continues. Educational psychologist Raymond Wlodkowski has summarized this cycle in the following chart.*

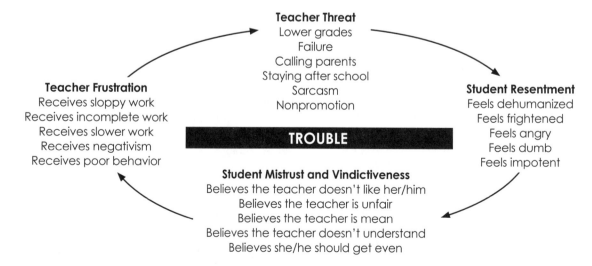

**Teacher Threat**
Lower grades
Failure
Calling parents
Staying after school
Sarcasm
Nonpromotion

**TROUBLE**

**Teacher Frustration**
Receives sloppy work
Receives incomplete work
Receives slower work
Receives negativism
Receives poor behavior

**Student Resentment**
Feels dehumanized
Feels frightened
Feels angry
Feels dumb
Feels impotent

**Student Mistrust and Vindictiveness**
Believes the teacher doesn't like her/him
Believes the teacher is unfair
Believes the teacher is mean
Believes the teacher doesn't understand
Believes she/he should get even

*From Wlodkowski, Raymond J. *Motivation and Teaching: A Practical Guide*. Washington, DC: National Education Association, 1986. Used with permission.

Some teachers at all levels of experience believe that controlling student behavior is an issue separate from curriculum or teaching methods. But in fact, we are not supposed to control our students at all. We are supposed to guarantee their learning. To do this, we must understand that behavior management, teaching methods, and curriculum are intertwined. If either of us were your principal, we would not let you send kids to our office until you had filled out a form that looked something like this:

---

**Student's Name:**_____

**Grade:**_____

**Teacher's Name:** _____

Describe the incident that prompted you to send this student to my office:

_____

_____

_____

_____

Describe what you as the teacher have done to match your lessons to this student's most successful learning modality:

_____

_____

_____

_____

Describe any evidence you have that the work you are expecting this student to do is neither too difficult nor too easy for the student:

_____

_____

_____

_____

---

After completing this imaginary form, most teachers would realize they could carefully choose and implement one more intervention in the classroom before sending the student to a higher authority.

This section describes several effective alternatives to coercion. If these strategies seem overwhelming to you—if you feel you lack the time or resources to use these strategies with your students—then ask yourself what kind of results you're achieving with what you're doing now. If you keep doing what you're doing, you'll keep getting what you're getting. Now is a good time to replace any methods that are not working well with those that will allow you to work smarter, not harder.

Remember that it took your students a long time to develop and practice their inappropriate behaviors. Progress toward change may be slow, with frequent setbacks. Real classroom behavior management is about changing the behavior of the adults. Changes in students come *after* changes in teachers and parents.

# Intervening with Inappropriate Behavior

If we were part of an accreditation team assessing a school's discipline program, we would evaluate it inversely to the size of the discipline manual. We believe that the thicker such a manual is, the less effective a discipline program will be. Many discipline programs are in use today by individual teachers and by entire schools and school systems. And yet the offices of those in charge of school discipline are always full of repeat offenders and other kids who seem unaware that rules even exist, let alone that they are expected to follow them. We can change this. Read on to learn how.

## Help All Students Feel That They Belong

Plan several activities for the beginning of the school year and throughout the year that are specifically designed to help all students feel that they belong to the group. See Chapter 1 for suggestions.

## Teach to Students' Learning Modality Strengths

If your students can't learn the way you are teaching them, you can either wait until they come around to your way of teaching or you can teach them the way they learn. See Chapters 3 and 4 for helpful strategies you can use to empower *all* your students to learn more effectively. Remind your students often that no actual learning would take place if we never made mistakes. Think out loud your own self-talk when you make a mistake. Making a mistake is always the best way to know that your current methods do not work.

## Teach Self-Regulation

Self-regulation is managing one's own emotions and behaviors. A successful student has learned how to do this. Students who have strong self-regulation skills in doing schoolwork can:

- locate needed information

- arrange their work area

- ask for help from peers

- organize and interpret information
- set goals and plans for completing tasks
- keep track of assignment due dates
- monitor achievement scores
- persevere to learn academic skills through practice
- self-evaluate work quality or progress
- self-reward for a doing a job well

Students who have strong behavioral self-regulation skills can:

- participate in class appropriately
- follow classroom routines and other expectations
- engage in calming and focusing self-talk
- adjust to schedule or teacher changes
- work effectively with peers and resolve conflicts
- control impulses by silently reciting a mantra such as *Stop! Think! Do!*
- remain on a path to self-control by recognizing triggers and learning to select appropriate behavior most of the time

## Unlocking Autism 🔒

Sensory processing is what allows your brain to comprehend what is going on inside your own body and in the world around you. It's how your brain understands what your senses perceive. Students with sensory processing disorders need to learn how to understand what is happening in their bodies, why they are feeling a certain way, and how to respond to the stimuli around them. Students who can learn effective self-regulation strategies are more successful at meeting school-related expectations.

Students with LD need to be explicitly taught these strategies if they are to be successful in school. Teaching students these skills requires them to break bad habits and replace them with good habits, and this does not happen without time and patience. We have listed six effective strategies you can use to teach self-regulation skills.

1. Set realistic short-term goals, such as *I will keep track of all my homework assignments today.*

2. Model how thinking aloud can keep one on track and can help students realize they are going down an ineffective thinking path.

3. Discuss problems in a small-group setting to have peers suggest a helpful behavior choice for the situation.

4. Scaffold your students' efforts by providing positive and specific prompts and corrective feedback on what the students are expected to learn.

5. Guide learners to make connections to abstract concepts through the use of hands-on and other concrete learning experiences.

6. Link new experiences to prior learning through the integration of information from multiple subject areas.

## Directly Teach and Coach Replacement Behaviors

Teaching and coaching can help a student replace undesirable behaviors with behaviors that are more appropriate and helpful. For example, Rosalie was in the habit of chewing pencils and erasers down to nothing. Her teacher chose, as a replacement behavior, giving Rosalie permission to chew on specially made chewing items, such as chewy tubes or chewable jewelry, that do not break down. (You can find such products at www.nationalautismresources.com or www.therapyshoppe.com.) Another student named Ivan always rocked in his chair—sometimes to the point of tipping over backward. His special education teacher helped the school purchase a fidget seat and also allowed Ivan to sit on a large exercise ball instead of a chair.

## Establish and Use Predictable Routines

Students with learning or social difficulties often create havoc for substitutes. If you understand that part of the problem is the students' uneasiness with the interrupted routine, you can come up with creative solutions. For example, you might leave detailed information on the established routines, including schedule, procedures, a request for the sub to maintain the established routine and schedule as much as possible, and the name of a person to contact in an emergency. Perhaps you could send a particularly disruptive student to work in a time-out area, another teacher's classroom, or the office of a person responsible for discipline—not as a punishment but as a preventive measure.

## Establish and Reinforce Simple Classroom Rules

Keep classroom rules simple and highly visible. We believe that the longer the list of rules, the more likely it is that kids will choose a misbehavior not specifically listed. (*Example:* If a rule states "No running in the halls," a student might skip down the hall, then argue that the rules don't forbid skipping.) The trick is to keep the rules simple and general. Post them on a chart displayed prominently in your room, and give your students frequent verbal reminders.

We have four favorite rules that generally get the job done:

1. Treat others the same way you want to be treated.

2. Don't bother anyone. (Chart examples with student input.)

3. Don't call attention to yourself. (Chart examples with student input.)

4. Do your work and record your progress in the manner requested by the teacher.

If students break a rule, ask them privately to identify which rule their behavior violates. If they can't identify that their behavior is against the rules, ask them to sit alone until they can either stop the undesirable behavior or talk with you about the needed change. Explain the effect the misbehavior has on others, including you, and outline the consequence that will be applied if they fail to choose more appropriate behavior. Tell them they can rejoin the class after they complete a "Behavior Change Plan" (page 218).

## Be Consistent and Fair

- Avoid overusing negative or hostile eye contact. Make sure that every student also receives positive facial expressions from you regularly.

- Anticipate situations that are likely to cause problems, and brainstorm possible solutions with the student before the next similar event. (*Example:* "Eric, we have to go into the auditorium for a program in an hour. Let's think of a plan so when you feel unable to sit and listen, you can leave before you call attention to yourself.")

- Set up conditions that allow students to save face. (*Example:* If you know that a student will resist a request to clean up the floor around her desk, work up to it gradually by preceding it with other less objectionable requests. "Josie, please pass out these pencils for me. . . . Thanks. Now would you please take the lunch count to the office for me. . . . Thanks. Now please pick up all the papers on the floor around your desk and put them in this box. . . . Thanks.")

- Help complainers by acknowledging that you hear their complaints and by challenging them to come up with workable solutions. They will either think of good solutions or stop complaining. **Tip:** Ask them to describe their complaint, writing down all the details they can think of, so you can understand the complexity of their problem. Chances are, the complaints will diminish or end soon.

## Make Sure the Curriculum Is Stimulating and Worth Learning

The Common Core State Standards link required learning to meaningful scenarios to increase student interest and help them see the reasons why they have to learn certain things. Even if your state is not using Common Core, you know that integrated learning experiences are usually much more interesting and motivating for students than basic skills lessons are. For example, instead of just reading about how fire stations work, build in math lessons about the typical menus and shopping lists or costs for a day or week at the station. Such lessons teach the same math skills in a much more motivating way, don't you agree? This method is more interesting for the teacher, too. For more information on how to infuse rigor into any type of curriculum, consult the book *Rigor and Engagement for Growing Minds* by Bertie Kingore. (Visit www.bertiekingore.com.)

We can't really *make* kids do anything; we can only provide opportunities and motivate kids to engage in the learning tasks we offer. See pages 66–73 for specific strategies that will help you provide a meaningful and challenging curriculum.

### Tech Tip 🖥

Technology is a great way to keep students engaged in learning, so they become too busy and interested in what's happening in the class to choose negative behaviors. Lessons that promote critical thinking and problem solving are good ways to achieve this goal. Prepare an annotated list of websites you think would be helpful for your students with LDs, and keep it near the computers they use.

One engaging game we recommend is Fantastic Contraption (fantasticcontraption.com). In this physics game, students move a piece from one area into a scoring zone by any means necessary, using rotating engines and rods of different kinds to change the world around them. The possibilities are endless, and the game provides kinesthetic experiences, which we know are essential to engaging students with LD.

## Keep Talk to a Minimum

For some kids with behavior disorders or language processing problems, too much teacher talk is frustrating and even annoying. Create several nonverbal cues that indicate what you want kids to do or stop doing, and use these cues instead of words whenever possible. Be sure to fully explain and model each signal. Use signals that require students to attend to you immediately, such as a specific segment of music or a clapping sequence that requires students to finish the sequence with their own clapping.

You might also teach your students how they can signal you when they have a specific need. One teacher tells her class, "If you are feeling like you need to move, please stand beside your desk. If you need a break, pantomime the time-out sign, and if you think we're too serious and need to lighten things up a little, wink at me." Students are more likely to honor your signals when the communication works both ways.

## Positive Time-Out

Used consistently and calmly, time-out is an effective strategy to teach students self-control without disrupting instruction in the classroom. For time-out to be effective, students must understand that it is not punitive, but rather a chance to calm down, regain self-control, and be welcomed back into the group when ready. Time-out is most effective when a designated area reserved for this purpose allows the student to have necessary separation while simultaneously keeping track of what is occurring in the classroom. Time-out should be used as soon as a student begins losing self-control, so that regaining control is easier. Instruct students in how to go to the time-out spot quickly and quietly, use learned strategies to regain self-control in a nondistracting manner, and rejoin the group when ready. Prompting a student to go to time-out should be done using a quiet voice and few words or gestures, so instruction is not interrupted.

Time-out should be brief—no more than five minutes—and used consistently with all students as a part of the classroom behavior plan. The goal is for students to learn to self-monitor their behavior so they can go to time-out voluntarily, whenever they sense that this would be a helpful thing to do for themselves or the rest of the class. If more than five minutes is needed, or if students' need for time-out does not diminish over time, another type of intervention is indicated. If students are allowed to stay in time-out indefinitely, some may manipulate the teacher so they can go to time-out more often.

## Help Students Stay Calm

- Be aware of situations that are likely to overstimulate students. Strive for a good balance between stimulating and calming activities.

- At the beginning of each work period, have students move through a controlled exercise or rhythmic activity to release pent-up energy. Many commercial products (audio recordings, videos, DVDs, and so on) are available for this purpose. One of our favorites is Brain Gym (www.braingym.org).

- Talk the class through progressive relaxation, an exercise in which they alternately tense and relax many parts of their body, from their head to their toes.

## Teach Students How to Handle Anger

Kids who get angry easily may not know how to express their anger in more acceptable ways. Hand out copies of the "Things You Can Do Instead of Staying Angry" form (page 217) for students to keep at their desks. Tell students they might mark the tips that work best for them, or circle the ones they would like to try the next time they get angry. Give positive reinforcement each time you notice students who have handled their anger appropriately.

If we want our students to handle their anger in healthy ways, we need to set a good example. Kids need to understand that their behavior leads to certain positive and negative consequences. But a teacher who gets upset should not be one of those negative consequences. Keep in mind that many struggling students, especially those with severe emotional problems, really can't choose more appropriate behaviors without direct instruction, proactive counseling, and support from qualified professionals. Deal with misbehavior quickly and fairly; apply logical consequences rather than threats and punishments.

## Teach Students How to Monitor Their Self-Talk

When kids engage in negative self-talk, it adversely affects their behavior and productivity. You can help your students develop a short script they can keep at their desks. Anytime they catch themselves using negative self-talk, they should take several deep breaths and read the script to themselves. After reading, they should close their eyes and visualize themselves in the more positive situation. Here's an example:

- Negative self-talk: "What if the teacher calls on me and I don't know the answer? What if the kids think I'm dumb? I'd better make them notice me for something else first."

- Positive self-talk: "Stop! I'm going to take three deep breaths and remember that the teacher doesn't call on anyone until we've had a chance to talk to our partner. I have a nice partner who always helps me think of what to say. I'll rehearse my answer so when I get called on, I'll be able to have a good answer."

Coach students to notice times when their behavior is correct and helpful and silently congratulate themselves for their success. Their self-talk might sound something like this: "I'm proud of myself for not touching anyone on my trip to and from the board." Arrange a nonverbal signal to use with students when you notice praiseworthy behavior, so you can let them know it's time for some silent self-praise.

## Use the WDEP Model

Based on Glasser's work in reality therapy, the WDEP model is a helpful guide to dialoguing with students who are engaging in inappropriate behavior. The acronym *WDEP* stands for the words *want, doing, evaluate,* and *plan*. WDEP can lead to a "Behavior Change Plan" (page 218).

The setting should be a private conference between you and the student. Sit beside the student rather than across from him. Suggest that you and the student can become partners in finding a solution to the student's problem. Visualize the problem in the empty space across from you both. Make sure the student understands that the purpose of your meeting is not to punish, but to make a plan for appropriate and productive behavior.

Tell the student that you are going to check in with radio station WDEP. Ask the following questions and listen respectfully to any and all responses:

- "What do you *want* to happen?"

- "What are you *doing* to get what you want?"

- "*Evaluate* how well your behavior is helping you reach your goal. Is what you are doing against the class rules? If so, which rule or rules?"

- "Think of a *plan* to change what you're doing so your new behavior has a better chance of helping you get what you want or need."

Try hard to avoid jumping in with a solution unless the student asks for your input. Then make just *one* suggestion at a time that specifically addresses *only* the behavior that is the focus of this conference. Arrange to

meet again in a day or two to see how well the plan is working and, if necessary, to guide the student to create a different plan. Magic happens with many students when we can illustrate they are truly in control of their own behavior and its consequences.

## Scenario: Charlie

Everyone knows someone like Charlie. Charlie was a seventh grader with a behavior disorder. He simply could not keep his hands to himself. Not only did he touch other kids at every opportunity; he sometimes hurt them. He was contrite immediately after each incident, but he seemed unable to translate being sorry into more appropriate behavior. It occurred to Susan that "keep your hands to yourself" was too vague an expectation for Charlie to understand.

Charlie and Susan met and agreed that he would carry a Koosh ball whenever he left his desk to remind him not to touch other kids. In between trips, he could use the ball to help get rid of his omnipresent excess energy. Susan showed Charlie how to keep track of his own progress on a chart he would keep at his desk. He would earn and record a plus (+) each time he left his desk and returned without touching anyone, and a minus (–) each time he touched someone. As soon as he accumulated three plusses and no more than two consecutive minuses, he would earn 10 minutes of free drawing time, which he seemed to greatly appreciate.

Susan attached a small chart to his desk and demonstrated how to enter a plus when he met his no-touching goal and a minus when he didn't. She explained that for the first few days, she would reinforce his behavior with a thumbs-up or thumbs-down signal.

The first time he left his desk and returned, Susan gave him a thumbs-up. He entered a plus on his chart.

The second time—thumbs-down. He had "accidentally" touched Brian at the pencil sharpener. Susan walked over to Charlie's desk, and they had a brief conversation:

*Susan:* "I noticed you touched Brian, so what mark will you record this time?"

*Charlie:* "It wasn't my fault. He touched me first!"

*Susan:* "You're not recording whose fault it was; you're recording whether you touched someone."

*Charlie:* "That's not fair."

*Susan (without emotion):* "Please record the minus you earned, and then we'll make a plan so the same thing doesn't happen again."

*Charlie:* "Okay—but it's still not fair."

After Charlie grudgingly recorded a tiny minus, Susan asked him to suggest a plan that would lead to more success the next time he left his seat. He decided that he would wait until no one else was at the pencil sharpener.

Charlie went on to record another plus, then two minuses in a row. After he had recorded the second minus, Susan prompted him:

*Susan:* "You know, if you have to record a minus the next time you leave your desk, the first two plusses won't count. Remember, our agreement requires you to have three plusses with no more than two minuses in a row. So tell me your plan to be sure not to touch anyone the next time you leave your desk."

*Charlie:* "I guess I should carry that ball you gave me with both hands."

*Susan:* "Sounds like a good plan. Hope it works."

Charlie held on tightly to his ball during each subsequent time he left his desk, and he was soon able to record the next plus. Susan bestowed his reward immediately, and Charlie looked proud as he took his 10 minutes to draw a picture of a kid desperately hanging on to a Koosh ball as he walked around the room.

In subsequent days, Charlie learned to record his tallies without any direct assistance, and he earned far more plusses than minuses. After several successes, we upped the ante to four, then five plusses in a row. It's not essential that kids record their marks totally honestly. The very act of being responsible for recording one's behavior ultimately leads to behavior change.

# Helping Students Learn to Choose Appropriate Behavior

## Catch Them Being Good and Doing Well

- Regularly scan the class to notice and reinforce students' appropriate behaviors. If students perceive that the only time they get your attention is when they are doing something wrong, you can expect problems. Simply calling everyone's attention to what's being done right can motivate students to borrow teacher-pleasing behaviors from other kids. Purposefully notice kids when they are behaving appropriately, and support that behavior in encouraging terms. (*Example:* "I notice that half the class is ready for directions. I'd love to see the rest of the class be ready, too." It's probably better not to use specific students' names in your praise.

Such kids may become targets for the hostility of others.)

- When you have coached a student to change a particular behavior, notice the preferred behavior privately as soon as it happens, even if at first it means leaving something else you are doing. Increase the duration of time between praising statements until eventually the student chooses the appropriate behaviors automatically.

- Praise is much more effective when it is focused on students' actions rather than on their personalities. (*Examples:* Instead of "You're such a good boy, Joseph," say, "Joseph, your improved behavior this week must be the result of all of your hard work." Instead of "This is the best class I've ever had," say, "Class, we are getting so much more work done when you follow the class rules and are considerate to each other.")

## Use Awareness Tallies

If students appear unaware that their behavior needs to change, use this strategy for a short time.

1. Identify and describe a behavior you would like a student to change.

2. Gather baseline data about the student's behavior. If the child's parent or caregiver approves, one way to do this is by making a video. Simply set up a video camera on a tripod and aim it at the target student; turn it on after the student stops noticing it. You can count the number of infractions at a later time, when you don't have to monitor the rest of the class.

3. Remember that a picture equals a thousand words. Don't show the video to anyone but the student (except, perhaps, the student's parents or guardians at a conference). When you show it to the student, use only a short segment and make sure that the student can view it in privacy. Have the student tally the inappropriate behaviors within a reasonable time period.

   **Variation:** Have the *student* tally his or her own inappropriate behaviors during a given time period. Afterward, discuss the frequency of the behavior with the student. Ask the student to set a goal of fewer times for the next tally period.

4. Repeat this process until the number of times the behavior is observed declines to a manageable amount.

| Awareness Tally | | | |
|---|---|---|---|
| Date/Time | Inappropriate behavior | During what class activity | Tally # of times |
| 4/6 9:45–10:15 | Talking out of turn | Class discussion about novel | 卌 |

## Use I-Messages

Rather than blaming students for their behavior, tell them how you feel about it. (*Example:* Instead of "If you don't stop calling Jason a 'retard,' you're going to have to work in the office!" say, "I worry that Jason will be embarrassed when you call him unpleasant names, which is not an acceptable behavior in this class.")

Follow this with a statement of exactly what you expect this student to do. (*Example:* "I need you to tell me a plan before recess of how you will solve this problem. If you can't come up with a plan, I'll make one for you.")

## Model the Behavior You Want Students to Emulate

1. Decide which positive behavior you would like the student to demonstrate. It's important to introduce requests for behavior change one at a time. Do not add other requests until each new behavior has been learned.

2. Model exactly what you want the student to do as you softly talk out loud about the steps you are taking. (*Example:* "I'm walking down the aisle on my way to the rug for a meeting with the teacher. I'm keeping my arms at my sides so I won't touch anyone. When I get all the way to the rug without touching anyone, I will say to myself, 'Congratulations to me for getting from my seat to the rug without touching anyone! I'm terrific!'")

3. Ask the student to perform the same task while you softly talk the student through it.

4. Have the student perform the same task while talking through it.

5. Have the student perform the same task while thinking or whispering the self-talk.

Students should keep tally charts at their desks so they can mark each time they complete the task correctly. If it seems necessary, you may have students choose a mutually acceptable reward they know they will earn after a certain number of tallies.

## Directly Teach Social Skills

1. Identify a skill the student lacks. Discuss with the student how having the skill will improve interactions with others.

2. Privately model how the skill should be used.

3. Ask the student to describe the components of the skill as modeled correctly.

4. Have the student role-play the skill with you or another student as you coach them through it.

5. Have the student role-play the skill while talking through it.

6. Have the student role-play the skill while whispering the self-talk.

7. Provide numerous opportunities for the student to continue practicing the skill.

8. Each time you notice the student using the skill correctly, say, "I noticed that you were [describe the skill] correctly. Good work!" Consistent, immediate positive feedback is essential to having the student form the habit of using the skill.

9. After the student calms down from exhibiting an inappropriate behavior, have the student think out loud about the better possible choices with you or another available staff person. To end this direct instruction intervention, have the student make a plan for a more effective choice if the behavior occurs again.

10. Whenever the student lapses into inappropriate behavior, ask the student to think out loud about all the better choices possible. Then, to add a little humor, have the student wonder aloud why, in this situation, such a silly choice was made. Have the student end this chat with a plan for how to make a more effective choice next time.

## Learn FAST to Make Good Choices

This mnemonic strategy helps students make appropriate choices and solve problems independently. It can also help students control impulsive behavior. You can say, "To keep out of trouble, you need to remember: learn FAST."

**F = Freeze:** Don't react right away. Stop and think.

**A = Alternatives:** Consider two or three choices for reacting and the consequences of each.

**S = Select:** Choose the best action from the alternatives.

**T = Try it:** Go with your plan for a week or two; if it's not working, try another plan.

## Use a Token Economy

In situations where inappropriate behavior persists, intervention should focus on positive reinforcement. One such method is a token economy. Target students earn tokens for demonstrating desired behaviors. When students choose not to follow their behavior management program, they earn no tokens for that particular time period. However, no previously earned tokens are ever taken away. If you feel the need to do that, you should suggest a positive time-out instead. (See page 204.)

Teachers "price" rewards for target students to "purchase" when they have accumulated enough tokens. In most schools, other students almost never take the earned tokens from target students because most kids prefer a class in which order is routine and privileges are consistently available for all. For this reason, all students perceive they are benefitting from the token economy system.

Some teachers make desired outcomes more likely when the entire class is given some reward, such as five minutes at the end of class for "groom and chat," because they either ignored inappropriate behaviors or helped the target student succeed.

To set up a token economy with a student, the following steps may be used:

1. The teacher confers with the student to determine the behavior that needs to be changed.

2. Together, they determine the number of tokens the student can earn for each time period during which the student refrains from exhibiting the undesired behavior.

3. The student keeps a record of tokens earned. The student experiences a feeling of gaining control in the learning environment.

4. Any teacher or adult overseeing the activity or lesson should be the person who physically hands the token to the student when the desired behavior is observed. That includes monitors who supervise lunch, recess, or other activities.

5. The student can earn a predetermined number of tokens during a designated time frame.

6. As the student's appropriate behavior increases, the tokens required to earn the rewards also increase, until this system is no longer needed and the desired behavior is automatic.

## Scenario: Boris

A third grader named Boris was extremely aggressive at recess. Traditional interventions had failed to change his behavior. His teachers created a behavior management program in which Boris could earn tokens for not being physically or verbally abusive to anyone during recess. The recess monitor would give him the tokens earned as soon as recess was over.

When Boris returned to his classroom, he placed his tokens in a designated container and recorded his progress on his "Token Record Sheet." (See page 219.) Boris could determine when he had earned the number of tokens needed to purchase a reward from a list he and his teacher had created. He could keep any unspent tokens and add them to the next day's earned tokens. Boris decided to see how many tokens he could earn during the entire school year without spending any, so the tokens became their own intrinsic rewards.

Boris's *class* also got a bonus of five minutes' "groom and chat time" on any day that Boris reached his token goal. This motivated his peers to help him ignore opportunities for negative behavior. They also came to understand that they could positively impact his behavior in general.

After implementing a token economy for at least two weeks, progress should be visible. If progress doesn't happen, revise or change the plan. For example, tokens may need to be given more frequently.

## Use Functional Behavior Assessment (FBA)

If a token economy and the other strategies previously described do not lead to the desired behavior changes, a functional behavior assessment (FBA) is the next logical step. FBA is a highly effective behavior management method, but it is also very time-consuming. It should be reserved only for students who need serious further interventions.

## Scenario: Javier

Javier was struggling in his fifth-grade class to follow the school-wide positive behavior support system (page 214) recently implemented in Lisa's district. He had trouble following the rules, even though he wanted to earn tickets to purchase rewards like his classmates.

His special education teacher, regular education teacher, and other staff who came in contact with him throughout his school day met to brainstorm interventions that might be effective in developing the positive behaviors Javier needed. After many intervention attempts, the team decided to complete a FBA to help them identify the antecedents of his behaviors, the conditions that were contributing to continuation of the inappropriate behaviors, and interventions that might be effective.

The first step was to have all the staff who worked with Javier complete an interview form (on pages 220–222) to gather information. Then, a form was developed and used to record data (page 223) through observing Javier's behaviors and the actions that occurred before and after these behaviors. The final step was to analyze this data and develop a plan (page 224).

Using the interview forms and the data collected through observations over ten school days, the team concluded that the antecedent to Javier's undesired behaviors was a request to complete work that involved writing, the area of his disability. The team developed a list of supports for Javier to remove his anxiety associated with written work. Some of these supports included sensory breaks to divide the assignment into smaller time chunks, a peer scribe for longer written responses, and use of a laptop with a speech-to-text app to complete written assignments more easily.

With these supports, plus the fact that he was experiencing rewards more frequently than he had been in the past, Javier's unacceptable behaviors began to decrease and were gradually replaced with appropriate behaviors. For Javier, as for many students, the appropriate behaviors stuck. Desired behaviors tend to stay in place with a plan formed through FBA because all parties are aware of the root of the problem (antecedents to undesirable behaviors). Staff can plan proactively to avoid predictable antecedents and continually provide appropriate supports for lasting change.

A functional behavior assessment is a process for identifying problem behaviors and developing interventions to eliminate them or replace them with appropriate behaviors. This process involves three steps:

- **Step 1:** Any teacher or staff member who has observed the behavior of the student provides written responses to interview questions focusing on antecedent behaviors and consequences, or what happens immediately before and immediately after the inappropriate behavior. (See "Step 1: FBA Interview Form" on pages 220–222.) The teacher also notices and records consequences that perpetuate the undesired behavior, any patterns in the behaviors, and the times behaviors most often occur. A classroom teacher can work alone or with a special education staff person for additional help in interpreting the information collected and developing a plan.

- **Step 2:** Collect data through direct observation of the student, using a direct observation form. (See "Step 2: Direct Observation Form" on page 223 and the sample form on page 211.) Compare the data collected on this form with the data collected on the FBA interview form and note any discrepancies.

- **Step 3:** Develop a summary based on the results of the interview (step 1) and the data collected during the direct observation (step 2) to build a positive behavior support plan. Ongoing analysis of the plan occurs and revisions are made as needed until the undesired behavior is eliminated or replaced with appropriate behavior. (See "Step 3: Positive Behavior Support Plan" on page 224 and the sample form on page 211.)

The information gathered through the interview and direct observation results in the following:

1. Specific, clear description of the inappropriate behavior(s)

2. Identification of the environmental factors, including antecedents and consequences, that correspond with the behavior(s)

3. Development of an action plan for the student that can allow effective teaching and learning to occur without inappropriate behaviors interfering

Keep a record of two or three of the student's most problematic behaviors for ten days using the FBA method. This helps staff make intelligent decisions about how to proceed with behavioral interventions. If needed, you may ask a special education staff member to help you create this summary by asking for specific suggestions regarding effective interventions. Also consult the chart on pages 212–213 for ideas. Reevaluate the action plan at the end of the first week and then every two weeks once it is working successfully.

The chart also lists some common inappropriate behaviors and suggested interventions. Examples for each behavior and effective interventions are also included to help clarify each one for you.

## Unlocking Autism 🔒

Applied behavior analysis (ABA), an intervention plan for increasing useful behaviors and reducing those that may cause harm or interfere with learning, can positively impact social and communication behaviors and other extreme behaviors associated with autism. Documenting trigger situations and related consequences can assist in developing appropriate replacement behaviors. Correctly implemented over time, ABA interventions can produce comprehensive, consistent, and lasting results. One excellent source for this information is www.autismspeaks.org.

## Use Behavior Contracts

When Susan's granddaughter Brooke was five years old, she and her parents came to visit Grandma and Grandpa. They stayed for three days, and on the morning they were supposed to return home, Brooke indicated rather emotionally that she wanted to extend her visit. It was a very busy time for Susan, and on several previous visits Brooke had desperately needed her mommy and daddy almost as soon as they walked out the door. She promised not to repeat that behavior this time.

"Well, if you want to stay, you have to sign a contract," Susan said.

Her eyes widened, and she asked, "What does that mean?"

"I write out the expectations I have for your behavior," Susan explained. "If you agree to do what I ask, you have to sign the contract. When you sign the contract, it means that you promise to do exactly what it says."

"Okay."

Susan took out a piece of paper and wrote down three expectations. She added a line to the left of each expectation so Brooke could initial it.

_____1. I promise not to cry for my mommy at night. If I want to talk to my mommy, I'll tell Grandma during the day.

_____2. I promise not to cry when I have to go to bed.

_____3. I won't ask how many days are left until I go home. Instead, Grandma and I will mark off every day on the calendar so I can count the days myself.

Susan and Brooke read through the contract together, and Brooke very seriously printed her initials next to each item. Then they put the contract on the refrigerator with a magnet, Brooke kissed her parents good-bye, and Brooke and Susan started a highly satisfying five-day stay together. During that whole time, Brooke never engaged in the inappropriate behaviors Susan had feared. Whenever Susan took Brooke someplace with her and someone asked Brooke, "Are you being a good girl while you are staying with Grandma?" she would reply seriously, "Yes, I am, because we have a contract."

You might want to move beyond the other strategies suggested in this chapter to a formal behavior contract. The power of a behavior contract is amazingly strong. Students take promises seriously when they've signed their name to a piece of paper. Even very young students can learn to use behavior contracts.

**1.** Identify the inappropriate behavior that you want the student to stop doing.

**2.** Collect baseline data for several days to establish how often the behavior occurs.

**3.** Meet with the student to share the data you've collected. Describe the behavior you have observed and ask the student to explain why the behavior is inappropriate. If the student can't do so, explain it yourself. Suggest a replacement behavior. *Be very specific in describing the behavior you want.* Model it if necessary.

**4.** Give the student a copy of the "Behavior Contract" handout on page 225. Include a description of the desired behavior and the number of times the student should exhibit the behavior. (**Tip:** Have the student choose this goal, and start small.) Explain that the student should make a tally mark on the contract each time he or she exhibits the behavior. Agree on an incentive the student will earn upon achieving the goal.

Notice that this contract asks the student to tally successes, not failures. Working to *increase* the frequency of what we *do* want is more effective than working to *decrease* the frequency of what we *don't* want.

**5.** Be prepared to deliver the incentive as soon as possible after the student satisfies the terms of the contract.

**Tips:**

- Keep the behavior contract between you and the student private. You may let parents know what you are doing, but don't involve them in the steps of the contract or require their signature, since you would then lose control over the contract terms.

- Make the initial contract short-term. On later contracts, you can gradually extend the time and increase the number of tallies needed to earn the incentive.

- Don't worry if kids don't record their behavior accurately. The act of recording in itself can lead to improved behavior.

- If the inappropriate behavior is causing harm to other kids or seriously interfering with the progress of the class, you may also need to identify a consequence to be imposed at the time the harm is done. Keep the consequence separate from the contract; it should not interfere with the contract's continuation.

## Step 2: Direct Observation Form (Sample)

| Student:<br>Kevin | Class or Subject:<br>Math | Staff Collecting Data: Mrs.<br>Jefferson | Date and Time:<br>Daily math period<br>10:00–11:30 a.m. |
| --- | --- | --- | --- |
| **Antecedent(s)<br>to Behavior:**<br><br>Asked to do academic task<br><br>Asked to work independently and without attention-seeking behaviors<br><br>Asked to focus on teacher during instructional lesson<br><br>Asked to work with a partner or group | **Behavior(s) of Concern:**<br><br>Focusing on instruction<br><br>Attending to tasks | **Consequence(s)**<br><br>Verbal redirection<br><br>Review assignments and directions one-on-one<br><br>Preferential seating<br><br>Offer choices | |

## Step 3: Positive Behavior Support Plan (Sample)

**A. Preventing the disruptive behavior (describe one to three options):**

1. Use limited, concise language with one-step direction using a gestural or visual cue.

2. Provide short tasks that do not require extended attention in order to be successful.

3. Increase opportunities for movement during learning tasks.

**B. Desirable behavior goal:**

Student will focus on instruction or attend to task for 15 minutes without needing verbal, visual, or gestural prompts.

**C. Reinforcement when the student performs the desirable behavior:**

1. Student will receive tokens toward a reward within a token economy system.

2. Student will receive verbal praise from the teacher for the desired behavior.

**D. Consequences when the student performs the undesirable behavior again:**

1. When the student first exhibits undesired behavior, show a warning card with the number 1 on it. If the student continues to exhibit the behavior after one minute, show a warning card with the number 2. If the student still continues after another minute, show a warning card with the number 3. Do not argue with the student at all during this time. When showing the third card, remove the student for a one-minute time-out to think.

2. Clearly describe and demonstrate to the other students how to ignore the student's undesired behavior in class. Then, when necessary, use a silent signal to prompt that a time has come for the class to engage in "planned ignoring" of a particular student's inappropriate behavior so as to remove the factor of a student seeking attention for himself.

3. Be equally purposeful in giving attention and subtle praise when the student engages in the desired behavior.

## Positive Behavioral Intervention Chart for Common Inappropriate Behaviors

| Inappropriate Behavior | Behavior Intervention | Description of Intervention | Example |
|---|---|---|---|
| Student is always touching others in annoying ways. | Teacher prompts student with a secret, agreed-upon signal. The student earns tokens for responding appropriately. | As student reaches out to touch a person, teacher uses the agreed-upon vocal or gestural signal as a warning. | Dom gets out of his seat during independent work time to sharpen his pencil. He slides his hand across several students' backs on the way to the pencil sharpener. The teacher prompts him by clearing her throat. On his way back to his seat, he does not touch any student. He earns one out of two possible tokens for making one-half a successful trip. |
| Student is often distracted from the task at hand. | Redirect to appropriate task. | Redirection occurs through predetermined visual, gestural, or verbal prompts. | Amy is not attending to her math instruction. A cue card (visual prompt) is placed on her desk to reengage her in the required task. |
| Student repeats negative behavior often throughout the day. | Ignore negative behavior and catch student being good, or send student to positive time-out. | Reward positive behaviors privately the moment you see them. | Roberto is seen offering another student a turn in the task rather than declaring it is always his turn. Mrs. Desario lets Roberto know she has noticed this and gives him five minutes to do an activity of his choice. |
| Student is inconsistent in following the classroom behavior plan. Note: The plan should be very brief. (See "Establish and Reinforce Simple Classroom Rules," page 202.) | Apply consequences as determined by the classroom behavior plan or send student to positive time-out. | Develop clear and simple classroom rules and make certain that all adults have consistent expectations for student behavior. | The substitute teacher communicates to the students that she is aware of the class rules and intends to follow them in the same way the regular teacher does. |
| Student has difficulty disengaging from the present task. | Give a five-minute warning when transitions are coming. | Five minutes before a transition is to occur, give a visual or verbal prompt to all students indicating the precise change in activity and related expectations. | At 2:10, Mrs. Rodriguez tells the class, "At 2:15, we will put away the map we are working on and start our work on the most common state products." |

| Student has a difficult time maintaining attention. | Give sensory breaks at predetermined times or as needed. | Allow the student to have appropriate sensory input or movement activities, such as wall push-ups, a Koosh ball, music, or a healthy snack. | To help Connor prepare to attend during math instruction, he moves to the back of the room to do wall push-ups beginning 5 minutes before the math lesson. |
|---|---|---|---|
| Student often blurts out silly remarks, causing a disruption for some classmates. | Use the Name Card Method (page 12) to significantly reduce blurting out, or send student to positive time-out. | Become familiar with the Name Card Method and use it for part of each lesson, one subject at a time. | Discussion buddies work together to be sure each student has an appropriate answer to each question, greatly increasing student participation. |
| Student behaves in an outrageously inappropriate way. | Removal from the classroom or environment. Note: Time-out is not a good choice here, since the student behavior has escalated to such a point that 5 minutes will never be enough time for regaining self-control. | Call for support that a student needs to be removed. | Josh refuses to perform the requested task and starts yelling and screaming. You call the office for assistance. A crisis team staff arrives to assist you. If Josh leaves with the staff, great. If not, remove the other students if safety is a concern. |

# Improving Behavior for the Whole Class

Although ideally we want to move away from external motivation for doing well in school, whole-class programs can be remarkably effective in persuading kids who misbehave to conform to reasonable expectations. Some teachers give points to the whole class when all students have met certain clearly defined and explained behavior expectations, usually for a given class or subject rather than for an entire school day. You may also give points to rows or small groups of kids seated together.

You might award points for categories, including attendance, bringing in homework, following class rules, completing expected tasks, and so on. Only *give* points—never take them away. Your students will soon begin putting pressure on their peers who are keeping them from getting the points. (It's fun to watch them take over some of the things *you* used to have to do to get positive results from everyone in the class.) Tally points regularly and let kids cash them in for treats, coupons, or privileges ranging from extra recess time to class celebrations.

With very young students, you might want to hand out colored cards or other tokens each time you recognize their good behavior. Just before class ends, have them turn in their cards or tokens for an incentive of their choice.

With older students, try the "positive points" system. Each student gets a card used to tally points earned by achieving personal behavioral goals. Whenever you notice a student engaging in a goal-related behavior, you acknowledge it verbally. (*Examples:* "Tracy, I noticed that you kept all your materials together in your folder today. Give yourself five positive points." "Jeffrey, I noticed that you followed directions. Give yourself three positive points.") You and the class decide in advance how many points a behavior is worth and work together to create a list of incentives (menu items) with specific point values. Vary the menu often to keep interest high. A card that is lost or destroyed is not replaced that day; points are not carried over from week to week; once points have been earned, they cannot be taken away later for inappropriate behavior. At the end of the week, students exchange their points for incentives of their choosing. Sometimes they might decide to pool their points toward a treat or activity for the whole class.

# Conflict Resolution and Peer Mediation

Many schools are using programs designed to reduce conflict before it escalates into violence. Some programs train teachers to mediate conflicts, but the most exciting programs train students in these skills. (See "References and Resources" on page 259.) When such programs are used successfully, the number of incidents involving inappropriate behavior drops dramatically, as does the number of discipline referrals.

Help your students learn to deal directly with each other when arguments or disagreements arise. Coach them through the process of thinking through the problem, explaining it clearly and simply, trying to imagine how the other person feels, and coming up with possible solutions in preparation for meeting face-to-face. The handout "Getting Ready to Talk: For People in Conflict" (page 226) invites students to put their thoughts on paper. Completing the handout, bringing it into a conflict resolution meeting, and consulting it during the meeting are excellent ways to keep things on track. You can learn more about the principles of both conflict resolution and peer mediation by consulting the resources on this topic listed in the "References and Resources" section on page 259.

# School-Wide Behavior Models

We have found that behavioral change programs applied to an entire school, including all students and staff, are the most effective. Although many such commercial programs are available, we have chosen to describe the process called school-wide positive behavior support (SWPBS). This approach is incorporated into many commercial programs, but it is okay to use it without formally purchasing any program. Please consult the website www.pbis.org for more information.

Many schools nationwide are using SWPBS to reduce discipline problems and increase instructional time. This proactive behavioral model uses three tiers, similar to RTI. As always, direct instruction in using appropriate social skills and applying problem-solving principles are key components of the successful implementation of this model.

The visual of the SWPBS model bears a close resemblance to the RTI model described on pages 63–65 of this book. This is an intentional move by the designers of the SWPBS model. When SWPBS and RTI are implemented together, both behavior and learning outcomes

PBS Leadership Team Meets Monthly
Administrative Involvement
Staff Buy-In
Use Data for Decision Making

FEW
SOME
ALL

## Tier III
- Functional behavior assessment and individual behavior plans
- Parent collaboration and education
- Collaboration with student's physician or mental health professional
- Intensive academic support

## Tier II
- Target social skills instruction
- Simple behavior plans
- Alternatives to suspension
- Increased academic support
- School-based mentors
- Classroom management support
- Newcomers club

## Tier I
- Teach school-wide positive behavior expectations and procedures
- Positive reinforcement for all students
- Consistent consequences for problem behaviors
- Effective procedures and supervision in non-classroom areas
- Effective instruction and classroom management

improve dramatically. Refer to the "References and Resources" on page 259 for more information.

In schools that use SWPBS, students are explicitly taught behaviors they are expected to demonstrate throughout the building, including the classroom, hallway, bathroom, bus, playground, cafeteria, and auditorium. After students learn these behaviors, they earn "star ticket" rewards for demonstrating "shining star" behaviors. Star tickets may be redeemed for prizes. Monthly assemblies are held to help reinforce the behaviors students are expected to demonstrate.

The expected behaviors are:

**S:** Support safety.

**T:** Take responsibility.

**A:** Always do your best.

**R:** Respect yourself and others.

# Dealing with Bullying in Your Class and School

We all have experienced bullying—as a recipient, bystander, or perpetrator—and can understand that both the kid who bullies and the target are experiencing discomfort. Bullying comes in many forms, including teasing, taunting, mocking, name-calling, insults, nasty emails and text messages, cyberbullying, threats, and physical violence. Kids bully for many reasons—to feel powerful and in control, to be the center of attention, because they have been bullied themselves, because they get pleasure from other people's pain, or because they feel little or no empathy for others.

It's a myth that kids bully because they have low self-esteem. Researchers have found that the hurtful behavior has more to do with the emotion of shame and less to do with self-esteem.* Students who attack, injure,

and even kill their schoolmates often have a history of being bullied themselves.**

Efforts to stop bullying vary by school district. The effectiveness of anti-bullying efforts has improved dramatically in recent years due to easier access to programs with proven success.

If bullying is a problem at your school, it's almost impossible to stop without a dedicated school-wide program that is accepted and supported by everyone in your school community, from the administration to the students and their families. Highly effective programs are based on the landmark work of David Olweus, a professor of psychology at the University of Oslo in Norway. When a series of bullying-related suicides shocked Norway into awareness of the problem, Olweus responded by creating a comprehensive program that is now widely used and respected. Another effective school-wide bullying prevention program is No Place for Hate by the Anti-Defamation League (www.adl.org /npfh). For more information on these and other anti-bullying programs, see "References and Resources" on page 259.

The very act of differentiating the curriculum communicates to all students that individual differences are to be honored in the classroom. The availability of differentiated learning tasks allows students to respect themselves just as they are, which in turn makes them more open to respecting others.

# Questions and Answers

*"Shouldn't kids just know how to behave more appropriately in school?"*

Never assume that students know how to substitute good behavior for bad. Students need to work with an adult to learn such basic skills as taking turns, sharing, asking for help, accepting suggestions, apologizing when necessary, and accepting praise or compliments. Several excellent books, including Arnold Goldstein's Skillstreaming series and Dorothy Rich's *MegaSkills*, can help you teach social skills directly. More excellent resources are described in the "References and Resources" section on pages 259–260.

*"How can I find time to try these interventions? When am I supposed to do all of the record-keeping involved?"*

For several days, try keeping a log of the amount of time you spend disciplining students with significant behavior problems. Then ask yourself if that time wouldn't be better spent teaching kids how to manage their own

---

*Psychology Today.* Mary Larnia. "Do Bullies Really Have Low Self Esteem?" October 22, 2010.

---

**American Psychological Association, "Being Bullied Throughout Childhood and Teens May Lead to More Arrests, Convictions, Prison Time." August 1, 2013, www.apa.org/news/press/releases/2013/08 /being-bullied.aspx

behavior more successfully. If students need to come to class early or stay beyond regular dismissal time, it's appropriate to use those times to teach the elements of the management systems. You'll probably observe that the amount of time needed per student actually decreases when the time is spent on management rather than punishment.

### *"What technology can we use to contribute positively to behavioral issues?"*

Check out YouTube and other sources to find some "groovy" examples (such as "Calm Down"; see www .youtube.com/watch?v=tIiZHH92DL0) of how to use music and humor to help kids make better behavioral choices.

### *"We have some parents who object to using behavior contracts or time-outs with their children. What can we do?"*

A conference among parents, teachers, the principal, and appropriate support staff may help all parties reach agreement on the need for certain interventions. When parents feel that they are active members of the intervention team and that their input is heard and respected, they are likely to be more agreeable to educational recommendations proposed at team meetings. Students' input on interventions can also be elicited and shared with the team.

### *"My students' parents want to be involved in their behavior contracts. Why do you recommend that parents not be involved?"*

A behavior contract should relate only to a child's behavior at school, and any incentives or consequences specified in the contract should be given only at school. When parents are expected to apply consequences at home for a child's inappropriate behavior at school, the teacher loses control of the situation, and its effectiveness at school is compromised. Parents can help by spending one-on-one time with their child—reading aloud, playing a game the child enjoys, or just talking about each other's experiences during the day. Parents can also make sure that the child spends time at home on activities related to learning, such as creating nutritious and affordable grocery lists and computing the cost, including any sales tax, while trying to stay within the family budget. In addition, parents can be invited to use any of the forms in this chapter for home-related behavior change needs.

# Things You Can Do Instead of Staying Angry

1. Close your eyes and count to 10 forward and backward. Or try counting backward from 100 by threes. You can't stay angry when you're concentrating on a learning task.

2. Think of positive words, such as *calm, open-minded, ready to learn, peaceful,* and *happy.*

3. Put your opinion in an I-statement. Tell the other person how what they have said or done makes you feel. Like this: "I feel _____ when you _____."

4. Try to see the problem from the other person's point of view. How would you feel if you were that person?

5. Ask the teacher or another student for help in getting over your anger.

6. Calm down with a relaxation technique. Take a deep breath through your nose, hold it as you count to six, and let it out slowly through your mouth as you count to six. Repeat several times.

7. Go to the listening center and listen to soothing music for a while.

8. Close your eyes and picture yourself in a place where you feel calm. Notice the details of this calming place and think of how you love to be there.

9. With the teacher's permission, run up and down a flight of stairs several times.

10. Think of how you would feel if the other person expressed anger at you the way you want to express it.

11. Take a voluntary time-out in the classroom or another time-out place. Don't forget the time-out pass.

12. Think of a joke. Say some silly tongue twisters. SMILE! It's hard to stay angry when you're smiling.

**Add other ideas that work for you or your classmates:**

_____

_____

_____

_____

_____

# Behavior Change Plan

My Name: _____

Date: _____  Time: _____

| | | |
|---|---|---|
| **What I did that was against the rules:** | **What I wanted to happen:** | **What really happened:** |
| **To get what I want, I must stop:** | **What I can do to behave more appropriately:** | **What I need from my teacher to help my plan:** |

# Token Record Sheet

**Name:** _____

| Week of _____ (Dates) | Tokens Earned | Tokens Spent | Tokens Remaining |
|---|---|---|---|
| Monday | | | |
| Tuesday | | | |
| Wednesday | | | |
| Thursday | | | |
| Friday | | | |

# Step 1: FBA Interview Form

**Student Name:** _____ **Date:** _____

**School:** _____ **Grade:** _____ **DOB:** _____

**Educational Program Description:**

_____

_____

_____

**Description of the Behavior of Concern** (specifically describe what the behavior looks and sounds like):

_____

_____

_____

*Instructions:* When the answer is YES, add details on the lines provided.

## I. Physiological and Medical Factors:

**1.** Could the behavior be the result of a medical or psychiatric condition or any form of physical discomfort?

☐ NO

☐ YES_____

**2.** Could the behavior be related to a side effect of medication?

☐ NO

☐ YES_____

**3.** Could the behavior be the result of some physical deprivation condition (thirst, hunger, lack of rest, and so on)?

☐ NO

☐ YES_____

## II. Antecedent Events:

**1.** Are there circumstances in which the behavior ALWAYS occurs?

☐ NO

☐ YES_____

**2.** Are there circumstances in which the behavior NEVER occurs?

☐ NO

☐ YES_____

**3.** Does the behavior occur only (or more often) during particular activities?

☐ NO

☐ YES_____

**4.** Does the behavior occur only with (or more likely with) certain people?

☐ NO

☐ YES_____

*continued* →

**5.** Does the behavior occur in response to certain stimuli (demands, termination of preferred activities, tone of voice, noise level, ignoring, change in routine, transitions, number of people in the room, and so on)?

☐ NO

☐ YES_____

**6.** Does the behavior occur only (or more likely) during a certain time of day (morning, afternoon, end of school day, evening)?

☐ NO

☐ YES_____

## III. Skill Deficits Related to Behavior of Concern:

Could the behavior be related to any skill deficits? (Check* all that apply.)

☐ **Academic skills:** Task requirements as presented are not at the student's instructional level in the core areas of reading, math, or writing.

☐ **Participation skills:** The student has difficulty participating in nondirected, semidirected, teacher-directed, or peer-directed activities. The student has difficulty in small or large group instruction.

☐ **Social skills:** The student has difficulty acquiring or maintaining peer friendships. The student often withdraws from social interaction. The student is often verbally or physically aggressive in social interactions.

☐ **Communication skills:** The student has difficulty expressing needs, including items, activities, attention, information, changes in the environment, or help. The student has difficulties in conversational skills and answering questions, understanding nonverbal or verbal language, or following directions.

☐ **Organizational skills:** The student has difficulty with organizing school supplies, class notes, study area, time, or project work, or dividing assignments into manageable tasks.

☐ **Self-regulation skills:** The student has difficulties with staying on task, completing work assignments, handling stressful situations, calming self when agitated, following rules, finding successful solutions to problems encountered with peers or teachers, and/or difficulty transitioning between activities, places, or people.

☐ **Study skills:** The student has difficulty with taking effective notes, using effective study techniques, studying for tests, taking tests, or participating in assessments.

☐ **Motor skills:** The student has difficulty with gross motor skills (running, raising arms, putting feet together, squatting, bending at waist, and so on) or fine motor skills (pointing, counting with fingers, holding a pencil or pen, holding a fork or spoon, pressing a computer key, using a mouse, and so on). The student has difficulty with imitating others' appropriate actions.

☐ **Functional skills:** The student has difficulty with performing activities of daily living (eating, dressing, toileting, grooming).

☐ **Play skills:** The student has difficulty with actively exploring activities or toys in the environment (inside or outside) to play with during leisure time, playing with the items as designated, or engaging in interactive play with peers during activities.

---

*For checked categories, please refer for further assessment (speech and language evaluation, occupational therapy evaluation, curriculum-based assessments, specific skills assessments).

*continued* ➔

## IV. Consequence Factors:

**1.** Does the behavior allow the student to gain something?

### A. Preferred activities or items?

*Indicators: The behavior often occurs when the student sometimes or always regains an item or activity that has been taken away or terminated. The behavior often occurs when the student sometimes or always gains access to an activity or item that the student was told he or she couldn't have. The behavior rarely occurs when the student is given free access to his or her favorite items or activities.*

☐ NO

☐ YES_____

### B. Peer or adult attention?

*Indicators: The student frequently approaches others. The student frequently initiates social interaction. When the behavior occurs, someone usually responds by interacting with the student in some way (verbal reprimand, redirection, comforting statements). The behavior rarely occurs when the student is receiving attention.*

☐ NO

☐ YES_____

**2.** Does the behavior allow the student to postpone, avoid, or escape something such as task demands, social interaction, and so on?

*Indicators: The behavior often occurs when the student sometimes or always postpones or escapes the task demands placed upon him or her. The behavior rarely occurs when few demands are placed on the student or when the student is left alone. The student is often noncompliant when asked to complete tasks. The behavior often occurs prior to predictable demands and the student sometimes or always avoids or postpones the tasks.*

☐ NO

☐ YES_____

**3.** Does the behavior provide stimulation as an alternative to the student's lack of active engagement in activities?

*Indicators: The behavior occurs frequently when the student is alone or unoccupied. The student seems to have few known reenforcers or rarely engages in social interaction activities. When the student engages in the behavior, peers have been taught not to respond by ignoring the behavior.*

☐ NO

☐ YES_____

# Step 2: Direct Observation Form

Prior to using this form, fill in a checklist of the predictions of the team so that the data collection person can check all that apply during the observation.

| Student: | Class or Subject: | Staff Collecting Data: | Date and Time: |
|---|---|---|---|
| | | | |

| Antecedent(s) to Behavior: | Behavior(s) of Concern: | Consequence(s) |
|---|---|---|
| | | |

# Step 3: Positive Behavior Support Plan

**A. Preventing the disruptive behavior (describe one to three options):**

**B. Desirable behavior goal:**

**C. Reinforcement when the student performs the desirable behavior:**

**D. Consequences when the student performs the undesirable behavior again:**

# Behavior Contract

**Made between**_____ **and** _____

**for the period**_____ **through**_____

The behavior I am agreeing to demonstrate:

_____

_____

_____

_____

_____

The incentive I am trying to earn:

_____

_____

_____

_____

The price of the incentive (number of tallies I need):_____

| **TALLY BOX** |
| :-: |
| |

Student's signature:_____

Teacher's signature: _____

# Getting Ready to Talk

**For People in Conflict**

My name: _____

Name of person I argued or disagreed with: _____

My explanation of the problem:

_____

_____

_____

_____

_____

_____

How the other person probably feels about the situation:

_____

_____

_____

_____

_____

_____

To solve this problem, I am willing to:

_____

_____

_____

_____

_____

_____

# CHAPTER 11

# Helping Parents Become Partners in Their Children's Learning

When parents* are supportive of the school's goals and communicate this support to their children, their children have a much better chance of succeeding in school than kids whose parents are unsupportive and uninvolved. As teachers, we need to help parents find a way to become team members in the goal of educating their children.

Having a child with severe learning difficulties can be challenging and stressful. Parents typically move through a series of emotions and attitudes, ranging from "Won't someone please help my child learn?" to "Why aren't the teachers doing their job?" to "What's wrong with this lazy kid?" On first finding out about their child's learning problems, some parents react with denial. Others, recognizing the similarities between their child's situation and their own history of struggling to learn, may think, "Look at me! I made it and I'm doing fine. Why can't my child do the same?" Still others may decide, "The schools I attended never helped me with my problem. This school can't help my child either." They may either become extremely demanding or withdraw entirely to save themselves from more pain.

Other problems arise if teachers come to the conclusion that parents who do not attend parent-teacher conferences or other school events simply don't care enough about their children's education. In fact, many of these parents are vitally interested in having the education system help their children find pathways to productive lives. It may be that the hours they have to work, a lack of childcare, or language barriers make it impossible for them to demonstrate their support in ways we would recognize.

Some parents may be reluctant to display their own language or learning inadequacies or may have personal memories of painful school experiences and consequently may be pessimistic about their children's experiences. Others feel perplexed by the ways in which their children are being taught and may not know how to become more involved. Some parents have experienced nightmarish school meetings at which no one on staff had anything kind to say about their child. Parents

## Unlocking Autism 🔒

Teachers and parents of students with autism need to develop a trusting partnership. A parent-teacher meeting should be held at the beginning of the year to share helpful information about the student. Translators should be present if needed. To assure that parents and teachers are working toward the same goals, such as consistently reinforcing appropriate social skills and rules, ongoing communication should occur frequently. Some schools have established support groups for families dealing with autism.

---

*Parents, caregivers, other relatives, foster parents—any adult a child lives with can be a partner in his or her learning.

who feel that the system isn't being fair may come to view the school as an enemy. Even when parents really don't want to get involved, we can't assume that the child doesn't want to learn. In many schools, formerly unsuccessful students are experiencing school success despite bleak conditions at home.

It's not enough to say that your school *wants* parent involvement. Your school must *work* proactively and assertively to invite parents for specific kinds of participation. Virtually any kind of parent involvement boosts student achievement, from creating learning materials for the classroom to joining a committee, from going on a field trip to volunteering in the classroom. When parents are present in school activities, they send a clear message to their children that school is worthwhile and valuable. This chapter describes several ways to reach out to parents and make them feel welcome at school.

## Ways to Promote Parent Involvement at School

1. All communication with parents, whether oral or written, should be available in the language spoken in the home. Efforts by your school to provide this service will go a long way toward making parents feel that the school is truly interested in communicating with them.

2. Regularly send home notes to parents in which you recognize something positive their child has done at school. When families have a history of hearing only bad or gloomy news about their children, the arrival of good news about any behavior, event, or work product can begin to reverse the fearful or negative impressions some parents have about school in general.

3. Frequently send home classroom or school newsletters. When written in a folksy manner without educational jargon, newsletters are effective communication tools. If students themselves write some of the articles and are excited about that, it is much more likely that parents will either read the text themselves or ask their children to translate for them. As a regular feature, you might describe activities that are designed for parents and students to do together. (*Examples:* Go through the house to find items that begin with certain letters or rhyme with certain words. Use family experiences as the impetus for language experience stories dictated by the children. [See pages 95–97.] Poll family members on their food preferences, TV-watching habits, job-related issues, and other topics of interest.)

4. Make your school family-friendly by raising awareness about the positive aspects of diversity. Diversity provides opportunities to learn about and appreciate our similarities and differences. Invite all families of children in your class to share information about their cultures, traditions, and observances with the students and one another, even if they are celebrated by an older generation and the students themselves were born in the United States. Suggest that families contact the principal if any school communications seem insensitive or confusing. Seek their input regarding alternative ways in which to send a message.

> It's not enough to say that your school *wants* parent involvement. Your school must *work* proactively and assertively to invite parents for specific kinds of participation.

5. Arrange for translators to be present at school meetings so parents for whom English is a second language can easily follow the agenda and receive the necessary information. If possible, have your school purchase or borrow a system that allows translators to speak through microphones to listeners wearing headsets. (You've seen this sort of thing in use during televised United Nations meetings.) All meeting documents should be available in the languages spoken in the home.

6. Fewer than half of America's households today fit the traditional family model. Therefore, it's important for us to accept many different kinds of family arrangements as normal, simply because those are the environments from which our students come. Avoid addressing verbal and written communications to "Mom and Dad." Use "to our parents" instead.

7. Be sensitive to the emotional trauma certain well-meaning assignments might cause. For example, asking students to discover their family's roots can be upsetting for adopted children or those whose families escaped from or disappeared in a violent conflict in another land. Having students write their autobiographies can be disturbing to those whose earlier lives were traumatic. Don't assume that all kids celebrate Christmas and Easter or take family vacations. When you ask kids to report on personal or family data, make several choices available.

8. Avoid attributing children's inappropriate behavior to their family situations. Since we can do very little to change what's going on in families, the least we can do is reduce the stress that children experience at school. When children become more positive about going to school and participating in school activities, one source

of aggravation and frustration for their family may diminish.

**9.** Consider making scheduled home visits, or providing conferences during their off-work times, to families who don't come to school when they are invited.

**10.** Help parents connect to parent support groups in your community. If possible, attend a few meetings yourself to get an insider's perspective. Call ahead for permission to sit in on the group.

**11.** Find out about literacy programs in your community. Some parents resist school involvement out of fear that their illiteracy might be revealed. Learning to read along with their children can be a satisfying experience.

**12.** Offer classes in effective parenting, even if only a few people show up. Advertise in several languages the fact that there will be translation services, and list the languages that will be available. Be sure to present the classes in a positive light. Explain that they're being offered as opportunities to learn something new and connect with other parents. Emphasize that there is no intent to criticize parenting styles and that everyone benefits from new learning.

**13.** Offer information nights on learning modalities, Common Core State Standards, or other educational topics, while slipping in a little advice on creating and maintaining positive parent-child-teacher relationships.

# Homework Issues

Time spent at home reviewing what has been learned at school may contribute to better school success. However, we can't assume that all kids have equal access to home conditions that make homework a positive experience. Homework can exacerbate the social and economic differences among students, since some parents are more able to give appropriate support for homework assignments than others are.

Parents play a critical role in determining whether and how effectively children do their homework. Damaging cycles develop when parents nag kids to do their homework or take on a teaching role. Often, when parents who themselves are classroom teachers try to teach their own children, the kids get the message that their parents would like them better if they were better students. The situation is made very confusing when parents use different teaching methods than those being used by the students' teachers.

Taking class time to correct homework is no longer considered an effective way to help struggling students learn content with more mastery. Students who find school difficult usually resist homework, in either active or passive ways, such as "forgetting" to return it to school. For decades, school systems and practices have been making these students endure feelings of guilt, shame, and hopelessness. Yet this problem continues in many classrooms nonetheless. So we have to consider that a different approach might lead to better outcomes. One method of solving the homework problem, the flipped classroom, is discussed on page 74. You may find it helpful to spend some time reading about this and other related topics. Search the Internet for the keywords *homework best practices*.

Since the topic of homework is such a huge issue for teachers, students, and parents, we present a brief summary of our beliefs about homework.

Work assigned to be done at home should:

1. be relevant, meaningful, manageable, and within students' ability to understand

2. provide time for students to gain confidence in standards the teacher has already directly taught them

3. be accepted even if students don't show their work, if the student can successfully complete a similar problem or exercise right there in class

4. be accepted even if the format is not exactly what the teacher required, since we must be sensitive to the common problems of kids with LDs regarding their executive functioning skills (described in Chapter 9).

5. not be assigned as finite amounts of work, but rather as a focus on the amount of time students should spend on homework for each particular school subject

6. never be counted against the student if the home environment is completely non-conducive to homework

7. never be graded, even as extra credit, since it is a part of the learning process

8. never be used to lower a student's grade

9. never take up class time for correcting; teachers should simply accept homework as evidence of time spent outside of class to reinforce what has been taught and to be prepared for continuing lessons that teach new concepts and skills

10. not be required at all if a student has an acceptable level of performance in any subject area (parents and kids can choose websites to visit instead)

## Scenario: Stacy

Stacy was a second grader who brought home hours of homework every night. Her mom had to meet the school bus to physically help Stacy get off, since the pile of books and papers she carried was so big.

Where did all this homework come from? Stacy's overhelpful parents had told her to bring home whatever was too hard for her to complete in school, so they could help. In fact, the parents had created learned helplessness in Stacy. Since she correctly perceived that her parents thought she was incapable of learning without their assistance, she had adopted that attitude as well. What made her situation especially ironic was that her mom was a teacher by profession. Naturally Stacy's mom was frustrated, because she knew she was helping her own students learn but felt powerless to help her own daughter.

Together, Stacy and her parents created the same painful scene at the kitchen table every night. Stacy would begin a task, look up with tears streaming down her face, and moan, "I can't do this! The teacher didn't explain it right. He wouldn't answer my questions. I need help!" Minutes turned into hours. Stacy's dad walked away in frustration, and her mom continued to help Stacy into total helplessness.

## Ways to Make Homework Meaningful and Manageable

**1.** Current practices focus on using homework time to make sure students have some practice between one class period and another. Homework expectations should be mindful of that goal.

**2.** If your school district has a homework policy, become familiar with it. Most policies are described in terms of how much *time* students should spend on homework. We believe teachers should follow this type of policy literally. Therefore, parents should monitor only that their kids record their beginning and ending work times, and should keep distractions away during homework times.

**3.** For students in the upper grades with lengthier homework assignments, the homework period for each subject should not exceed 15 minutes, and students should be able to have a snack or some exercise between work periods. If students reach a point of serious frustration with homework tasks, they can dictate a note to the teacher to describe their problem. If the school's homework policy is different from this suggested procedure, the school might consider changes at your suggestion or after reading some of the articles on homework in the "References and Resources" on pages 260–261.

**4.** Homework assignments should never be very difficult and should require only materials that are generally available in the home. Unless your child is experiencing a flipped classroom (see page 74), never expect students to learn new concepts on their own as homework. Instead, use the assignments to reinforce and extend concepts that you have taught at school.

**5.** Tailoring homework assignments to students' learning modality strengths can immediately lead to better results. Help parents understand and appreciate their children's learning modalities by sharing with them the information in Chapter 3. Offer several product alternatives so students can select products that complement their learning modalities; see page 51 for ideas.

---

Parents should monitor only that their kids record their beginning and ending work times, and should keep distractions away during homework times.

---

**6.** Give parents the help and encouragement they need to support their children during homework time. On pages 235–239 you'll find several handouts to copy and send home, include in your classroom newsletter, hand out at conferences, or make available at open houses. Be sure to include copies of the "Homework Contract" handout on page 237 or make it available on your school's general website or on your own Web page.

**7.** Never let students believe that homework is assigned just to keep them busy. Preface each assignment by explaining its educational purpose. (*Examples:* "These problems relate to the math skill we learned today." "This story is required reading for your biography project.") If an assignment doesn't have a clear purpose, don't give it.

**8.** Use a consistent system to assign homework, such as a regular or digital assignment notebook used by all teachers in your school. (See page 190.) Allow several minutes at the end of each class for students to write

### Tech Tip 🖥

Find out what homework assistance is available from your school. Some schools provide homework assistance websites. Others recommend sites that parents and students can visit together. Other sites, such as www.khanacademy.org, provide *free*, easy-to-understand tutorials for kids.

down their assignments. Tell parents to expect this assignment notebook to be available at home each day, and ask them to sign off each evening to indicate that the student worked for the agreed-upon period of time. Suggest ways for parents to help their children remember to return their notebooks and assignments to school if they are not digital.

**9.** If students move from class to class during the day, work with the other teachers to coordinate your homework schedules so students (and their families) won't have a heavy load at some times and little or nothing at other times.

**10.** Don't get into the habit of sending notes home to parents explaining the homework a child is expected to do. The only time you might send home a note for a student with learning difficulties is when the child has *no* homework. This implies that homework time should be a regularly scheduled part of the family's routine, and that having no homework is the exception.

**11.** Even after introducing a new concept at school, don't have students practice it at home with more than eight examples. After that many repetitions, some students have gained complete understanding while others are likely to have learned it *incorrectly* very well.

**12.** It's more productive to expect students to work for a certain period of time on an assignment than to assign an arbitrary number of problems or activities. Students should get partial credit for attempting the work or for completing some part of the assignment during the expected time period. See "Goal Setting" on pages 61–63 for an explanation of why this works well for struggling students. Then send home the "Homework Goal Chart" handout (page 238) weekly. The first time you send home the chart (and anytime you think this is needed or appropriate), include a note to parents explaining the goal-setting method. Encourage them to work with their children to set a consistent homework time each day. **Tip:** Be sure to keep your expectations realistic—and remember that struggling students should not spend too much time on homework in general.

**13.** Have students end each homework assignment by completing these sentences: *The part of this assignment I understood well was _____. The part I didn't understand at all was _____.*

**14.** For long-term assignments, consider using chunking (page 187) and backward planning (page 190). These methods help students learn to redefine success for an entire project as the ability to set and accomplish realistic short-term goals one learning session at a time, and teach them that long-term success happens by combining the outcomes of these goals.

**15.** When students fail to complete a homework assignment, the problem might be that they simply didn't understand what they were supposed to do. Homework should never be used as punishment, nor should assignments be made longer to make up for previously missed assignments.

**16.** Be aware that the typical problems associated with traditional homework assignments usually diminish or even disappear when a flipped classroom model is used. Please see page 74 for a description of this model.

### Tech Tip for Parents 🖥

New apps for smartphones and tablets are being developed all the time. Learn how to evaluate them to see whether or not one might provide the right kind of support for your child. You might find the form on pages 78–79 helpful for this task.

# Productive Parent-Teacher Meetings

We should always be sensitive to the likelihood that many parents of struggling students won't expect parent-teacher meetings to be pleasant experiences. Some will have a history of painful conferences, and there are almost certainly bad feelings at home when children are not doing well at school.

- Some teachers send home a form that helps parents prepare for conferences. When parents have a chance to think about a conference ahead of time, and when they know that the teacher will want their input and perspective, they may feel less apprehensive. Send home a copy of the "Parent-Teacher Conference Questionnaire" handout (page 240) several days before a scheduled conference. Refer to it during the conference.

- When telling parents about their child's school experience, be as matter-of-fact and objective as you can.

- Avoid sending messages through third parties. (*Examples:* Don't ask the child to remind the parent to come to a conference; contact the parent yourself. Don't ask the parent to pass along your suggestions from a parent-teacher conference to the child; give those messages directly to the child. In this way, all communications will be open and clear, and both you and the parent will give the child similar messages.) At best, third-party communication creates confusion; at worst, it aggravates problems. It enables students to play teacher and parents against one another instead of focusing on student problems. When students see that you and their parents agree on problems and what to do about them, negative behaviors almost always subside.

You may find it helpful to follow an agenda when meeting with parents, whether in person or by telephone, formally or informally. Naturally you won't need to include *all* the following items listed in *every* meeting, but a quick read-through in advance will help ensure that you don't omit anything important. If the purpose of the meeting is to set up a plan to monitor the student's work or behavior, the student should be present.

1. Always begin by giving examples of the child's positive traits. Share something about the child that you find particularly attractive or engaging. **Tip:** Try to identify a strength that may have been overlooked in the past because it didn't develop in positive ways. For example, many kids who get into trouble are excellent leaders.

2. Ask the parents to tell you about their child's strengths and strong interests. Tell them that you can't possibly know everything about their child, and you see them as partners in helping you understand their child's personality and needs. Write down this information for future reference. If the parents have completed a "Parent-Teacher Conference Questionnaire" (page 240), you can use that as your written record, with your notes added.

3. Explain your homework policies. (*Example:* "I will assign 30 minutes of homework on most school nights. On days when I don't assign any homework, I'll send home a note to let you know. On days when I don't assign any homework or when your child forgets the homework at school, your child should spend 30 minutes on a self-selected learning task found on the Internet or in any books or learning materials you have at home." Reassure the parents that you won't assign homework that is beyond the child's ability to do independently. Give them one or more of the homework-related handouts on pages 235–239.

4. Share what you know about the child's learning modalities. Help the parents understand that their child is intelligent and can be a better learner when learning modality strengths are taken into consideration—at home and at school.

5. Share the information and examples you have about the child's progress to date. Parents enjoy seeing evidence of what their child is doing in school. Include references to any forms related to schoolwork or homework that the parents have filled out and returned to you. Avoid discussing the child's rank in class. This would be a good time to share the child's "Achievement Data Recording Chart" (page 182) with the parents so they are aware of their child's goals.

6. Identify only one behavior you would like the student to focus on in an effort to improve learning or personal behavior. Be specific. (*Examples:* "I would like Howard to work on the computer for 20 minutes each day as part of his writing time." "I would like Dao to make two positive comments to her classmates every day.") Ask parents for suggestions.

7. If you are using a behavior management program with the student, give the parents a progress report. If the student hasn't been observing the conditions of the plan, it's all right to tell the parents, but make it very clear that you don't expect them to impose any consequences at home for work or behavior plans not met at school. (*Example:* Some kids really shine during out-of-school experiences, such as music lessons or membership on a sports team. Those shining moments should not depend on positive results at school.)

8. Encourage parents to support their child's interests outside of school. Share what you know about related programs offered by community organizations at nominal or no cost.

---

Always conclude by thanking the parents for taking the time to come to the meeting. Tell them that their presence shows that they are interested in their child's education. Explain that this interest is vital in helping their child develop and maintain a positive attitude about learning.

---

9. If you have any articles, books, or other materials you think might be helpful to the parents, offer them in a friendly manner. Consult the "References and Resources" at the end of this book for possibilities. Give parents copies of the handouts at the end of this chapter. **Tip:** Be careful not to inundate them with too much information at any one time. And be sure that you are thoroughly familiar with the handouts before you give them to parents, in case they have questions.

**10.** Always conclude by thanking the parents for taking the time to come to the meeting. Tell them that their presence shows that they are interested in their child's education. Explain that this interest is vital in helping their child develop and maintain a positive attitude about learning.

Throughout the meeting, use active and reflective listening. When parents share something about their child, paraphrase it back to them. This shows that you value them as sources of information and that you're willing to see their child from their point of view. More and more schools are including students in some or all parent-teacher conferences. After all, students are the ones who have to make certain changes, and their input into setting up the conditions of those changes is pertinent to the ultimate success of any plan.

Always make notes immediately after each meeting rather than relying on your memory later. If several meetings are scheduled very close together, dictate your comments into a recording device.

# Open Houses

Open houses have two purposes:

1. For children and their families to become familiar with the school, the classroom, the teacher(s), and the administration

2. For teachers to communicate their expectations and routines to the parents

In a perfect world, schools should not try to accomplish both these objectives in the same evening. If your school wishes to accomplish several objectives through the open house procedure, it's better to hold several open houses during the school year. The first open house might be held during the first weeks of school. Parents can have the chance to tour the learning environment, say hello to teachers, and become familiar with the school calendar. Children attend, too, and there is no formal presentation by the teacher.

The next open house is when teachers introduce their programs, expectations, policies, and teaching styles to parents. (Some schools call this "Meet-the-Teacher Night.") The teachers clearly explain how parents can get in touch with them and encourage parents to initiate contact rather than waiting for formal conferences. Translators should be present to communicate with parents who speak different languages. Since the purpose of this meeting is for teachers to talk directly to parents, children should not attend. Provide childcare services for families who might not be able to attend otherwise.

A third open house might be held near the end of the school year. This is the time when students share their portfolios and other schoolwork with their parents and demonstrate the progress they have made during that year.

# Questions and Answers

*"What can we do about parents who never show up at school, despite our best efforts to include them?"*

Send home specific suggestions telling parents how they can support their children's learning at home. If the parents really won't come to you, ask if it's all right for you to visit them at home. Be sensitive to the fact that some parents may feel inadequate about their own abilities. Never give up on a student because the parents can't or won't get involved with the school.

There is no doubt that students do better in school when their parents actively support their learning. Anything you can do to strengthen parental support will pay off big. Some parents need to be told this directly; we can't assume all parents know how important their involvement is. Many programs have successfully increased parent involvement. Search the Internet for such programs so you can contact them and emulate their successful strategies. For more ideas, see "References and Resources" on page 260.

*"What should I do if parents are overly interested in their child's grades and appear not to understand the importance of goal setting and slow, steady progress?"*

Go back to pages 61–63 to read about the function that effective goal setting plays in people's lives. Explain that the most motivated students and adults are those who perceive the direct relationship between efforts and outcomes. Describe your goal of motivating students to learn that hard work pays off in evidence of better achievement. Explain the danger of allowing kids to believe that they can get high grades with little effort. When we give kids grades they don't deserve, we communicate our perception that they aren't capable of doing really well.

*"How can we entice parents who usually don't attend school events to do so?"*

Always provide translators in the most common languages spoken by families in your school. Advertise this availability in all the information provided about the event. Offer free childcare by high school students who need community service hours for graduation, so families can bring small children. *Always feed families who attend!* Include items that reflect the cultures represented in your school.

# Schoolwork Sign-Off Form

*Dear Parent or Caregiver:*

This form is being sent to you along with a folder of your child's schoolwork. Please complete and sign this form and return it to school by _____ (date). You may keep your child's work at home.

**Student's Name:** _____ **Today's Date:** _____

Check all statements that are true:

_____ My child explained to me the work he or she brought home.

_____ I noticed something that was done well and I complimented my child.

_____ I have questions about my child's schoolwork.


Write your questions here:

_____

_____

_____

_____

_____

_____

_____

_____

_____

_____

_____

If your child had trouble understanding the homework assignment, ask your child to describe the problem here:

_____

_____

_____

_____

_____

_____

_____

_____

_____

_____

**Your signature:** _____

# How to Be a Homework Helper

## Tips for Parents and Caregivers

Children are more likely to succeed in school when parents support their homework efforts. This handout describes ways for you to encourage your child to accept homework as a fact of life—and support your child to get it done.

1. Communicate your belief that homework is an important part of learning. When you show that you're serious about homework, your child will take it more seriously.

2. Make an agreement with your child about how much after-school time your child will spend doing homework each day. Guidelines for maximum times:

   ■ for children in the primary grades (first through third): 15 to 30 minutes

   ■ for children in the upper elementary grades (fourth through sixth): 30 to 45 minutes

   ■ for middle-school students: up to one hour

   ■ for high-school students: up to two hours

3. Work with your child to establish a homework schedule and do your part to honor it. (*Example:* If your child is supposed to do homework from 5:00 to 6:00 each night, don't serve dinner at 5:45.)

4. Provide a place where your child can work. It should be comfortable, adequately lit, and free from distractions. Give your child some choices. If your child wants to listen to soft instrumental music, sit on the floor, or work in low light, that's okay—as long as your child works for the expected amount of time and keeps up with the teacher's expectations. If these conditions are not met, your child should do homework at a table or desk in a quiet place until the work improves. When favorable reports start coming home from the teacher, let your child make choices again about the homework environment.

5. Create a homework kit. Include pencils, rulers, glue, tape, erasers, a dictionary, a thesaurus—any materials your child needs to do his homework. Keep everything together in a plastic storage bin or tote. Put smaller items in a zippered case.

6. Remember that your child's homework is your child's responsibility, not yours. You are only responsible for providing an uninterrupted time and place where your child can work. Monitor the use of electronic devices such as mobile phones and tablets, and don't allow visitors.

7. What if the teacher doesn't give any homework on a particular day? Or what if your child forgets to bring it home? Your child should use regularly scheduled homework time to work on some other type of learning activity (*examples:* looking at a newspaper, reading a book or a magazine, watching an educational TV program, writing a story, or learning about an interesting topic).

# How to Use the Homework Contract

## Guidelines for Parents and Caregivers

The "Homework Contract" is an effective way to help your child manage homework time. It gives your child immediate positive feedback for accomplishing specific goals. Several copies of a blank contract are included along with this how-to sheet. If you need more copies, just ask.

For the first few contracts, you can sit with your child and make sure your child understands what to do. After that, the contract is your child's responsibility.

### Three Simple Steps

1. The child sets a goal for each time segment. (The blank contract allows for three time segments, but it's okay if your child chooses fewer or more.)

2. You and your child decide together on rewards he or she will earn after:

   A. working for an entire time segment without complaining, arguing, or procrastinating (five-minute rewards)

   B. completing all of his or her goals

3. Whenever your child completes a goal, your child enjoys a reward.

### Recommended Rewards
Five-minute rewards:

- a healthful snack
- a stretch break
- listening to a favorite song
- a comic book break
- something else your child enjoys doing

All-goals-completed rewards:

- The best reward for children up to adolescence is to spend quality one-on-one time with you or another parent or caregiver. When this isn't possible, the reward might be to watch a favorite television show or video.

- For adolescents who don't consider one-on-one time with adults a reward, allow time with friends on the phone or the computer, or time to work on an ongoing project or passionate interest.

> **Important:**
> The reward should never
> be money!

# Homework Contract

**Name:**_____ **Today's Date:** _____

How much time I will spend doing homework:_____

My goal for the FIRST time segment: _____

_____

_____

My five-minute reward for reaching that goal: _____

_____

_____

My goal for the SECOND time segment: _____

_____

_____

My five-minute reward for reaching that goal: _____

_____

_____

My goal for the THIRD time segment: _____

_____

_____

My five-minute reward for reaching that goal: _____

_____

My reward if I complete ALL my goals: _____

_____

_____

**Student's Signature:**_____

# Homework Goal Chart

**Name:** _____

**Week of:** _____

**Directions:** Decide how much time you will spend each day on homework for each subject. Write a fraction in each box you use. The *denominator* (bottom number) is the amount of time you will spend on that subject. The *numerator* (top number) is the number of pages you will read, problems you will work, sentences you will write, and so on in that time period. (*Example:* If you plan to read 10 pages of a novel in 30 minutes on Monday, write 10/30 in the "Reading" box for Monday.) When the time is up, write your comments in the box at the far right.

| Number ⁄ Time | Math | Reading | Writing | Other | Comments |
|---|---|---|---|---|---|
| Monday | ___\|___ | ___\|___ | ___\|___ | ___\|___ | |
| Tuesday | ___\|___ | ___\|___ | ___\|___ | ___\|___ | |
| Wednesday | ___\|___ | ___\|___ | ___\|___ | ___\|___ | |
| Thursday | ___\|___ | ___\|___ | ___\|___ | ___\|___ | |
| Friday | ___\|___ | ___\|___ | ___\|___ | ___\|___ | |
| Weekend | ___\|___ | ___\|___ | ___\|___ | ___\|___ | |

# How to Handle Homework Problems

## Strategies for Parents and Caregivers

**Problem:** Your child refuses to do homework.

**What to do:** First, find out if the material is too easy or too difficult. If it's too easy, your child might be bored and unwilling to work. If it's too hard, the work might be impossible for your child to do. Ask for a conference with the teacher to request homework that is appropriately challenging without being overwhelming.

**Problem:** Your child always asks you for help with homework.

**What to do:** It's okay to spend a small amount of time with your child to clarify the homework directions. But please *don't* tutor or teach your child. You are not responsible for teaching what your child hasn't learned in school. If your child tries to work on an assignment for a reasonable amount of time but still seems totally perplexed, let your child stop working on it. Help your child write a note to the teacher explaining the situation and asking for help.

**Problem:** You know that your child is capable of doing the homework but just won't do it.

**What to do:** The best thing you can do is let your child experience the natural consequences of this decision. If your child has to stay after school, receive a lower grade, or miss a field trip, that's your child's problem, not yours. When parents constantly rescue kids from failure, the kids get hooked on their parents' help. Children learn to take responsibility by learning what happens when they avoid responsibility. Help your child by not helping.

**Problem:** Your child forgets to bring homework home from school.

**What to do:** Once you have established a regular after-school homework time, your child should always use that time to work on *something* related to improving skills or increasing learning. Insist that your child spend the designated time on some type of learning activity (*examples:* reading a book, checking up on the news, visiting educational websites such as Khan Academy, spending imaginary money on catalog purchases, and so on). *Caution:* Don't make the alternatives to homework too much fun, or your child might prefer them and keep forgetting to bring homework home—on purpose.

# Parent-Teacher Conference Questionnaire

**Student's name:** _____

*Dear Parent or Caregiver:*

Our parent-teacher conference is scheduled for: _____ (date) at _____ (time). Please take a few moments to answer the following questions, and please bring the completed questionnaire to the conference.

1. What are your child's strengths at home? What is your child really good at doing?
2. What are your child's chores at home?
3. How does your child spend spare time? What are your child's hobbies and interests?
4. What is your child like to live with?
5. What is your child's personality outside of school?
6. What is your child's social life outside of school?
7. How do you and your child handle homework time?

Please list any questions you would like to have answered during our conference:

_____
_____
_____
_____
_____
_____
_____

Please list any concerns you would like to talk over during our conference:

_____
_____
_____
_____
_____
_____
_____

Thank you for taking the time to complete this questionnaire. I look forward to seeing you at our conference.

**Teacher's signature:** _____

## Tips for Parents and Caregivers

1. Try to spend 10 to 15 minutes of uninterrupted time with your child every day. Give your child your undivided attention. Don't talk about school unless your child brings it up; instead, talk about things your child is interested in. Listen with your ears, your eyes, and your body language, and resist asking questions or giving advice. Use phrases like these to let your child know that you want to know and understand her or him better:

   "Tell me about . . ."

   "So, what you are saying is . . ."

   "It sounds like you are feeling _____ about _____ . . ."

2. If your child has nothing to say during your time together, share something positive about your own day.

3. If you have a large family, set up a buddy system and encourage children to share information with their buddies. During dinner, invite everyone to share something positive about their day.

4. Monitor your child's media use. Restrict or prohibit violent games and programs, including some cartoons. Help your child choose games and programs that educate. Play and watch them together when you can, and ask questions along the way. Encourage kids to ask questions, too. If no one knows the answer to a particular question, the child might be motivated to look it up.

5. Help your child develop a skill he or she is interested in and shows a natural talent for. Excellence in sports, the arts, crafts, volunteer work, or anything else kids feel passionate about can help develop high self-esteem.

6. Never imply that your child should somehow be different in order to be a better person or better student. Help your child learn how to separate her or his identity from any problems at school. Praise your child's positive qualities at every opportunity. (*Examples:* What makes your child special? His ability to make people laugh? Her singing? His honesty? Her talent at drawing? What else can you think of?)

7. Use words sparingly when giving your child directions. Always demonstrate what you want your child to do. Give one direction at a time, never a string of directions all at once. Show what you mean, give an example, and offer positive reinforcement as soon as your child completes the task.

8. Predictability, consistency, and routines increase children's sense of security. Strive for regular bedtimes and mealtimes. Provide as much structure as possible—chores to do, homework schedules, time spent together.

9. Instead of doing things *for* your child, work *with* your child. Coach your child to tell you when your help is no longer needed.

# How to Help Your Child Become a Better Reader

## If your child is very young:

1. Hold your child in your lap as you look at and read a book. If you don't have books available, use other reading material—greeting cards, catalogs, newspapers, magazines, shopping lists. The more your child sees that print is important, the more likely it is that your child will develop a positive attitude about reading.

2. Before you read a story to your child, have your child look through it and predict what will happen by looking at the pictures and other clues. Stop reading at frequent intervals to ask your child to guess or predict what will happen next or what a certain character will do. This helps your child realize that there are many possible ways for stories to end, and that good readers keep guessing as a story progresses.

3. Leave off the last word or words of certain phrases or sentences as you read aloud. Your child will learn to anticipate what's coming and supply the missing words. Reinforce this behavior by saying "Isn't reading fun?" or "You are such a good reader!" Even though your child isn't really reading, she or he will feel like a reader and perceive reading as pleasant and positive.

4. Right after you finish reading a story, have your child read it to you. Listen eagerly and pay no attention to accuracy. You'll probably notice that your child is mimicking your expression and pacing, and that's exactly what your child should be doing. Praise these efforts: "What a good reader you are!" "I love it when you read to me." "I'm so proud of the way you're trying to help yourself learn to read."

## For all ages:

1. Read to and with your child every day. If possible, spend the last 10 to 15 minutes of each day together sharing a book. It's a great way to get closer and improve your child's reading skills.

2. Take regular trips together to the public library. Get your child a personal library card. Ask the librarian to show both of you how to find information your child is interested in. You'll both be amazed at how easy it is to find out almost anything once you know where to look.

3. Ask your child's teacher to show you how to use whisper reading.

4. When your child is reading to you, don't rush in to supply missing words. Give your child plenty of time to think of an appropriate word to insert in that spot. It's better for your child to guess a word that makes sense than to keep struggling over the right word.

5. If your child asks for help while reading, you might say, "Let's look at the picture and see if we can figure out what that word might be." Or "Skip over this word for now and keep on reading until you get to the end of the sentence. Then come back and try to figure it out." Or simply tell your child the word. During the early stages of reading development, don't expect your child to sound out every word accurately. This is a struggle and can lead to a negative attitude about reading in general.

# How to Help Your Child Become a Better Writer

1. Encourage *all* your child's writing efforts, accurate or not. Let the teacher worry about the accuracy. Focus on helping your child develop a positive attitude about writing.

2. Show your child how to make "Happy Birthday" or "Get Well" cards for relatives. Suggest writing a few things down in a diary or journal at the end of the day as part of a bedtime routine. Have your child keep a "Things-to-Do" or "My Goals" list and update it daily.

3. Whenever your child writes something, give it the proper attention. Put it on the refrigerator and praise your child's efforts: "I'm so proud of you for learning how to write!"

4. Call your child's attention to the many times in a day or week when you need writing (*examples:* sending and receiving communications from family members and people at work, reading and responding to letters and email, making a grocery list, writing out a check).

5. Work with your child to write a letter to the editor of your local newspaper. Express your feelings and opinions about an article or event. This demonstrates that writing is a way to communicate thoughts.

6. Work with your child to write a letter to a neighbor or relative who would enjoy receiving mail. Ask for a mailed reply addressed to your child.

# How to Help Your Child Become Better in Math

1. Use playing cards in simple games like War and Go Fish. Show your child how to figure out the value of the cards by counting the spots. Teach your child how cards with more spots win over cards with fewer spots. **Tip:** To avoid confusion, remove the picture cards and the aces until your child has mastered the number cards. Then return the other cards to the deck.

2. Playing board games is an excellent way to learn about numbers. Have your child count out loud the number of spaces to move for each turn. Call attention to whose piece is closest to the beginning and end of the game. You might slip in a few addition and subtraction facts while playing.

3. Many children can learn math facts more quickly (and remember them longer) when music, rhyme, and rhythm are used to teach them. Make up counting chants together. Set math facts to familiar tunes.

4. Encourage your child to notice the numbers in everyday things. For example:

   - Count the items as you put them into the grocery cart.

   - Count the items as you set the table.

   - Count the laundry items as you fold them.

   - Ask, "What number comes after 5? Before 4?"

   - Count backward instead of forward from 10 (or 20, and so on).

   - Ask, "How many wheels are on your toy dump truck? How many are on your bike? Which has more wheels?"

   - Ask, "How old are you? How old is your brother or sister? Who is older? By how many years?"

   - Ask, "How many kids should we invite to your birthday party? How many pieces will we have to cut from the cake? If everyone gets six pieces of candy, how many pieces will we need?"

# References and Resources

## Introduction

Dweck, Carol. *Mindset: The New Psychology of Success: How We Can Learn to Fulfill Our Potential.* New York: Ballantine, 2008.

Haberman, Martin. *Star Teachers: The Ideology and Best Practice of Effective Teachers of Diverse Children and Youth in Poverty.* Milwaukee: Haberman Educational Foundation, 2005.

Olweus Bullying Prevention Program (www.clemson.edu/olweus). A comprehensive, school-wide program designed for use in elementary, middle, junior high, and high schools (K–12).

The President's Committee for People with Intellectual Disabilities (PCPID) (www.acl.gov/programs/aidd/Programs/PCPID/index.aspx). Formerly the President's Committee on Mental Retardation (PCMR). The U.S. Department of Health and Human Services' online entry point to this public federal program.

Rimm, Sylvia. *How to Parent So Children Will Learn: Strategies for Raising Happy, Achieving Children.* Tucson: Great Potential Press, 2008.

Rosenthal, Robert, and Lenore Jacobson. *Pygmalion in the Classroom: Teacher Expectation and Pupils' Intellectual Development.* Norwalk, CT: Crown House Publishing, 2003.

## Chapter 1: Creating Active Learning for All Students

Autism Speaks (autismspeaks.org). A world-leading autism advocacy and science organization dedicated to increasing awareness of this global health crisis and funding biomedical research on treatments and cures for autism.

everythingESL.net. The website of ESL (English as a Second Language) teacher Judie Haynes includes lesson plans, teaching tips, downloads, discussion topics, and resource picks for teachers grades K–12.

Friends Who Care. Developed by Easter Seals, this awareness-building curriculum helps teachers, parents, and young people develop a better understanding of what it means to have a disability. Search for "Friends Who Care" on the Easter Seals website (www.easterseals.com).

MegaSkills National Education Center (www.ripin.org/fsce/Megaskills/index.html). Based on the lifework of educator Dr. Dorothy Rich, this organization and its website offer resources for teachers and parents to convey essential skills for achieving one's potential. The MegaSkills are confidence (feeling able to do it), motivation (wanting to do it), responsibility (doing what's right), effort (being willing to work hard), initiative (moving into action), perseverance (completing what you start), caring (showing concern for others), teamwork (working with others), common sense (using good judgment), problem solving (putting what you know and what you can do into action), focus (concentrating with a goal in mind), and respect (showing good behavior, courtesy, and appreciation).

National Clearinghouse for English Language Acquisition (NCELA) (www.ncela.us). Information and resources for teachers, parents, and community members; supports the U.S. Department of Education's Office of English Language Acquisition, Language Enhancement, and Academic Achievement for Limited English Proficient Students (OELA).

Stokes, Susan. "Structured Teaching: Strategies for Supporting Students with Autism?" National Association of Special Education Teachers. *www.naset.org/2758.0.html* (accessed May 21, 2014).

Taubman, Mitchell, Ron Leaf, and John McEachin. *Crafting Connections: Contemporary Applied Behavior Analysis for Enriching the Social Lives of Persons with Autism Spectrum Disorder.* New York: DRL Books, 2011. A useful book for providing direct instruction in social skills for students who need it, including issues faced by people on the autism spectrum such as teasing and bullying, conversational development, and social comprehension.

Teachers of English to Speakers of Other Languages (www.tesol.org). Tips, strategies, and more for grades K–12. An organization devoted to maintaining professional expertise in teaching English language learners.

Think-Pair-Share SmartCard (www.kaganonline.com). Describes many variations of Dr. Frank Lyman's Think-Pair-Share part of the Name Card Method. A similar SmartCard is available for Lyman's ThinkTrix Model.

## Chapter 2: Understanding Learning Difficulties and Intervening Effectively

Birth Defect Research for Children (www.birthdefects.org). Information and support services for children born with birth defects and their families.

Brain Gym International (www.braingym.org). Help for kinesthetic learners. The Brain Gym program has been used successfully by parents and teachers to significantly improve learning attitudes and achievement through non-academic means. It works on the assumption that people with learning difficulties have immature nerve networks in the brain that can be significantly improved through certain forms of exercise. Teachers have found that if they precede each learning activity with two to three minutes of Brain Gym exercise, kids are more able to focus on the actual lesson. The key to these exercises is that participants must watch their hands move across the midlines of their bodies. *Two sample exercises:* Cross Crawl: Have students march in place while touching the right hand to the left knee and the left hand to the right knee. Lazy 8s: Draw an infinity sign ∞ on a chart. Have students draw it in unison several times by starting in the middle of the figure and moving down and to the left, up and to the right, back to the middle, down and to the right, up and back down to the left center, just like drawing an 8 lying on its side. Visit the website to find certified Brain Gym instructors and classes in your area, as well as Brain Gym books and learning materials by Paul E. Dennison and Gail E. Dennison.

Brewer, Chris. *Soundtracks for Learning.* Bellingham, WA: LifeSounds Educational Services, 2008. Book and CD. There is proof that music stimulates parts of the brain, enhances memory and increases one's ability to focus. Brewer's lifework has been devoted to helping parents and teachers make those connections. His LifeSounds website is www.musicandlearning.com.

Hornik-Beer, Edith Lynn. *For Teenagers Living with a Parent Who Abuses Alcohol/Drugs.* Lincoln, NE: iUniverse.com, 2001.

Lucas, Cheri. "Boost Memory and Learning With Music." PBS.org. www.pbs.org/parents/education/music-arts/boost-memory-and-learning-with-music (accessed May 21, 2014).

March of Dimes Foundation (www.marchofdimes.com). Materials to support the development and education of children born with birth defects.

McMurchie, Susan. *Understanding My Learning Differences.* Verona, WI: IEP Resources, 2003. Twenty-three lesson plans help students with LD become more aware of their learning differences and develop coping and self-help skills.

National Center for Learning Disabilities (NCLD) (ncld.org). An excellent resource from the NCLD includes the LD Navigator (ldnavigator.ncld.org), an online resource guide with comprehensive information about learning disabilities for professionals and parents. There are also demonstrations of successful lessons for working with kids with LD.

The President's Committee for People with Intellectual Disabilities (PCPID) (see page 245).

Reif, Sandra F. *How to Reach and Teach Children with ADD/ADHD.* San Francisco: Jossey-Bass, 2005.

Rich, Dorothy. *MegaSkills: Building Our Children's Character and Achievement for School and Life.* Naperville, IL: Sourcebooks, 2008. How to teach children basic competency skills such as confidence, motivation, effort, responsibility, perseverance, focus, and common sense. Dr. Rich's materials have been used for many years to teach appreciation, kindness and respect in schools (see Chapter 1 Resources, page 245).

Winebrenner, Susan, with Dina Brulles. *Teaching Gifted Kids in Today's Classroom: Strategies and Techniques Every Teacher Can Use.* Minneapolis: Free Spirit Publishing, 2012. The definitive guide to meeting the learning needs of gifted students in the mixed-ability classroom.

## ADD/ADHD

A.D.D. WareHouse (addwarehouse.com). A comprehensive catalog of materials for and about children with attention deficits and other learning problems. Many are designed to be used by kids themselves.

Attention Deficit Disorder Association (ADDA) (www.add .org). Materials and services to help people with attention deficit disorders.

Burge, Martha, and Allen Frances. *The ADD Myth: How to Cultivate the Unique Gifts of Intense Personalities.* San Francisco: Conari Press, 2012.

The Center for Speech and Language Disorders (www.csld .org). This nonprofit organization offers family-centered services for children with language/communication disorders so that they may reach their potential. The website has definitions of speech and language disorders and links to resources on the topic.

Children and Adults with Attention-Deficit/Hyperactivity Disorder (CHADD) (www.chadd.org). One of the most nationally recognized sources of information and support for parents and teachers of children with ADD.

Council for Exceptional Children (CEC) (www.cec.sped.org). Services, articles, and resources for helping young people with all types of learning difficulties.

Goldstein, Arnold P. et al. The Skillstreaming Series (www .skillstreaming.com; www.researchpress.com). Books, skill cards, CD-ROMs, and videos help kids of different age levels learn appropriate social/interactive skills and make good behavior choices. The series includes *Skillstreaming in Early Childhood, Skillstreaming the Elementary School Child,* and *Skillstreaming the Adolescent.*

The Hallowell Centers (www.drhallowell.com). Founded by Dr. Edward Hallowell, a psychologist and leading national expert in ADD in both children and adults, the centers help people with ADD lead happier, more productive lives. Dr. Hallowell also manages a national system of life coaches to assist those with ADD to live one day at a time.

Hallowell, Edward M., and John J. Ratey. *Delivered from Distraction: Getting the Most out of Life with Attention Deficit Disorder.* New York: Ballantine, 2005. The follow-up to Hallowell and Ratey's *Driven to Distraction* is an up-to-date guide to living a successful life with ADD.

———. *Driven to Distraction: Recognizing and Coping with Attention Deficit Disorder from Childhood to Adulthood.* New York: Anchor Books, 2011. This practical and useful book is considered a classic in the field.

Kravets, Marybeth, and Imy F. Wax. *The K&W Guide to Colleges for Students with Learning Disabilities or Attention Deficit Disorder: A Resource Book for Students, Parents, and Professionals.* The Princeton Review, 2003. This important book details many post-secondary colleges with programs that continue the support which students with LD received in grades preK–12.

Mahr, Krista. "ADHD Kids Can Get Better." *Time Magazine.* content.time.com/time/health/article/0,8599,1683069,00 .html. November 12, 2007 (accessed May 21, 2014).

Quinn, Patricia O., and Judith M. Stern. *Putting On the Brakes: Understanding and Taking Control of Your ADD or ADHD.* Washington, DC: Magination Press, 2012. A students' activity book is also available.

## Autism Spectrum Disorder

Autism Society (www.autism-society.org). Information, support, and advocacy for individuals within the autism spectrum and their families.

Autism Speaks (www.autismspeaks.org) This organization is an excellent resource for families dealing with autism.

National Association of Special Education Teachers (www.naset.org). "Exceptional teachers teaching exceptional children": There are many resources here, including e-newsletters, about issues that concern parents and teachers of people on the autism spectrum. (Read the excellent article on this site by Susan Stokes—see Chapter 1 Resources, page 245.) Structured teaching is an approach in instructing children with autism. It allows for implementation of a variety of instructional methods such as visual support strategies, Picture Exchange Communication System (PECS), sensory integration strategies, discrete trial, music/rhythm intervention strategies, Greenspan's Floortime, and more. Structured teaching is one of many approaches to consider in working with children with autism.

National Autism Resources (nationalautismresources.com). Books, DVDs, toys, pressure jackets, kits and other equipment for raising children on the autism spectrum, as well as children with Asperger's Syndrome.

National Institutes of Health (www.nimh.nih.gov). The "News" category at this website for the National Institute of Mental Health, one of the National Institutes of Health, is worth checking regularly for updates on brain and mental-health science.

## Learning Disabilities and Other Learning Challenges

Alexander Graham Bell Association for the Deaf and Hard of Hearing (www.agbell.org). Resources for people with hearing disabilities.

American Academy of Child & Adolescent Psychiatry (www.aacap.org). Information about the understanding and treatment of developmental, behavioral, and mental disorders that affect children and adolescents.

American Association on Intellectual and Developmental Disabilities (www.aaidd.org). Help for families with persons who have mental retardation, including Downs syndrome.

American Foundation for the Blind (www.afb.org). Information, help, and advocacy for those living with vision loss and for their families, coworkers and friends.

Harwell, Joan M., and Rebecca Williams Jackson. *The Complete Learning Disabilities Handbook: Ready-to-Use Strategies & Activities for Teaching Students with Learning Disabilities.* San Francisco: Jossey-Bass, 2008.

International Dyslexia Association (www.interdys.org). An international organization dedicated to the study and treatment of dyslexia. Formerly the Orton Dyslexia Society.

Irlen Institute (www.irlen.com). Diagnostic testing and help for children and adults with perceptual reading and learning problems whose brains are not getting the correct information when they try to read. For some children, the Irlen Method of using colored overlays or lenses for eyeglasses dramatically improves learning success by overcoming scotopic sensitivity and improving reading skills. The Irlen color-based technology filters out offensive light waves so that the brain can accurately process visual information. This technology can improve reading fluency, comfort, comprehension, attention, and concentration while reducing light sensitivity. The institute can recommend a testing center for assessment; you can also search YouTube for video demonstrations.

Lavoie, Rick. *How Difficult Can This Be? The F.A.T. City Workshop.* Arlington, VA: PBS Distribution, 2004. DVD. Lavoie's video is a must-see for teachers and parents of kids with LD (available at www.shoppbs.org).

LDOnline (www.ldonline.org). This comprehensive website should be your first stop when you need information about children or teens with learning challenges.

RickLavoie.com (www.ricklavoie.com). Rick Lavoie's influential books, videos (see *How Difficult Can This Be? The F.A.T. City Workshop,* above), articles, and workshops are fabulous resources for anyone who lives and works with students with learning difficulties. Lavoie really understands these kids, and he helps parents and teachers do the same. His work will open the eyes of families and friends who are desperately trying to understand and respond appropriately to the learning and emotional needs of children with LD. Furthermore, parents of these kids may recognize themselves in these resources and get helpful information they can use themselves, regardless of their age.

## Children of Alcoholics

American Academy of Child & Adolescent Psychiatry (AACAP) (www.aacap.org) has a wealth of facts, figures, advice and resources for those who treat children living in homes with an alcoholic, or for the families or youth themselves.

Hornik-Beer, Edith Lynn. *For Teenagers Living with a Parent Who Abuses Alcohol/Drugs.* Lincoln, NE: iUniverse.com, 2001.

Lee, Christopher, and Rosemary F. Jackson. *Faking It: A Look into the Mind of a Creative Learner.* Portsmouth, NH: Heinemann, 1992. Lee learned how to deal with his serious learning challenges after evading the issue until college. Despite the publication date of this book, his story is timeless, taking the reader into his brain to describe exactly what happens when he tries to read, write, and just learn in general. This book could be read out loud to students experiencing similar challenges.

## Children in Poverty

The Efficacy Institute (www.efficacy.org), founded by Dr. Jeff Howard, offers training and services for measurable improvement in academic performance and character development. Designed with low-income students in mind, it teaches that "smart is something you can *get*" and success depends on the level and quality of one's effort. Adults are advised not to indicate that they are judging students' abilities, even when young people confront difficulty, but to model excitement and determination about figuring out what the problem is.

The Haberman Educational Foundation (www.haberman foundation.org). This nonprofit organization works to teach and implement research-based models for identifying educators who serve students at risk and in poverty.

Haberman, Martin. *Star Teachers of Children in Poverty.* Indianapolis: Kappa Delta Pi Publications, 1995.

——. *Star Teachers: The Ideology and Best Practice of Effective Teachers of Diverse Children and Youth in Poverty.* Milwaukee: Haberman Educational Foundation, 2005.

Kannapel, Patricia et al. "Inside the Black Box of High-Performing, High-Poverty Schools." Prichard Committee for Academic Excellence. www.prichardcommittee.org /wp-content/uploads/2013/02/Inside-the-Black-Box.pdf. February 2005 (accessed May 21, 2014). This fascinating study documents the characteristics that are found in low-income, high-poverty schools, suggesting that learning success can be accomplished regardless of adverse social and economic conditions.

Suskind, Ron. *A Hope in the Unseen: An American Odyssey from the Inner City to the Ivy League.* New York: Broadway Books, 1998. Suskind's book is based on a Pulitzer Prize–winning true story about how one teen from the inner city of Washington, DC, was able to move out of the cycle of poverty into a college education. This story, and others like it, are very inspirational and give hope to children in poverty and ideas about assistance to the people who read it.

## Dyslexia

Davis, Ronald D., and Eldon M. Braun. *The Gift of Dyslexia: Why Some of the Smartest People Can't Read . . . And How They Can Learn.* New York: Perigee, 2010.

Hultquist, Alan M., and Lydia T. Corrow. *What Is Dyslexia? A Book Explaining Dyslexia for Kids and Adults to Use Together.* Philadelphia: Jessica Kingsley, 2008. Explains four different types of dyslexia in children and adults.

Learning Ally (www.learningally.org). This organization makes available recordings of most textbooks and some literature used in schools throughout the United States, at nominal fees. Formerly Reading for the Blind and Dyslexic.

## Intellectual Disabilities

*Educating Peter* (www.films.com). This 1992 Academy Award–winning documentary follows a child with Downs syndrome who is mainstreamed into a public school. It vividly captures Peter's achievements as he makes a place for himself among his peers. *Graduating Peter* (2001) highlights Peter's experiences in sixth grade, eighth grade,

and high school, then follows his progress in building a meaningful life. Both are HBO productions available for purchase on www.films.com, but briefer segments may also be viewed on YouTube.

The President's Committee for People with Intellectual Disabilities (PCPID) (see page 245).

## Twice Exceptional

Baum, Susan, and Hank Nicols. "Student Personality Prototype Test," International Center for Talent Development (www.internationalcenterfortalentdevelopment.com). Baum and Nicols's free resource gives educators additional information about why certain students behave as they do. Dr. Baum has expertise in teaching twice-exceptional children.

Baum, Susan M., and Steven V. Owen. *To Be Gifted and Learning Disabled: Strategies for Helping Bright Students with LD, ADHD, and More.* Waco, TX: Prufrock Press, 2004.

Smart Kids with Learning Disabilities (www.smartkidswithld .org). A highly valuable website for kids who are twice exceptional (gifted learners with accompanying learning difficulties) and their parents and teachers.

*2e (Twice-Exceptional) Newsletter* (www.2enewsletter.com). This e-newsletter focuses on practical things adults can do to help themselves understand and support their children who are twice exceptional.

## Recommended Readings for Students

Carlson, Nancy. *This Morning Sam Went to Mars: A Book About Paying Attention.* Minneapolis: Free Spirit Publishing, 2013. A story about a daydreaming boy who learns strategies to focus, stay organized, eat better food, and ask for help when he needs it. For ages 5–9.

Carlson, Nancy, and Armond Isaak. *Armond Goes to a Party: A Book About Asperger's and Friendship.* Minneapolis: Free Spirit Publishing, 2014. A story for ages 5–9 about a boy with Asperger's who attends a birthday party. Helpful for students with Asperger's and for raising classmates' awareness.

Chesner, Jonathan. *ADHD in HD: Brains Gone Wild.* Minneapolis: Free Spirit Publishing, 2012. An autobiographical collection of essays and anecdotes about living with ADHD, with an optimistic perspective on the fun aspects of having a "wild brain" and advice on how ADHD kids can focus and organize. Ages 13 and up.

Gordon, Michael. *I Would If I Could: A Teenager's Guide to ADHD/Hyperactivity.* DeWitt, NY: GSI Press, 1992.

Hayes, Marnell L. *The Tuned-In, Turned-On Book About Learning Problems.* Novato, CA: High Noon Books, 1994. Written directly to adolescents with LD, this book helps kids identify and capitalize on their individual learning styles.

Janover, Caroline. *Josh: A Boy with Dyslexia.* Lincoln, NE: iUniverse, 2004. Young readers go into the mind and heart of a fifth grader with LD. Includes questions and answers about dyslexia and LD. For ages 8–12.

——. *Zipper: The Kid with ADHD.* Lincoln, NE: iUniverse, 2004.

Levine, Melvin D. *Keeping a Head in School: A Student's Book About Learning Abilities and Learning Disorders.* Cambridge, MA: Educators Publishing Service, 1991. Helps students develop and use effective strategies for getting better results with schoolwork.

Moss, Deborah. *Lee, the Rabbit with Epilepsy.* Bethesda, MD: Woodbine House, 1989. For ages 4–9.

——. *Shelley, the Hyperactive Turtle.* Bethesda, MD: Woodbine House, 2006. For ages 4–9.

Quinn, Patricia O., and Judith M. Stern. *Putting On the Brakes Activity Book for Kids with ADD or ADHD.* Companion to the bestselling *Putting On the Brakes* classic. Washington, DC: Magination Press, 2009. Pictures, puzzles, questionnaires, and games teach kids how to get organized, follow directions, study effectively, and more.

——. *Putting On the Brakes: Understanding and Taking Control of Your ADD or ADHD.* Washington, DC: Magination Press, 2012. Written for kids by a pediatrician and a special education teacher, this book clearly explains ADHD and offers practical suggestions for coping with the problems it presents. For ages 8–13.

Taylor, John F. *The Survival Guide for Kids with ADHD.* Minneapolis: Free Spirit Publishing, 2013. Helps kids diagnosed with ADD or ADHD succeed in school, get along better at home, and form healthy and enjoyable relationships with peers. Includes a special message for parents. For ages 8–12.

Verdick, Elizabeth, and Elizabeth Reeve. *The Survival Guide for Kids with Autism Spectrum Disorders (And Their Parents).* Minneapolis: Free Spirit Publishing, 2012. Positive in tone, this straightforward handbook helps kids with ASD understand their condition and build a skill set for communicating and succeeding. Ages 8–13.

## Chapter 3: Using Students' Learning Styles to Facilitate Learning Success

Note: An Internet search can lead you to many resources for helping children with learning disorders, particularly for those on the autism spectrum. This list is therefore not comprehensive.

### Learning Styles

Brain Gym International (see Chapter 2 Resources, page 245).

CAPSOL Styles of Learning (stylesoflearning.com). An assessment that measures learning strengths and weaknesses so that you can adjust instruction.

Freed, Jeffrey, and Laurie Parsons. *Right-Brained Children in a Left-Brained World: Unlocking the Potential of Your ADD Child.* New York: Simon and Schuster, 1998. Freed shares his techniques for teaching compensation learning strategies to children who have trouble learning. The strategies work whether or not the child has ADD. A related book from Jeffrey Freed and Joan Shapiro is *4 Weeks to an Organized Life with AD/HD* (Taylor Trade Publishing, 2007).

HowardGardner.com. Creator of the Multiple Intelligence Model, Dr. Gardner maintains a website for information about multiple intelligences, with current research, findings, papers, books, projects, talks, presentations, and more.

Kingore, Bertie. *Rigor and Engagement for Growing Minds.* Austin, TX: Professional Associates Publishing, 2013. Dr. Kingore's book describes how to increase rigor in all classrooms using a variety of strategies designed for students of various learning abilities, with special emphasis on rigor for advanced or gifted students. Read other books by Kingore as well—they are all totally practical and provide endless ideas for all teachers (see www.bertiekingore.com).

LDOnline (see Chapter 2 Resources, page 247).

Maslow, Abraham H. *Motivation and Personality.* New York: Pearson, 1997. Still very relevant, and available on Amazon.com.

National Reading Styles Institute (NRSI) (www.nrsi.com). The NRSI's Power Reading Online (PRO) K–12 program helps teachers assess and accommodate students' reading styles and teach reading skills in ways that are friendly to tactile-kinesthetic learners. Director and developer Dr. Marie Carbo has years of research proving that students make amazing gains in reading comprehension in relatively short periods of time with her methods. Susan Winebrenner has taught the Carbo Method for years and can validate Carbo's reported results. Whereas previously teachers were responsible for preparing the recorded segment kids needed to learn to read fluently, PRO has all the selections already recorded for you by Carbo and her associates. Check this resource out for potentially miraculous results for your struggling readers.

Salend, Spencer J. *Creating Inclusive Classrooms: Effective and Reflective Practices for All Students.* Upper Saddle River, NJ: Prentice Hall, 2004.

SuccessMaker: A Digital Learning Curriculum (pearsonschool.com). This programmed digital skill work for grades K–8 individualizes instruction to the specific needs of each student, automatically presenting instruction at the level at which a student is ready to learn and creating a successful learning experience. Aligns with district, local, and national standards, and is supported by a comprehensive management system.

### Social Skills Issues

Baum and Nicols, "Student Personality Prototype Test" (see Chapter 2 Resources, page 248).

Edutopia (edutopia.org). This site's Resources for Technology Integration (www.edutopia.org/technology-integration-guide -resources) are designed to address many of the National

Educational Technology Standards (NETS) established by the International Society for Technology in Education (www.iste.org/standards).

Learning Style (Modality) Inventories: Use your search engine on your Internet browser to discover various types of learning style (modality) assessment tools.

Madrigal, Stephanie, and Michelle Garcia Winner. *Superflex . . . A Superhero Social Thinking Curriculum.* San Jose, CA: Think Social Publishing, 2008. Superflex teaches social thinking skills through the use of superheroes that defeat the challenges in different social situations arising throughout the day both in and outside of school. It teaches children in grades 3–5 how to regulate their behaviors and become stronger social problem-solvers. Kids come to understand that everyone has an inner Superflex to help him or her engage in flexible social thinking. Also presented are related strategies children can use to prevail over various social challenges, represented by Unthinkable characters, whose behavior they can learn to outwit and outsmart when the going gets tough.

Miller, M. J., K. L. Lane, and J. Wehby. "Social Skills Instruction for Students with High-Incidence Disabilities: A School-Based Intervention to Address Acquisition Deficits." *Preventing School Failure* 49, no. 2 (Winter 2005): 27–37.

National Center for Learning Disabilities (www.ncld.org) has short videos of successful teachers of students with LD sharing tips and techniques.

### Recommended Reading for Students

Armstrong, Thomas. *You're Smarter Than You Think: A Kid's Guide to Multiple Intelligences.* Minneapolis: Free Spirit Publishing, 2014. Helps kids ages 9–14 understand Howard Gardner's theory of multiple intelligences, what it means to them, and how to make the most of their own abilities and potential.

Fisher, Gary, and Rhoda Cummings. *The Survival Guide for Kids with LD (Learning Differences).* Minneapolis: Free Spirit Publishing, 2002. Helps young people with LD succeed in school and prepare for life as adults. For ages 8 and up.

Galbraith, Judy. *The Survival Guide for Gifted Kids.* Minneapolis: Free Spirit Publishing, 2013. For ages 10 and under. Incorporates new technology tips to the array of self-help concepts on communication, brain power, creativity, anxiety, and other issues affecting gifted children.

Galbraith, Judy, and Jim Delisle. *The Gifted Teen Survival Guide.* Minneapolis: Free Spirit Publishing, 2011. For ages 11 and up. Based on new surveys of nearly 1,400 gifted teenagers, this guide offers teens many strategies to manage their education and lives—including discussions of perfectionism, twice-exceptionality, and bullying.

## Chapter 4: Ensuring That All Students Make At Least One Year's Academic Growth During Each School Year

Accelerated Schools Plus (www.acceleratedschools.net). Accelerated Schools Plus is a process for accelerating the achievement of all students by developing accelerated learning environments and empowering learners through academic rigor and inquiry-based instruction. The goal is for all students to successfully participate in learning experiences usually applied only to gifted students.

Anderson, Lorin, W. et al. *A Taxonomy for Learning, Teaching, and Assessing: A Revision of Bloom's Taxonomy of Educational Objectives.* New York: Pearson, 2000. Note: *A Taxonomy for Learning* does not include the Depth of Knowledge information from Karin Hess, which may be found on page 67 of this book.

Barton, Linda G. *Quick Flip Questions for the Revised Bloom's Taxonomy.* Madison, WI: Edupress, 2007. This spiral-bound flip book can help teachers by ensuring they use questions with their students from the higher levels of the taxonomy to stimulate rigorous thinking and learning.

Kingore, *Rigor and Engagement* (see Chapter 3 "Learning Styles" Resources, page 249).

National Center for the Improvement of Educational Assessment (www.nciea.org). Dr. Karin Hess and several other assessment specialists work for this agency to provide current assessment information for all educators.

Rivkin, Steven G., Eric A. Hanushek, and John F. Kain. "Teachers, Schools, and Academic Achievement." *Econometrica* 73, no. 2 (March 2005): 417–458. This report on a landmark study of Texas schools discusses the effects that poor teaching can have on target students over a period of several years. The document states that "high quality instruction throughout primary school could substantially offset disadvantages associated with low socioeconomic background."

### Teaching Strategies

The Accelerated Reader program at Renaissance Learning (www.renlearn.com). Students learn new words in context through reading, then use this computer program that offers quizzes on books from many popular series to help stimulate vocabulary acquisition. Also allows teachers to provide each student with an individualized list of learned vocabulary words.

Coil, Carolyn. *Teaching Tools for the 21st Century.* Marion, IL: Pieces of Learning, 2005. Includes CD.

Delta Education (delta-education.com). Inquiry-based, hands-on science and math curricula, supplemental teaching materials, classroom accessories, and reading materials that integrate the language arts with science.

Edutopia (see "Social Skills Issues" Resources above).

Fairfax Network (fcps.edu/fairfaxnetwork). Distance learning enrichment programs for grades K–12, staff development, teacher training, and parent programs. Sample titles: *Giant Pandas, She's Got It!* (about women inventors), and *Universal Words.* Programs are available for purchase on DVD, video, and streaming video.

Freed and Parsons, *Right-Brained Children* (see Chapter 3 "Learning Styles" Resources, page 249).

Hallerman, Sara, John Larmer, and John Mergendoller. *PBL in the Elementary Grades: Step-by-Step Guidance, Tools and Tips for Standards-Focused K–5 Projects.* Novato, CA: Buck Institute for Education, 2011.

Higher Order Thinking Skills (HOTS) (www.hots.org). A general thinking-skills program for Title I and LD students in grades 4–8 that accelerates learning, test scores, and social confidence. Demo units are available to download. Dr. Stanley Pogrow has been working for many years to convince educators that higher-order thinking skills should be present in the learning activities for all students. Common Core puts that belief into general practice.

Holt, Tim. "Why Problem Based Learning is Better." Powerful Learning Practice. plpnetwork.com/2013/01/10/problem-vs-project-based-learning (accessed May 21, 2014). A comprehensive essay on the differences between Problem Based Learning and Project Based Learning, with an excellent list of arguments that explain why it is inevitable that Common Core and more rigor had to finally become part of the regular curriculum for all students.

HyperStudio at Mackiev.com (www.mackiev.com/hyperstudio/index.html). A multimedia thinking tool for project-based learning. Includes brainstorming tools, visual organizers, project planners, desktop publishing features, multimedia presentation capabilities, and authoring tools for CD-ROMs and website development.

International Society for Technology in Education (www.iste.org). Technology information and resources for educators and education leaders, serving more than 100,000 education stakeholders worldwide.

Krauss, Jane, and Suzie Boss. *Thinking Through Project-Based Learning: Guiding Deeper Inquiry.* Thousand Oaks, CA: Corwin, 2013.

LD Resources (www.ldresources.com). Resources for the LD community on this website include articles, commentaries, and lists of tools, schools, organizations, and professionals. Browsable categories include "Technology Issues and Ideas" and "Computers and Software."

Levine, Mel. *A Mind at a Time.* New York: Simon and Schuster, 2002. Explains how parents and teachers can encourage children's learning strengths and bypass their learning weaknesses.

National Reading Styles Institute (see Chapter 3 Resources, page 249).

News Currents (www.newscurrents.com). A weekly current-events discussion program written on three levels for grades 3–12. Learning the news in teams with the information provided by this company can significantly accelerate students' interest in current events.

Sweet, Michael, and Larry K. Michaelson. *Team-Based Learning in the Social Sciences and Humanities: Group Work That Works to Generate Critical Thinking.* Sterling, VA: Stylus Publishing, 2012.

Soup2Nuts (www.soup2nuts.tv). Formerly Tom Snyder Productions, this award-winning animation studio offers multimedia resources to support active learning in science, math, social studies, reading, and language arts. A Scholastic company.

Sunburst Technology (www.sunburst.com). The reliable publisher of educational software programs makes technology skills products, including a Type to Learn 4 program—increasingly important once again with keyboarding so deeply embedded in the Common Core and other technology-driven learning programs. Sunburst also offers programs in most other subject areas.

Think-Pair-Share and ThinkTrix SmartCards (www.kaganonline.com). Each laminated 8.5" x 11" four-fold card describes many variations of Dr. Frank Lyman's Think-Pair-Share and ThinkTrix Models.

The U.S. Department of Labor and the Secretary's Commission on Achieving Necessary Skills (wdr.doleta.gov/SCANS). This commission advises the Secretary of Labor on the level of skills required to enter employment. It builds on the work of six special panels established by the commission to examine all manner of jobs, from manufacturing to government employment. Researchers were also commissioned to conduct lengthy interviews with workers in a wide range of jobs. In carrying out this charge, the commission was asked to define the skills needed for employment; propose acceptable levels of proficiency; suggest effective ways to assess proficiency; and develop a dissemination strategy for the nation's schools, businesses, and homes.

Rivkin, Hanushek, and Kain, "Teachers, Schools, and Academic Achievement" (see Chapter 4 Resources, page 250).

## Resources for RTI

Center on Response to Intervention at American Institutes for Research (www.rti4success.org).

Allain, Joanne Klepeis, and Nancy Chapel Eberhardt. *RTI: The Forgotten Tier, A Practical Guide for Building a Data-Driven Tier 1 Instructional Process.* Stockton, KS: Rowe Publishing and Design, 2011.

Bender, William N., and Cara Shores. *Response to Intervention: A Practical Guide for Every Teacher.* Thousand Oaks, CA: Corwin, 2007. For educators new to the RTI approach, *Response to Intervention* presents an overview of key concepts with guidelines for accountability practices that benefit students in inclusive classrooms.

Brown-Chidsey, Rachel, Louise Bronaugh, and Kelly McGraw. *RTI in the Classroom: Guidelines and Recipes for Success.* New York: Guilford Press, 2009.

Esteves, Kelli J., and Elizabeth Whitten. *RTI in Middle School Classrooms.* Minneapolis: Free Spirit Publishing, 2014. Provides practical, research-based response to intervention strategies for middle school educators in a diversity of settings.

Mellard, Darryl F., and Evelyn Johnson. *RTI: A Practitioner's Guide to Implementing Response to Intervention.* Thousand Oaks, CA: Corwin Press, 2008.

"Response to Intervention Resources for Teachers." Use your search engine to locate helpful RTI resources for teachers to use just by entering this phrase in the search field.

SmartTutor Education Program. RTI Resources: 2013. Available at http://thinkonline.smarttutor.com

Weaver, Brenda M. *RTI: Assessments & Remediation for K–2.* New York: Scholastic Teaching Resources, 2009.

Whitten, Elizabeth, Kelli J. Esteves, and Alice Woodrow. *RTI Success: Proven Tools and Strategies for Schools and Classrooms.* Minneapolis: Free Spirit Publishing, 2009. This all-in-one resource includes step-by-step guidelines for implementing RTI, as well answering many educators' questions about a variety of RTI issues.

## Chapter 5: Teaching Integrated Language Arts, Including Literature, Sounds, and Writing

Akhavan, Nancy L. *Teaching Writing in a Title I School, K–3.* Portsmouth, NH: Heinemann, 2009. This author has many books designed to help students who need assistance to access Common Core content. Her topics include accelerated vocabulary development, phonemic competency, strategies for nonfiction, and other strands of skills essential to the CCSS.

Carbo, Marie. *Becoming a Great Teacher of Reading: Achieving High Rapid Reading Gains with Powerful, Differentiated Strategies.* Thousand Oaks, CA: Corwin, 2007.

———. *What Every Principal Should Know About Teaching Reading: How to Raise Test Scores and Nurture a Love of Reading.* Syosset, NY: National Reading Styles Institute, 1997. Classroom-based, research-proven examples of how to strengthen reading programs using students' reading styles, achieve high reading gains, evaluate reading programs, and start an exemplary reading program.

Clicker (www.cricksoft.com/us). A talking word processor that allows students to start writing with a picture, then helps them turn it into text.

Cunningham, Patricia M., and Richard L. Allington. *Classrooms That Work: They Can All Read and Write.* New York: Pearson, 2010. Integrates phonics and literature-based process writing and reading instruction for a balanced approach to literacy.

Daily Oral Language (DOL) (www.greatsource.com). The teacher's manual for this program contains a year's worth of sentences (two per day) with errors in them that students edit. When paired with the Name Card Method on page 12, it is a very effective tool for teaching editing to kids.

Graves, Donald H. *Writing: Teachers and Children at Work.* Portsmouth, NH: Heinemann, 2003. Many people feel that this book revolutionized writing instruction.

The Great Books Foundation (www.greatbooks.org). Great Books Workshops for adults teach *shared inquiry,* a collaborative, question-driven method of discussion.

Harvey, Stephanie, and Anne Goudvis. *Strategies That Work: Teaching Comprehension to Enhance Understanding.* Portland, ME: Stenhouse Publishers, 2000. Excellent presentation of specific strategies classroom teachers can use to improve comprehension.

International Dyslexia Association (www.interdys.org). An international organization dedicated to the study and treatment of dyslexia. Many of their methods are successful for kids with reading problems, whether or not they have been diagnosed as dyslexic. Formerly the Orton Dyslexia Society.

International Literacy Association (www.literacyworldwide .org). Books, brochures, videos, and journals to support the teaching of reading and writing.

Irlen, Helen. *Reading by the Colors: Overcoming Dyslexia and Other Reading Disabilities Through the Irlen Method.* New York: Perigee, 2005. Describes the Irlen Method of using colored overlays or lenses for eyeglasses for overcoming scotopic sensitivity and improving reading skills (see Chapter 2 Resources, page 247, for more information on the method and the Irlen Institute).

Keyboarding programs for writers with learning difficulties:

- Keyboarding Skills (www.epsbooks.com). This approach uses the multisensory "alphabet method" to teach keyboarding skills to students of varying ages.

- SpongeBob SquarePants Typing (www.broderbund.com). Ages 7 and up. A wet and wacky romp through the world of keyboarding that both kids and adults will enjoy.

- Type to Learn and Type to Learn Jr. (www.smartkidssoft ware.com). Comprehensive keyboarding courses covering grades 1–6.

- UltraKey 6 (www.bytesoflearning.com). All ages. Teaches touch-typing and safe keyboarding using voice, animation, video, and virtual reality. Provides options that adapt to a broad range of age groups and special needs.

Learning Ally (www.learningally.org). This organization makes available, for nominal fees, recordings of most textbooks and some literature used in schools throughout the United States.

Lyman, Donald E. *Making the Words Stand Still.* Boston: Houghton Mifflin, 1988. Writing from his own experience, Lyman describes the anguish that kids with LD feel as they try to learn, then describes his own unique teaching methods.

Merit Software (www.meritsoftware.com). This educational software company sells products for home and school use, including Grammar Fitness, Write It Right, ESL Fitness, and Vocabulary Fitness. Merit also maintains several interactive websites where students can learn basic writing skills for free. English Grammar Connection (www.englishgrammar connection.com) has online lessons help improve students' English grammar skills. Essay Punch (www.essaypunch. com) takes users through the actual steps of writing a basic essay. Paragraph Punch (www.paragraphpunch.com) takes users through the actual steps of writing a basic paragraph.

Morsink, C. V. *Teaching Special Needs Students in Regular Classrooms.* Boston: Little, Brown and Co., 1984.

National Reading Styles Institute (see Chapter 3 Resources, page 249).

Palincsar, Annemarie. Palincsar is the designer of Reciprocal Teaching, a comprehension strategy that has enjoyed a great reputation for its effectiveness for many years. A multimedia literacy initiative called Reading Rockets (www.reading rockets.org) sells several products based on her work. The work of Lori Oczkus shows how to translate Reciprocal Teaching for primary-age students. Oczkus introduces powerful comprehension strategies—Predict, Question, Clarify, and Summarize—with four unique puppets: Paula the Powerful Predictor thinks about what will come next; game-show-host Quincy Questioner asks questions about text; Clara Clarifier monitors understanding; and friendly cowboy Sammy Summarizer lassoes the main idea. Oczkus demonstrates how to use the puppets for reciprocal teaching with the whole class, guided reading groups, or reading buddies. Visit Oczkus's website www.primaryconcepts.com for more information.

Parents Active for Vision Education (P.A.V.E.) (www.pavevision.org). Helps parents and educators locate services to diagnose reading problems that stem from vision problems.

*Promoting Vocabulary Development: Components of Effective Vocabulary Instruction.* Austin, TX: Texas Education Agency, 2002. One of five downloadable PDFs available in the Red Book Series of the Texas Education Agency's Reading Initiative program (www.tea.state.tx.us). The series provides information and resources on reading topics (including vocabulary development, comprehension, and content-area reading) to assist parents, educators, school board members, and others with an interest in education and children's reading development.

Read-Write-Think (www.readwritethink.org). In partnership with the International Reading Association (IRA), the National Council of Teachers of English (NCTE), and Verizon Thinkfinity, this online source offers lesson plans, standards, student materials, a calendar of classroom activities, and online resources associated with events, literacy, literature, and more.

Readers' Theater Series (www.evan-moor.com). Scripts and plays to help students practice reading aloud with fluency and expression.

Rico, Gabrielle. *Writing the Natural Way.* New York: Tarcher/ Putnam, 2000. Demonstrates a visual technique to increase fluency for writers and turn the task of writing into the joy of writing. The revised edition is newly illustrated and includes updated, field-tested exercises.

Shaywitz, Sally. *Overcoming Dyslexia: A New and Complete Science-Based Program for Reading Problems at Any Level.* New York: Vintage, 2003. Dr. Shaywitz, a professor at Yale, has spent many years developing a scientific approach to understanding and "treating" dyslexia and other reading problems. This book is exceptionally valuable.

Simon S.I.O. (Sounds It Out) (www.donjohnston.com). Very helpful in teaching phonemic awareness and phonics. The program engages students with an animated personal tutor.

6+1 Trait Writing (educationnorthwest.org/traits). The Northwest Regional Educational Laboratory's (NWREL's) unique approach to presenting the Six-Trait Writing model and training teachers in its use. Teachers and students can use this framework to pinpoint areas of strength and weakness as they continue to focus on improved writing.

Stevenson Learning Skills (www.stevensonlearning.com). Materials that take a multisensory approach to teaching reading and related skills, as well as math facts and concepts.

Tibbett, Teri. *Listen to Learn: Using American Music to Teach Language Arts and Social Studies (Grades 5–8).* San Francisco: Jossey-Bass, 2004. Book and music CD. Offers teachers a dynamic way to use the history of American music to engage their students. Features a variety of activities that encourage students to write about their favorite music, investigate songs as poetry, research the lives of famous musicians, and more.

Vacca, Richard T., Jo Anne L. Vacca, and Maryann Mraz. *Content Area Reading: Literacy and Learning Across the Curriculum.* New York: Pearson, 2013. Reading, writing, speaking, and listening processes to help students learn subject matter across the curriculum. This respected text is designed to be an active learning tool, complete with real-world examples and research-based practices, and has been updated to incorporate topics related to contemporary issues such as content standards, assessments, No Child Left Behind, and Reading First.

Winebrenner, Susan, with Dina Brulles. *Teaching Gifted Kids in Today's Classroom: Strategies and Techniques Every Teacher Can Use.* Minneapolis: Free Spirit Publishing, 2012. Chapter 4, "Extending Reading and Writing Instruction," gives several suggestions for implementing and managing a flexible and responsive reading program.

Winsor Learning (www.winsorlearning.com). A source for multisensory phonics instruction based on the Orton-Gillingham approach, which has been an integral part of special education instruction for decades. It combines a technique called the Sonday system with RTI and applies it to reading comprehension.

WordMaker (www.donjohnston.com). This phonics, phonemic awareness, and spelling program based on the work of Dr. Patricia Cunningham helps students remember words they have learned and use them in their writing.

Word Quests for Word Seekers (www.wordquests.info). An online resource providing etymologies for English words derived from Latin and Greek.

The Word Within the Word (www.rfwp.com). Michael Clay Thompson's vocabulary-building curriculum uses etymology, not memorization, in a systematic approach to the study of vocabulary. Student and teacher volumes are available, each containing thirty lessons, as well as class sets and alternative test books (to reduce the possibility of cheating). Published by Royal Fireworks Press.

Write:OutLoud (www.donjohnston.com). Helps younger and older students by saying words as they are being typed, so students can both read and hear what they have written. This and other assistive technologies are available from Don Johnston Inc. (www.donjohnston.com).

## Visual Organizers

Enchanted Learning (www.enchantedlearning.com). Nondigital versions of graphic organizers.

Inspiration Software (www.inspiration.com). Inspiration (for older students) and Kidspiration (for younger kids) create graphic organizers from text students enter so they can see what they are thinking. The programs then help students transfer information from the graphic organizers to written documents.

Nuttall, James, and Linda Nuttall. *Dyslexia and the iPad.* CreateSpace Independent Publishing Platform, 2013.

Tate, Marcia L. *Engage the Brain: Graphic Organizers and Other Visual Strategies.* 9 vols. Thousand Oaks, CA: Corwin, 2007.

## Technology Integration

Bookshare (bookshare.org). Online digital library available for free to all print-disabled students in the United States.

Center on Teaching and Learning (dibels.uoregon.edu). University of Oregon's DIBELS (Dynamic Indicators of Basic Early Literacy Skills) Data System.

The Comic Creator (readwritethink.org/files/resources /interactives/comic). Hosted by Read-Write-Think (see Chapter 5 Resources, page 253), this online application allows users to create comic-book-style panels of their own.

Comics in the Classroom (comicsintheclassroom.net). For educators interested in using comics as teaching aids, this site has reviews of comic books suitable for classroom use, as well as offering a selection of lesson plans and links to the comics featured in them.

De Bono, Edward. *Six Thinking Hats.* New York: Back Bay Books, 1999. Lateral thinking.

Edutopia (edutopia.org). Presents ideas for using technology in the classroom and at home to improve learning, encourage collaboration, and increase student engagement.

Kingore, Bertie. *Tiered Learning Stations in Minutes!* Austin, TX: Professional Associates Publishing, 2011. Includes CD-ROM.

Learning Ally (learningally.org). Provider of free audiobooks, including student textbooks.

Lyman, Donald E. *Making the Words Stand Still.* Boston: Houghton Mifflin, 1988.

Madrigal and Winner, *Superflex* (see Chapter 3 Resources, page 250).

Miller, Lane, and Wehby, "Social Skills Instruction" (see Chapter 3 Resources, page 250).

Make Beliefs Comix (makebeliefscomix.com). Bill Zimmerman and Tom Bloom's site allows users to create their own comic strips, complete with characters, objects, background colors and dialogue. The site includes lesson plans, writing prompts, aids for parents, and other educational resources, and accepts characters keyed in other languages, such as Spanish and French.

National Autism Resources (see Chapter 2 Resources, page 247).

The National Center for Learning Disabilities (www.ncld .org) has videos of successful teachers of students with LD sharing their "tips" in short videos.

Oczkus, Lori. *Interactive Think-Aloud Lessons.* New York: Scholastic, 2009. Oczkus has created other resources for using Reciprocal Teaching, published by the International Reading Association and available at Amazon.com.

Peck, Alec F., and Stan Scarpati, eds. *Autism Spectrum Disorders: Family, Community, Social Skills, and Behavior, A Collection of Articles from Teaching Exceptional Children.* Arlington, VA: Council for Exceptional Children, 2011. This compilation of articles from the *TEACHING Exceptional Children* (TEC) journal reviews the latest practices, dialogue, and critical issues affecting educators working with children with autism spectrum disorders.

———. *Classroom Instruction and Students with Autism Spectrum Disorders: A Collection of Articles from Teaching Exceptional Children.* Arlington, VA: Council for Exceptional Children, 2011. This second collection of articles about autism spectrum disorders from *TEACHING Exceptional Children* provides the keys to creating collaborative environments and designing successful interventions in the effective education of students with autism spectrum disorders.

Proloquo2Go (assistiveware.com) is an award-winning Augmentative and Alternative Communication (AAC) solution for iPad, iPhone, and iPod touch for people who have difficulty speaking.

Reading Styles Inventory: Dr. Marie Carbo has good resources on her Reading Styles Inventory on her website NRSI.com. Do a web search on Reading Styles Inventory for other resources that are specific to early childhood, reading, etc.

Read-Write-Think (readwritethink.org). At this website, teachers can use thousands of documents, including lesson plans, rubrics, etc.

Smart Kids with Learning Disabilities (www.smartkidswithld .org). A highly valuable website for kids who are twice exceptional (gifted learners with accompanying learning difficulties) and their parents and teachers.

Sunburst Technology (see Chapter 4 Resources, page 251).

Top 100 Special Needs Resources on the Web: phdinspecialeducation.com/special-needs

Typing.com (www.typing.com). A free online typing tutor and keyboarding tutorial for typists of all skill levels. The website includes entertaining typing games and typing tests.

Weaver, Constance. *Reading Process and Practice.* Portsmouth, NH: Heinemann 2002.

Write:OutLoud (see page 254).

Vatterott, Cathy. *Rethinking Homework: Best Practices That Support Diverse Needs.* Alexandria, VA: ASCD, 2009. A book that contains much helpful information, but we have one caution: The author states that unfinished homework is useless and does not contribute positively to learning. We would ask you to qualify that to believe, as we do, that homework assigned by elapsed time may be returned to class for full homework credit, whether or not an arbitrary number of problems/lines/exercises were completed.

## Common Core State Standards

Calkins, Lucy. Author of over thirty books on reading and writing education, including *The Art of Teaching Reading*, *The Art of Teaching Writing*, and *Raising Lifelong Learners: A Parent's Guide,* Dr. Calkins is Founding Director of The Teachers College Reading and Writing Project and Robinson Professor of Children's Literature at Teachers College. The project is a think tank that develops state-of-the-art methods and provides professional development for hundreds of schools. As the leader of this world-renowned organization, Calkins works closely with superintendents, district leaders, and school principals to reimagine what is possible when school leadership is aligned with professional development. She also works with particular teachers and their vibrant, quirky classes full of children. Calkins's books grow out of her work with her staff and a small cadre of New York City teachers who joined her in a year-long study group in primary writing. Particularly recommended are Calkins's

coauthored Units of Study series and the books *The Nuts and Bolts of Teaching Writing, The Conferring Handbook,* and *Resources for Primary Writing,* which includes a CD-ROM of supporting print and video material.

Graves, Donald, "All Children Can Write," available at www.ldonline.org. In this classic article, Dr. Graves, author of many books and articles on writing, describes his philosophies and effective writing practices, including a section devoted to teaching reluctant writers.

Hyerle, David. *Visual Tools for Transforming Information into Knowledge.* Thousand Oaks, CA: Corwin, 2009.

Jones, Fred. *Tools for Teaching: Discipline-Instruction-Motivation.* Santa Cruz, CA: Fredric H. Jones & Associates, 2007.

McKnight, Katherine. *The Common Sense Guide to the Common Core.* Minneapolis: Free Spirit Publishing, 2014. Forty clearly presented tools tested by educators across the country guide teachers, administrators, coaches, and other educators through every stage of implementing the CCSS across the curriculum.

National Reading Styles Institute (see Chapter 3 Resources, page 249).

Palincsar, A. S., A. L. Brown, and S. Martin. "Peer Interaction in Reading Comprehension Instruction." *Educational Psychologist* 22, no. 3–4 (1987): 231–253. Enter "Reciprocal Teaching" into the search field on Reading Rockets (www.readingrockets.org) for a video demonstration of this technique.

Pinterest has two good sources for knowledge, general information, and lesson planning resources on the Common Core: pinterest.com/teachervision/common-core, and TeacherVision's Pinterest board (enter "TeacherVision" in the search field).

Prince, Cynthia D. et al. "Research Synthesis: A. General Compensation Questions." Center for Educator Compensation Reform. www.cecr.ed.gov/researchSyntheses /Research%20Synthesis_Q%20A1.pdf (accessed May 21, 2014).

## Chapter 6: Reading and Learning with Informational Text

Discovery Education (www.discoveryeducation.com). Digital textbooks and online experiences in science, social studies and mathematics.

Edutopia (see Chapter 3 Resources, page 250).

Hallerman, Larmer, and Mergendoller, *PBL in the Elementary Grades* (see Chapter 4 Resources, page 251).

Larmer, John, David Ross, and John Mergendoller. *PBL Starter Kit: To-the-Point Advice, Tools and Tips for Your First Project in Middle or High School.* Novato, CA: Buck Institute for Education, 2009.

Larmer, John, and John R. Mergendoller. "Seven Essentials for Project-Based Learning." *Educational Leadership* 68, no. 1 (September 2010): 34–37.

Newbridge Educational Publishing (newbridgeonline.com). A complete resource for curriculum-based nonfiction.

Project-Based Learning: Building motivation, checklists, and tools at the 4Teachers.org website (pblchecklist.4teachers .org/more.shtml, accessed May 21, 2014).

Prufrock Press (www.prufrock.com) offers resources for critical and creative thinking, real-world problem solving, and mathematics.

"Reading in the Content Areas: Strategies for Success." Teaching Today: Glencoe Online/McGraw-Hill. www.teachingtoday.glencoe.com. September 2006 (accessed May 21, 2014).

Reading Rockets (www.readingrockets.org) is an excellent place to search for Reciprocal Teaching summaries.

Read-Write-Think (see Chapter 5 Resources, page 255).

Thinking Maps (www.thinkingmaps.com). Visual teaching tools that foster and encourage lifelong learning, the Thinking Maps provide a common visual language for learning within and across disciplines.

Vacca, Vacca, and Mraz, *Content Area Reading* (see Chapter 5 Resources, page 253).

## Chapter 7: All Students Can Be Successful in Math

Algeblocks (www.hand2mind.com). Grades 6–12. Hands-on algebra with manipulatives. Classroom kits and training videos are available.

AplusMath (www.aplusmath.com). Helps students improve their math skills interactively. Offers online interactive worksheets, flash cards, and games covering a variety of topics. The site also has custom flash cards and worksheets that can be printed.

Bley, Nancy S., and Carol A. Thornton. *Teaching Mathematics to Students with Learning Disabilities*. Austin, TX: PRO-ED, 2001. A gold mine of information about and strategies for helping students with learning disabilities learn math.

Cooper, Richard. *Alternative Math Techniques: When Nothing Else Seems to Work*. Sopris West, 2005.

Council for Economic Education (CEE) (www.councilfor econed.org) Delivers economic education and financial literacy to K–12 students by educating the educators. The CEE has a wealth of classroom resources, competitions, webinars, professional development opportunities and more.

FASTT Math (fasttmath.com). Grades 2 and up. Research-validated methods help struggling students to develop fluency with basic math facts in addition, subtraction, multiplication, and division. The software, from Scholastic, provides an adaptive program that increases fact fluency in customized, 10-minute daily sessions. Examination packets, including a disk that shows how the lessons work, are available upon request. District site licenses are available.

Gardner, Martin. *The Colossal Book of Short Puzzles and Problems*. New York: W. W. Norton, 2006. Videos of Gardner's entertaining math "tricks" may be accessed through YouTube.

Georgia Standards (www.georgiastandards.org). Managed by the Georgia Department of Education, this site offers a year's worth of lesson plans for a variety of grades and subjects. Its teacher resource links provide access to dozens of math-related sites and products.

Hands-On Equations: Making Algebra Child's Play (www.borenson.com). Grades 3–8. A visual and kinesthetic teaching system for introducing algebraic concepts. Students balance both parts of equations to understand the concept of "equal." In addition to its products, the company offers instructional workshops throughout the United States.

Higher Order Thinking Skills (HOTS) (see Chapter 4 Resources, page 251).

Kamii, Constance, with Linda Leslie Joseph. *Young Children Continue to Reinvent Arithmetic (2nd Grade): Implication of Piaget's Theory*. New York: Teachers College Press, 2004. Kamii's book series features educational strategies for early elementary-aged students based on Jean Piaget's scientific ideas of how children develop logico-mathematical thinking. Available at store.tcpress.com.

Kolpas, Sidney J. "Let Your Fingers Do the Multiplying," *Mathematics Teacher* 95, no. 4 (April 2002): 246–251.

LD Online (ldonline.org) has an LD Topic resource page entitled "Math & Dyscalculia."

Lieberthal, Edwin M. *The Complete Book of Fingermath*. New York: McGraw-Hill, 1979. This book is out of print but worth tracking down on the Internet and in libraries.

The Math Forum @ Drexel (www.mathforum.org). Affiliated with Drexel University, this site features dozens of math lessons on fractions and other concepts. Click on "Ask Dr. Math" to ask your own questions and search through questions that have already been posted on the site.

"Mathematics Interventions: What Strategies Work for Struggling Learners or Students With Learning Disabilities?" Education Northwest (educationnorthwest.org).

MathLine Concept-Building System (www.howbrite.com). A manipulative that combines the number line with the abacus, showing how math operations actually work.

Math Notes (www.mathsongs.com). This series of audio CDs uses a sing-along format to teach math concepts to kinesthetic learners. Each CD comes with a book of math objectives and directions for using the material in the classroom, as well as a copy of the song for use as an overhead master. No previous math skills are required to use the songs. Inquiries: (936) 624-6231.

National Center for Improving Student Learning and Achievement in Mathematics and Science (NCISLA) (ncisla .wceruw.org). Home of Cognitively Guided Instruction (CGI) and source of teacher training in the method.

National Council of Teachers of Mathematics (NCTM) (www.nctm.org). Books, journals, materials, videos, and collections of math lessons for many topics and grade levels. NCTM Standards *(Principles & Standards for School Mathematics)* are available on this website.

Paula's Special Education Resources (paulabliss.com). Click "My Math Page" for materials on mathematics LDs.

*Schoolhouse Rock! (Special 30th Anniversary Edition).* Orlando: Walt Disney Studios Home Entertainment, 2010. This two-DVD set collects all 46 of the musical cartoons that have helped students with LD for decades, including math classics such as "My Hero Zero" and "Three Is a Magic Number."

SuccessMaker: A Digital Learning Curriculum (pearsonschool.com). This scalable digital courseware for grades K–8 individualizes instruction to the specific needs of each student, automatically presenting material at the level at which a student is ready to learn and creating a successful learning experience. Aligns with district, local, and national standards, and is supported by a comprehensive management system. Used in more than 16,000 schools in the United States and 1,500 abroad. Courseware is available in customizable bundles. Program costs vary depending on the software purchased, the range of grade levels to be covered, and the amount of professional development services requested.

Teacher2Teacher (www.mathforum.org/t2t). Part of the Math Forum @ Drexel (see page 256), this question-and-answer service connects teachers and parents who have questions about teaching math.

TouchMath (www.touchmath.com). Multisensory teaching approach that bridges manipulation and memorization. Offered are comprehensive programs for Common Core and RTL/Sp. Ed., including workbooks, technology, and classroom aids.

Trade-Offs (www.ait.net/catalog). Grades 5–8. Fifteen 20-minute video programs and a teacher's guide to explain basic economics to middle school students. From the Agency for Instructional Technology.

The 24 Game (www.24game.com) demonstrates that math can be powerful fun. The answer is always 24, which alleviates students' anxiety about finding the right answer and puts the emphasis on the process—the method behind the math.

Twin Sisters Productions (www.twinsisters.com) has a variety of educational children's music for ages 6–12. Kids learn addition, subtraction, multiplication, and division with musical/rhythmic assistance. Additional school subject areas are available; many products are on CD.

The University of Chicago School Mathematics Project (UCSMP) (ucsmp.uchicago.edu). Offers information,

training, and teaching assistance. Materials are available for all grade levels.

"What Are Strategies for Teaching a Student with a Math-Related Learning Disability?" AccessSTEM (The Alliance for Students with Disabilities in Science, Technology, Engineering, and Mathematics). www.washington.edu /doit/Stem/articles?322. January 25, 2013 (accessed May 21, 2014).

YouTube (www.youtube.com) features many fascinating mathematics demonstrations, TouchMath and Finger Math among them. Timothy Basaldua provides interesting math and geometry videos.

## Chapter 8: Using Assessments to Support Student Learning

BertieKingore.com (www.bertiekingore.com). The website of Bertie Kingore, Ph.D., a national consultant who has worked with students, their teachers, and their parents for over 30 years, is dedicated to providing educational materials that enrich learning experiences for all students. Kingore continues to work in classrooms to model the differentiation of instruction for all learners.

Bolt, Sarah E., and Andrew T. Roach. *Inclusive Assessment and Accountability: A Guide to Accommodations for Students with Diverse Needs.* New York: Guildford Press, 2009. Information on policy mandates, detailed case studies, and reproducibles. This resource provides step-by-step guidelines for choosing appropriate accommodations and alternative testing practices.

Hess, Karen. K. "A New Lens for Examining Cognitive Rigor in Standards, Curriculum, and Assessments." National Center for the Improvement of Educational Assessment. www.nciea.org/publications/rigorpresentation_KH11.pdf (accessed May 21, 2014). Dr. Hess, a senior associate at the National Center for the Improvement of Educational Assessment, coaches on learning how to differentiate using the Little Red Riding Hood story, including the T-BEAR Graphic Organizer.

Kannapel, Patricia et al. "Inside the Black Box of High-Performing, High-Poverty Schools." The Prichard Committee for Academic Excellence, 2005. www.prichardcommittee. org/wp-content/uploads/2013/02/Inside-the-Black-Box. pdf (accessed May 21, 2014). The report details how high-performing schools in high-poverty areas facilitate consistent student achievement regardless of ethnicity or social or economic class.

Kohn, Alfie. *Beyond Discipline: From Compliance to Community.* Alexandria, VA: ASCD, 2006.

———. *The Homework Myth: Why Our Kids Get Too Much of a Bad Thing.* Boston: Da Capo Press, 2006.

———. *Punished by Rewards.* New York: Houghton Mifflin, 1999.

The Leadership and Learning Center (www.leadandlearn .com). Founder Douglas Reeves identified five factors present in schools with performance at or above the 90th percentile in which 90-plus percent of students come from combined minorities and 90-plus percent are on free or reduced lunch. The factors are: strong emphasis on achievement, focus on essential curricular areas, frequent assessments with multiple chances for students to show improvement, writing across the curriculum, and use of consistent rubrics across all classes for assessment.

Learner Profile (learnerprofile.com). This computerized assessment management tool allows you to track students' grades and assignments, organize student information, and develop reports on your computer.

Product Guide Kits (curriculumproject.com). A unique collection of assessment rubrics that help students plan how to earn high grades for their projects and products.

Rubistar (rubistar.4teachers.org). A terrific free tool for teachers who want to use rubrics but don't have the time to develop them from scratch. The site is also available in Spanish; click the "Rubistar en Español" window. A project of the High Plains Regional Technology in Educational Consortium (HPR*TEC), one of ten RTECS funded by the Department of Education.

Schumm, Jeanne Shay, Ph.D. *School Power: Study Skill Strategies for Succeeding in School*. Minneapolis: Free Spirit Publishing, 2001. A lively, popular eBook for ages 11 and up that teaches a reliable set of skills students need to do well in school, such as test-taking, speech preparation, handling long-range assignments, and more.

Wormeli, Rick. *Fair Isn't Always Equal: Assessing & Grading in the Differentiated Classroom*. Portland, ME: Stenhouse, 2006.

## Chapter 9: Improving Students' Executive Functioning Skills

### Executive Functioning

Cooper-Kahn, Joyce, and Laurie Dietzel. *Late, Lost, and Unprepared*. Bethesda, MD: Woodbine House, 2008.

Dawson, Peg, and Richard Guare. *Executive Skills in Children and Adolescents: A Practical Guide to Assessment and Intervention*. New York: Guilford Press, 2010.

Kaufman, Christopher. *Executive Function in the Classroom: Practical Strategies for Improving Performance and Enhancing Skills for All Students*. Baltimore: Paul H. Brookes Publishing, 2010.

Meltzer, Lynn. *Promoting Executive Function in the Classroom*. New York: Guilford Press, 2010.

Moss, Samantha, and Lesley Schwartz. *Where's My Stuff: The Ultimate Teen Organizing Guide*. San Francisco: Zest Books, 2007.

Mullin, Melissa, and Karen Fried. *Executive Functioning Workbook*. Santa Monica: The K&M Center, 2013.

Zeigler Dendy, Chris A. "Executive Function . . . What Is This Anyway?" www.chrisdendy.com/executive.htm (accessed May 21, 2014). This author has emerged as a definitive expert on ADD/ADHD and executive functioning. Visit her website (www.chrisdendy.com) for helpful information on these topics. She reports that kids with ADD/ADHD may be experiencing a situation in which their brains are maturing several years later than the brains of age peers. This would indicate that the better our intervention efforts with these kids, the faster they would catch up. The study is reported in "Brain Maturation Delayed, Not Deviant, in Kids With ADHD," *Psychiatric Times* (www.psychiatrictimes.com /articles/brain-maturation-delayed-not-deviant-kids-adhd; accessed May 21, 2014).

### General Resources

Cash, Richard M. *Advancing Differentiation*. Minneapolis: Free Spirit Publishing, 2010. Guides educators in developing rigorous, concept-based curriculum that is differentiated for all learners across content areas.

Coil, Carolyn. *Differentiation, RTI, and Achievement: How They Work Together*. Marion, IL: Pieces of Learning, 2009. All of Carolyn Coil's work is extremely practical and helpful to teachers and parents (visit PiecesofLearning.com to learn more about her books).

Heacox, Diane. *Differentiating Instruction in the Regular Classroom*. Minneapolis: Free Spirit Publishing, 2012. The ultimate go-to resource and practical introduction to providing variety and challenge in differentiated classes. Includes digital content.

——. *Making Differentiation a Habit: How to Ensure Success in Academically Diverse Classrooms*. Minneapolis: Free Spirit Publishing, 2009. Expanding on her trusted guide *Differentiating Instruction in the Regular Classroom,* Diane Heacox offers new ideas, fresh perspectives, and additional research-based strategies to help teachers seamlessly integrate differentiation practices.

——. *Up from Underachievement: How Teachers, Students, and Parents Can Work Together to Promote Student Success*. Minneapolis: Free Spirit Publishing, 1991. Describes a step-by-step program that helps students in all grades break the failure chain.

Kohn, Alfie. *Unconditional Parenting: Moving from Rewards and Punishments to Love and Reason*. New York: Atria Books, 2005.

Learning to Learn (www.learningtolearn.com). A research-based learning and thinking skills system recommended for national use by the U.S. Department of Education. Students move away from rote learning towards inquiry-based learning and acquire skills that help them use their natural visual learning abilities. Delivered in schools through teacher training.

Levine, Mel. *A Mind at a Time*. New York: Simon & Schuster, 2002. Dr. Levine, a pediatrician, teaches how to identify kids' individual learning patterns and use that information to strengthen their abilities or overcome their weaknesses, producing positive results instead of repeated frustration and failure.

——. *The Myth of Laziness*. Simon & Schuster, 2003.

Pieces of Learning (www.piecesoflearning.com) publishes books on differentiation, standards-based teaching, assessment, and raising student achievement, including Carolyn Coil's *Becoming an Achiever: A Student Guide* and *Motivating Underachievers*.

### Recommended Readings for Students

Carlson, Richard. *Don't Sweat the Small Stuff for Teens*. New York: Hyperion, 2000.

Covey, Sean. *The Seven Habits of Highly Effective Teens: The Ultimate Teenage Success Guide*. New York: Simon & Schuster, 1998. For teens ages 13 and up, parents, grandparents, and any adult who influences young people.

Fox, Annie, and Ruth Kirschner. *Too Stressed to Think? A Teen Guide to Staying Sane When Life Makes You Crazy*. Minneapolis: Free Spirit Publishing, 2005. This eBook helps teens choose effective responses to stress by illustrating dozens of realistic scenarios.

Johnson, Spencer. *Who Moved My Cheese? for Teens*. New York: Putnam, 2002. Presents the author's parable about change framed in a story about a group of high school friends trying to handle change in their lives.

Shumsky, Ron, Susan M. Islascox, and Rob Bell. *The Survival Guide for School Success*. Minneapolis: Free Spirit Publishing, 2014. The habits of successful students are presented as ten smartphone-style mental "Apps" aimed at teenagers for enhancing concentration, organization and positivity.

## Chapter 10: Helping Students Choose Appropriate Behaviors

American Psychological Association. "Being Bullied Throughout Childhood and Teens May Lead to More Arrests, Convictions, Prison Time." www.apa.org/news/press /releases/2013/08/being-bullied.aspx. August 1, 2013 (accessed May 21, 2014).

Baker, Beth, and Char Ryan. *The PBIS Team Handbook*. Minneapolis: Free Spirit Publishing, 2014. A detailed, plain-language guide to implementing and sustaining positive behavior interventions and supports. Includes downloadable digital content.

Brewster, Cori, and Jennifer Railsback. *Schoolwide Prevention of Bullying*. Portland, OR: Northwest Regional Educational Laboratory, 2001. This booklet is available for free download at www.wrightslaw.com/advoc/articles/prevention.of .bullying.pdf (accessed May 21, 2014).

Curwin, Richard L., Allen N. Mendler and Brian D Mendler. *Discipline with Dignity: New Challenges, New Solutions*. Alexandria, VA: ASCD, 2008.

DeBruyn, Robert L., and Jack L. Larson. *You Can Handle Them All: A Discipline Model for Handling 124 Student Behaviors at School and at Home*. Manhattan, KS: The Master Teacher, 2009. There are two versions of this book,

one for teachers, another for parents. Describes many common "misbehavior" challenges and prescribes effective interventions for them.

Goldstein et al. The Skillstreaming Series (see Chapter 2 Resources, page 246).

Gootman, Marilyn E. *The Caring Teacher's Guide to Discipline*. Thousand Oaks, CA: Corwin Press, 2008.

The Honor Level System (www.honorlevel.com). A software system for school discipline that stresses positive reinforcement for appropriate behavior and academic achievement. Created to meet the needs of one middle school in Washington more than 20 years ago, the software program is now used with more than 90,000 high school, junior high, middle school, and elementary students in the United States.

Illinois PBIS (Positive Behavior Intervention and Support) Network. "Effective Bullying Prevention (BP) within a School-wide System of Positive Behavior Interventions and Supports." www.isbe.net/learningsupports/pdfs/bully-prev-pbis-brief .pdf. December 2010 (accessed May 21, 2014). Also check out www.pbis.org: the National Technical Assistance Center on Positive Behavioral Interventions and Supports.

Larnia, Mary C. "Do Bullies Really Have Low Self-Esteem?" *Psychology Today*. www.psychologytoday.com/blog/intense -emotions-and-strong-feelings/201010/do-bullies-really -have-low-self-esteem. October 22, 2010 (accessed May 21, 2014).

Lavoie, *How Difficult Can This Be?* (see Chapter 2 Resources, page 247).

Managing the Disruptive Classroom (www.ait.net). A program for teachers based on reality therapy, produced by the Agency for Instructional Technology (AIT) and Phi Delta Kappa. Includes a sixty-minute DVD or VHS program and a thirty-two-page facilitator's guide.

McIntyre, Thomas. *The Survival Guide for Kids with Behavior Challenges*. Minneapolis: Free Spirit Publishing, 2013. Written in language kids ages 9–14 can relate to, this handbook helps them make good choices, get along with teachers, and work toward positive change.

Migliore, Eleanor T. "Eliminate Bullying in Your Classroom." *Intervention in School & Clinic* 38: 3 (January 2003): 172–177.

Olweus Bullying Prevention Program (see page 245).

Rational Emotional Behavior Therapy (REBT) (www.albert ellis.org). REBT by Albert Ellis teaches kids (and adults) that they are guided by the thoughts they choose, and that changing one's thoughts will change one's emotions and behaviors. This theory is now compatible with many "New Age" teachings, but it is interesting to know it has a basis in the study of psychology.

Responsible Thinking Process (www.responsiblethinking .com). A behavior management and classroom discipline process that teaches respect for others by fostering responsible thinking. Created by Edward E. Ford, the company's publishing arm is Brandt Publishing. One recommended Edward Ford book is *Discipline for Home and School, Book One.* (Brandt Publishing, 2003). Susan has seen this program in action and continues to be highly impressed with its precepts and outcomes. A Time-Out room, staffed (sometimes with a parent or other community member) provides students who are making inappropriate behavior choices in their classroom with a programmed approach to understanding why their behavior was chosen, why it was not acceptable, and how to make a plan to make better behavior choices when they return to the classroom. It is especially effective for small schools.

Rich, *MegaSkills: Building Our Children's Character* (see Chapter 2 Resources, page 246).

RickLavoie.com (see Chapter 2 Resources, page 247).

## Chapter 11: Helping Parents Become Partners in Their Children's Learning

Brewster and Railsback, *Schoolwide Prevention of Bullying* (see Chapter 10 Resources, page 259).

DeBruyn and Larson, *You Can Handle Them All* (see Chapter 10 Resources, page 259).

Dreikurs, Rudolf, and Vicki Soltz. *Children: The Challenge.* New York: Hawthorn, 1964.

Ford, Edward E. *Discipline for Home and School, Fundamentals.* Scottsdale, AZ: Brandt Publishing, 2004.

———. *Discipline for Home and School, Book One: Teaching Disruptive Children How to Look Within Themselves, Decide the Way They Want to Be, and Then Think of Ways to Achieve Their Goals Without Violating the Rights of Others.* Scottsdale, AZ: Brandt Publishing, 2003.

Froschl, Merle et al. *Quit It! A Teacher's Guide on Teasing and Bullying for Use with Students in Grades K–3.* New York: Educational Equity Concepts, 1998. The book-and-two-CD teaching packet is available from Wellesley College's Educational Equity Center (www.edequity.org).

Glasser, William. *The Quality School: Managing Students without Coercion.* New York: HarperCollins, 1998.

Gootman, *The Caring Teacher's Guide to Discipline* (see Chapter 10 Resources, page 259).

The Honor Level System (see Chapter 10 Resources, page 259).

Lavoie, *How Difficult Can This Be?* (see Chapter 2 Resources, page 247).

Managing the Disruptive Classroom (see Chapter 10 Resources, page 259).

Migliore, "Eliminate Bullying in Your Classroom" (see Chapter 10 Resources, page 260).

Olweus Bullying Prevention Program (see Introduction Resources, page 245).

Powers, William T. *Behavior: The Control of Perception.* New Canaan, CT: Benchmark Publications, 2005.

Responsible Thinking Process (see Chapter 10 Resources, page 260).

RickLavoie.com (see Chapter 2 Resources, page 247).

Sjostrom, Lisa, and Nan Stein. *Bullyproof: A Teacher's Guide on Teasing and Bullying for Use with Fourth and Fifth Grade Students.* Wellesley, MA: Wellesley College Center for Research on Women, 1996. Available from the Wellesley Centers for Women (www.wcwonline.org).

Teacher Learning Center (tlc-sems.com). The skills and strategies you need to deal with disruptions while teaching kids responsibility for their own actions.

### Homework

Berger, Eugenia Hepworth, and Mari Riojas-Cortez. *Parents as Partners in Education: Families and Schools Working Together.* New York: Pearson, 2011.

Cline, Foster, and Jim Fay. *Parenting with Love and Logic.* Colorado Springs: NavPress, 2006. The advice given in the famous series by Cline and Fay is practical, easy to use, and has long been proven effective.

Faber, Adele, and Elaine Mazlish. *How to Talk So Kids Will Listen and Listen So Kids Will Talk.* New York: Scribner, 2012.

Gootman, Marilyn E. *The Loving Parents' Guide to Discipline.* New York: Berkley Trade, 2000.

Henderson, Anne T. et al. *Beyond the Bake Sale: The Essential Guide to Family/School Partnerships.* New York: W. W. Norton, 2007.

Homework Lady (www.homeworklady.com). The website of Dr. Cathy Vatterott, a longtime expert on the subject of homework.

Johnson, Mary. *The 21st Century Parent: Multicultural Parent Engagement Leadership Strategies Handbook.* Charlotte, NC: Information Age Publishing, 2012.

Kelly, Kate, and Peggy Ramundo. *You Mean I'm Not Lazy, Stupid or Crazy?!* New York: Scribner, 2006.

KidsHealth from Nemours (kidshealth.org/parent/positive /learning/homework.html). This site gives helpful homework advice for parents.

National Center for School Engagement (NCSE). "Parental Involvement in Schools." www.schoolengagement.org /index.cfm/index.cfm/Parental Involvement in Schools (accessed May 21, 2014).

National Educational Association (NEA). "Research Spotlight on Parental Involvement in Education." www.nea.org/tools/17360.htm (accessed May 21, 2014).

Ridnouer, Katy. *Everyday Engagement: Making Students and Parents Your Partners in Learning.* Alexandria, VA: ASCD, 2011.

Romain, Trevor. *How to Do Homework Without Throwing Up.* Minneapolis: Free Spirit Publishing, 1997. Kids ages 8–13 can learn a variety of simple techniques for getting homework done. Serious suggestions delivered with wit and humor.

Vatterott, Cathy. *Rethinking Homework: Best Practices that Support Diverse Needs.* Alexandria, VA: ASCD, 2001.

Wallis, Claudia. "The Myth About Homework." *Time Magazine.* content.time.com/time/magazine/article/0,9171,1376208,00.html. August 29, 2006 (accessed May 21, 2014). Major points from this article: Homework does not measurably improve academic achievement for kids in grade school (based on a study by Harris Cooper, Ph.D., of Duke University), and too much homework (more than sixty to ninety minutes per night in total from all teachers) actually leads to lower test scores.

Washington State Family and Community Engagement Trust (www.wafamilyengagement.org). This organization aims to improve parents' participation in their children's education. Another good resource is to search "Parental Involvement in Education" on About.com's Teaching channel (teaching.about.com).

# Index

Note: Page references in *italics* refer to figures; those in **boldface** refer to reproducible templates.

# About the Authors

**Susan Winebrenner, M.S.,** is a former classroom teacher and current full-time consultant in staff development. She is the author and coauthor of several books and teaching resources, including *Teaching Gifted Kids in Today's Classroom* and *The Cluster Grouping Handbook.* Through her consulting and workshop business, Education Consulting Service, Susan presents seminars nationally and internationally, helping educators translate education research into classroom practice. She has served on the faculty of New Leaders for New Schools, a national organization dedicated to training and supporting a new generation of outstanding school principals for urban schools. Susan lives in San Marcos, California. Visit Susan's website at susanwinebrenner.com.

**Lisa M. Kiss, M.Ed.,** is the director of special education at Tulpehocken School District in Berks County, Pennsylvania. Previously, she taught in special education and gifted education for over 20 years. She has supervised numerous student teachers and has presented at several state conferences on the topics of cluster grouping and inclusion to help all students be successful. She lives in Lebanon, Pennsylvania.

Download the free PLC/Book Study Guide at freespirit.com/teaching-kids-with-LD-PLC.

# More Great Books from Free Spirit

### Teaching Gifted Kids in Today's Classroom Professional Development Multimedia Package
*by Susan Winebrenner, M.S., and Dina Brulles, Ph.D.*

Package includes:

- DVD (100+ minutes)
- *Study Group Leader's Guide*
  PB, spiral bound, 8½" x 11", 96 pp.
- *Teaching Gifted Kids in Today's Classroom*
  PB, 8½" x 11", 256 pp., with digital content
- Shelf storage box with magnetic closure

*Teaching Gifted Kids in Today's Classroom also sold separately.*

### The Cluster Grouping Handbook: A Schoolwide Model
**How to Challenge Gifted Students and Improve Achievement for All**
*by Susan Winebrenner, M.S., and Dina Brulles, Ph.D.*

224 pp., PB, 8½" x 11". For teachers and administrators, grades K–8. Includes digital content.

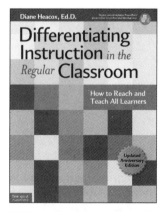

### Differentiating Instruction in the Regular Classroom
**How to Reach and Teach All Learners (Updated Anniversary Edition)**
*by Diane Heacox, Ed.D.*

176 pp., PB, 8½" x 11". For teachers, grades K–12. Includes digital content.

### Making Differentiation a Habit
**How to Ensure Success in Academically Diverse Classrooms**
*by Diane Heacox, Ed.D.*

192 pp., PB, 8½" x 11".
For teachers and administrators, grades K–12. Includes digital content.

## Advancing Differentiation
**Thinking and Learning for the 21st Century**

*by Richard M. Cash, Ed.D.,*
*foreword by Diane Heacox, Ed.D.*

*208 pp., PB, 8½" x 11" . Teachers and administrators, grades K–12. Includes digital content.*

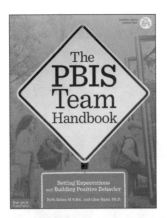

## The PBIS Team Handbook
**Setting Expectations and Building Positive Behavior**

*by Beth Baker, M.S.Ed., with Char Ryan, Ph.D.*

*208 pp., PB, 8½" x 11". For K–12 PBIS coaches and team members, including special educators, teachers, paraprofessionals, school psychologists, social workers, counselors, administrators, parents, and other school staff members. Includes digital content.*

## RTI Success
**Proven Tools and Strategies for Schools and Classrooms**

*by Elizabeth Whitten, Ph.D., Kelli J. Esteves, Ed.D., and Alice Woodrow, Ed.D.*

*256 pp., PB, 8½" x 11". For teachers and administrators, grades K–12. Includes digital content.*

## RTI in Middle School Classrooms
**Proven Tools and Strategies**

*by Kelli J. Esteves, Ed.D., and Elizabeth Whitten, Ph.D.*

*224 pp., PB, 8½" x 11". For middle school teachers and administrators. Includes digital content.*

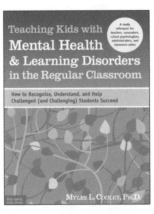

## Teaching Kids with Mental Health & Learning Disorders in the Regular Classroom
**How to Recognize, Understand, and Help Challenged (and Challenging) Students Succeed**

*by Myles L. Cooley, Ph.D.*

*224 pp., PB, 8½" x 11". For grades K–12.*

## Self-Regulation in the Classroom
**Helping Students Learn How to Learn**

*by Richard M. Cash, Ed.D.*

*184 pp., PB, 8½" x 11". K–12 teachers, administrators, counselors. Includes digital content.*

---

**Interested in purchasing multiple quantities and receiving volume discounts?**
Contact edsales@freespirit.com or call 1.800.735.7323 and ask for Education Sales.

**Many Free Spirit authors are available for speaking engagements, workshops, and keynotes.**
Contact speakers@freespirit.com or call 1.800.735.7323.

For pricing information, to place an order, or to request a free catalog, contact:

**6325 Sandburg Road • Suite 100 • Minneapolis, MN 55427-3674**
**toll-free 800.735.7323 • local 612.338.2068 • fax 612.337.5050**
**help4kids@freespirit.com • www.freespirit.com**